T0315493

Complex-Valued
Neural Networks

Complex-Valued Neural Networks

Advances and Applications

Edited by

Akira Hirose
The University of Tokyo

IEEE Press Series on Computational Intelligence
David B. Fogel, Series Editor

IEEE PRESS

WILEY

Published by John Wiley & Sons, Inc., Hoboken, New Jersey.
Published simultaneously in Canada.

For general information on our other products and services please contact our Customer Care Department within the United States at (800) 762-2974, outside the United States at (317) 572-3993 or fax (317) 572-4002.

Wiley also publishes its books in a variety of electronic formats. Some content that appears in print, however, may not be available in electronic formats. For more information about Wiley products, visit our web site at www.wiley.com.

Library of Congress Cataloging-in-Publication Data is available.

ISBN 9781118344606

10 9 8 7 6 5 4 3 2 1

CONTRIBUTORS

CHAPTER 1
AKIRA HIROSE, The University of Tokyo, Tokyo, Japan

CHAPTER 2
SIMONE FIORI, Università Politecnica delle Marche, Ancona, Italy

CHAPTER 3
TOHRU NITTA, National Institute of Advanced Industrial Science and Technology (AIST), Tsukuba, Japan

CHAPTER 4
MD. FAIJUL AMIN, University of Fukui, Fukui, Japan; Khulna University of Engineering and Technology, Khulna, Bangladesh
KAZUYUKI MURASE, University of Fukui, Fukui, Japan

CHAPTER 5
TEIJIRO ISOKAWA,   University of Hyogo, Hyogo, Japan
HARUHIKO NISHIMURA,   University of Hyogo, Hyogo, Japan
NOBUYUKI MATSUI,   University of Hyogo, Hyogo, Japan

CHAPTER 6
YASUAKI KUROE,   Kyoto Institute of Technology, Kyoto, Japan

CHAPTER 7
RAMASAMY SAVITHA,   Nanyang Technological University, Singapore
SUNDARAM SURESH,   Nanyang Technological University, Singapore
NARASIMHAN SUNDARARAJAN,   Sri Jaya Chamarajendra College of Engineering (SJCE), Mysore, India

CHAPTER 8
NIKOLAY MANYAKOV,   KU Leuven, Leuven, Belgium
IGOR AIZENBERG,   Texas A&M University–Texarkana, Texarkana, Texas, U.S.A.
NILOLAY CHUMERIN,   KU Leuven, Leuven, Belgium
MARK M. VAN HULLE,   KU Leuven, Leuven, Belgium

CHAPTER 9
XIA HONG,   University of Reading, Reading, U.K.
SHENG CHEN,   University of Southampton, Southampton, U.K.; King Abdulaziz University, Jeddah, Saudi Arabia
CHRIS J. HARRIS,   University of Southampton, Southampton, U.K.

CHAPTER 10
WAI KIT WONG,   Multimedia University, Melaka, Malaysia
GIN CHONG LEE,   Multimedia University, Melaka, Malaysia
CHU KIONG LOO,   University of Malaya, Kuala Lumpur, Malaysia
WAY SOONG LIM,   Multimedia University, Melaka, Malaysia
RAYMOND LOCK,   Multimedia University, Melaka, Malaysia

CONTENTS

3 N-Dimensional Vector Neuron and Its Application to the N-Bit Parity Problem   **59**
Tohru Nitta

4 Learning Algorithms in Complex-Valued Neural Networks using Wirtinger Calculus   **75**
Md. Faijul Amin and Kazuyuki Murase

7 Meta-cognitive Complex-valued Relaxation Network and its Sequential Learning Algorithm 153

Ramasamy Savitha, Sundaram Suresh, and Narasimhan Sundararajan

10   Quaternionic Fuzzy Neural Network for View-invariant Color Face Image Recognition   235

Wai Kit Wong, Gin Chong Lee, Chu Kiong Loo, Way Soong Lim, and Raymond Lock

PREFACE

Complex-valued neural networks (CVNNs) have continued to open doors to various new applications. The CVNNs are the neural networks that deal with complex amplitude, i.e. signal having phase and amplitude, which is one of the most core concepts in science and technology, in particular in electrical and electronic engineering. A CVNN is not equivalent to a double-dimensional real-valued neural network. It has different dynamics and characteristics such as generalization, which is significantly useful in treatment of complex-amplitude information and wave-related phenomena. This is a critical point in applications in engineering fields. It is also crucial for developing new devices in the future. That is, the CVNN framework will play an important role in introduction of learning and self-organization into future quantum devices dealing with electron waves and photonic waves.

We can further expect that broad-sense CVNNs such as quaternion neural networks break ground in unique directions respectively. Quaternion has been essential in computer graphics to render three-dimensional moving objects. When we introduce learning and self-organization in virtual realities and computer-aided amenities, quaternion neural networks will surely bring an important fundamental basis. CVNNs may be useful even in physiological analysis and modeling where the researchers suggest, for example, that the phase information of neuron firing timing against the theta wave in electroencephalography possesses a close relationship to short-term position memory in the brain.

This book includes recent advances and applications of CVNNs in the following ten chapters. Chapter 1 presents historical and latest advances in applications of CVNNs first. Then it illustrates one of the most important merits of CVNNs, namely, the suitability for adaptive processing of coherent signals. Chapter 2 deals with complex-valued parameter manifolds and with applications of CVNNs in which the connection parameters work in complex-valued manifolds. Successful applications are also shown, such as blind source separation of complex-valued sources, multichannel blind deconvolution of signals in telecommunications, nondestructive evaluation of materials in industrial metallic slab production, and a purely algorithmic problem of averaging the parameters of a pool of cooperative CVNNs. Chapter 3 describes the N-dimensional vector neuron, which can deal with N signals as one cluster, by extending the three-dimensional vector neuron to N dimensions. The N-bit parity problem is solved with a signal N-dimensional vector neuron with an orthogonal decision boundary. It is shown that the extension of the dimensionality of neural networks to N dimensions originates the enhancement of computational power in neural networks. Chapter 4 discusses the Wirtinger calculus and derives several algorithms for feedforward and recurrent CVNNs. A functional dependence diagram is shown for visual understanding of respective derivatives. For feedforward networks, two algorithms are considered, namely, the gradient descent (backpropagation) and the Levenberg–Marquardt (LM) algorithms. Simultaneously, for recurrent networks, the authors discuss the complex versions of the real-time recurrent learning (RTRL) and the extended Kalman filter (EKF) algorithms.

Chapter 5 presents quaternion associative memories. Quaternion is a four-dimensional hypercomplex number system and has been extensively employed in the fields of robotics, control of satellites, computer graphics, and so on. One of its benefits lies in the fact that affine transforms in three-dimensional space can be compactly and consistently represented. Thus neural networks based on quaternion are expected to process three-dimensional data with learning or self-organization more successfully. Several schemes to embed patterns into a network are presented. In addition to the quaternion version of the Hebbian learning scheme, the projection rule for embedding nonorthogonal patterns and local iterative learning are described. Chapter 6 extends neural networks into the Clifford algebraic domain. Since geometric product is non-commutative, some types of models are considered possible. In this chapter three models of fully connected recurrent networks are i nvestigated, in particular from the viewpoint of existence conditions of an energy function, for two classes of the Hopfield-type Clifford neural networks.

Chapter 7 presents a meta-cognitive learning algorithm for a single hidden layer CVNN called Meta-cognitive Fully Complex-valued Relaxation Network (McFCRN). McFCRN has two components, that is, cognitive and meta-cognitive components. The meta-cognitive component possesses a self-regulatory learning mechanism which controls the learning stability of FCRN by deciding *what to learn*, *when to learn*, and *how to learn* from a sequence of training data. They deal with the problem of explicit minimization of magnitude and phase errors in logarithmic error function. Chapter 8 describes a multilayer feedforward neural network equipped with multi-valued neurons and its application to the domain of brain–computer interface (BCI). A new methodology for electroencephalogram (EEG)-based BCI is developed with which subjects can issue commands by looking at corresponding targets that are flickering at the same frequency but with different initial phase. Chapter 9 develops a complex-valued (CV) B-spline (basis-spline) neural network approach for efficient identification of the CV Wiener system as well as the effective inverse of the estimated CV Wiener model. Specifically, the CV nonlinear static function in the Wiener system is represented using the tensor product from two univariate B-spline neural networks. The effectiveness is demonstrated using the application of digital predistorter for high-power amplifiers with memory. Chapter 10 presents an effective color image processing system for persons' face image recognition. The system carries out the recognition with a quaternion correlator and a max-product fuzzy neural network classifier. The performance is evaluated in terms of accuracy, calculation cost, and noise and/or scale tolerance.

This is the first book planned and published by the Complex-Valued Neural Networks Task Force (CVNN TF) of the IEEE Computational Intelligence Society (CIS) Neural Networks Technical Committee (NNTC). The CVNN TF has been established to promote research in this developing field. The authors expect readers to get more interested in this area, to send feedback in any form, and to join us. Please visit our website http://www.eis.t.u-tokyo.ac.jp/news/NNTC_CVNN/.

AKIRA HIROSE

Tokyo
January 2013

CHAPTER 1

APPLICATION FIELDS AND FUNDAMENTAL MERITS OF COMPLEX-VALUED NEURAL NETWORKS

Akira Hirose

The University of Tokyo, Tokyo, Japan

This chapter presents historical and latest advances in applications of complex-valued neural networks (CVNNs) first. Then it also shows one of the most important merits of CVNNs, namely, the suitability for adaptive processing of coherent signals.

1.1 INTRODUCTION

This chapter presents historical and latest advances in applications of complex-valued neural networks (CVNNs) first. Then it also shows one of the most important merits of CVNNs, namely, the suitability for adaptive processing of coherent signals.

CVNNs are effective and powerful in particular to deal with wave phenomena such as electromagnetic and sonic waves, as well as to process wave-related information. Regarding the history of CVNNs, we can trace back to the middle of the 20th century. The first introduction of phase information in computation was made by Eiichi Goto in 1954 in his invention of "Parametron" [17, 18, 61]. He utilized the phase of a high-frequency carrier to represent binary or multivalued information. However, the computational principle employed there was "logic" of Turing type, or von Neumann type, based on symbol processing, so that he could not make further extensive use of the phase. In the present CVNN researches, contrarily, the researchers extend the world of computation to pattern processing fields based on a novel use of the structure of complex-amplitude (phase and amplitude) information.

We notice that the above feature is significantly important when we give thought to the fact that various modern technologies centered on electronics orient toward coherent systems and devices rather than something incoherent. The feature will lead to future general probability statistics, stochastic methods, and statistical learning and self-organization framework in coherent signal processing and information analysis. The fundamental idea is applicable also to hypercomplex processing based on quaternion, octonion, and Clifford algebraic networks.

Some parts of the following contents of this chapter were published in detail in *the Journal of Society of Instrument and Control Engineers* [29], *the Frontiers in Electrical and Electronic Engineering in China* [28], and *IEEE Transactions in Neural Networks and Learning Systems* [35].

1.2 APPLICATIONS OF COMPLEX-VALUED NEURAL NETWORKS

Complex-valued neural networks (CVNNs) have become widely used in various fields. The basic ideas and fundamental principles have been published in several books in recent years [27, 22, 26, 41, 53, 2]. The following subsections present major application fields.

1.2.1 Antenna Design

The most notable feature of CVNNs is the compatibility with wave phenomena and wave information related to, for example, electromagnetic wave, lightwave, electron wave, and sonic wave [28]. Application fields include adaptive design of antennas such as patch antennas for microwave and millimeter wave. Many researches have been reported on how to determine patch-antenna shape and sub-element arrangement, as well as on the switching patterns of the sub-elements [46, 10, 47]. A designer assigns desired frequency-domain characteristics of complex amplitude, or simply amplitude, such as transmission characteristics, return loss, and radiation patterns. A CVNN mostly realizes a more suitable design than a real-valued network does even when he/she presents only simple amplitude. The reason lies in the elemental dynamics consisting of phase rotation (or time delay × carrier frequency) and amplitude increase or decrease, based on which dynamics the CVNN learning or self-organization works. As a result, the generalization characteristics (error magnitude at nonlearning points in supervised learning) and the classification manner often become quite different from those of real-valued neural networks [28, 35]. The feature plays the most important role also in other applications referred to below.

1.2.2   Estimation of Direction of Arrival and Beamforming

The estimation of direction of arrival (DoA) of electromagnetic wave using CVNNs has also been investigated for decades [67, 6]. A similar application field is the beamforming. When a signal has a narrow band, we can simply employ Huygens' principle. However, in an ultra-wideband (UWB) system, where the wavelength is distributed over a wide range, we cannot assume a single wavelength, resulting in unavailability of Huygens' principle. To overcome this difficulty, an adaptive method based on a CVNN has been proposed [60] where a unit module consists of a tapped-delay-line (TDL) network.

1.2.3   Radar Imaging

CVNNs are widely applied in coherent electromagnetic-wave signal processing. An area is adaptive processing of interferometric synthetic aperture radar (InSAR) images captured by satellite or airplane to observe land surface [59, 65]. There they aim at solving one of the most serious problems in InSAR imaging that there exist many rotational points (singular points) in the observed data so that the height cannot be determined in a straightforward way.

Ground penetrating radar (GPR) is another field [21, 66, 43, 44, 49, 34]. GPR systems usually suffer from serious clutter (scattering and reflection from non-target objects). Land surface as well as stones and clods generate such heavy clutter that we cannot observe what are underground if we pay attention only to the intensity. Complex-amplitude texture often provides us with highly informative features that can be processed adaptively in such a manner that we do in our early vision.

1.2.4   Acoustic Signal Processing and Ultrasonic Imaging

Another important application field is sonic and ultrasonic processing. Pioneering works were done into various directions [69, 58]. The problem of singular points exists also in ultrasonic imaging. They appear as speckles. A technique similar to that used in InSAR imaging was successfully applied to ultrasonic imaging [51].

1.2.5   Communications Signal Processing

In communication systems, we can regard CVNNs as an extension of adaptive complex filters, i.e., modular multiple-stage and nonlinear version. From this viewpoint, several groups work hard on time-sequential signal processing [15, 16], blind separation [68], channel prediction [12], equalization [63, 36, 55, 40, 33, 7, 8], and channel separation in multiple-input multiple-output (MIMO) systems [37]. Relevant circuit realization [13] is highly inspiring not only as working hardware but also for understanding of neural dynamics.

1.2.6   Image Processing

There are many ideas based on CVNNs also in image processing. An example is the adaptive processing for blur compensation by identifying point scattering function in the frequency domain [3]. In such a frequency-domain processing of images, we often utilize the fact that the phase information in frequency domain corresponds to position information in spatial domain. On the other hand, CVNN spatial-domain processing is also unique and powerful. A highly practical proposal was made for quick gesture recognition in smart phones by dealing with finger angle information adaptively by a CVNN [19]. Biological imaging is another expanding field. There we can find, for example, a classification of gene-expression stages in gene images [1], along with adaptive segmentation of magnetic resonance image (MRI) by placing a dynamic boundary curve (so-called "snake") in the obtained complex-amplitude MRI image for segmentation of blood vessels and other organs [20]. Since there are various types of active and coherent imaging systems in medicine, we can expect further applications of CVNNs to deal with complex-amplitude images.

1.2.7   Social Systems Such as Traffic and Power Systems

Recent applications expand more multi-directionally even to social systems. In traffic systems, a CVNN will be effectively used for controlling mutual switching timing of traffic lights in complicatedly connected driving roads [50]. Since traffic lights have periodic operation, some CVNN dynamics is suitable for their adaptive control. Green energy and smart grid are also the fields. A CVNN-based prediction of wind strength and direction has been demonstrated for efficient electric power generation [14] in which amplitude and phase in the complex plane represent the strength and the direction, respectively.

1.2.8   Quantum Devices Such as Superconductive Devices

Applications to quantum computation using quantum devices such as superconductivity have also been investigated in many groups [57, 39, 48]. Their results suggest the future realization of intrinsically non-von Neumann computers including pattern-information representing devices. Conventional quantum computation is strictly limited in its treatable problems. Contrarily, CVNN-based quantum computation can deal with more general problems, which leads to wider applications of quantum computation.

1.2.9   Optical/Lightwave Information Processing Including Carrier-Frequency Multiplexing

Learning optical and lightwave computer is another field of CVNN applications. There are researches such as frequency-domain multiplexed learning [38] and real-time generation of a three-dimensional holographic movie for interactively controllable optical tweezers [32, 62]. In these networks, a signal has its carrier frequency, equivalent to a band signal in communications, and therefore the learning and processing dynamics is controllable by modulating the carrier frequency. The idea can be adapted to complex filters. It led to a novel developmental learning of motion control combined with reinforcement learning [30]. The success suggests further a possible influence of frequency modulation of brain wave on biological brain activity, indicating a new door to CVNN-related physiology.

1.2.10 Hypercomplex-Valued Neural Networks

Hypercomplex-valued neural networks have also been actively investigated [5]. An example is the adaptive learning in three-dimensional color space by using quaternion [45]. An adaptive super-high-sensitive color camera (so-called night vision) has been produced that realizes a compensation of nonlinear human color-vision characteristics in extremely dark environment. More generalized hypercomplex networks, namely, Clifford algebraic neural networks, are also discussed very actively in, e.g., special sessions in conferences [54].

1.3 WHAT IS A COMPLEX NUMBER?

In this section, we look back the history of complex numbers to extract the essence influential in neural dynamics.

1.3.1 Geometric and Intuitive Definition

Throughout history, the definition of the complex number has changed gradually [11]. In the 16th century, Cardano tried to work with imaginary roots in dealing with quadratic equations. Afterward, Euler used complex numbers in his calculations intuitively and correctly. It is said that by 1728 he knew the transcendental relationship $i \log i = -\pi/2$. The Euler formulae appear in his book as

$$\cos x = \frac{e^{ix} + e^{-ix}}{2} \quad \text{and} \quad \sin x = \frac{e^{ix} - e^{-ix}}{2i} \tag{1.1}$$

In 1798, Wessel described representation of the points of a plane by complex numbers to deal with directed line segments. Argand also interpreted $\sqrt{-1}$ as a rotation through a right angle in the plane, and he justified this idea on the ground that two $\sqrt{-1}$ rotations yields a reflection, i.e., -1. It is also believed that, in early 1749, Euler already had a visual concept of complex numbers as points of a plane. He described a number x on a unit circle as $x = \cos g + i \sin g$, where g is an arc of the circle. Gauss was in full possession of the geometrical theory by 1815. He proposed to refer to $+1$, -1, and $\sqrt{-1}$ as direct, inverse, and lateral unity, instead of positive, negative, and imaginary or "impossible" elements.

1.3.2   Definition as Ordered Pair of Real Numbers

The geometrical representation is intuitively simple and visually understandable, but may be weak in strictness. In 1835, Hamilton presented the formal definition of the complex number as an "ordered pair of real numbers," which also led to the discovery of quaternions, in his article entitled "Theory of conjugate functions, or algebra as the science of pure time." He defined addition and multiplication in such a manner that the distributive, associative, and commutative laws hold. The definition as the ordered pair of real numbers is algebraic, and it can be stricter than the intuitive rotation interpretation.

At the same time, the fact that a complex number is defined by two real numbers may lead present-day neural-network researchers to consider a complex network equivalent to just a doubled-dimension real-number network effectively. However, in this paper, the authors would like to clarify the merit by focusing on the rotational function even with this definition.

Based on the definition of the complex number as an ordered pair of real numbers, we represent a complex number z as

$$z \equiv (x, y) \tag{1.2}$$

where x and y are real numbers. Then the addition and multiplication of z_1 and z_2 are defined in *complex domain* as

$$(x_1, y_1) + (x_2, y_2) \equiv (x_1 + x_2, y_1 + y_2) \tag{1.3}$$
$$(x_1, y_1) \cdot (x_2, y_2) \equiv (x_1 x_2 - y_1 y_2, x_1 y_2 + y_1 x_2) \tag{1.4}$$

As a reference, the addition and multiplication (as a step in correlation calculation, for example) of *two-dimensional real values* is expressed as

$$(x_1, y_1) + (x_2, y_2) = (x_1 + x_2, y_1 + y_2) \tag{1.5}$$
$$(x_1, y_1) \cdot (x_2, y_2) = (x_1 x_2, y_1 y_2) \tag{1.6}$$

In the comparison, the addition process is identical. Contrarily, the complex multiplication seems quite artificial, but this definition (1.4) brings the complex number with its unique function, that is, the angle rotation, as well as amplitude amplification/attenuation, which are the result of the intermixture of the real and imaginary components.

It is easily verified that the commutative, associative, and distributive laws hold. We have the unit element $(1, 0)$ and the inverse of z ($\neq 0$), which is

$$
\begin{aligned}
z^{-1} &\equiv \left(\frac{x}{x^2 + y^2}, \frac{-y}{x^2 + y^2} \right) \\
&= \left(\frac{x}{|z|^2}, \frac{-y}{|z|^2} \right)
\end{aligned} \tag{1.7}
$$

where $|z| \equiv \sqrt{x^2 + y^2}$.

1.3.3 Real 2×2 Matrix Representation

We can also use real 2×2 matrices, instead of the ordered pairs of real numbers, to represent complex numbers [11, 9]. With every complex number $c = a + ib$, we associate the C-linear transformation

$$T_c : C \to C, \quad z \mapsto cz = ax - by + i(bx + ay) \tag{1.8}$$

which includes a special case of $z \to iz$ that maps 1 into i, i into -1, ..., with a rotation with right angle each. In this sense, this definition is a more precise and general version of Argand's interpretation of complex numbers. If we identify C with R^2 by

$$z = x + iy = \begin{pmatrix} x \\ y \end{pmatrix} \tag{1.9}$$

it follows that

$$T_c \begin{pmatrix} x \\ y \end{pmatrix} = \begin{pmatrix} ax - by \\ bx + ay \end{pmatrix}$$
$$= \begin{pmatrix} a & -b \\ b & a \end{pmatrix} \begin{pmatrix} x \\ y \end{pmatrix} \tag{1.10}$$

In other words, the linear transformation T_c determined by $c = a + ib$ is described by the matrix $\begin{pmatrix} a & -b \\ b & a \end{pmatrix}$. Generally, a mapping represented by a 2×2 matrix is noncommutative. However, in the present case, it becomes *commutative*. By this real matrix representation, the imaginary unit i in C is given as

$$I \equiv \begin{pmatrix} 0 & -1 \\ 1 & 0 \end{pmatrix}, \quad I^2 = \begin{pmatrix} -1 & 0 \\ 0 & -1 \end{pmatrix} = -E \tag{1.11}$$

In the days of Hamilton, we did not have matrices yet. Even after the advent of matrices, it is very rare to define complex numbers in terms of real 2×2 matrices [11] (Chapter 3, §2, 5.), [9]. The introduction of complex numbers through 2×2 matrices has the advantage, over introducing them through ordered pairs of real numbers, that it is unnecessary to define an ad hoc multiplication. What is most important is that this matrix representation clearly expresses the function specific to the complex numbers—that is, the rotation and amplification or attenuation as

$$\begin{pmatrix} a & -b \\ b & a \end{pmatrix} = r \begin{pmatrix} \cos\theta & -\sin\theta \\ \sin\theta & \cos\theta \end{pmatrix} \tag{1.12}$$

where r and θ denote amplification/attenuation of amplitude and rotation angle applied to signals, respectively, in the multiplication calculation. On the other hand, addition is rather plain. The complex addition function is identical to that in the case of doubled-dimension real numbers.

In summary, the phase rotation and amplitude amplification/attenuation are the most important features of complex numbers.

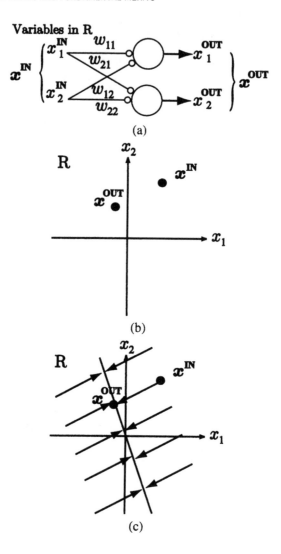

Figure 1.1 (a) A simple real-valued single-layered two-input two-output feedforward network to learn (b) a mapping that maps x^{IN} to x^{OUT} and (c) a possible but degenerate solution that is often unuseful [28].

1.4 COMPLEX NUMBERS IN FEEDFORWARD NEURAL NETWORKS

We consider intuitively what feature emerges in the dynamics of complex-valued neural networks. Here we first take a layered feedforward neural network. Then we consider metrics in correlation learning.

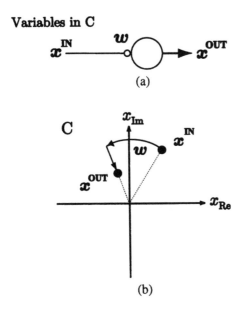

Figure 1.2 (a) A complex-valued neural network seemingly identical to Fig. 1.1(a) to learn the mapping shown in Fig. 1.1(b), and (b) a solution obtained in this small-degree-of-freedom case [28].

1.4.1 Synapse and Network Function in Layered Feedforward Neural Networks

In wave-related adaptive processing, we often obtain excellent performance with learning or self-organization based on the CVNNs. As already mentioned, the reason depends on situations. However, the discussion in Section 1.3 suggests that the origin lies in the complex rule of arithmetic. That is to say, the merit arises from the functions of the four fundamental rules of arithmetic of complex numbers, in particular the multiplication, rather than the representation of the complex numbers, which can be geometric, algebraic, or in matrices. Moreover, the essence of the complex numbers also lies in the characteristic multiplication function, the phase rotation, as overviewed in Section 1.3 [27].

Let us consider a very simple case shown in Fig. 1.1(a), where we have a single-layer 2-input 2-output feedforward neural network in real number. For simplicity, we omit the possible nonlinearity at the neurons, i.e., the activation function is the identity function, where the neurons have no threshold. We assume that the network should realize a mapping that transforms an input x^{IN} to an output x^{OUT} in Fig. 1.1(b) through supervised learning that adjusts the synaptic weights w_{ji}. Simply, we have only a single teacher pair of input and output signals. Then we can describe a general input–output relationship as

$$\begin{pmatrix} x_1^{OUT} \\ x_2^{OUT} \end{pmatrix} = \begin{pmatrix} a & b \\ c & d \end{pmatrix} \begin{pmatrix} x_1^{IN} \\ x_2^{IN} \end{pmatrix} \tag{1.13}$$

We have a variety of possible mapping obtained by the learning because the number of parameters to be determined is larger than the condition; i.e., the learning task is an ill-posed problem. The functional difference emerges as the difference in the generalization characteristics. For example, learning can result in a degenerate mapping shown in Fig. 1.1(c), which is often unuseful in practice.

Next, let us consider the mapping learning task in the one-dimensional complex domain, which transforms a complex value $x^{IN} = (x_1^{IN}, x_2^{IN})$ to another complex value $x^{OUT} = (x_1^{OUT}, x_2^{OUT})$. Figure 1.2(a) shows the complex-valued network, where the weight is a single complex value. The situation is expressed just like in (1.13) as

$$\begin{pmatrix} x_1^{OUT} \\ x_2^{OUT} \end{pmatrix} = \begin{pmatrix} |w| \cos \theta & -|w| \sin \theta \\ |w| \sin \theta & |w| \cos \theta \end{pmatrix} \begin{pmatrix} x_1^{IN} \\ x_2^{IN} \end{pmatrix} \tag{1.14}$$

where $\theta \equiv \arg(w)$. The degree of freedom is reduced, and the arbitrariness of the solution is also reduced. Figure 1.2(b) illustrates the result of the learning. The mapping is a combination of phase rotation and amplitude attenuation. This example is truly an extreme. The dynamics of a neural network is determined by various parameters such as network structure, input–output data dimensions, and teacher signal numbers. However, the above characteristics of phase rotation and amplitude modulation are embedded in the complex-valued network as a universal elemental process of weighting.

The essential merit of neural networks in general lies in the high degree of freedom in learning and self-organization. However, if we know *a priori* that the objective quantities include "phase" and/or "amplitude," we can reduce possibly harmful portion of the freedom by employing a complex-valued neural network, resulting in a more meaningful generalization characteristics. The "rotation" in the complex multiplication works as an elemental process at the synapse, and it realizes the advantageous reduction of the degree of freedom. This feature corresponds not only to the geometrical intuitive definition of complex numbers but also to the Hamilton's definition by ordered pairs of real numbers, or the real 2×2 matrix representation.

Though we considered a small feedforward network in this section, the conclusion is applicable also to other CVNNs such as complex-valued Hebbian-rule-based network and complex correlation learning networks, where the weight is updated by the multiplication results. The elemental process of phase rotation and amplitude modulation results in the network behavior consistent with phase rotation and amplitude modulation in total. The nature is a great advantage when we deal with not only waves such as electromagnetic wave and lightwave, but also arbitrary signals with the Fourier synthesis principle, or in the frequency domain through the Fourier transform.

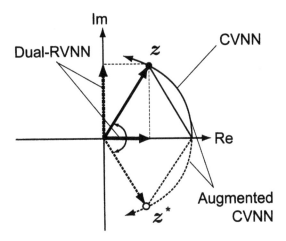

Figure 1.3   Conceptual illustration of the relationship among bases in the respective neural networks to deal with complex signal z [35].

1.4.2 Circularity

The circularity of the signals to be processed is also an important factor. To deepen the discussion, we refer to the wide sense linear (or widely linear: WL) systems which introduce conjugate signals in addition to direct complex signals [56, 41]. WL systems well learn complex data distributed anisotropically in the complex plane, i.e., noncircular data. For example, it is useful for predicting wind strength and direction by assuming the axes of the complex number plane represent north, south, east, and west, and the distance from the origin expresses the strength. Augmented complex-valued neural networks have been proposed in such a context [64]. Wind has high anisotropy in general. The augmented complex-valued networks does not lead to the reduction of the degree of freedom. The degree is the same as that of real-valued networks, resulting in dynamics similar to that of real-valued ones [42].

Figure 1.3 is a conceptual illustration showing the bases of the respective networks. The number of the bases of the augmented complex networks becomes that of the real-valued networks back, and its dynamics approaches that of real networks. This situation is analogous to the fact that the combination of positive and negative frequency spectra generates almost real-valued signals. In other words, if we compare the relationship to the polarization of lightwave, we come to the following. Complex-valued neural networks deal with only right- or left-handed circular polarized light, which are suitable for circular signal processing. Note that the signal in total can be out of complete circularity, but only each frequency component has the circularity. Since any waveform can be synthesized by sinusoidal components through Fourier synthesis, the signals that the complex networks can deal with are not limited to completely coherent signals. In contrast, the augmented complex-valued networks deal with both the right- and left-handed circular polarized light.

They are more flexible because of the larger degree of freedom, which is too much for circular signals. Dual univariate networks have the same degree of freedom; however, in this case, the bases are linear polarization corresponding to the real and imaginary parts, instead of the right- and left-handed circular bases in the augmented networks. In this manner, they are similar to each other.

Consequently, complex-valued neural networks are suitable for processing analytic signals, which consist of a real component and its consistent imaginary component that has the same amplitude but 90-degree shifted phase. The analytic signal is essentially circular. Analytic signals exist widely in electronics—for example, at the output of heterodyne or homodyne mixers and at the output of digital signal processing using the Hilbert transform. Complex-valued networks have the ability to process such analytic signals appropriately.

1.5 METRIC IN COMPLEX DOMAIN

1.5.1 Metric in Complex-Valued Self-Organizing Map

Among various neurodynamics in the complex domain, the complex-valued self-organizing maps (CSOMs) may possess fewer features which reflect the complex multiplication mentioned in Section 1.4 since most of SOMs have two subprocesses in the operation, i.e., winner determination and weight update, both of which may consist of only addition and subtraction in its arithmetic without any multiplication that utilizes the complex nature of phase rotation.

However, the circumstances depend on the metric we use to determine the dynamics. If we employ complex inner product, instead of conventional Euclidean metric in double-dimensional real space, we can utilize the characteristics specific to complex space [4]. The general dynamics of a SOM will be explained in Section 1.5. In this section, we discuss the metric we use in feature vector space.

1.5.2 Euclidean Metric

In SOM in general, the metric most widely used to determine the *winner* neuron whose weight w_c is nearest to an input feature vector z is the Euclidean metric. Even in a complex-valued SOM (CSOM) where z and w are complex, we can express them with imaginary unit i as

$$z \equiv \begin{bmatrix} |z_1| \exp(i\theta_1) \\ |z_2| \exp(i\theta_2) \\ \vdots \end{bmatrix} \tag{1.15}$$

$$w_c \equiv \begin{bmatrix} |w_{c\,1}| \exp(i\psi_{c\,1}) \\ |w_{c\,2}| \exp(i\psi_{c\,2}) \\ \vdots \end{bmatrix} \tag{1.16}$$

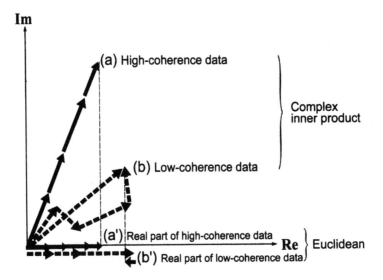

Figure 1.4   Conceptual illustration to compare the inner product z^*w_c and the real-part inner product $\mathbf{Re}(z^*w_c)$ to calculate $||z - w_c||^2$ [4].

The Euclidean process to choose a winner is expressed as

$$\hat{c} = \arg\min_c ||z - w_c|| \quad (c : \text{class index}) \tag{1.17}$$

where $\arg\min_c \cdots$ chooses a c that minimizes $\cdots$, and $||\cdot||$ denotes norm (amplitude), i.e.,

$$
\begin{aligned}
||z - w_c||^2 &= (z - w_c)^* (z - w_c) \\
&= ||z||^2 + ||w_c||^2 - (z^*w_c + w_c^*z) \\
&= ||z||^2 + ||w_c||^2 - 2\mathbf{Re}(z^*w_c)
\end{aligned}
\tag{1.18}
$$

Though (1.18) deals with complex numbers, this arithmetic is identical to the calculation of real-valued Euclidean distance and also of the real-valued inner product; i.e., when $x, w_c \in \mathbf{R}^m$,

$$
\begin{aligned}
||x - w_c||^2 &= ||x||^2 + ||w_c||^2 - 2x^T w_c \\
&= ||x||^2 + ||w_c||^2 - 2\sum_i |x_i||w_{c\,i}| \cos(\psi_{c\,i} - \theta_i)
\end{aligned}
\tag{1.19}
$$

Then, when $||z||^2$ and $||w_c||^2$ are almost constants, as is often the case, and/or we pay attention to phase information, the distance (1.19) is detemined by the cosine component (real part) $|z_i||w_{c\,i}| \cos(\psi_{c\,i} - \theta_i)$.

1.5.3 Complex Inner-Product Metric

Instead, we can also employ a complex inner-product metric for use in determination of a winner in the CSOM as

$$\hat{c} = \arg\max_c \left(\left| \frac{z^* w_c}{||z||\,||w_c||} \right| \right) \quad (c : \text{class index}) \tag{1.20}$$

This process is better understandable in equations by employing the polar representation. That is, the numerator of the complex-valued inner product (1.20) is given as

$$z^* w_c = \sum_i \left(|z_i| \exp(-i\theta_i) \right) \left(|w_{c\,i}| \exp(i\psi_{c\,i}) \right) \tag{1.21}$$

$$= \sum_i |z_i||w_{c\,i}| \exp(i(\psi_{c\,i} - \theta_i)) \tag{1.22}$$

where the summation takes into account the phase values directly, that is, the direction of the arrows [4].

In other words, the metric (1.22) takes both the cosine and sine components (real and imaginary parts) into consideration. That is, when we express the vectors as $z = (x_1 + iy_1, x_2 + iy_2, ...)$ and $w = (u_1 + iv_1, u_2 + iv_2, ...)$, omitting suffix c, we obtain

$$
\begin{aligned}
z^* w &= [x_1 - iy_1 \quad x_2 - iy_2 \quad ... \quad] [u_1 + iv_1 \quad u_2 + iv_2 \quad ... \quad]^T \\
&= x_1 u_1 + y_1 v_1 + x_2 u_2 + y_2 v_2 + ... \quad \Longleftarrow \text{cos component} \\
&\quad + i\,(x_1 v_1 - y_1 u_1 + x_2 v_2 - y_2 u_2 + ...) \quad \Longleftarrow \text{sin component} \tag{1.23}
\end{aligned}
$$

1.5.4 Comparison Between Complex Inner Product and Euclidean Distance

Figure 1.4 is a conceptual illustration to show the merit of this complex inner-product metric. In active imaging such as the ground penetrating radars described in Section 1.2.3, we obtain coherent signals consisting of amplitude and phase. The feature vector is defined in complex domain. For a set of high-coherence signals, i.e., signals having similar phases, the summation to generate inner product grows straightforward as shown by arrows (a) in Fig. 1.4. Contrarily, in a low-coherence case, having random phases, the summation does not grow so much as shown by arrows (b). This effect emerges also in the Euclidean metric to some extent. However, the Euclidean metric is related only to the cosine component as shown in Fig. 1.4(a') and (b'), resulting in a partial treatment of phase directions. The evaluation results can be different from (a) and (b). The complex inner-product metric is then more sensitive to signal coherence and, therefore, enhances the distinction among various objects compared with the case of Euclidean metric described below.

In addition, the complex inner product is inherently less sensitive to the norm of signal vectors. This is simply because of the normalization. It is desirable in particular in coherent imaging systems where we often suffer from distortion in intensity caused by the mirror glaring and speckles.

1.5.5 Metric in Correlation Learning

Correlation learning, used widely in neural networks such as associative memories [24] described in Section 1.5.5, also possess the same feature of the complex-valued learning. The correlation learning embeds the correlation between output signals z_s and input signals z_t in synaptic weights w. For simplicity of expression, we consider one of the output signals z_s out of $\boldsymbol{z_s}$. As shown in detail in Section 1.5.5, the learning dynamics is expressed as

$$\tau \frac{dw}{dt} = -w + z_s\, z_t^* \tag{1.24}$$

where τ is the learning time constant in the time t domain. Various pairs of input z_t and output z_s teacher signals are presented to the network for the training. The correlation is accumulated into w, converging at

$$w \longrightarrow K < z_s\, z_t^* > \tag{1.25}$$

where K is a real constant.

Here we express the teacher signal pairs in real and imaginary parts as

$$z_s = x_s + j y_s \tag{1.26}$$
$$z_t = [x_{t1} + j y_{t1}, x_{t2} + j y_{t2}, \ldots, x_{tN} + j y_{tN}]^T \tag{1.27}$$

where j and N are the imaginary unit and the input terminal number. Then the product in the correlation in (1.25) is rewritten as

$$
\begin{aligned}
z_s\, z_t^* = [\ &(x_s x_{t1} + y_s y_{t1}) + j(y_s x_{t1} - x_s y_{t1}), \\
&(x_s x_{t2} + y_s y_{t2}) + j(y_s x_{t2} - x_s y_{t2}), \\
&\qquad \cdots \\
&(x_s x_{tN} + y_s y_{tN}) + j(y_s x_{tN} - x_s y_{tN})\ ]^T
\end{aligned}
\tag{1.28}
$$

The real and imaginary parts mix with each other. The meaning becomes obvious when we express the pixel values in amplitude and phase as

$$z_s = r_s e^{i\theta_s} \tag{1.29}$$
$$z_t = [r_{t1} e^{j y_{t1}}, r_{t2} e^{j y_{t2}}, \ldots, r_{tN} e^{j y_{tN}}]^T \tag{1.30}$$

and rewrite (1.28) as

$$z_s\, z_t^* = [\ r_s r_{t1} e^{j(\theta_s - \theta_{t1})}, r_s r_{t2} e^{j(\theta_s - \theta_{t2})}, \ldots, r_s r_{tN} e^{j(\theta_s - \theta_{tN})}\ ]^T \tag{1.31}$$

The product yields the phase difference as well as the amplitude product, which is compatible with the signal circularity.

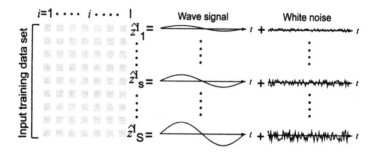

Figure 1.5   A set of teacher signals [35] (See color insert.).

On the contrary, if we regard the neural network as a real-valued network having double input terminals and two output neurons corresponding to real and imaginary parts, the dynamics for double-dimensional real signals z_s and z_t are expressed as

$$z_s = [x_s, y_s] \tag{1.32}$$
$$z_t = [x_{t1}, y_{t1}, x_{t2}, y_{t2}, \dots, x_{tN}, y_{tN}]^T \tag{1.33}$$

and the product as a step to calculate correlation becomes

$$z_s z_t = [x_s x_{t1}, y_s y_{t1}, x_s x_{t2}, y_s y_{t2}, \dots, x_s x_{tN}, y_s y_{tN}]^T \tag{1.34}$$

We can find that the product (1.34) is different from (1.28) or (1.31). That is, the dynamics of the real-valued network is completely different from that of the complex-valued one. The difference originates from the very basic arithmetic operation, and is therefore very fundamental. This property may also be called circularity as one of the characteristics of the complex-valued neural network. The circularity is one of the most essential features of the complex-valued neural networks.

1.6 EXPERIMENTS TO ELUCIDATE THE GENERALIZATION CHARACTERISTICS

To elucidate the generalization characteristics in feedforward layered neural networks described in Section 1.4, we conducted a set of experiments. The details were reported in Ref. 35. The outline is explained as follows.

- Input signals: Weighted summation of the following (A) and (B) as shown in Fig. 1.5.
  (A) Sinusoid: completely coherent signal.
  (B) White Gaussian noise (WGN): completely incoherent data having random amplitude and phase (or real and imaginary parts).

- Task to learn: Identity mapping, which is expected to show the learning characteristics most clearly for the above signals with various degrees of coherence.

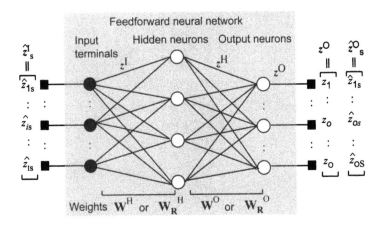

Figure 1.6   Basic construction of the complex- and real-valued feedforward neural networks [35]. (See color insert.)

- Evaluation of generalization: Observation of the generalization error when the input signals shift in time, or when the amplitude is changed.

1.6.1   Forward Processing and Learning Dynamics

1.6.1.1 Complex-Valued Neural Network (CVNN)   Figure 1.6 shows the general construction of the neural network to be considered here. It is a layered feedforward network having input terminals, hidden neurons, and output neurons. In a CVNN, we first employ a phase amplitude-type sigmoid activation function and the teacher-signal-backpropagation learning process, [23, 31] with notations of

$$z^I = [z_1, ..., z_i, ..., z_I, z_{I+1}]^T$$
$$\text{(Input signal vector)} \tag{1.35}$$

$$z^H = [z_1, ..., z_h, ..., z_H, z_{H+1}]^T$$
$$\text{(Hidden-layer output signal vector)} \tag{1.36}$$

$$z^O = [z_1, ..., z_o, ..., z_O]^T$$
$$\text{(Output-layer signal vector)} \tag{1.37}$$

$$\mathbf{W}^H = [w_{hi}] \quad \text{(Hidden neuron weight matrix)} \tag{1.38}$$

$$\mathbf{W}^O = [w_{oh}] \quad \text{(Output neuron weight matrix)} \tag{1.39}$$

where $[\cdot]^T$ means transpose. In (1.38) and (1.39), the weight matrices include additional weights $w_{h\ I+1}$ and $w_{o\ H+1}$, equivalent to neural thresholds, where we add formal constant inputs $z_{I+1} = 1$ and $z_{H+1} = 1$ in (1.35) and (1.36), respectively. Respective signal vectors and synaptic weights are connected with one an-

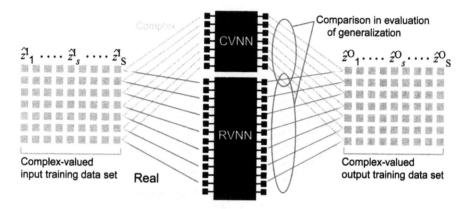

Figure 1.7   Schematic diagram of the learning process for pairs of input–output teachers [35]. (See color insert.)

other through an activation function $f(z)$ as

$$z^{\mathrm{H}} = f\left(\mathbf{W}^{\mathrm{H}} z^{\mathrm{I}}\right) \tag{1.40}$$

$$z^{\mathrm{O}} = f\left(\mathbf{W}^{\mathrm{O}} z^{\mathrm{H}}\right) \tag{1.41}$$

where $f(z)$ is a function of each vector element $z \ (\in \boldsymbol{C})$ defined as

$$f(z) = \tanh\left(|z|\right)\exp\left(i \arg z\right) \tag{1.42}$$

Figure 1.7 is a diagram to explain the supervised learning process. We prepare a set of teacher signals at the input $\hat{z}_s^{\mathrm{I}} = [\hat{z}_{1s}, ..., \hat{z}_{is}, ..., \hat{z}_{Is}, \hat{z}_{I+1\ s}]^T$ and the output $\hat{z}_s^{\mathrm{O}} = [\hat{z}_{1s}, ..., \hat{z}_{os}, ..., \hat{z}_{Os}]^T$ $(s = 1, ..., s, ...S)$ for which we employ the teacher-signal backpropagation learning. We define an error function E to obtain the dynamics by referring to Refs. [31, 23, 27] as

$$E \equiv \frac{1}{2}\sum_{s=1}^{S}\sum_{o=1}^{O}\left|z_o(\hat{z}_s^{\mathrm{I}}) - \hat{z}_{os}\right|^2 \tag{1.43}$$

$$\left|w_{oh}^{\mathrm{new}}\right| = \left|w_{oh}^{\mathrm{old}}\right| - K\frac{\partial E}{\partial\left|w_{oh}\right|} \tag{1.44}$$

$$\arg w_{oh}^{\mathrm{new}} = \arg w_{oh}^{\mathrm{old}} - K\frac{1}{|w_{oh}|}\frac{\partial E}{\partial(\arg w_{oh})} \tag{1.45}$$

$$\frac{\partial E}{\partial |w_{oh}|} =$$

$$\left(1 - |z_o|^2\right) \left(|z_o| - |\hat{z}_o| \cos\left(\arg z_o - \arg \hat{z}_o\right)\right) |z_h|$$
$$\cdot \cos\left(\arg z_o - \arg \hat{z}_o - \arg w_{oh}\right)$$
$$- |z_o||\hat{z}_o| \sin\left(\arg z_o - \arg \hat{z}_o\right) \frac{|z_h|}{\tanh^{-1}|z_o|}$$
$$\cdot \sin\left(\arg z_o - \arg \hat{z}_o - \arg w_{oh}\right) \tag{1.46}$$

$$\frac{1}{|w_{oh}|} \frac{\partial E}{\partial(\arg w_{oh})} =$$

$$\left(1 - |z_o|^2\right) \left(|z_o| - |\hat{z}_o| \cos\left(\arg z_o - \arg \hat{z}_o\right)\right) |z_h|$$
$$\cdot \sin\left(\arg z_o - \arg \hat{z}_o - \arg w_{oh}\right)$$
$$+ |z_o||\hat{z}_o| \sin\left(\arg z_o - \arg \hat{z}_o\right) \frac{|z_h|}{\tanh^{-1}|z_o|}$$
$$\cdot \cos\left(\arg z_o - \arg \hat{z}_o - \arg w_{oh}\right) \tag{1.47}$$

where $(\cdot)^{\text{new}}$ and $(\cdot)^{\text{old}}$ indicates the update of the weights from $(\cdot)^{\text{old}}$ to $(\cdot)^{\text{new}}$, and K is a learning constant. The teacher signals at the hidden layer $\hat{z}^H = [\hat{z}_1, ..., \hat{z}_h,$ $..., \hat{z}_H]^T$ is obtained by making the output teacher vector itself $\hat{z}^O$ propagate backward as

$$\hat{z}^H = \left(f\left(\left(\hat{z}^O\right)^* \hat{w}^O\right)\right)^* \tag{1.48}$$

where $(\cdot)^*$ denotes Hermite conjugate. Using $\hat{z}^H$, the hidden layer neurons change their weights by following (1.44) (1.47) with replacement of the suffixes o,h with h,i [25, 27].

1.6.1.2 Complex-Valued Neural Network Having Real–Imaginary Separate-Type Activation Function (RI-CVNN)
We also investigate the characteristics of complex-valued neural networks having real-imaginary separate-type activation function. Instead of (1.42), a neuron has an activation function expressed as

$$f(z) = \tanh(\mathbf{Re}[z]) + i \tanh(\mathbf{Im}[z]) \tag{1.49}$$

The structure and the dynamics of feedforward processing and backpropagation learning are those described in, for example, Ref. 52.

1.6.1.3 Real-Valued Neural Network Having Double Input Terminals and Output Neurons for Bivariate Procesing (RVNN)
Similarly, the forward processing and learning of a RVNN having double input terminals and output neurons are explained as follows. Figure 1.7 includes also this case. We represent a complex number as a pair of real numbers as $z_i = x_{2i-1} + ix_{2i}$. Then we have a double number of terminals for real and imaginary parts of input signals z_R^I and a double number of

output neurons to generate real and imaginary parts of output signals z_R^O. We also prepare a double number of hidden neurons for hidden-layer signals z_R^H so that the equivalent number of neurons is the same as that of the above CVNN.

Forward signal processing connects the signal vectors as well as hidden neuron weights $\mathbf{W}_R^H$ and output neuron weights $\mathbf{W}_R^O$ through a real-valued activation function f_R as

$$
z_R^I = [\ \overbrace{x_1,\ x_2}^{\text{real \& imaginary}},\ ...,\ x_{2i-1}, x_{2i}, ...,
$$
$$
x_{2I-1}, x_{2I}, x_{2I+1}, x_{2I+2}]^T
$$
$$
\left(= z^I\right)\quad \text{(Input signal vector)} \tag{1.50}
$$

$$
z_R^H = [x_1, x_2, ..., x_{2h-1}, x_{2h}, ...,
$$
$$
x_{2H-1}, x_{2H}, x_{2H+1}, x_{2H+2}]^T
$$
$$
\text{(Hidden-layer output signal vector)} \tag{1.51}
$$

$$
z_R^O = [x_1, x_2, ..., x_{2o-1}, x_{2o}, ..., x_{2O-1}, x_{2O}]^T
$$
$$
\text{(Output-layer signal vector)} \tag{1.52}
$$

$$
\mathbf{W}_R^H = [w_{Rhi}]\quad \text{(Hidden neuron weight matrix)} \tag{1.53}
$$

$$
\mathbf{W}_R^O = [w_{Roh}]\quad \text{(Output neuron weight mateix)} \tag{1.54}
$$

$$
z_R^H = f_R\left(\mathbf{W}_R^H z_R^I\right) \tag{1.55}
$$

$$
z_R^O = f_R\left(\mathbf{W}_R^O z_R^H\right) \tag{1.56}
$$

$$
f_R(x) = \tanh(x) \tag{1.57}
$$

where the thresholds are $w_{R\,h\,2I+1}$, $w_{R\,h\,2I+2}$, $w_{R\,h\,2H+1}$, and $w_{R\,h\,2H+2}$ with formal additional inputs $x_{2H+1} = 1$, $x_{2H+2} = 1$, $x_{2H+1} = 1$, and $x_{2H+2} = 1$. We employ the conventional error backpropagation learning. That is, we define an error function E_R for a set of input and output teacher signals $(\hat{z}_s^I, \hat{z}_s^O)$ to obtain the learning dynamics as

$$E_{\text{R}} \equiv \frac{1}{2} \sum_{s=1}^{S} \sum_{o=1}^{2O} \left| x_o(\hat{z}_{\text{R}_s}^{\text{I}}) - \hat{x}_{os} \right|^2 \quad (= E) \tag{1.58}$$

$$w_{\text{R}oh}^{\text{new}} = w_{\text{R}oh}^{\text{old}} - K \frac{\partial E_{\text{R}}}{\partial w_{\text{R}oh}} \tag{1.59}$$

$$w_{\text{R}ji}^{\text{new}} = w_{\text{R}hi}^{\text{old}} - K \frac{\partial E_{\text{R}}}{\partial w_{\text{R}hi}} \tag{1.60}$$

$$\frac{\partial E_{\text{R}}}{\partial w_{\text{R}oh}} = (x_o - \hat{x}_o)\left(1 - x_o^2\right) x_h \tag{1.61}$$

$$\frac{\partial E_{\text{R}}}{\partial w_{\text{R}hi}} = \left(\sum_{o}^{2O} (x_o - \hat{x}_o)\left(1 - x_o^2\right) w_{oh} \right)\left(1 - x_h^2\right) x_i \tag{1.62}$$

1.6.1.4 *Dual Real-Valued Neural Networks for Real–Imaginary Separate Processing (dual-RVNN)*   We consider another type of real-valued neural network in which the real and imaginary parts of input signals are processed separately. It is an extension of dual univariate real-valued neural network having single-layer structure. We may have a variety of ways of mixing and separation of real and imaginary variables in multiple-layer networks. With this network, we examine a completely separate case where the neurons in the real-part network have no connections to those in the imaginary-part network. The learning and processing dynamics are identical to that of the above RVNN except that the numbers of input terminals and output neurons are the same as the CVNNs for the respective real and imaginary networks.

1.6.2 Experimental Setup

1.6.2.1 *Simulation Setup*   Figure 1.8 shows schematically how to observe the generalization characteristics of the networks. We conducted the learning process as follows. We chose the identity mapping as the task to be learned to show the network characteristics most clearly. That is, we take a set of input and output teacher signals as $\hat{z}_s^{\text{I}} = \hat{z}_s^{\text{O}}$ ($s = 1, 2, ..., S$) with the following conditions. For a signal set showing high coherence, we choose its wavelength in such a manner that a unit wave spans just over the neural input terminals $i = 1, ..., I$, and discrete I points are fed to the network evenly with a constant interval in the unit wave. In more detail, we choose multiple amplitude values between 0 to 1 evenly for $s_{\text{A}} = 1, ..., S_{\text{A}}$ teacher signals as well as multiple time shift amount between 0 to half-wave duration (phase shift in a sinusoidal case between 0 to π evenly for $s_{\text{t}} = 1, ..., S_{\text{t}}$ teachers. Consequently we generate $S = S_{\text{A}} \times S_{\text{t}}$ points of discrete teacher-signal sets $\hat{z}_{is}$ ($s = 1, 2, ..., S$) as

$$z_{is} \equiv \frac{s_{\text{A}}}{S_{\text{A}} + 1} \exp\left(i \left(\frac{s_{\text{t}}}{2S_{\text{t}}} + \frac{i}{I} \right) 2\pi \right) \tag{1.63}$$

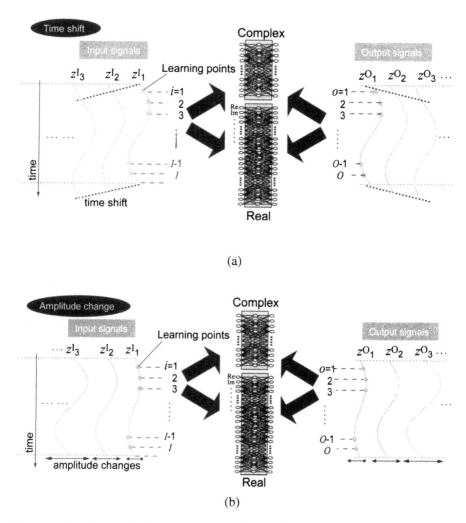

Figure 1.8   Schematic diagrams showing how to feed signals to observe (a) time-shift and (b) amplitude-change generalizations [35]. (See color insert.)

Note that the wavelength, and then the signal frequency, are unchanged. Figure 1.5 includes the manner of the amplitude variation. We add WGN to the sinusoidal wave with various weighting. The noise power is adjusted depending on the signal power and the expected signal-to-noise ratio SNR which is determined in each learning trial.

The dots on the continuous signals in Fig. 1.8 indicates the discrete teacher signal points $\hat{z}_{is}$. We observe the generalization characteristics by inputting signals other than the teachers and evaluate the output errors. Figure 1.8(a) illustrates the observation of outputs when the input signal is shifted in time. The continuous time signal

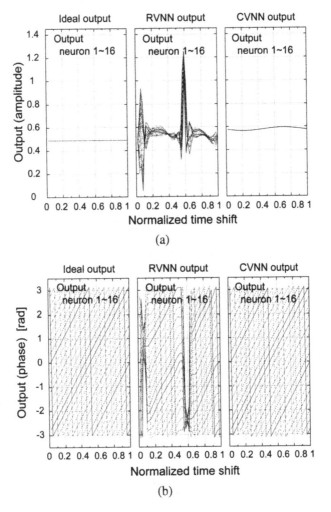

Figure 1.9 Example of (a) amplitude and (b) phase when the input signal gradually shifts in time in the real-valued and complex-valued neural networks (RVNN and CVNN) when no noise is added to sinusoidal signals ($SNR= \infty$) [35].

was generated by the Lagrange interpolation. Figure 1.8(b) shows the observation when the amplitude is changed. We combine the time shift and the amplitude change to evaluate the generalization. In the experiment below, $S_A = 4$, $S_t = 4$, and the neural network parameters are listed in Table 1.1. The learning iteration is 3,000.

1.6.2.2 Heterodyne Signal Experiment We process a heterodyne signal observed in a sonar imaging system. The signal has a carrier of 100 kHz with thermal noise. It is converted into 100 Hz in-phase and quadrature-phase (IQ) intermediate-frequency (IF) signals through an IQ mixer. The imbalance of the IQ mixer is less than 0.3 dB

Table 1.1   Parameters in the neural networks [35]

	CVNN or RI-CVNN	RVNN or dual-RVNN
Number of input neurons	$I = 16$	$2I = 32$
Number of hidden neurons	$H = 25$	$2H = 50$
Number of output neurons	$O = 16$	$2O = 32$
Learning constant	$K = 0.01$	$K = 0.01$

in amplitude and 3 degrees in phase, which is common in this type of systems. The IF signal is recorded by a personal computer (PC) through an analogue/digital converter with 600 k Sample/s sampling frequency. We aim at appropriate interpolation of the signals in time and/or space domain for post-processing to generate high-quality time–space images. When the 100 kHz carrier signal power changes, the SNR also changes for a constant noise power.

1.6.3   Results

1.6.3.1   Examples of Output Signals for Inputs Having Various Coherence Degrees   Figure 1.9 displays typical examples of the output signals of the CVNN and RVNN for a single learning trial when $SNR = \infty$, i.e., the signal is completely sinusoidal and coherent. After a learning process, we use other input signal points to investigate the generalization. As mentioned above, the wavelength is adjusted to span over the 16 neural input terminals. For example, we gradually move the input signal forward in time while keeping the amplitude unchanged at $a = 0.5$. Figures 1.9(a) and (b) present the output amplitude and phase, respectively, showing from left-hand side to the right-hand side the ideal output of the identity mapping, the RVNN outputs, and CVNN outputs of the 16 output neurons. The horizontal axes present the time shift t normalized by the unit-wave duration.

In Fig. 1.9(b), we find that the output signals of the RVNN locally deviate greatly from the ideal ones. The learning points are plotted at $t = 0$ (no time shift), where the output amplitude is almost 0.5 for all the neurons. However, with the time course, the amplitude values fluctuate largely. Contrarily, the CVNN amplitude stays almost constant. At the learning point $t = 0$, the value is slightly larger than 0.5, corresponding to the slight nonzero value of the residual error in the learning curve.

In Fig. 1.9(c), the ideal output phase values on the left-hand side exhibit linear increase in time. In the RVNN case, though the phase values at $t = 0$ are the same as those of ideal outputs, the values sometimes swing strongly. In contrast, the CVNN output phase values increase orderly, which is almost identical with the ideal values. In summary, the CVNN presents much better generalization characteristics than the RVNN when the coherence is high, i.e., $SNR = \infty$.

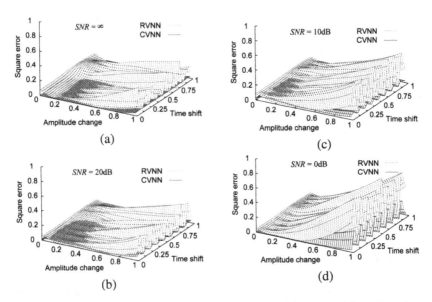

Figure 1.10   Squared generalization errors averaged for 100 trials as functions of amplitude change and time shift for $SNR=$ (a) ∞, (b) 20 dB, (c) 10 dB, and (d) 0 dB, respectively [35].

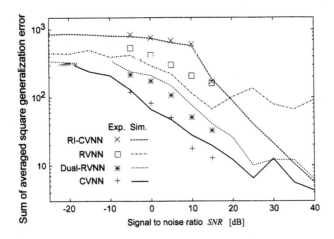

Figure 1.11   Squared generalization errors summed up for all the sampling amplitude-time points shown in Fig. 1.10 versus signal SNR for the real-valued and complex-valued neural networks (CVNN, RI-CVNN, RVNN, and dual-RVNN; curves denote simulations, marks denote experiments) [35].

1.6.3.2 Generalization Error and Its Dependence on the Coherence Here we present statistic results obtained by repeating the above simulations as well as the real-world experiment dealing with the heterodyne signals explained in Section 1.6.2.2.

Figure 1.10 is a three-dimensional representation of the square errors as the average of 100 learning trials for various coherence degree, namely, $SNR=$ (a) ∞, (b) 20 dB, (c) 10 dB, and (d) 0 dB, as functions of time shift and amplitude change. The learning points exist at $t = 0$ and amplitude values of $a = 0.2, 0.4, 0.6$, and 0.8. At these points we can find the errors are very small, which corresponds to the almost zero residual errors in the learning curves. However, the errors at the teacher points for lower SNRs are obviously positive. This is because the learning error in some trials fails to converge at zero. As a whole, we notice in Fig. 1.10 that the generalization error of the RVNN are larger than those of the CVNN, in particular in the cases of higher SNR. When SNR is low ($\sim$0 dB), the error of the CVNN also increases.

Figure 1.11 compares quantitatively the generalization errors, summed up for all the sampling amplitude-phase points shown in Fig. 1.10, for the CVNN, RI-CVNN, RVNN, and dual-RVNN as functions of the coherence degree, i.e., SNR. The four curves show the results of the simulation, while the marks indicate experimental results. In all the neural network cases, the generalization error reduces according to the increase of the coherence (increase of SNR). The CVNN curve shows lower errors than other network ones over a wide range of SNR. The dual-RVNN also shows low errors though, at the middle SNR ($SNR = -5$ to 15 dB) the value is 3 to 6 dB larger than that of the CVNN. The error of the simulated RVNN is about 2 dB larger than the dual-RVNN in the low and middle SNR range. The experimental results (marks) of the RVNN are slightly larger. It is remarkable that, in the higher coherence region ($SNR > 10$ dB), the RVNN curve holds a floor at a nonnegligible level. The RI-CVNN shows a large generalization error in the low coherence region. This is not only because of the errors at non-teacher points but also because of the errors at teacher points. That is, the learning sometimes fails. In the high coherence region ($SNR > 20$ dB), however, the generalization error decreases and approaches to the curves of the CVNN and dual-RVNN. In summary, we found that the four neural networks present generalization characteristics different among them. The experimental results have been found mostly near to the simulation results. In total, the CVNN shows good generalization characteristics.

1.7 CONCLUSIONS

This chapter first presented recent advances in applications of complex-valued neural networks in various engineering fields, in particular in coherent systems. We also mentioned the history briefly by referring to Parametron. Then we discussed their merits intuitively concerning the degree of freedom in the learning in feedforward layered neural networks as well as the metric specific to the complex-valued networks such as complex inner product. We also considered widely linear systems and circularity not only in data but also in neural dynamics. In the latter part, we examined the generalization characteristics of complex-valued networks in comparison with real-valued ones. We observed that the complex-valued neural networks show smaller generalization error in the feedforward network to deal with coherent signals. This fact leads to great merits in electronics and engineering fields that deal with wave phenomena and wave-related information such as communications, imaging and sensing, social systems such as traffic signals, frequency-domain processing including frequency-domain multiplexing, and quantum computation and devices. Hypercomplex-valued networks are also promising in the fields related to three-dimensional motion, color processing, and other high-dimensional space information.

REFERENCES

1. I. Aizenberg, E. Myasnikova, M. Samsonova, and J. Reinitz. Temporal classification of drosophila segmentation gene expression patterns by the multi-valued neural recognition method. *Journal of Mathematical Biosciences*, 176(1):145–159, 2002.

2. Igor Aizenberg. *Complex-Valued Neural Networks with Multi-Valued Neurons*. Springer, 2011.

3. Igor Aizenberg, Dimitriy V. Paliy, Jacek M. Zurada, and Jaakko T. Astola. Blur identification by multilayer neural network based on multivalued neurons. *IEEE Transactions on Neural Networks*, 19(5):883–898, May 2008.

4. Takashi Aoyagi, Damri Radenamad, Yukimasa Nakano, and Akira Hirose. Complex-valued self-organizing map clustering using complex inner product in active mmillimeter-wave imaging. In *Proceedings of the International Joint Conference on Neural Networks (IJCNN) 2010 Barcelona*, pages 1346–1351, Barcelona, July 2010. IEEE/INNS.

5. Eduardo Bayro-Corrochano. *Geometric Computing for Wavelet Transforms, Robot Vision, Learning, Control and Action*. Springer, 2010.

6. Ann-Chen Chang, Chih-Wei Jen, and Ing-Jiunn Su. Robust adaptive array beamforming based on independent component analysis with regularized constraints. *IEICE*, E90-B(7):1791–1800, July 2007.

7. Sheng Chen, Lajos Hanzo, and S. Tan. Symmetric complex-valued RBF receiver for muptiple-antenna-aided wireless systems. *IEEE Transactions on Neural Networks*, 19(9):1657–1663, September 2008.

8. Sheng Chen and Xia Hong. Modeling of complex-valued Wiener systems using B-spline neural network. *IEEE Transactions on Neural Networks*, 22(5):818–825, 2011.

9. E. T. Copson. *An Introduction to the Theory of Functions of a Complex Variable*. Oxford: Clarendon Press, 1935.

10. K. L. Du, A. K. Y. Lai, K. K. M. Cheng, and M. N. S. Swamy. Neural methods for antenna array signal processing: A review. *Signal Processing*, 82:547–561, 2002.

11. H.-D. Ebbinghaus, H. Hermes, F. Hirzebruch, M Koecher, K. Mainzer, J. Neukirch, A. Prestel, and R. Remmert. *Numbers*. Springer-Verlag, (Chapter 3, Section 2), 1983.

12. Q. Gan, P. Saratchandran, N. Sundararajan, and K. R. Subramanian. A complex valued radial basis function network for equalization of fast time varying channels. *IEEE Transactions on Neural Networks*, 10(4):958–960, July 1999.

13. George M. Georgiou and Cris Koutsougeras. Complex domain backpropagation. *IEEE Transactions on Circuits and Systems II*, 39(5):330–334, 1992.

14. S. L. Goh, M. Chen, D. H. Popovic, K. Aihara, and Danilo P. Mandic. Complex valued forecasting of wind profile. *Renewable Energy*, 31:1733–1750, 2006.

15. S. L. Goh and Danilo P. Mandic. Nonlinear adaptive prediction of complex valued nonstationary signals. *IEEE Transactions on Signal Processing*, 53(5):1827–1836, 2005.

16. S.L. Goh and Danilo P. Mandic. An augmented extended kalman filter algorithm for complex-valued recurrent neural networks. *Neural Computation*, 19(4):1–17, 2007.

17. Eiichi Goto. The parametron – A new circuit element which utilizes non-linear reactors (in Japanese). *Paper of Technical Group of Electronic Computers and Nonlinear Theory, IECE*, July 1954.

18. Eiichi Goto. On the application of parametrically excited non-linear resonators (in Japanese). *The Journal of the Institute of Electrical Communication Engineers of Japan (IECE)*, 38(10):2761, October 1955.

19. Abdul Rahman Hafiz, Md. Faijul Amin, and Kazuyuki Murase. Real-time hand gesture recognition using complex-valued neural network (CVNN). In *International Conference on Neural Information Processing (ICONIP) 2011 Shanghai*, pages 541–549, November 2011.

20. Astri Handayani, Andriyan Bayu Suksmono, Tati L. R. Mengko, and Akira Hirose. Blood vessel segmentation in complex-valued magnetic resonance images with snake active contour model. *International Journal of E-Health and Medical Communications*, 1:41–52, 2010.

21. Takahiro Hara and Akira Hirose. Plastic mine detecting radar system using complex-valued self-organizing map that deals with multiple-frequency interferometric images. *Neural Networks*, 17(8-9):1201–1210, November 2004.

22. Akira Hirose. Complex-valued neural networks (Tutorial, International Joint Conference on Neural Networks (IJCNN) 2009 Atlanta) (IEEE Computational Intelligence Society (CIS) Video Archive.

23. Akira Hirose. Continuous complex-valued back-propagation learning. *Electronics Letters*, 28(20):1854–1855, 1992.

24. Akira Hirose. Dynamics of fully complex-valued neural networks. *Electronics Letters*, 28(16):1492–1494, 1992.

25. Akira Hirose. Applications of complex-valued neural networks to coherent optical computing using phase-sensitive detection scheme. *Information Sciences –Applications–*, 2:103–117, 1994.

26. Akira Hirose, editor. *Complex-Valued Neural Networks: Theories and Applications*. World Scientific Publishing Co. Pte. Ltd., 2003.

27. Akira Hirose. *Complex-Valued Neural Networks*. Springer-Verlag, Heidelberg, Berline, New York, 2006.

28. Akira Hirose. Nature of complex number and complex-valued neural networks. *Frontiers of Electrical and Electronic Engineering in China*, 6(1):171–180, 2011.

29. Akira Hirose. Advances in applications of complex-valued neural networks. *Journal of the Society of Instrument and Control Engineering*, 51(4):351–357, April 2012.

30. Akira Hirose, Yasufumi Asano, and Toshihiko Hamano. Developmental learning with behavioral mode tuning by carrier-frequency modulation in coherent neural networks. *IEEE Transactions on Neural Networks*, 17(6):1532–1543, November 2006.

31. Akira Hirose and Rolf Eckmiller. Behavior control of coherent-type neural networks by carrier-frequency modulation. *IEEE Transactions on Neural Networks*, 7(4):1032–1034, 1996.

32. Akira Hirose, Tomoaki Higo, and Ken Tanizawa. Efficient generation of holographic movies with frame interpolation using a coherent neural network. *IEICE Electronics Express*, 3(19):417–423, 2006.

33. Akira Hirose and Tomoyuki Nagashima. Predictive self-organizing map for vector quantization of migratory signals and its application to mobile communications. *IEEE Transactions on Neural Networks*, 14(6):1532–1540, 2003.

34. Akira Hirose and Yukimasa Nakano. Adaptive identification of landmine class by evaluating the total degree of conformity of ring-SOM. *Australian Journal of Intelligent Information Processing Systems*, 12,(1):23–28, 2010.

35. Akira Hirose and Yoshida Shotaro. Generalization characteristics of complex-valued feedforward neural networks in relation to signal coherence. *IEEE Transactions on Neural Networks and Learning Systems*, 23(4):541–551, April 2012.

36. Deng Jianping, Narasimhan Sundararajan, and P. Saratchandra. Communication channel equalization using complex-valued minimal radial basis fuction neural networks. *IEEE Transactions on Neural Networks*, 13(3):687–696, May 2002.

37. Mitsuru Kawamoto and Yujiro Inouye. Blind deconvolution of MIMO-FIR systems with colored inputs using second-order statistics. *IEICE Transactions on Fundamentals*, E86-A(3):597–604, March 2003.

38. Sotaro Kawata and Akira Hirose. Frequency-multiplexing ability of complex-valued Hebbian learning in logic gates. *International Journal of Neural Systems*, 12(1):43–51, 2008.

39. Mitsunaga Kinjo, Shigeo Sato, Yuuki Nakamiya, and Koji Nakajima. Neuromorphic quantum computation with energy dissipation. *Physical Review A*, 72:052328, 2005.

40. Shin'ichi Koike and Seiichi Noda. Pre-compensation of transmitter nonlinearity with memory effects in digital QAM systems. *IEICE Transactions on Fundamentals*, E87-A(10):2744–2754, October 2004.

41. Danilo P. Mandic and Vanessa Su Lee Goh. *Complex Valued Nonlinear Adaptive Filters – Noncircularity, Widely Linear and Neural Models*. Wiley, April 2009.

42. Danilo P. Mandic, Susanne Still, and Scott C. Douglas. Duality between widely linear and dual channel adaptive filtering. In *IEEE Internatinal Conference on Acoustics, Speech, and Signal Processing 2009 Taipei*, pages 1729–1732, 2009.

43. Soichi Masuyama and Akira Hirose. Walled LTSA array for rapid, high spatial resolution, and phase sensitive imaging to visualize plastic landmines. *IEEE Transactions on Geoscience and Remote Sensing*, 45(8):2536–2543, August 2007.

44. Soichi Masuyama, Kenzo Yasuda, and Akira Hirose. Multiple mode selection of walled-ltsa array elements for high resolution imaging to visualize antipersonnel plastic landmines. *IEEE Geoscience and Remote Sensing Letters*, 5(4):745–749, October 2008.

45. Nobuyuki Matsui, Teijiro Isokawa, Hiromi Kusamichi, Ferdinand Peper, and Haruhiko Nishimura. Quaternion neural network with geometrical operators. *Journal of Intelligent and Fuzzy Systems*, 15:149–164, 2004.

46. R. K. Mishra and A. Patnaik. Neurospectral computation for input impedance of rectangular microstrip antenna. *Electronics Letters*, 35:1691–1693, 1999.

47. R. K. Mishra and A. Patnaik. Designing rectangular patch antenna using the neurospectral method. *IEEE Transactions on Antennas and Propagation*, 51:1914–1921, 2003.

48. Y. Nakamiya, M. Kinjo, O. Takahashi, S. Sato, and K. Nakajima. Quantum neural network composed of kane's qubits. *Japanese Journal of Applied Physics*, 45(10A):8030–8034, October 2006.

49. Yukimasa Nakano and Akira Hirose. Improvement of plastic landmine visualization performance by use of ring-csom and frequency-domain local correlation. *IEICE Transactions on Electronics*, E92-C(1):102–108, January 2009.

50. Ikuko Nishikawa and Yasuaki Kuroe. Dynamics of complex-valued neural networks and its relation to a phase oscillator system. In *International Conference on Neural Information Processing (ICONIP) 2004 Calcutta*, pages 122–129, Berlin, November 2004. Springer.

51. Tomohiro Nishino, Ryo Yamaki, and Akira Hirose. Ultrasonic imaging for boundary shape generation by phase unwrapping with singular-point elimination based on complex-valued Markov random field model. *IEICE Transactions on Fundamentals*, E93-A(1):219–226, January 2010.

52. Tohru Nitta. An extension of the back-propagation algorithm to complex numbers. *Neural Networks*, 10:1391–1415, 1997.

53. Tohru Nitta, editor. *Complex-Valued Neural Networks: Utilizing High–Dimensional Prarameters*. Information Science Reference, Pensylvania, February 2009.

54. Tohru Nitta and Yasuaki Kuroe. Special session on Clifford algebraic neural networks. In *International Conference on Neural Information Processing (ICONIP) 2011 Shanghai*. Springer, 2011.

55. Dong-Chul Park and Tae-Kyun Jung Jeong. Complex-bilinear recurrent neural networks for equilization of a digital satellite channel. *IEEE Transactions on Neural Networks*, 13(3):711–725, March 2002.

56. Bernard Picinbono and Pascal Chevalier. Widely linear estimation with complex data. *IEEE Transactions on Signal Processing*, 43(8):2030–2033, August 1995.

57. Shigeo Sato, Mitsunaga Kinjo, and Koji Nakajima. An approach for quantum computing using adiabatic evolution algorithm. *Jpnanese Journal of Appl.ied Physics 1*, 42(11):7169–7173, 2003.

58. H. Sawada, R. Mukai, S. Araki, and S. Makino. Polar coordinate based nonlinear function for frequency-domain blind source separation. *IEICE Transactions on Fundamentals of Electronics, Communications, and Computer Sciences*, E86A:590–596, 2003.

59. Andriyan Bayu Suksmono and Akira Hirose. Adaptive noise reduction of insar image based on complex-valued mrf model and its application to phase unwrapping problem. *IEEE Trans. on Geoscience and Remote Sensing*, 40(3):699–709 (followed by publisher's errata on Fig.12), 2002.

60. Andriyan Bayu Suksmono and Akira Hirose. Beamforming of ultra-wideband pulses by a complex-valued spatio-temporal multilayer neural network. *International Journal of Neural Systems*, 15(1):1–7, 2005.

61. Hidetosi Takahasi. An exerimental decimal calculator (in Japanese). *Paper of Technical Group of Electronic Computers, IECE*, March 1956.

62. Chor Shen Tay, Ken Tanizawa, and Akira Hirose. Error reduction in holographic movies using a hybrid learning method in coherent neural networks. *Applied Optics*, 47(28):5221–5228, 2008.

63. Xiaoqiu Wang, Hua Lin, Jianming Lu, and Takashi Yahagi. Combining recurrent neural networks with self-organizing map for channel equalization. *IEICE Transactions on Communications*, E85-B(10):2227–2235, October 2002.

64. Yili Xia, Beth Jelfs, Marc M. Van Hulle, Jose C. Principe, and Danilo P. Mandic. An augumented echo state network for nonlinear adaptive filetering of complex noncircular signals. *IEEE Transactions on Neural Networks*, 22(1):74–83, January 2011.

65. Ryo Yamaki and Akira Hirose. Singular unit restoration in interferograms based on complex-valued Markov random field model for phase unwrapping. *IEEE Geoscience and Remote Sensing Letters*, 6(1):18–22, January 2009.

66. Chih-Chung Yang and N.K. Bose. Landmine detection and classification with complex-valued hybrid neural network using scattering parameters dataset. *IEEE Transactions on Neural Networks*, 16(3):743–753, May 2005.

67. W.H. Yang, K.K. Chan, and P.R. Chang. Complex-valued neural-network for direction-of-arrival estimation. *Electronics Letters*, 30:574–575, 1994.

68. Cheolwoo You and Daesik Hong. Nonlinear blind equalization schemes using complex-valued muptilayer feedforward neural networks. *IEEE Transactions on Neural Networks*, 9:1442–1455, 1998.

69. Yanwu Zhang and Yuanliang Ma. CGHA for principal component extraction in the complex domain. *IEEE Transactions on Neural Networks*, 8:1031–1036, 1997.

CHAPTER 2

NEURAL SYSTEM LEARNING ON COMPLEX-VALUED MANIFOLDS

Simone Fiori

Università Politecnica delle Marche, Ancona, Italy

An instance of artificial neural learning is by criterion optimization, where the criterion to optimize measures the learning ability of the neural network either in supervised learning (the adaptation is supervised by a teacher) or in unsupervised learning (the adaptation of network parameters proceeds on the basis of the information that the neural system is able to extract from the inputs). In some circumstances of interest, the space of parameters of the neural system is restricted to a particular feasible space via suitable bounds, which represent the constraint imposed by the learning problem at hand. In this case, the optimization rules to adapt the parameters of the neural network must be designed according to the known constraints. If the set of feasible parameters form a smooth continuous set, namely, a differentiable manifold, the design of adaptation rules falls in the realm of differential geometrical methods for neural networks and learning and of the numerical geometric integration of learning equations. The present chapter deals with complex-valued parameter-manifolds and with applications of complex-valued artificial neural networks whose connection-parameters live in complex-valued manifolds. The successful applications of such neural networks, which are described within the present chapter, are to blind source separation of complex-valued sources and to multichannel blind deconvolution of signals in telecommunications, to nondestructive evaluation of materials in industrial metallic slabs production and to the purely algorithmic problem of averaging the parameters of a pool of cooperative complex-valued neural networks. The present chapter recalls those notions of differential geometry that are instrumental in the definition of a consistent learning theory over complex-valued differentiable manifolds and introduces some learning problems and their solutions.

2.1   INTRODUCTION

Complex-valued neural systems are made of basic processing elements with complex-valued weights and complex-valued activation functions. A number of signal/data processing methods based on complex-valued neural systems are nowadays made use of in pattern recognition and classification, in artificial neural information processing and in image processing. The use of complex-valued weights and complex-valued activation functions is not simply a theoretical generalization of the real-valued case but it makes it possible to extend the functionality of a single basic neural processing element and of an artificial neural system to solve applied problems that do not accommodate well in the framework of real-valued neural systems [1]. Complex-valued neural systems find applications in adaptive signal processing for highly functional sensing and imaging, in automatic control in unknown and changing environment, in brain-like information processing and in robotics inspired by human neural systems [32]. In the field of signal processing, for example, complex-valued neural systems are widely applied, as in land-surface classification, in the generation of digital elevation maps and in speech synthesis.

An instance of artificial neural system learning is by criterion optimization, where the criterion to optimize measures the learning ability of the neural system either in supervised learning or in unsupervised learning (i.e., information-theoretic-based learning). In some applications, the parameters of the neural system are restricted to lay in a particular feasible space. In such a case, the optimization rules to adapt the parameters of the artificial neural system must be designed according to the structure of the feasible space. If the feasible space forms a smooth manifold, the design of adaptation rules falls in the realm of differential geometrical methods for neural systems and learning and of the numerical geometric integration of learning equations.

The present chapter deals with complex-valued parameter-manifolds and with applications of complex-valued artificial neural systems whose adaptable parameters lay on complex-valued manifolds. The successful applications of such neural systems, which are described within the present chapter, are to blind source separation of complex-valued sources, to optimal pre-coding of MIMO broadcast channels and to the purely algorithmic problem of averaging the parameters of a pool of cooperative complex-valued neural systems. The present chapter fits within the research line of differential geometrical methods for machine learning and neural networks design [2]. In particular, the present chapter lays on the intersection between the author's research line about learning by optimization on Riemannian (as well as pseudo-Riemannian) manifolds with application, e.g., to blind signal deconvolution

[15, 19], blind source separation, latent variable analysis and independent component analysis [17, 26], unsupervised machine learning by optimization on differentiable manifolds and Lie groups [6, 14, 18, 21, 23, 24], and the author's research line about complex-valued neural systems [10, 16, 20].

The present chapter recalls those notions of differential geometry that are instrumental in the definition of a consistent learning theory over complex-valued differentiable manifolds and introduces some learning problems and their solutions. A reference on differential geometry is [39].

Notation. Throughout the present chapter, symbol $\mathbb{C}$ denotes the field of complex numbers, symbol $\mathbb{C}^{n \times p}$ denotes the set of $n \times p$ matrices with complex-valued entries, superscript ^{H} denotes hermitian transpose, operator tr denotes matrix trace, operator det denotes matrix determinant and symbol $\Re$ denotes real part.

2.2 LEARNING AVERAGES OVER THE LIE GROUP OF UNITARY MATRICES

Unitary matrices play a prominent role in engineering. For instance, unitary matrices are involved in almost all modern multi-antenna transceiver techniques and in sensor array applications to biomedicine and to astronomy. A typical application in signal processing is to array and multichannel signal processing techniques, which appear to be key technologies in wireless communication systems [43]. An interesting signal processing application involving sets of unitary matrices is the design of symbol constellations with maximal diversity [30]. Multiple antennas can enhance the data rate for wireless communication systems without increasing the error probability. Fully diversified constellations with large diversity are playing an important role in improving the data rate of systems with multiple antennas. The involved design problem may be cast as follows: Given a diversity measure for unitary matrices, find a constellation of given cardinality such that the diversity of the unitary matrices in the constellation is as large as possible. Another interesting application of unitary matrices is to holographic memory design and analysis [45, 46]. Volume holographic data storage based on phase-code multiplexing appears to be a promising technology for the next generation of optical storage devices, because volume holographic memories offer high storage capacities and short data access times.

In some applications, several estimates of a sought-for unitary matrix are available. An example found in the field of artificial neural network learning is provided by a set of different algorithms that were designed for the same purpose and that are run on the same data set in order to perform a unitary-matrix learning task. Another example is provided by the repeated run of an adaptive algorithm on the same data set from different initial conditions. Allegedly, the available estimates of the actual unitary matrix will differ only slightly one to another, except for a few outliers. A concern that might arise in this case is how to merge the obtained unitary matrix estimates in order to obtain an *average matrix* that is close to the actual unitary matrix.

2.2.1 Differential-Geometric Setting

The notion of mean value of objects belonging to a curved space arises as a generalization of mean values of real numbers. When the space that the objects to be averaged belong to is a smooth manifold M endowed with a Riemannian metric, a possible definition of average value is given by the Riemannian mean. Given a set of N points $x_k \in M, k \in \{1, \ldots, N\}$, their Riemannian mean is defined as

$$\mu \stackrel{\text{def}}{=} \arg \min_{x \in M} \sum_{k=1}^{N} d^2(x, x_k) \tag{2.1}$$

where $d : M \times M \to \mathbb{R}_0^+$ is a distance function. In general, this definition does not guarantee the average $\mu \in M$ to be unique. As long as a suitable geometrical characterization of the space M is available and a distance function is available in closed form, the Riemannian-mean problem (2.1) may be tackled. This would be the case, for example, for the matrix-hypersphere that will be introduced in Section 2.3.

In the present section, a different approach is adopted, based on the assumption that the manifold of interest is a Lie group. The average element in the Lie group G is characterized as the one corresponding to the *arithmetic mean* in the Lie algebra of G.

A Lie group G is an algebraic group that also possesses the structure of a smooth manifold. In particular, the set G is endowed with a differential manifold structure, which is further supposed to be Riemannian. The tangent space of the manifold G at a point $g \in G$ is denoted by $T_g G$. The tangent bundle associated with the Lie group G is denoted here as TG. The Lie group G is associated with a Lie algebra $\mathfrak{g} \stackrel{\text{def}}{=} T_e G$.

Recall that an algebraic group structure (G, m, i, e) is made of a set G endowed with multiplication operation m, inverse operator i and an identity element e, such that for every $g_1, g_2 \in G$, it holds that $m(g_1, g_2) \in G, m(g_1, i(g_1)) = m(i(g_1), g_1) = e$ and $m(g_1, e) = m(e, g_1) = g_1$. Also, group identity and inverse need to be unique and the group multiplication needs to be associative, namely $m(g_1, m(g_2, g_3)) = m(m(g_1, g_2), g_3), \forall g_1, g_2, g_3 \in G$. In addition, it is necessary to ensure that the algebraic and differential structures are compatible, namely, that the map $(g_1, g_2) \mapsto m(g_1, i(g_2))$ be infinitely differentiable for every $g_1, g_2 \in G$.

A left translation about an element $g \in G$, $\ell_g : G \to G$, may be associated with the Lie group G, which is defined by

$$\ell_g(g_1) = m(i(g), g_1), \ \forall g, g_1 \in G \tag{2.2}$$

The inverse of operator $\ell_g(\cdot) : G \to G$ is defined as

$$\ell_g^{-1}(g_1) = m(g, g_1) \tag{2.3}$$

As G is a Riemannian manifold, it is endowed with a inner product $\langle \cdot, \cdot \rangle_g : T_g G \times T_g G \to \mathbb{R}$. A geodesic line with normal parameterization $\gamma : [0, 1] \to G$ connecting two points $g_1, g_2 \in G$ is the shortest path on G having g_1 and g_2 as endpoints. Namely it solves the variational problem:

$$\delta \int_0^1 \langle \dot{\gamma}^G(t), \dot{\gamma}^G(t) \rangle_{\gamma^G(t)} \, dt, \tag{2.4}$$

where the overdot stands for derivative with respect to the parameter t and symbol δ denotes variation. The geodesic curve γ can also be specified in terms of an endpoint $g \in G$ and a tangent vector $v \in T_g G$, namely it satisfies the conditions $\gamma^G(0) = g$ and $\dot{\gamma}^G(0) = v$. In this case, the geodesic curve is specified as $\gamma_{g,v}^G(t)$. The quantity $d_\gamma(g_1, g_2)$ defined as:

$$d_\gamma(g_1, g_2) \stackrel{\text{def}}{=} \int_0^1 \sqrt{\langle \dot{\gamma}^G(t), \dot{\gamma}^G(t) \rangle_{\gamma^G(t)}} \, dt, \tag{2.5}$$

is termed geodesic distance. Exponential maps may be associated to a manifold by the help of geodesic curves. The exponential map: $TG \rightarrow G$ associated to any geodesic $\gamma_{g,v}^G : [0, 1] \rightarrow G$ emanating from $g \in G$ with tangent $v \in T_g G$ at the origin is defined by $\exp_g^G(v) \stackrel{\text{def}}{=} \gamma_{g,v}^G(1)$. The exponential $\exp_g^G$ maps a point of $T_g G$ into a point in G. The exponential map at the origin of a Lie group, $\exp_e^G$, is simply denoted by $\exp^G$ and its inverse operator is denoted by $\log^G$.

2.2.2 An Averaging Procedure over the Lie Group of Unitary Matrices

The set of samples to average consists of N independent estimates $g_k \in G$ belonging to a Lie group G. It is assumed that the estimates $g_k \in G$ are sufficiently close to each other for them to make sense to average. The procedure to compute a mean element μ is independent of the estimation problem as well as of the estimation algorithms through which the estimates were computed.

An algorithm to learn averages, as developed in Ref. [27], reads:

1. Shift the whole set of available patterns in a neighborhood of the identity $e \in G$ by left-translation about the sought-after average element μ. The shifted set of patterns is then given by $\ell_\mu(g_n) = m(i(\mu), g_n) \in G, n = 1, \ldots, N$.

2. As the elements $\ell_\mu(g_n)$ belong to a neighborhood of the identity e, then they may be shifted to the Lie algebra $\mathfrak{g}$ by applying operator $\log^G$, which yields $u_n \stackrel{\text{def}}{=} \log^G(m(i(\mu), g_n)) \in \mathfrak{g}, n = 1, \ldots, N$.

3. In the Lie algebra $\mathfrak{g}$, averaging may be computed by the *arithmetic mean* $\frac{1}{N} \sum_{n=1}^N u_n$.

4. The mean element $\frac{1}{N} \sum_{n=1}^N u_n$ in $\mathfrak{g}$ must correspond – upon exponentiation and inverse left-translation – to the mean element $\mu \in G$.

Ultimately, an element $\mu \in G$ is sought, which satisfies the condition

$$\mu = m\left(\mu, \exp^G\left(\frac{1}{N} \sum_n \log^G(m(i(\mu), g_n))\right)\right) \tag{2.6}$$

In some circumstances of interest, Eq. (2.6) may be solved in closed form. Otherwise, it might be solved by means of a fixed-point iteration algorithm.

In the present context, the Lie group of interest has the structure $(U(p), \cdot, ^H, I_p)$, where $U(p)$ is the set of $p \times p$ unitary matrices, namely:

$$U(p) \overset{\text{def}}{=} \{g \in \mathbb{C}^{p \times p} | g^H g = I_p\} \tag{2.7}$$

and I_p denotes the $p \times p$ identity matrix. The Lie algebra $\mathrm{u}(p)$ associated to the unitary group is made of skew-Hermitian matrices, namely:

$$\mathrm{u}(p) \overset{\text{def}}{=} \{u \in \mathbb{C}^{p \times p} | u^H = -u\} \tag{2.8}$$

Also, it holds that

$$T_g U(p) = \{gu | u \in \mathrm{u}(p)\} \tag{2.9}$$

The unitary group is endowed with the canonical inner product:

$$\langle v_1, v_2 \rangle_g \overset{\text{def}}{=} \Re\mathrm{tr}(v_1^H v_2) \tag{2.10}$$

associated to the Frobenius norm, for every $v_1, v_2 \in T_g U(p)$. The exponential map exp coincides with the matrix exponential function while the inverse exponential map coincides with the matrix logarithm function.

Here $Gl(p, \mathbb{C})$ denotes the general linear Lie group of $p \times p$ invertible complex-valued matrices and by $\mathfrak{gl}(p, \mathbb{C})$ its associated Lie algebra (namely, the set of $p \times p$ complex-valued matrices). The exponential of a matrix $u \in \mathfrak{gl}(p, \mathbb{C})$ is given by the convergent series:

$$\exp(u) = I_p + \sum_{k=1}^{\infty} \frac{u^k}{k!}$$

It is worth recalling that, given matrices $u_1, u_2 \in \mathfrak{gl}(p, \mathbb{C})$, it holds that $\exp(u_1 + u_2) \neq \exp(u_1) \exp(u_2)$ unless matrices u_1 and u_2 commute. Logarithms of a matrix g are solutions of the matrix equation $\exp(u) = g$. A matrix has a logarithm if and only if it is invertible. The logarithm is not unique, but if a matrix has no negative real eigenvalues, then it has a unique logarithm known as the *principal logarithm*, which is denoted by $\log(g)$. Furthermore, if, for any given matrix norm $\| \cdot \|$ it holds $\|g - I_p\| < 1$, where I_p denotes the identity element in $Gl(p)$, then it holds that

$$\log(g) = -\sum_{k=1}^{\infty} \frac{(I_p - g)^k}{k}$$

In general, given matrices $g_1, g_2 \in Gl(p, \mathbb{C})$, it holds that $\log(g_1 g_2) \neq \log(g_1) + \log(g_2)$. In practice, matrix exponential and logarithm may be computed efficiently by making use of the spectral decomposition of matrices or by various approximate methods [9, 31].

Condition (2.6) gives rise to the fixed-point learning algorithm:

$$\mu_{k+1} = \mu_k \exp\left(\sum_n \log \sqrt[N]{(\mu_k)^H g_n}\right) \tag{2.11}$$

Algorithm 1 Pseudocode to implement the averaging method (2.11) over the unitary group.

Set $k = 0$
Set μ_0 to an initial guess in $U(p)$
Set ε to desired precision
repeat
    Update $\mu_{k+1} = \mu_k \exp\left(\frac{1}{N} \sum_{n=1}^{N} \log((\mu_k)^H g_n) \right)$
    Set $k = k + 1$
until $d_\gamma(\mu_k, \mu_{k-1}) \leq \varepsilon$

A geodesic curve on the manifold $U(p)$ endowed with the metric (2.10) departing from the point $g \in U(p)$ with tangent direction $v = gu$, with $u \in \mathfrak{u}(p)$, has expression $\gamma_{g,gu}^{U(p)}(t) = g \exp(tu)$, $t \in [0, 1]$. Therefore, as it holds that $\dot{\gamma}_{g,gu}^{U(p)}(t) = \gamma_{g,gu}^{U(p)}(t)u$, the geodesic arclength is given by

$$d_\gamma = \int_0^1 \sqrt{\mathrm{tr}((\gamma_{g,gu}^{U(p)}(t)u)^H (\gamma_{g,gu}^{U(p)}(t)u)))}\, dt = \sqrt{-\mathrm{tr}(u^2)}$$

If the geodesic curve is specified in terms of endpoints $\gamma(0) = g_1 \in U(p)$ and $\gamma(1) = g_2 \in U(p)$, then it must hold that $g = g_1$ and $u = \log(g_1^H g_2)$; therefore,

$$d_\gamma(g_1, g_2) = \sqrt{-\mathrm{tr}((\log(g_1^H g_2))^2)} \tag{2.12}$$

The discussed averaging procedure may be summarized by the pseudocode listed in the Algorithm 1.

A first set of numerical tests was conducted by generating a random matrix $\bar{g} \in U(p)$ and N matrices $g_k \in U(p)$ by means of the relationship $g_n = \bar{g} \exp(u_n)$, where the $u_n \in \mathfrak{u}(p)$ are random matrices defined by $u_n \overset{\text{def}}{=} \frac{1}{2}(b_n - b_n^H)$ and the $b_n \in \mathbb{C}^{p \times p}$ are, in turn, random matrices whose real-part and imaginary-part entries are drawn from a zero-mean Gaussian distribution with variance σ_u^2. With the aim of objectively measuring the behavior of the average-learning algorithm, two indices were defined:

$$\text{Relative distance} \overset{\text{def}}{=} \frac{\sum_n d_\gamma(\mu, g_n)}{\sum_n d_\gamma(\bar{g}, g_n)}, \tag{2.13}$$

which measures how far apart the average pattern lies from the pattern set with respect to the original point $\bar{g}$, and

$$\text{Closeness}_n \overset{\text{def}}{=} \frac{d_\gamma(\mu, g_n)}{d_\gamma(\bar{g}, g_n)} \tag{2.14}$$

which measures how far the average point lies from each of the nth sample relatively to the original point $\bar{g}$. Figure 2.1 displays the result of a run when $p = 5$, $N = 100$ and $\sigma_u^2 = 0.25$. Figure 2.1(a) shows that the algorithm converges steadily and

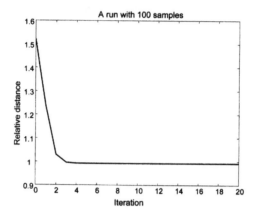

(a) Relative distance versus iteration.

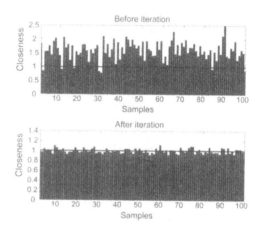

(b) Closeness indices.

Figure 2.1   Experiment on the Lie group $G = U(5)$ with $N = 100$ samples to average. In Figure 2.1(b), the top panel shows closeness indices before iteration, namely, with $\mu = \mu_0$, while the bottom panel shows closeness indices after iteration. The straight line on both panels denotes the value 1.

in a few iterations. Figure 2.1(b) shows the distribution of normalized distances $d_\gamma(\mu_0, g_n)$, which differ considerably from 1 as the initial guess is chosen randomly, and the distribution of normalized distances $d_\gamma(\mu, g_n)$ after completion of learning, which are close to 1, a fact that confirms that the learned average matrix truly locates as close as possible to all samples at a time.

A second kind of numerical result allows a better visualization of the behavior of the discussed averaging algorithm. An useful illustration consists in seeing the *cloud* of points representing the matrices g_n to get a nice view of how these points distribute around the actual solution $\bar{g}$ and how close to it the mean solution μ locates. However, in general an element of a Lie group $U(p)$ involves several parameters and it is impossible to get a nice graphical point-wise representation of the elements g_n. A special case is the one of the group of unitary unimodular matrices $SU(2)$, defined as

$$SU(2) = \{g \in \mathbb{C}^{2\times2} \,|\, g^H g = I_2, \; \det(g) = 1\} \tag{2.15}$$

Any $SU(2)$ matrix may be represented as [20]

$$g = \begin{bmatrix} z_1 & z_2 \\ -z_2^* & z_1^* \end{bmatrix} \tag{2.16}$$

where $z_1, z_2 \in \mathbb{C}$ are the Cayley–Klein parameters, which have to satisfy the constraint $|z_1|^2 + |z_2|^2 = 1$, where symbol $|\cdot|$ denotes complex-valued number modulus and superscript * denotes complex conjugation. The manifold $SU(2)$ is a subgroup of the manifold $U(2)$ under matrix multiplication/inversion. The Lie algebra $\mathfrak{su}(2)$ associated with the Lie group $SU(2)$ is the set of 2×2 complex-valued, skew-Hermitian, traceless matrices. As a numerical case study, a central random matrix $\bar{g} \in SU(2)$ may be generated and then N matrices $g_n \in SU(2)$ may be further generated by the rule

$$g_n = \bar{g} \exp(u_n) e^{-\mathrm{tr}(u_n)} \tag{2.17}$$

where $u_n \in \mathfrak{u}(2)$ are random matrices defined by $u_n \overset{\text{def}}{=} \frac{1}{2}(b_n - b_n^H)$ and the $b_n \in \mathbb{C}^{2\times2}$ are, in turn, random matrices whose real-part and imaginary-part entries are drawn from a zero-mean Gaussian distribution with variance σ_u^2. In fact, it holds that

$$\det(g_n) = \det(\bar{g}) \det(\exp(u_n)) e^{-\mathrm{tr}(u_n)} = 1 \cdot e^{\mathrm{tr}(u_n)} \cdot e^{-\mathrm{tr}(u_n)} = 1 \tag{2.18}$$

Complex variables z_1, z_2 in (2.16) comprise a total of 4 real parameters and the constraint on their moduli makes the representation have in total 3 independent parameters. Therefore, any matrix in $G = SU(2)$ may be represented by a point of $\mathbb{R}^3$: For graphical representation purpose only, the representation $g \to [\Re z_1 \; \Im z_1 \; \Re z_2]^T$ is made use of, where symbol $\Im$ denotes imaginary part. Figure 2.2 displays the result of a single run when $N = 100$, $\sigma_u = 0.5$ and the samples set contains 10% of outliers (i.e., elements generated with $\sigma_u = 5$), after 10 iterations of the algorithm. From Figure 2.2 it is readily appreciated how the computed empirical mean does lay very close to the actual center of the distribution, in spite of the outliers.

2.3 RIEMANNIAN-GRADIENT-BASED LEARNING ON THE COMPLEX MATRIX-HYPERSPHERE

A signal-processing problem posed in Ref. [33] concerns the computation of an optimal precoding matrix via maximization of a weighted sum rate in MIMO broadcast

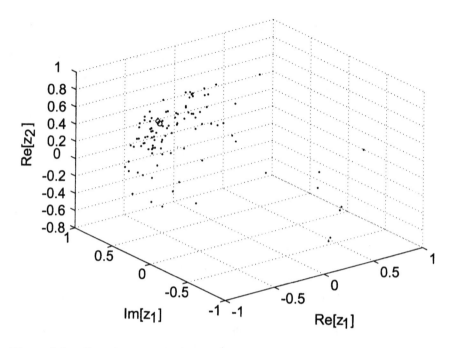

Figure 2.2   Experiment on $SU(2)$ with $N = 100$ and with outliers: The open circle (○) denotes the computed average solution μ, the diamond (◇) denotes the point $\bar{g}$, while the cloud of dots (·) denotes the patterns g_n.

channels. For a recent review of weighted sum rate in MIMO broadcast channels see, e.g., Refs. [29, 34, 35]. The main focus of the present contribution is to develop a suitable algorithm to learn a precoding matrix. The present analysis of the above problem starts by casting it as an optimization problem of a regular criterion function over the complex-valued matrix-hypersphere $\mathbb{S}^\alpha_{n,p}(\mathbb{C})$, defined as

$$\mathbb{S}^\alpha_{n,p}(\mathbb{C}) \stackrel{\text{def}}{=} \{x \in \mathbb{C}^{n \times p} | \text{tr}(x^H x) = \alpha\} \tag{2.19}$$

where $n \geq p$ and $\alpha > 0$.

As the real line $\mathbb{R}$ is a subfield of the complex plane $\mathbb{C}$, the developed optimization algorithm translates to the real-valued parameter space $\mathbb{S}^\alpha_{n,p}(\mathbb{R})$ in a straightforward way, which proves useful in certain applications. An application of learning by optimization on the manifold $\mathbb{S}^1_{n,p}(\mathbb{R})$ is to dimension reduction for image retrieval [47], which was designed to optimize class separation with respect to metrics derived from cross-correlation of spectral histograms. A problem formally similar to the one discussed in Ref. [33] tailored to the real line was discussed in Ref. [42] under the name of "maximum relative uncertainty theory" for linear-neural-networks' unsupervised learning. Moreover, optimization problems over the manifold $\mathbb{S}^\alpha_{n,1}(\mathbb{R})$ arise in applications such as blind channel deconvolution [15, 19] and one-unit principal/independent component analysis [22].

The sought-after learning rule over the manifold $\mathbb{S}^\alpha_{n,p}(\mathbb{C})$ is formulated in terms of Riemannian-gradient-based optimization of a regular criterion function, as the space of interest $\mathbb{S}^\alpha_{n,p}(\mathbb{C})$ is a smooth manifold that may be endowed with a Riemannian geometry. The discussed Riemannian-gradient-based optimization theory is implemented by a geodesic-stepping method [28, 36]. Geodesic stepping is based on the calculation of geodesic arcs in closed form and provides a geometrically sound way of moving from a point along a given direction on a Riemannian manifold proportionally to a learning stepsize. A method to compute a numerically optimal learning stepsize schedule is discussed as well, which resembles the line-search method on Euclidean spaces, termed *geodesic-search* method. An advantage of the devised geodesic-search method is that, in the space $\mathbb{S}^\alpha_{n,p}(\mathbb{C})$, the geodesic curve is periodic of finite period, hence the learning stepsize belongs to a closed interval. Moreover, unlike other methods previously adopted [19], it does not rely on any local approximation of the criterion function and hence does not limit to short steps.

2.3.1 Geometric Characterization of the Matrix Hypersphere

The tangent space to the manifold $\mathbb{S}^\alpha_{n,p}(\mathbb{C})$ at a point $x \in \mathbb{S}^\alpha_{n,p}(\mathbb{C})$ is denoted by $T_x\mathbb{S}^\alpha_{n,p}(\mathbb{C})$. Given any smooth curve $\gamma(t)$ such that $\gamma : [-a, a] \to \mathbb{S}^\alpha_{n,p}(\mathbb{C})$, with $a > 0$ and $\gamma(0) = x$, the tangent space $T_x\mathbb{S}^\alpha_{n,p}(\mathbb{C})$ is spanned by the vectors $\dot{\gamma}(0)$, where an overdot denotes derivative with respect to parameter t. Hand-by-hand derivation of the condition $\mathrm{tr}(\gamma^H(t)\gamma(t)) = \alpha$ gives, for any $t \in [-a, a]$,

$$\mathrm{tr}(\dot{\gamma}^H(t)\gamma(t) + \gamma^H(t)\dot{\gamma}(t)) = 2\Re\mathrm{tr}(\dot{\gamma}^H(t)\gamma(t)) = 0$$

where symbol $\Re$ denotes real part. Setting $v \overset{\mathrm{def}}{=} \dot{\gamma}(0) \in T_x\mathbb{S}^\alpha_{n,p}(\mathbb{C})$, it is found that the tangent space of the smooth manifold $\mathbb{S}^\alpha_{n,p}(\mathbb{C})$ at a point $x \in \mathbb{S}^\alpha_{n,p}(\mathbb{C})$ is described by

$$T_x\mathbb{S}^\alpha_{n,p}(\mathbb{C}) = \{v \in \mathbb{C}^{n\times p} | \Re\mathrm{tr}(v^H x) = 0\} \tag{2.20}$$

By embedding the manifold $\mathbb{S}^\alpha_{n,p}(\mathbb{C})$ into the ambient space $\mathbb{C}^{n\times p}$ equipped with the inner product $\langle z, w\rangle \overset{\mathrm{def}}{=} \Re\mathrm{tr}(z^H w)$, $z, w \in \mathbb{C}^{n\times p}$, the normal space $N_x\mathbb{S}^\alpha_{n,p}(\mathbb{C})$ to the manifold $\mathbb{S}^\alpha_{n,p}(\mathbb{C})$ at a point $x \in \mathbb{S}^\alpha_{n,p}(\mathbb{C})$ may be defined as the collection of vectors that are orthogonal to the tangent space $T_x\mathbb{S}^\alpha_{n,p}(\mathbb{C})$, namely as

$$N_x\mathbb{S}^\alpha_{n,p}(\mathbb{C}) \overset{\mathrm{def}}{=} \{z \in \mathbb{C}^{n\times p} | \Re\mathrm{tr}(z^H v) = 0, \forall v \in T_x\mathbb{S}^\alpha_{n,p}(\mathbb{C})\} \tag{2.21}$$

The normal space $N_x\mathbb{S}^\alpha_{n,p}(\mathbb{C})$ admits the following characterization:

$$N_x\mathbb{S}^\alpha_{n,p}(\mathbb{C}) = \{\lambda x | \lambda \in \mathbb{R}\} \tag{2.22}$$

In fact, $\Re\mathrm{tr}(z^H v) = \Re\mathrm{tr}((\lambda x)^H v) = \Re\mathrm{tr}(\lambda x^H v) = \lambda\Re\mathrm{tr}(x^H v) = 0$, for all $v \in T_x\mathbb{S}^\alpha_{n,p}(\mathbb{C})$ and $\lambda \in \mathbb{R}$.

Endowing the smooth manifold $\mathbb{S}^\alpha_{n,p}(\mathbb{C})$ with a inner product turns it into a Riemannian manifold. The following inner product at every point $x \in \mathbb{S}^\alpha_{n,p}(\mathbb{C})$ is chosen:

$$\langle u, v\rangle_x \overset{\mathrm{def}}{=} \Re\mathrm{tr}(u^H v), \quad u, v \in T_x\mathbb{S}^\alpha_{n,p}(\mathbb{C}) \tag{2.23}$$

The above inner product defines the norm $\|v\|_x \overset{\text{def}}{=} \sqrt{\text{tr}(v^H v)}$, $v \in T_x \mathbb{S}^\alpha_{n,p}(\mathbb{C})$, at every point $x \in \mathbb{S}^\alpha_{n,p}(\mathbb{C})$.

The Riemannian gradient of a regular function $f : \mathbb{S}^\alpha_{n,p}(\mathbb{C}) \to \mathbb{R}$ is denoted as $\nabla_x f$ and satisfies the following conditions:

- *Tangency*: It holds that $\nabla_x f \in T_x \mathbb{S}^\alpha_{n,p}(\mathbb{C})$.

- *Compatibility with the metric*: It holds that $\langle v, \nabla_x f \rangle_x = \Re\text{tr}(v^H \partial_x f)$, for all $v \in T_x \mathbb{S}^\alpha_{n,p}(\mathbb{C})$,

where the gradient $\partial_x f$ represents the matrix of partial derivatives:

$$[\partial_x f]_{ab} = \frac{\partial f}{\partial x_{ab}} \tag{2.24}$$

From the metric compatibility condition, it follows that $\Re\text{tr}(v^H \nabla_x f) = \Re\text{tr}(v^H \partial_x f)$, $\forall v \in T_x \mathbb{S}^\alpha_{n,p}(\mathbb{C})$, which clearly implies that $\nabla_x f - \partial_x f \in N_x \mathbb{S}^\alpha_{n,p}(\mathbb{C})$, namely, that $\nabla_x f = \partial_x f + \lambda_x x$ for some $\lambda_x \in \mathbb{R}$. In addition, the tangency condition implies that $0 = \Re\text{tr}(x^H \nabla_x f) = \Re\text{tr}(x^H \partial_x f) + \lambda_x \Re\text{tr}(x^H x) = \Re\text{tr}(x^H \partial_x f) + \alpha \lambda_x$. Thus, applying both conditions yields the Riemannian gradient on the manifold $\mathbb{S}^\alpha_{n,p}(\mathbb{C})$:

$$\nabla_x f = \partial_x f - \frac{x}{\alpha} \Re\text{tr}(x^H \partial_x f) \tag{2.25}$$

A smooth curve $\gamma : [0,\ 1] \to \mathbb{S}^\alpha_{n,p}(\mathbb{C})$ is referred to as *geodesic line with normal parameterization* if it solves the following variational problem:

$$\delta \int_0^1 \langle \dot\gamma(t), \dot\gamma(t) \rangle_{\gamma(t)}\, dt = 0 \tag{2.26}$$

In the above expression, symbol δ denotes again the variation of the integral as in subsection 2.2.1. The variation $\delta\gamma \in T_\gamma \mathbb{S}^\alpha_{n,p}(\mathbb{C})$ is arbitrary, except at the boundaries of the curve, $\gamma(0)$ and $\gamma(1)$, where the variation vanishes to zero. The variation of the integral in (2.26) may be written explicitly as:

$$\int_0^1 \delta\text{tr}(\dot\gamma^H \dot\gamma)\, dt = 2 \int_0^1 \Re\text{tr}\left(\dot\gamma^H \frac{d\delta\gamma}{dt}\right) dt = -2 \int_0^1 \Re\text{tr}(\ddot\gamma^H \delta\gamma)\, dt$$

upon integration by parts. As the last integral must vanish to zero for any admissible variation $\delta\gamma$, the geodesic line is characterized by the condition $\ddot\gamma \in N_x \mathbb{S}^\alpha_{n,p}(\mathbb{C})$, namely $\ddot\gamma = \lambda_\gamma \gamma$ for $\lambda_\gamma \in \mathbb{R}$. As $\gamma(t) \in \mathbb{S}^\alpha_{n,p}(\mathbb{C})$, it must hold that $\Re\text{tr}(\gamma^H(t)\gamma(t)) = \alpha$ for any $t \in [0,\ 1]$. Deriving twice with respect to the parameter t gives the condition $\Re\text{tr}(\ddot\gamma^H \gamma + \dot\gamma^H \dot\gamma) = 0$. Replacing the term $\ddot\gamma$ with $\lambda_\gamma \gamma$ in the last equation gives $\Re\text{tr}(\lambda_\gamma \gamma^H \gamma + \dot\gamma^H \dot\gamma) = 0$ from which $\lambda_\gamma = -\alpha^{-1} \text{tr}(\dot\gamma^H \dot\gamma)$. Therefore, the equation of the geodesic curve reads

$$\ddot\gamma + \alpha^{-1} \text{tr}(\dot\gamma^H \dot\gamma)\gamma = 0 \tag{2.27}$$

The solution $\gamma_{x,v}^{\alpha} : \mathbb{R} \to \mathbb{S}_{n,p}^{\alpha}(\mathbb{C})$ of the variational problem (2.26) with initial conditions $\gamma(0) = x$ and $\dot{\gamma}(0) = v$ reads

$$\gamma_{x,v}^{\alpha}(t) = x \cos\left(t\sqrt{\frac{\mathrm{tr}(v^H v)}{\alpha}}\right) + v\sqrt{\frac{\alpha}{\mathrm{tr}(v^H v)}} \sin\left(t\sqrt{\frac{\mathrm{tr}(v^H v)}{\alpha}}\right) \qquad (2.28)$$

for $v \neq 0$, while $\gamma_{x,0}^{\alpha}(t) = x$.

The distance between the endpoints of a geodesic line in a matrix-hypersphere is defined as follows:

$$d_{\gamma}(\gamma_{x,v}^{\alpha}(0), \gamma_{x,v}^{\alpha}(1)) \overset{\mathrm{def}}{=} \int_0^1 \|\dot{\gamma}_{x,v}^{\alpha}(t)\|_{\gamma_{x,v}^{\alpha}(t)} \, \mathrm{d}t = \|v\|_x \qquad (2.29)$$

Such an expression is used to compute the distance between two points as the length of the geodesic line that connects them.

2.3.2 Geodesic-Stepping Optimization Method

Given a regular function $f : \mathbb{S}_{n,p}^{\alpha}(\mathbb{C}) \to \mathbb{R}$, a gradient-steepest ascent algorithm to compute its maximum (or a local maximum) compatible with the geometrical structure of the parameter space is the geodesic-stepping method (see, for instance, Refs. [28, 36]).

Geodesic-stepping methods are regarded as the counterparts of Euler stepping methods on curved spaces. Euler-stepping-based optimization consists in moving in the direction of the gradient of a criterion function along a straight line. Geodesic stepping extends Euler stepping by replacing the notion of straight line with the notion of geodesic line. Geodesic steepest-gradient-ascent stepping may be expressed as

$$\begin{cases} x_{k+1} = \gamma_{x_k, \nabla_{x_k} f}^{\alpha}(h_k) \text{ for } k \geq 0, \\ h_k = \arg\max_{t>0}\{f(\gamma_{x_k, \nabla_{x_k} f}^{\alpha}(t))\} \end{cases} \qquad (2.30)$$

where $x_k \in \mathbb{S}_{n,p}^{\alpha}(\mathbb{C})$ denotes a sequence of discrete steps on the manifold of parameters with step-counter $k \in \mathbb{N}$. The term $h_k > 0$ denotes a sequence of optimization stepsizes. Likewise in Euler stepping methods, in the context of geodesic stepping methods, the length of a step is proportional to the learning stepsize. In fact, from the definition of geodesic distance (2.29), it follows that

$$d_{\gamma}(x_k, x_{k+1}) = h_k \|\nabla_{x_k} f\|_{x_k} \qquad (2.31)$$

By setting $\omega_k \overset{\mathrm{def}}{=} \alpha^{-\frac{1}{2}} \|\nabla_{x_k} f\|_x$, the geodesic-stepping algorithm (2.30) may be implemented on the manifold $\mathbb{S}_{n,p}^{\alpha}(\mathbb{C})$ as:

$$x_{k+1} = x_k \cos(h_k \omega_k) + \nabla_{x_k} f \sin(h_k \omega_k) \omega_k^{-1} \text{ for } k \geq 0 \qquad (2.32)$$

as long as $\omega_k \neq 0$, otherwise the algorithm stops. The condition $\omega_k = 0$ corresponds to a critical point of the criterion function f.

The choice of the learning-stepsize schedule h_k is facilitated by the observation that the geodesic function (2.28), with $\|v\|_x \neq 0$, is periodic in the argument t of period $\Theta \stackrel{\text{def}}{=} \frac{2\pi\sqrt{\alpha}}{\|v\|_x}$. Namely, given a smooth function $f : \mathbb{S}_{n,p}^\alpha(\mathbb{C}) \to \mathbb{R}$ to optimize, it holds that $f(\gamma_{x,\nabla_x f}^\alpha(t + \Theta)) = f(\gamma_{x,\nabla_x f}^\alpha(t))$. The search of an optimal learning stepsize may thus be restricted to the interval $(0, \Theta]$. Numerically, for a fixed matrix $x \in \mathbb{S}_{n,p}^\alpha(\mathbb{C})$, the optimal stepsize in (2.30) may be approximated by sampling the function $f(\gamma_{x,\nabla_x f}^\alpha(t))$ at points $t = \frac{s\Theta}{S}$, where the integer constant S denotes the number of sampling locations and $s = 1, 2, \ldots, S$. The stepsize is selected as the value $\frac{s\Theta}{S}$ that guarantees the maximum increase of the function f with respect to the preceding learning step, namely, with respect to value $f(x)$. If no increase can be achieved, the learning process stops.

2.3.3 Application to Optimal Precoding in MIMO Broadcast Channels

Consider a discrete, memoryless communication channel model, $y = Hz + w$, where $z \in \mathbb{C}^n$ is the input vector, $y \in \mathbb{C}^m$ is the output vector, $H \in \mathbb{C}^{m \times n}$ is the channel matrix and $w \in \mathbb{C}^m$ is a Gaussian random noise vector. Without making any further assumptions, this is a general Multiple Input Multiple Output (MIMO) channel. In a multiple-input multiple-output (MIMO) communication channel, transmitters and receivers may cooperate [4]. The transmitters can cooperate if the messages to be sent through the communication channel is jointly encoded into the components of the input vector z, and the receivers can cooperate if the whole output vector y instead of each individual entries of y is used to decode the message. The channel can have four different interpretations, according to whether either side cooperates. If both transmitters and receivers are allowed to cooperate, it represents a single-user MIMO Gaussian channel, arising in multiple antenna wireless systems. If only the receivers are allowed to cooperate and the transmitters are constrained to encode their signals independently, then the MIMO system represents a Gaussian multiple-access channel, arising in code-division multiple access (CDMA). If only the transmitters are allowed to cooperate and the receivers are constrained to decode their signals independently, it represents a Gaussian *MIMO broadcast channel*, arising in the downlink of a wireless system where the base station is equipped with an antenna array.

When a base station of a MIMO broadcast channel does not have enough antennas for full multiplexing, a precoding matrix is sought for that maps the data streams to the antenna elements of the user that does not apply full multiplexing [33]. All other variables like power allocation and covariance matrices of fully multiplexing users are already completely determine; therefore, the weighted sum rate solely depends on the precoder matrix. As the particular choice of the precoding matrix defines the subspace that the transmitted signals lay in, it has also a considerable impact on the achievable rates of the other users.

The learning problem discussed in the present section, concerning the maximization of a weighted sum rate in the context of MIMO broadcast channels, may be cast as the *maximization* of the criterion function $F : \mathbb{S}_{n,p}^{\alpha}(\mathbb{C}) \to \mathbb{R}$ defined as [33]

$$F(x) \stackrel{\text{def}}{=} \frac{\det^{\beta}(x^H B x)}{\det(x^H A x)} \tag{2.33}$$

where $x \in \mathbb{S}_{n,p}^{\alpha}(\mathbb{C})$ denotes a precoding matrix, matrix $A \in \mathbb{C}^{n \times n}$ is Hermitian positive-definite, matrix $B \in \mathbb{C}^{n \times n}$ is Hermitian positive-semidefinite and such that $\operatorname{rank}(B) \geq p$ and the exponent $\beta > 1$.

In order to put into effect the learning scheme described in Section 2.3.2, it is necessary to compute the gradient $\partial_x F$ of the learning criterion (2.33). For $K \in \mathbb{C}^{n \times n}$ Hermitian and $x^H K x \in \mathbb{C}^{p \times p}$ nonsingular, it holds that

$$\partial_x \det(x^H K x) = 2 \det(x^H K x) K x (x^H K x)^{-1} \tag{2.34}$$

In fact, the gradient $\partial_x \det(x^H K x)$ must satisfy

$$\det((x + y)^H K (x + y)) - \det(x^H K x) = \Re\operatorname{tr}(y^H \partial_x \det(x^H K x)) + o(\|y\|)$$

where symbol $o(\cdot)$ denotes higher-order infinitesimal. Calculations show that:

$$
\begin{aligned}
&\det((x + y)^H K (x + y)) \\
&= \det(x^H K x + y^H K x + x^H K y + o(y)) \\
&= \det(x^H K x(e_p + (x^H K x)^{-1} y^H K x + (x^H K x)^{-1} x^H K y + o(y))) \\
&= \det(x^H K x) \det(e_p + (x^H K x)^{-1} y^H K x + (x^H K x)^{-1} x^H K y + o(y))
\end{aligned}
$$

where symbol e_p denotes a $p \times p$ identity matrix. For an arbitrary small $y \in \mathbb{C}^{p \times p}$, the following identity holds true:

$$\det(e_p + y) = 1 + \operatorname{tr}(y) + o(\|y\|) \tag{2.35}$$

Hence, it is found that:

$$
\begin{aligned}
&\det((x + y)^H K (x + y)) - \det(x^H K x) \\
&= \det(x^H K x) \operatorname{tr}((x^H K x)^{-1} y^H K x + (x^H K x)^{-1} x^H K y) + o(\|y\|) \\
&= 2 \det(x^H K x) \Re\operatorname{tr}(y^H K x (x^H K x)^{-1}) + o(\|y\|)
\end{aligned}
$$

The last term must equate $\Re\operatorname{tr}(y^H \partial_x \det(x^H K x))$, up to an high-order infinitesimal, hence (2.34) follows.

The result (2.34) holds true at every point $x \in \mathbb{S}_{n,p}^{\alpha}(\mathbb{C})$ such that $\det(x^H K x) \neq 0$. It may be extended to the whole matrix space $\mathbb{S}_{n,p}^{\alpha}(\mathbb{C})$ thanks to the notion of *adjugate* matrix [40]. The adjugate of a matrix $z \in \mathbb{C}^{p \times p}$, denoted as $\mathcal{A}(z)$, satisfies the identities $\mathcal{A}(z)z = z\mathcal{A}(z) = \det(z)e_p$. If $x^H K x$ is nonsingular, it holds that:

$$(x^H K x)^{-1} \det(x^H K x) = \mathcal{A}(x^H K x) \tag{2.36}$$

Algorithm 2 Pseudocode to implement the proposed procedure to optimize the criterion function.

Set $k = 0$

Set x_0 to an initial guess in $\mathbb{S}_{n,p}^{\alpha}(\mathbb{C})$

Set ε to desired precision

repeat

   Set $a_k = \det(x_k^H A x_k)$ and $b_k = \det(x_k^H B x_k)$

   Set $g_k = 2\frac{b_k^{\beta-1}}{a_k^2}[\beta a_k B x_k A(x_k^H B x_k) - b_k A x_k A(x_k^H A x_k)]$

   Set $v_k = g_k - \frac{x_k}{\alpha}\Re\mathrm{tr}(x_k^H g_k)$

   Set $\omega_k = \alpha^{-\frac{1}{2}}\|v_k\|$

   Set $\Theta_k = 2\pi/\omega_k$ and determine the stepsize h_k according to the method explained in Section 2.3.2

   Set $x_{k+1} = x_k \cos(\omega_k h_k) + v_k \sin(\omega_k h_k)\omega_k^{-1}$

   Set $k = k + 1$

until $\|v_k\| \leq \varepsilon$

The right-hand side of the above equation is defined for every $x \in \mathbb{S}_{n,p}^{\alpha}(\mathbb{C})$, hence the gradient (2.34) may be prolonged to the whole space $\mathbb{S}_{n,p}^{\alpha}(\mathbb{C})$ and reads

$$\partial_x \det(x^H K x) = 2K x A(x^H K x) \qquad (2.37)$$

Such result allows computing the gradient of the criterion function (2.33) that takes on the form

$$\partial_x F(x) = 2\frac{\det^{\beta-1}(x^H B x)}{\det^2(x^H A x)}$$
$$\times [\beta \det(x^H A x) B x A(x^H B x) - \det(x^H B x) A x A(x^H A x)] \qquad (2.38)$$

The above expression together with the general expression (2.25) of the Riemannian gradient on the hypersphere $\mathbb{S}_{n,p}^{\alpha}(\mathbb{C})$ gives the Riemannian gradient of the criterion function (2.33).

The proposed procedure to optimize the criterion function (2.33) may be summarized by the pseudocode listed in the Algorithm 2, where the quantity g_k denotes the gradient of the learning criterion function (2.33) while the quantity v_k denotes its Riemannian gradient. To start the iteration (2.32), an initial guess x_0 may be picked up randomly in $\mathbb{S}_{n,p}^{\alpha}(\mathbb{C})$. The learning progress may be monitored by computing iteratively the value of the learning criterion function $F(x_k)$. As the range of values of the criterion function may vary considerably, the following performance index may be considered instead:

$$10\log_{10}\left[\frac{F(x_k)}{F(x_0)}\right] \text{ for } k \geq 0 \qquad (2.39)$$

Figure 2.3 shows a result of learning on the manifold $\mathbb{S}_{8,5}^5(\mathbb{C})$. In the test-problem, the matrix A is generated by the rule $A = UPU^H$ with U being the orthogonal

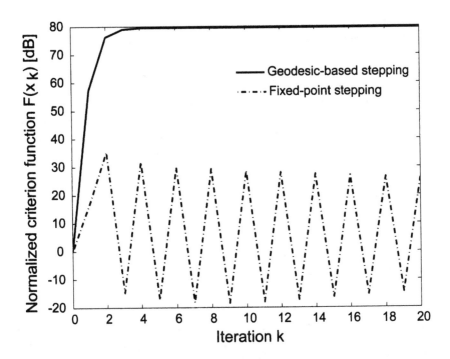

Figure 2.3   Result of a run of the algorithm (2.32) on the manifold $\mathbb{S}^5_{8,5}(\mathbb{C})$.

projection of a 8×8 random matrix $C + iD$ with C and D having random entries drawn from a normal distribution (here $i^2 = -1$) and P being a 8×8 diagonal matrix whose in-diagonal elements are drawn from a uniform distribution with support $[0, \frac{8}{10}]$. Likewise, the matrix B is generated by the rule $B = VRV^H$ with V being randomly generated likewise U and R being a diagonal matrix with at least 5 nonzero in-diagonal entries which are again drawn from a uniform distribution with support $[0, \frac{8}{10}]$. The rank of the matrix B, namely, the number of nonzero in-diagonal entries, is randomly selected in the integer-set $\{5, 6, 7, 8\}$. The number of sampling locations to approximate the optimal stepsize was set to $S = 50$. The obtained numerical result shows that the optimization algorithm (2.32) converges steadily and in a few iterations.

Figure 2.3 also shows a comparison of the learning ability of the proposed algorithm and that of the fixed-point learning method proposed in Ref. [29] to tackle the precoding matrix calculation problem. Though effective in the case $p = 1$, in the general case that $p > 1$ the fixed-point algorithm seems unsuitable.

2.4   COMPLEX ICA APPLIED TO TELECOMMUNICATIONS

Fiori [14] introduced a new class of learning rules for linear as well as nonlinear neural systems, arising from the study of the dynamics of an abstract rigid bodies in high-dimensional spaces, and experimentally proved their suitability for solving some learning problems such as optimal reduced-dimension data representation and blind source separation from instantaneous mixtures of real-valued independent signals. The studies on *rigid-body learning dynamics* are in close relationship with other contributions, such as the work of Qian [38] on second-order systems for learning. The mentioned class of learning algorithms is a subset of a larger family of adaptation rules that originated a general theoretical framework which encompasses several contributions found in the scientific literature [11]. The rigid-body theory may also be viewed as a special case of learning on Riemannian manifolds by the dynamical system theory, which has recently been developed in Refs. [24, 25].

The rigid-body learning paradigm arises from the equations describing the dynamics of an abstract rigid body embedded in a high-dimensional Euclidean space. The base-manifold for a single-unit system is the unit hypersphere $\mathbb{S}_{n,1}^1(\mathbb{R})$. For a single-unit neural system, the single-neuron learning equations read

$$\begin{cases} \dot{x} = \Omega x, \; q = -\mu \Omega x, \; f = -2 \nabla_x V, \\ \dot{\Omega} = \frac{1}{4}[(f+q)x^T - x(f+q)^T] \end{cases} \tag{2.40}$$

where $x(t) \in \mathbb{S}_{n,1}^1(\mathbb{R})$ describes the neuron's connection pattern at time t, superscript T denotes transposition, $\Omega \in \mathbb{R}^{n \times n}$ is a kind of angular speed, $q \in \mathbb{R}^n$ represents the braking effect produced by the fluid permeating the space that the body moves within, whose viscosity is denoted by μ, and $f \in \mathbb{R}^n$ represents the force field which makes the body move. It is further supposed that the force field derives from a potential energy function $V : \mathbb{S}_{n,1}^1(\mathbb{R}) \to \mathbb{R}$ that describes the neural system's task.

The basic properties of dynamical learning system (2.40) may be summarized as follows:

- Denote by $SO(n, \mathbb{R})$ the special orthogonal group, which is the subset of $\mathbb{R}^{n \times n}$ of the orthogonal matrices with unitary determinant. The manifold $SO(n, \mathbb{R})$ is a Lie group with Lie algebra $\mathfrak{so}(n, \mathbb{R})$, which is known to be the set of skew-symmetric matrices. It is immediate to verify that if $\Omega(0) \in \mathfrak{so}(n, \mathbb{R})$, then the equations (2.40) make $\dot{\Omega}(t) \in \mathfrak{so}(n, \mathbb{R})$ and thus $\Omega(t) \in \mathfrak{so}(n, \mathbb{R})$.

- Because of the skew-symmetry of the matrix field $\Omega(t)$, it follows that if $x(0) \in \mathbb{S}_{n,1}^1(\mathbb{R})$, then $x(t) \in \mathbb{S}_{n,1}^1(\mathbb{R})$ for all t. Also note that, by definition, it holds that $q, f \in T_x \mathbb{S}_{n,1}^1(\mathbb{R})$.

- The equilibrium conditions for the system (2.40) are that $\Omega x = 0$ and $f(t)x^T(t) - x(t)f^T(t) = 0_n$, where symbol 0_n denotes the null element of $\mathbb{R}^{n \times n}$. It is important to recall that the force field $f(t)$ is in general a nonlinear function of the parameters of the neural system.

- A rigid body, stimulated by a force field derived by a potential energy function, tends to *minimize* its potential energy V; therefore, the set of learning equations (2.40) for a neural unit with weight-vector x may be regarded as a nonconventional optimization algorithm.

An indicator of neuron's internal state, inspired by the rigid-bodie parallelism, is the neural system's *kinetic energy*, defined as

$$K(t) \overset{\text{def}}{=} \frac{1}{2}\|\dot{x}(t)\|^2_{x(t)} = -\frac{1}{2}x^T(t)\Omega^2(t)x(t) \geq 0 \qquad (2.41)$$

This is an important function in the theory of dynamical system because it may be proven that the sum $K + V$ of the kinetic energy and the potential energy – that is, the neural system's total energy – may be taken as a valid Lyapunov function for the system, ensuring the convergence of its connection pattern during the learning phase to a local optimum of the potential function V. Also, at these stable equilibria the kinetic energy vanishes. It is important to note that, because of the braking effect of the viscous fluid permeating the space that the abstract rigid body moves within, the rigid body is subject to energy loss.

2.4.1   Complex-Weighted Rigid-Body Learning Equations for ICA

Complex-valued independent component analysis (ICA) aims at extracting independent signals from their linear mixtures or to extract independent features (as latent variables) from signals having complex structure. A theoretical review as well as some interesting applications are reported in Refs. [7, 8, 12, 37, 44]. A way to define the independent components is to employ the maximum or minimum kurtosis principle: Under some conditions, the output of a linear neuron with n inputs $z(t) \in \mathbb{C}^n$ described by $y(t) = x^H(t)z(t)$ contains an independent component of the input if the weight-vector x maximizes or minimizes the fourth moment of neuron response [5]. The signal model is $z(t) = Ms(t)$, where $s(t) \in \mathbb{C}^n$ is a vector-signal with statistically independent components, and $M \in \mathbb{C}^{m \times n}$ is a matrix describing the mixing of the independent components into the observable signal or the expected relationship between the latent variables and the observable variables. Apart from special cases, the number of observations m should exceed or equate the number of independent sources n. With the convention that $s_r(t)$ denotes the rth independent component of $s(t)$, usually the hypotheses are that each s_r is a random signal and is statistically independent of each other at any time. Following Therrien [41], the kurtosis of signal $s(t) \in \mathbb{C}$ may be defined as $\kappa_4 \overset{\text{def}}{=} E[|s|^4] - 2E^2[|s|^2] - |E[s^2]|^2$. When s is white, i.e. $E[|s|^2] = 1$ and the real part and imaginary part of s have identical variance and are uncorrelated, the above expression simplifies into $E[|s|^4] - 2$.

The aim of the present section is to investigate the behavior of an extension of the rigid-body learning theory to the manifold $\mathbb{S}^1_{n,1}(\mathbb{C})$, in order to apply the neural ICA signal processing technique to blind separation of complex-valued signals [3, 7, 13]. The rigid-bodies-dynamics-based learning theory may be extended with little theoretical difficulty to the complex-valued case. The first step is to rewrite equations (2.40) for $x \in \mathbb{S}^1_{n,1}(\mathbb{C})$:

$$\begin{cases} \dot{x} = \Omega x, \; q = -\mu\Omega x, \; f = -2\nabla_x V, \\ \dot{\Omega} = \frac{1}{4}[(f+q)x^H - x(f+q)^H] \end{cases} \qquad (2.42)$$

Algorithm 3 Pseudocode to implement the complex-valued one-unit rigid-body learning procedure.

Set $k = 0$
Set x_0 to an initial guess in $\mathbb{S}^1_{n,1}(\mathbb{C})$ and $\Omega_0 = 0$
Set ε to desired precision
repeat

   Set $v_k = \Omega_k x_k$ and $\omega_k = \sqrt{\text{tr}(v_k^H v_k)}$
   Update $x_{k+1} = x_k \cos(h\omega_k) + v_k \sin(h\omega_k)\omega_k^{-1}$
   Set $q_k = -\mu v_k$ and $f_k = -2\eta E_z[|x_k^H z|^2 (x_k^H z)^* z]$
   Update $\Omega_{k+1} = \Omega_k + \frac{h}{4}[(f_k + q_k)x_k^H - x_k(f_k + q_k)^H]$
   Set $k = k + 1$
until $\|v_k\| \leq \varepsilon$

The field $\Omega(t)$ is a skew-Hermitian matrix field as it holds that $-\Omega(t) = \Omega^H(t)$ for any t. It is worth clarifying that, if $x = u + iv$ ($i^2 = -1$) and $V : \mathbb{C}^n \to \mathbb{R}$, then the ordinary gradient defines as $\partial_x V(x) \overset{\text{def}}{=} \partial_u V(u,v) + i\partial_v V(u,v)$. In the complex domain the system's kinetic energy writes $K = -\frac{1}{2}x^H \Omega^2 x$.

The basic conditions in complex-valued ICA are that the components of the source signal $s(t) \in \mathbb{C}^n$ in the model $z(t) = Ms(t) \in \mathbb{C}^n$ are IID and statistically independent at any time, and that the observed multivariate signal is white, i.e., the conditions $E_z[zz^H] = I_n$ and $E_z[zz^T] = 0_n$ are fulfilled [41]. The objective function which may be associated to complex-valued ICA is a kurtosis-based one [5], formally $E_z[|y|^4] - 2$, where $y(t) = x^H(t)z(t) \in \mathbb{C}$ is the response of a linear complex-weighted neuron having connection pattern z. In the rigid-body learning context it is, thus, assumed that

$$V(x) = \frac{1}{4}\eta\{E_z[|x^H z|^4] - 2\} \Rightarrow f = -2\eta E_z[|y|^2 y^* z] \qquad (2.43)$$

where the superscript $*$ denotes again complex conjugation. The sign of the constant $\eta \in \mathbb{R}$ determines whether maximization or minimization of the objective function is carried on.

The complex-valued rigid-body learning theory (2.42) may be implemented numerically by a geodesic-stepping algorithm as follows:

$$\begin{cases} x_{k+1} = \gamma^1_{x_k, \Omega_k x_k}(h), & q_k = -\mu\Omega_k x_k, \quad f_k = -2\nabla_{x_k}V, \\ \Omega_{k+1} = \Omega_k + \frac{h}{4}[(f_k + q_k)x_k^H - x_k(f_k + q_k)^H] \end{cases} \qquad (2.44)$$

where h denotes a fixed learning stepsize and the geodesic line equation is (2.28) with $\alpha = 1$. The discussed learning procedure may be summarized by the pseudocode listed in the Algorithm 3.

2.4.2 Application to the Blind Separation of QAM/PSK Signals

In order to test the explained ICA algorithm, computer simulations inspired by the work of Cardoso and Laheld [5] about blind separation of complex-valued QAM/PSK signals are shown and discussed in the following.

The input sequence $z \in \mathbb{C}^4$ is formed by a linear mixture of four independent signals arranged in a vector $s \in \mathbb{C}^4$. Signal s_1 is a QAM4, signal s_2 is a QAM16, signal s_3 is a PSK8, while signal s_4 is a Gaussian noise. The mixture is computed as $z = Ms$, where M is a randomly generated 4×4 complex-valued matrix.

As a measure of separation, the signal-to-interference ratio (SIR) was defined as

$$\mathrm{SIR} \stackrel{\mathrm{def}}{=} \frac{\|x^H M\|_2^2}{\|x^H M\|_1^2} - 1$$

where $\| \cdot \|_1$ denotes the L_1 (max-abs) norm.

A linear neuron with four inputs and one output, trained by the learning rule (2.42), will be able to recover one independent source signal except for arbitrary amplitude change and phase shift. An experimental result on blind separation is shown in Figure 2.4. The first row shows the original source signals, the second row shows the mixtures and the third row show the separation results of the neuron trained by the algorithm (2.44) with parameters $\eta = 0.5$, $\mu = 4$, and the sampling step to discretize the continuous-time learning equations was $h = 0.001$. The kinetic energy of the neuron vanishes to zero after learning, while the extracted signal is the PSK.

2.5 CONCLUSION

The present book chapter deals with artificial neural systems whose adaptable parameters lay on complex-valued manifolds and with their application to signal-processing problems. In particular, the present chapter recalled notions from differential geometry that are instrumental in the development of a consistent learning theory over complex-valued differentiable manifolds and introduced some applications in signal processing and their solutions based on learning.

A first application concerns averaging over a curved manifold. A committee of learning machines is a set of adaptive systems that work independently toward the solution of the same learning problem. Every machine in the committee learns a parameter pattern that differs only slightly one to another, except for a few outliers. A natural concern that arises in this case is how to merge the available patterns in order to obtain an *average* pattern that is closer to the optimal solution of the learning problem than the single parameter patterns. In this chapter, averaging is selected as a possible merging technique. In the case that the parameter space is curved, the averaging procedure should be designed on the basis of its geometric properties. It is known that curved parameter spaces provide a natural way to incorporate learning constraints pertaining to learning problems of interest. The present book-chapter treated in details the problem of designing an averaging procedure in the case that

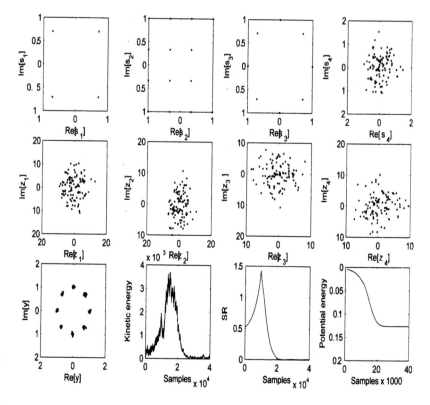

Figure 2.4   Top panels: Independent source signals. Middle panels: Observed mixed signals. Bottom panel (from left to right): Separated signal, neuron kinetic energy $K(t)$, signal-to-interference ratio (SIR) versus time, and potential energy function $V(t)$, versus time.

the parameter space shared by learning machines belonging to a committee exhibits the structure of the unitary group of matrices.

The second application discussed within present chapter is about learning the optimal precoding matrix for MIMO-broadcast channels. Numerical results about the solution of the formal problem related to the optimal precoding for MIMO-broadcast-channels show the effectiveness of the proposed learning method and of its numerical implementation. The obtained numerical results show that the developed optimization algorithm converges steadily and in a few iterations. The discussed method proves advantageous over the fixed-point learning method originally suggested in Ref. [29].

The third application is about blind separation of complex-valued signals from their linear complex-valued mixtures by a one-unit system complex-valued rigid-body learning theory. The numerical results show that a source signal can be correctly extracted from a mixture and that, in the special case of PSK/QAM source signals, the symbols of a PSK constellation are well-recognizable after separation.

REFERENCES

1. I. Aizenberg, Book Reviews: Complex-Valued Neural Networks: Theories and Applications. A. Hirose, ed. World Scientific Publishing Co., 2004). *IEEE Transactions on Neural Networks*, 17(2):534, March 2006.

2. S.-i. Amari and S. Fiori, Editorial: Special issue on Geometrical methods in neural networks and learning. *Neurocomputing*, 67:1–7, August 2005.

3. E. Bingham and A. Hyvärinen, ICA of complex valued signals: a fast and robust deflationary algorithm. In *Proceedings of the International Joint Conference on Neural Networks*, Vol. III, pp. 357–362, July 2000.

4. G. Caire and S. Shamai, On the achievable throughput of a multi-antenna Gaussian broadcast channel. *IEEE Transactions on Information Theory*, 49(7):1691–1705, July 2003.

5. J.F. Cardoso and B. Laheld, Equivariant adaptive source separation. *IEEE Transactions on Signal Processing*, 44(12):3017–3030, December 1996.

6. E. Celledoni and S. Fiori, Neural learning by geometric integration of reduced 'rigid-body' equations. *Journal of Computational and Applied Mathematics (JCAM)*, 172(2):247–269, December 2004.

7. G. Desodt and D. Muller, Complex ICA applied to the separation of radar signals. In *Proceedings of the European Conference on Signal Processing (EUSIPCO'90)*, Vol. I, Barcelona, Spain, September 1990, pp. 665–668.

8. Y. Deville, Towards industrial applications of blind source separation and independent component analysis. *First International Workshop on Independent Component Analysis and Signal Separation (ICA'99)*, Aussois, France, January 11-15, 1999, pp. 19–24.

9. L. Dieci, B. Morini and A. Papini, Computational techniques for real logarithms of matrices. *SIAM Journal of Matrix Analysis and Applications*, 17:570–593, 1996.

10. S. Fiori, Blind separation of circularly distributed source signals by the neural extended APEX algorithm. *Neurocomputing*, 34(1-4):239–252, August 2000.

11. S. Fiori, A theory for learning by weight flow on Stiefel-Grassman manifold. *Neural Computation* 13(7):1625–1647, July 2001.

12. S. Fiori, P. Burrascano, E. Cardelli, and A. Faba, A blind separation approach to electromagnetic source localization and assessment. In *Proceedings of the 7th International Conference on Engineering Applications of Neural Networks (EANN'2001)*, July 16-18, 2001, pp. 188–191.

13. S. Fiori, On blind separation of complex-valued sources by extended Hebbian learning. *IEEE Signal Processing Letters*, 8(8):217–220, August 2001.

14. S. Fiori, A theory for learning based on rigid bodies dynamics. *IEEE Transactions on Neural Networks* 13(3):521–531, May 2002.

15. S. Fiori, A fast fixed-point neural blind deconvolution algorithm. *IEEE Transactions on Neural Networks* 15(2):455–459, March 2004.

16. S. Fiori, Non-linear complex-valued extensions of hebbian learning: An essay. *Neural Computation* 17(4):779–838, 2005.

17. S. Fiori, Quasi-geodesic neural learning algorithms over the orthogonal group: A tutorial. *Journal of Machine Learning Research*, 6:743–781, May 2005.

18. S. Fiori, Formulation and integration of learning differential equations on the Stiefel manifold. *IEEE Transactions on Neural Networks* 16(6):1697–1701, November 2005.

19. S. Fiori, Geodesic-based and projection-based neural blind deconvolution algorithms. *Signal Processing*, 88(3):521–538, March 2008.

20. S. Fiori, A study on neural learning on manifold foliations: The case of the Lie group SU(3). *Neural Computation*, 20(4):1091–1117, April 2008.

21. S. Fiori, Lie-group-type neural system learning by manifold retractions. *Neural Networks*, 21(10):1524–1529, December 2008.

22. S. Fiori, On vector averaging over the unit hyphersphere. *Digital Signal Processing*, 19(4):715–725, July 2009.

23. S. Fiori, Learning by natural gradient on noncompact matrix-type pseudo-Riemannian manifolds. *IEEE Transactions on Neural Networks*, 21(5):841–852, May 2010.

24. S. Fiori, Extended Hamiltonian learning on Riemannian manifolds: Theoretical aspects. *IEEE Transactions on Neural Networks*, 22(5):687–700, May 2011.

25. S. Fiori, Extended Hamiltonian learning on Riemannian manifolds: Numerical Aspects. *IEEE Transactions on Neural Networks and Learning Systems*, 23(1):7–21, January 2012.

26. S. Fiori and P. Baldassarri, Approximate joint matrix diagonalization by Riemannian-gradient-based optimization over the unitary group (with application to neural multichannel blind deconvolution). In *Neural Computation and Particle Accelerators: Research, Technology and Applications*, E. Chabot and H. D'Arras editors, Series of Neuroscience Research Progress, NOVA Publisher, 2009.

27. S. Fiori and T. Tanaka, An algorithm to compute averages on matrix Lie groups. *IEEE Transactions on Signal Processing*, 57(12):4734–4743, December 2009.

28. D. Gabay, Minimizing a differentiable function over a differentiable manifold. *Journal of Optimization Theory and Applications*, 37(2):177–219, 1982.

29. C. Guthy, W. Utschick, R. Hunger and M. Joham, Efficient weighted sum rate maximization with linear precoding. *IEEE Transactions on Signal Processing*, 58(4):2284–2297, April 2010.

30. G. Han, K. Portman and J. Rosenthal, Unitary matrices with maximal or near maximal diversity product. In *Proceedings of the* 39th *Allerton Conference on Communication, Control and Computing, Allerton House, Monticello, Illinois, October 3-5, 2001*, pp. 82–91.

31. N.J. Higham, The scaling and squaring method for the matrix exponential revisited. *SIAM Journal of Matrix Analysis and Applications*, 26:1179–1193, 2005.

32. A. Hirose, *Complex-Valued Neural Networks*. Studies in Computational Intelligence, Vol. 32, Springer-Verlag, Berlin, 2006.

33. R. Hunger, P. de Kerret and M. Joham, An algorithm for maximizing a quotient of two Hermitian form determinants with different exponents. In *Proceedings of the International Conference on Acoustics, Speech and Signal Processing (ICASSP 2010, Dallas (TX, USA), March 2010)*, pp. 3346–3349.

34. M. Kobayashi and G. Caire, An iterative water-filling algorithm for maximum weighted sum-rate of Gaussian MIMO-BC. *IEEE Journal on Selected Areas in Communications*, 24(8):1640–1646, 2006.

35. J. Liu, Y.T. Hou and H.D. Sherali, On the maximum weighted sum-rate of MIMO Gaussian broadcast channels. In *Proceedings of the IEEE International Conference on Communications (ICC, Beijing (China), May 2008)*, pp. 3664–3668.

36. D.G. Luenberger, The gradient projection methods along geodesics. *Management Science*, 18:620–631, 1972.

37. A. Paraschiv-Ionescu, C. Jutten, and G. Bouvier, Neural network based processing for smart sensor arrays. In *Proceedings of International Conference on Artificial Neural Networks (ICANN)*, pp. 565–570, 1997.

38. N. Qian, On the momentum term in gradient descent learning algorithms. *Neural Networks*, 12:145–151, 1999.

39. M. Spivak, *A Comprehensive Introduction to Differential Geometry*, Vol. 1, 2nd edition, Publish or Perish Press, Berkeley, CA, 1979.

40. G.W. Stewart, On the adjugate matrix. *Linear Algebra and Its Applications*, 283(1-3):151–164, November 1998.

41. C.W. Therrien, *Discrete Random Signals and Statistical Signal Processing*, Prentice-Hall, Engelwood Cliffs, NJ, 1992.

42. L. Xu, Theories for unsupervised learning: PCA and its nonlinear extension. In *Proceedings of the International Joint Conference on Neural Networks (IJCNN 1994, Orlando (FL, USA), June 1994)*, Vol. II, pp. 1252–1257.

43. T. Yang and W.B. Mikhael, Baseband image rejection for diversity superheterodyne receivers. In *Proceedings of the 2004 IEEE Wireless Communications and Networking Conference (Atlanta, Georgia, USA)*, pp. 2232–2234.

44. A. Ypma and P. Pajunen, Rotating machine vibration analysis with second-order independent component analysis. In *Proceedings of First International Workshop on Independent Component Analysis and Signal Separation (ICA'99, Aussois, France, January 11-15, 1999)*, pp. 37–42, 1999.

45. X. Zhang, G. Berger, M. Dietz and C. Denz, Cross-talk in phase encoded volume holographic memories employing unitary matrices. *Applied Physics B, Lasers and optics*, 85(4):575–579, 2006.

46. X. Zhang, G. Berger, M. Dietz and C. Denz, Unitary matrices for phase-coded holographic memories. *Optics Letters*, 31(8):1047–1049, April 2006.

47. Y. Zhu, W. Mio and X. Liu, Optimal dimension reduction for image retrieval with correlation metrics. In *Proceedings of the International Conference on Neural Networks (IJCNN 2009, Atlanta (GA, USA), June 2009)*, pp. 3565–3570.

CHAPTER 3

N-DIMENSIONAL VECTOR NEURON AND ITS APPLICATION TO THE N-BIT PARITY PROBLEM

Tohru Nitta

National Institute of Advanced Industrial Science and Technology (AIST), Tsukuba, Japan

We describe a new neuron model, N-dimensional vector neuron, which can deal with N signals as one cluster, by extending the three-dimensional vector neuron to N dimensions naturally. The N-bit parity problem, which cannot be solved with a single usual real-valued neuron, can be solved with a single N-dimensional vector neuron with the orthogonal decision boundary, which reveals the potent computational power of N-dimensional vector neurons. Rumelhart, Hinton, and Williams showed that increasing the number of layers made the computational power of neural networks high. In this chapter, we show that extending the dimensionality of neural networks to N dimensions originates the similar effect on neural networks.

3.1 INTRODUCTION

In order to provide a high computational power, there have been many attempts to design neural networks, taking account of task domains. For example, complex-valued neural networks have been researched since the 1970s [1, 2]. Complex-valued neural networks whose parameters (weights and threshold values) are all complex numbers are suitable for the fields dealing with complex numbers such as telecommunications, speech recognition, and image processing with the Fourier transformation. Actually, we can find many applications of the complex-valued neural networks to various fields such as telecommunications and image processing in the literature [3, 4, 5]. For example, the fading equalization problem has been successfully solved with a single complex-valued neuron with the highest generalization ability [6], using the property that the decision boundary for the real part of an output of a single complex-valued neuron and that for the imaginary part intersect orthogonally [7]. The exclusive-or (XOR) problem and the detection of symmetry problem which cannot be solved with a single real-valued neuron [8] can be solved with a single complex-valued neuron with the orthogonal decision boundaries [6].

This chapter is organized as follows: Section 3.2 reviews various neuron models with high-dimensional parameters. Section 3.3 proposes an N-dimensional neuron, shows its property on decision boundaries, and provides a solution to the N-bit parity problem. Discussions are given in Section 3.4. Finally, we give some conclusions.

3.2 NEURON MODELS WITH HIGH-DIMENSIONAL PARAMETERS

In this section, various neuron models with high-dimensional parameters and their properties are reviewed briefly.

3.2.1 Complex-Valued Neuron

A usual real-valued neuron can be extended to complex numbers, which is the second lowest dimension [1, 2, 3, 4, 5, 9].

Consider an n-input complex-valued neuron with weights $w_k = w_k^r + iw_k^i \in C$ $(1 \leq k \leq n)$ (C denotes the set of complex numbers, $i = \sqrt{-1}$) and a threshold value $\theta = \theta^r + i\theta^i \in C$. Given input signals $x_k + iy_k \in C$ $(1 \leq k \leq n)$, the neuron generates a complex-valued output value $X + iY$, where

$$
\begin{aligned}
X + iY &= f_C\left(\sum_{k=1}^{n}(w_k^r + iw_k^i)(x_k + iy_k) + (\theta^r + i\theta^i)\right) \\
&= f\left(\sum_{k=1}^{n}(w_k^r x_k - w_k^i y_k) + \theta^r\right) \\
&\quad + if\left(\sum_{k=1}^{n}(w_k^i x_k + w_k^r y_k) + \theta^i\right), \quad\quad (3.1)
\end{aligned}
$$

$$
f_C(z) = f(x) + if(y), \quad z = x + iy \quad\quad (3.2)
$$

and $f : R \rightarrow R$ is a real-valued function such as a sigmoidal function (R denotes the set of real numbers). Although various types of activation functions $f_C : C \rightarrow C$ have been proposed, this chapter focuses on a split-type activation function described above. Equation (3.1) can be rewritten as

$$\begin{bmatrix} X \\ Y \end{bmatrix} = F_C\left(\sum_{k=1}^{n} \begin{bmatrix} w_k^r & -w_k^i \\ w_k^i & w_k^r \end{bmatrix} \begin{bmatrix} x_k \\ y_k \end{bmatrix} + \begin{bmatrix} \theta^r \\ \theta^i \end{bmatrix} \right) \qquad (3.3)$$

where

$$F_C\left(\begin{bmatrix} x \\ y \end{bmatrix} \right) = \begin{bmatrix} f(x) \\ f(y) \end{bmatrix}, \qquad \begin{bmatrix} w_k^r & -w_k^i \\ w_k^i & w_k^r \end{bmatrix} \in O_2(\mathbf{R}) \qquad (3.4)$$

and $O_2(\mathbf{R})$ is the two-dimensional orthogonal group.

The complex-valued neuron has different nature from that of the real-valued neuron. One of them is the decision boundary. Decision boundary is a boundary by which the pattern classifier classifies patterns, and it generally consists of hypersurfaces. In Ref. 10, the decision boundaries of the complex-valued neural network have been analyzed mathematically. A decision boundary of a single complex-valued neuron consists of two hypersurfaces which intersect orthogonally, and it divides a decision region into four equal sections.

3.2.2 Hyperbolic Neuron

Buchholtz and Sommer first formulated a hyperbolic neuron model using hyperbolic numbers [11]. Hyperbolic numbers, another second lowest dimension, are numbers of the form

$$w = a + ub \qquad (3.5)$$

where $a, b \in \mathbf{R}$ and u is called *unipotent* which has the algebraic property that $u \neq \pm 1$ but $u^2 = 1$ [12].

The input and output signals, as well as the weights and threshold values of the hyperbolic neuron, are all hyperbolic numbers, and the activation function f_H of the hyperbolic neuron is defined to be

$$f_H(z) = f(x) + uf(y) \qquad (3.6)$$

where $z = x + uy$ is a hyperbolic-valued net input to the hyperbolic neuron, and $f : \mathbf{R} \rightarrow \mathbf{R}$ (for example, $f(s) = 1/(1 + \exp(-s))$ for $s \in \mathbf{R}$). Various types of activation functions other than Eq. (3.6) can be considered naturally.

The decision boundary of a hyperbolic neuron consists of two hypersurfaces which can intersect orthogonally or be parallel depending on the values of the hyperbolic-valued weight vectors [13]. One of the advantages of hyperbolic neurons is that the angle between the decision boundary for the real part and that for the unipotent part can be easily controlled by changing the weight parameters.

3.2.3 Three-Dimensional Vector Neuron

The three-dimensional vector neuron is a natural extension of the complex-valued neuron to three dimensions, which can deal with three signals as one cluster: The input signals, thresholds, and output signals are all 3D real-valued vectors, and the weights are all 3D orthogonal matrices [14]. The activity a of neuron is defined to be

$$a = \sum_k W_k s_k + t \tag{3.7}$$

where s_k is the kth 3D real-valued vector input signal, W_k is the 3D orthogonal weight matrix for the kth input signal s_k (that is, an element of the three-dimensional orthogonal group $O_3(R)$: $W_k \cdot {}^t W_k = {}^t W_k \cdot W_k = I_3$ where I_3 denotes the three-dimensional identity matrix), and t is the 3D real-valued vector threshold value. The output signal $F(a)$ is defined to be

$$F(a) = \begin{bmatrix} f(a_1) \\ f(a_2) \\ f(a_3) \end{bmatrix}, \quad \text{where} \quad a = \begin{bmatrix} a_1 \\ a_2 \\ a_3 \end{bmatrix}$$

$$\text{and} \quad f(a_i) = \frac{1}{1 + \exp(-a_i)} \tag{3.8}$$

In the above formulation, various restrictions can be imposed on the 3D matrix; e.g., it can be regular, symmetric, or orthogonal, etc., which will influence the behavioral characteristics of the neuron. The weights are assumed to be orthogonal matrices because this assumption is a natural extension of the weights of the complex-valued neuron. Considering Eqs. (3.3) and (3.4), the formulation of a neuron as given in Eqs. (3.7) and (3.8) above is natural.

The 3D vector neural network constructed with the 3D vector neurons has the ability to learn 3D affine transformations [15].

3.2.4   Three-Dimensional Vector Product Neuron

The three-dimensional vector product neuron [16] is a three-dimensional neuron different from the 3D vector neuron described in Section 3.2.3: The computation is performed using a 3D vector product that is invented by the demands of sciences, e.g. dynamics.

The input signals, weights, thresholds and output signals are all 3D real-valued vectors. The activity a of neuron is defined to be

$$a = \sum_k (w_k \times s_k) + t \tag{3.9}$$

where s_k is the 3D real-valued vector input signal coming from the output of neuron k, w_k is the 3D real-valued vector weight for the kth input signal s_k, t is the 3D real-valued vector threshold value of neuron, and $x \times y$ denotes vector product of $x = {}^t[x_1 \ x_2 \ x_3]$ and $y = {}^t[y_1 \ y_2 \ y_3]$, i.e. $x \times y = {}^t[x_2 y_3 - x_3 y_2 \ x_3 y_1 - x_1 y_3 \ x_1 y_2 - x_2 y_1]$. To obtain the (3D real-valued vector) output signal, convert the activity value a into its three components as follows.

$$a = \begin{bmatrix} a_1 \\ a_2 \\ a_3 \end{bmatrix} \tag{3.10}$$

The output signal $F(a)$ is defined to be

$$F(a) = \begin{bmatrix} f(a_1) \\ f(a_2) \\ f(a_3) \end{bmatrix}, \quad \text{where } f(a_i) = \frac{1}{1 + \exp(-a_i)} \tag{3.11}$$

Kobayashi proposed a three-dimensional associative memory using the 3D vector product neuron [17]. The vector product neuron could be effectively used in the field dealing with three-dimensional vectors, especially vector product operation.

3.2.5   Quaternary Neuron

Quaternary neurons were proposed in the mid-1990s [18, 19]. The weights, threshold values, input and output signals are all quaternions where a quaternion is a four-dimensional number and was invented by W. R. Hamilton in 1843 [20]. The activity a of neuron is defined to be

$$a = \sum_n s_n w_n + t \tag{3.12}$$

where s_n is the quaternary input signal coming from the output of neuron n, w_n is the quaternary weight for the nth input signal, and t is the quaternary threshold value of neuron. To obtain the quaternary output signal, convert the activity value a into its four parts as follows.

$$a = a_1 + a_2 i + a_3 j + a_4 k \tag{3.13}$$

where $i^2 = j^2 = k^2 = -1$, $ij = -ji = k$, $jk = -kj = i$, $ki = -ik = j$. The output signal $f_Q(a)$ is defined to be

$$f_Q(a) = f(a_1) + f(a_2)i + f(a_3)j + f(a_4)k,$$
$$\text{where } f(a_l) = \frac{1}{1 + \exp(-a_l)} \tag{3.14}$$

The multiplication $s_n w_n$ in Eq. (3.12) should be carefully treated because the equation $s_n w_n = w_n s_n$ does not hold (the noncommutative property of quternions on multiplication), which produces two kinds of quaternary neurons: One calculates $a = \sum_n s_n w_n + t$, and the other calculates $a = \sum_n w_n s_n + t$. Kobayashi and Nakajima proposed a twisted quaternary neural network (TQNN) which consisted of both of the two kinds of neurons, and they discussed the properties of the TQNN vis-a-vis the ability to learn and the reducibility [21]. On the other hand, Isokawa et al. proposed a multistate Hopfield neural network model using *commutative quaternions* [22]. Nitta proved that the 4-bit parity problem which cannot be solved with a single usual real-valued neuron can be solved with a single quaternary neuron with the orthogonal decision boundary, resulting in the highest generalization ability [23].

3.2.6   Clifford Neuron

The Clifford neuron is a 2^n-dimensional neuron [24, 25, 26]. First, we briefly describe the Clifford algebra or geometric algebra [27]. Clifford algebra $Cl_{p,q}$ is an extension of real, complex numbers, and quaternions to higher dimensions, and has 2^n basis elements. The subscripts p, q such that $p + q = n$ determine the characteristics of the Clifford algebra. Note that commutativity does not hold generally. For example, in the case of $n = 2, p = 0, q = 2$, the number of basis is $2^2 = 4$, which corresponds to the basis of quaternions.

Let the space $\mathbf{R}^{n+1}$ be given with the basis $\{e_0, \ldots, e_n\}$. And also, let $p \in \{0, \ldots, n\}, q \overset{\text{def}}{=} n - p$ be given. Assume that the following rules on the multiplication hold:

$$e_0 e_i = e_i e_0 = e_i \quad (i = 1, \ldots, n), \tag{3.15}$$

$$e_i e_j = -e_j e_i \quad (i \neq j; \ i, j = 1, \ldots, n), \tag{3.16}$$

$$e_0^2 = e_1^2 = \cdots = e_p^2 = 1, \tag{3.17}$$

$$e_{p+1}^2 = \cdots = e_{p+q}^2 = -1 \tag{3.18}$$

Then, the 2^n basis elements of the Clifford algebra $Cl_{p,q}$ are obtained:

$$e_0; \ e_1, \ldots, e_n; \ e_1 e_2, \ldots, e_{n-1} e_n; \ e_1 e_2 e_3, \ldots; \ \ldots; \ e_1 e_2 \ldots e_n \tag{3.19}$$

where e_0 is a unit element. The addition and the multiplication with a real number are defined coordinatewise. Furthermore, we assume that the following condition holds:

$$e_1 e_2 \cdots e_n \neq \pm 1 \quad \text{if } p - q \equiv 1 \ (\text{mod } 4) \tag{3.20}$$

The algebra thus obtained is called Clifford algebra $Cl_{p,q}$.

The Clifford neuron is a 2^n-dimensional neuron where the input signals, weights, thresholds and output signals are all Clifford numbers. The activity a of neuron is defined to be

$$a = \sum_k w_k s_k + t \tag{3.21}$$

where s_k is the Clifford-valued input signal coming from the output of neuron k, w_k is the Clifford-valued weight for the kth input signal, and t is the Clifford-valued threshold of neuron. To obtain the Clifford-valued output signal, convert the activity value a into its 2^n parts as follows.

$$a = a_1 \cdot e_0 + \cdots + a_{2^n} \cdot e_1 \cdots e_n \tag{3.22}$$

The output signal $f_{Cl_{p,q}}(a)$ is defined to be

$$f_{Cl_{p,q}}(a) = f(a_1) \cdot e_0 + \cdots + f(a_{2^n}) \cdot e_1 \cdots e_n$$

$$\text{where} \quad f(a_l) = \frac{1}{1 + \exp(-a_l)} \tag{3.23}$$

Pearson formulated a multilayered Clifford neural network model, derived a Clifford back-propagation learning algorithm, and clarified the ability on approximate functions [24, 25]. Buchholz formulated another multilayered Clifford neural network with a split-type activation function which is different from that Pearson adopted [28]. Kuroe first proposed models of recurrent Clifford neural networks and discussed their dynamics from the point of view of the existence of energy functions [29, 30].

3.3 *N*-DIMENSIONAL VECTOR NEURON

It is a matter of common occurrence that a vector is used in the real world, which represents a cluster of something, – for example, a four-dimensional vector consisting of height, width, breadth, and time, along with a N-dimensional vector consisting of N particles and so on. Then, we formulate a model neuron that can deal with N signals as one cluster, called *N-dimensional vector neuron*, by extending the three-dimensional vector neuron described in Section 3.2.3 to N dimensions naturally [31].

3.3.1 *N*-Dimensional Vector Neuron Model

We will consider the following N-dimensional vector neuron with M inputs. The input signals, thresholds, and output signals are all N-dimensional real-valued vectors, and the weights are all N-dimensional orthogonal matrices. The net input u to a N-dimensional vector neuron is defined as

$$u = \sum_{k=1}^{M} W_k x_k + \theta \tag{3.24}$$

where x_k is the kth N-dimensional real-valued vector input signal, W_k is the N-dimensional orthogonal weight matrix for the kth input signal x_k (that is, an element of the N-dimensional orthogonal group $O_N(R)$), and θ is the N-dimensional real-valued vector threshold value. The N-dimensional real-valued vector output signal is defined to be

$$1_N(u) = \begin{bmatrix} 1_R(u^{(1)}) \\ \vdots \\ 1_R(u^{(N)}) \end{bmatrix}, \text{ where } u = \begin{bmatrix} u^{(1)} \\ \vdots \\ u^{(N)} \end{bmatrix}$$

$$\text{and } 1_R(u) = \begin{cases} 1 & \text{if } u \geq 0 \\ 0 & \text{if } u < 0 \end{cases} \tag{3.25}$$

For the sake of simplicity, the step function 1_R is used. Naturally, the activation function 1_R can be replaced with a nonlinear function.

3.3.2 Decision Boundary

We can find that a decision boundary of a N-dimensional vector neuron consists of N hyperplanes which intersect each other orthogonally, and it divides a decision region into N equal sections, as that of a complex-valued neuron case [10]. The net input u (Eq. (3.24)) to a N-dimensional neuron with M inputs can be rewritten as

$$u = \sum_{k=1}^{M} W_k x_k + \theta$$

$$= \begin{bmatrix} [w_1^{(1)} \cdots w_M^{(1)}] \begin{bmatrix} x_1 \\ \vdots \\ x_M \end{bmatrix} + \theta^{(1)} \\ \vdots \\ [w_1^{(N)} \cdots w_M^{(N)}] \begin{bmatrix} x_1 \\ \vdots \\ x_M \end{bmatrix} + \theta^{(N)} \end{bmatrix} \qquad (3.26)$$

where $w_k^{(i)}$ is the ith row vector of W_k ($i = 1, \cdots, N; k = 1, \cdots, M$), and $\theta = {}^t[\theta^{(1)} \cdots \theta^{(N)}]$. Thus,

$$u^{(i)}(x_1, \cdots, x_M) \overset{\text{def}}{=} [w_1^{(i)} \cdots w_M^{(i)}] \begin{bmatrix} x_1 \\ \vdots \\ x_M \end{bmatrix} + \theta^{(i)}$$

$$= 0 \qquad (3.27)$$

is the decision boundary for the ith component of an output of the N-dimensional vector neuron with M inputs ($i = 1, \cdots, N$). That is, input signals ${}^t[x_1, \cdots, x_M] \in R^{MN}$ are classified into two decision regions

$$\{{}^t[x_1, \cdots, x_M] \in R^{MN} \mid u^{(i)}(x_1, \cdots, x_M) \geq 0\} \qquad (3.28)$$

and

$$\{{}^t[x_1, \cdots, x_M] \in R^{MN} \mid u^{(i)}(x_1, \cdots, x_M) < 0\} \qquad (3.29)$$

by the hyperplane given by Eq. (3.27) ($i = 1, \cdots, N$). The normal vector $q^{(i)}$ of the decision boundary for ith component (Eq. (3.27)) is given by ${}^t[{}^t w_1^{(i)} \cdots {}^t w_M^{(i)}]$ ($i = 1, \cdots, N$), and it follows from the orthogonal property of the weight matrix W_k (i.e., $W_k \cdot {}^t W_k = {}^t W_k \cdot W_k = I_N$($N$-dimensional identity matrix)) that the inner product of the normal vectors of the decision boundaries for any two distinct components is zero: for any $1 \leq i, j \leq N$ such that $i \neq j$,

$$^t q^{(i)} \cdot q^{(j)} = [w_1^{(i)} \cdots w_M^{(i)}] \cdot \begin{bmatrix} {}^t w_1^{(j)} \\ \vdots \\ {}^t w_M^{(j)} \end{bmatrix} = 0 \qquad (3.30)$$

Thus, the decision boundary of a N-dimensional vector neuron consists of N hyperplanes which intersect orthogonally each other.

3.3.3 *N*-Bit Parity Problem

We will find a solution to the *N*-bit parity problem, using a single *N*-dimensional vector neuron with the orthogonal decision boundary with the highest generalization ability. Minsky and Papert clarified the limitations of a single real-valued neuron: In a large number of interesting cases, a single real-valued neuron is incapable of solving the problems [8]. The most difficult problem among them is the parity problem, in which the output required is 1 if the input pattern contains an odd number of 1s and 0 otherwise.

Rumelhart, Hinton, and Williams showed that the *3-layered* real-valued neural network (i.e., with one hidden layer) can solve the parity problem [32, 33]. As described above, the parity problem cannot be solved with a single real-valued neuron. Then, it will be proved that the parity problem can be solved by a single *N*-dimensional vector neuron with the orthogonal decision boundary. Rumelhart, Hinton, and Williams showed that increasing the number of layers made the computational power of neural networks high. We will show that extending the dimensionality of neural networks to *N* dimensions originates the similar effect on neural networks.

3.3.4 A Solution

The input-output mapping in the *N*-bit parity problem is shown in Table 3.1. In order to solve the *N*-bit parity problem with *N*-dimensional vector neurons, the input-output mapping is encoded as shown in Table 3.2, where the outputs ${}^t[\,0\ 0\ 0\ \cdots\ 0\ 0\ 0\,], {}^t[\,0\ 0\ 0\ \cdots\ 0\ 1\ 1\,], {}^t[\,0\ 0\ 0\ \cdots\ 1\ 0\ 1\,], {}^t[\,0\ 0\ 0\ \cdots\ 1\ 1\ 0\,], \ldots$ are interpreted to be 0, and ${}^t[\,0\ 0\ 0\ \cdots\ 0\ 0\ 1\,], {}^t[\,0\ 0\ 0\ \cdots\ 0\ 1\ 0\,], {}^t[\,0\ 0\ 0\ \cdots\ 1\ 0\ 0\,], \ldots$ are interpreted to be 1 of the original *N*-bit parity problem (Table 3.1), respectively. We use a single *N*-dimensional vector neuron with only one input with a weight

$$W = \begin{bmatrix} w_{11} & \cdots & w_{1N} \\ \vdots & & \vdots \\ w_{N1} & \cdots & w_{NN} \end{bmatrix} \in O_N(\mathbf{R}) \qquad (3.31)$$

(we assume that it has no threshold parameters). The decision boundary of the *N*-dimensional vector neuron described above consists of the following *N* hyperplanes which intersect orthogonally each other:

$$[w_{11} \ \cdots \ w_{1N}] \begin{bmatrix} x_1 \\ \vdots \\ x_N \end{bmatrix} = 0,$$

$$\vdots \qquad\qquad (3.32)$$

$$[w_{N1} \ \cdots \ w_{NN}] \begin{bmatrix} x_1 \\ \vdots \\ x_N \end{bmatrix} = 0$$

for any input signal $x = {}^t[x_1 \cdots x_N] \in \mathbf{R}^N$. The N equations of Eq. (3.32) are the N decision boundaries for the N components of the output of the N-dimensional vector neuron, respectively. Figure 3.1 shows an example of the decision boundary of the N-dimensional vector neuron ($N = 2$ for the sake of simplicity).

Table 3.1   The *N*-bit parity problem

			Input				Output,
x_1	x_2	x_3	$\cdots$	x_{N-2}	x_{N-1}	x_N	y
0	0	0	$\cdots$	0	0	0	0
0	0	0	$\cdots$	0	0	1	1
0	0	0	$\cdots$	0	1	0	1
0	0	0	$\cdots$	1	0	0	1
$\vdots$	$\vdots$	$\vdots$	$\vdots$	$\vdots$	$\vdots$	$\vdots$	$\vdots$
0	0	1	$\cdots$	0	0	0	1
0	1	0	$\cdots$	0	0	0	1
1	0	0	$\cdots$	0	0	0	1
0	0	0	$\cdots$	0	1	1	0
0	0	0	$\cdots$	1	0	1	0
0	0	0	$\cdots$	1	1	0	0
$\vdots$	$\vdots$	$\vdots$	$\vdots$	$\vdots$	$\vdots$	$\vdots$	$\vdots$
0	1	1	$\cdots$	0	0	0	0
1	0	1	$\cdots$	0	0	0	0
1	1	0	$\cdots$	0	0	0	0
$\vdots$	$\vdots$	$\vdots$	$\vdots$	$\vdots$	$\vdots$	$\vdots$	$\vdots$
1	1	1	$\cdots$	1	1	1	$\begin{cases} 1 & \text{(if } N \text{ is odd)} \\ 0 & \text{(if } N \text{ is even)} \end{cases}$

Letting $w_{ii} = 1$ $(i = 1, \cdots, N)$ and $w_{ij} = 0$ $(i \neq j)$ (i.e., the weight $\mathbf{W}$ is the N-dimensional identity matrix), we can find that the N-dimensional vector neuron implements the input-output mapping shown in Table 3.2, the decision boundary of which consists of the orthogonal N hyperplanes

$$x_1 = 0,$$
$$\vdots \qquad\qquad (3.33)$$
$$x_N = 0$$

and divides the input space (the decision region) into 2^N equal sections, and has the highest generalization ability for the N-bit parity problem. Figure 3.2 shows an example of the decision boundary for the 2-bit parity case.

Table 3.2   An encoded N-bit parity problem

Input							Output,
x_1	x_2	x_3	$\cdots$	x_{N-2}	x_{N-1}	x_N	y
-1	-1	-1	$\cdots$	-1	-1	-1	$^t[0\ 0\ 0 \cdots 0\ 0\ 0]$
-1	-1	-1	$\cdots$	-1	-1	1	$^t[0\ 0\ 0 \cdots 0\ 0\ 1]$
-1	-1	-1	$\cdots$	-1	1	-1	$^t[0\ 0\ 0 \cdots 0\ 1\ 0]$
-1	-1	-1	$\cdots$	1	-1	-1	$^t[0\ 0\ 0 \cdots 1\ 0\ 0]$
$\vdots$	$\vdots$	$\vdots$	$\vdots$	$\vdots$	$\vdots$	$\vdots$	$\vdots$
-1	-1	1	$\cdots$	-1	-1	-1	$^t[0\ 0\ 1 \cdots 0\ 0\ 0]$
-1	1	-1	$\cdots$	-1	-1	-1	$^t[0\ 1\ 0 \cdots 0\ 0\ 0]$
1	-1	-1	$\cdots$	-1	-1	-1	$^t[1\ 0\ 0 \cdots 0\ 0\ 0]$
-1	-1	-1	$\cdots$	-1	1	1	$^t[0\ 0\ 0 \cdots 0\ 1\ 1]$
-1	-1	-1	$\cdots$	1	-1	1	$^t[0\ 0\ 0 \cdots 1\ 0\ 1]$
-1	-1	-1	$\cdots$	1	1	-1	$^t[0\ 0\ 0 \cdots 1\ 1\ 0]$
$\vdots$	$\vdots$	$\vdots$	$\vdots$	$\vdots$	$\vdots$	$\vdots$	$\vdots$
-1	1	1	$\cdots$	-1	-1	-1	$^t[0\ 1\ 1 \cdots 0\ 0\ 0]$
1	-1	1	$\cdots$	-1	-1	-1	$^t[1\ 0\ 1 \cdots 0\ 0\ 0]$
1	1	-1	$\cdots$	-1	-1	-1	$^t[1\ 1\ 0 \cdots 0\ 0\ 0]$
$\vdots$	$\vdots$	$\vdots$	$\vdots$	$\vdots$	$\vdots$	$\vdots$	$\vdots$
1	1	1	$\cdots$	1	1	1	$^t[1\ 1\ 1 \cdots 1\ 1\ 1]$

3.4 DISCUSSION

The N-dimensional vector neuron throws the framework '*number field*' to the winds whereas the Clifford neuron described in Section 3.2.6 maintains the framework '*algebra*' firmly. This difference between the N-dimensional vector neuron and the Clifford neuron yields different properties.

Since the dimension of the Clifford neuron is 2^n, it can have 1, 2, 4, 8, 16, 32, ... dimensions, depending on the value of n. For example, one must use a Clifford neuron with $16 = 2^4$ dimensions to express 9-dimensional information (note that $2^3 = 8 < 9$). In this case, the remaining 7 dimensions lie idle. That is, the Clifford neuron has a redundancy as its nature in this sense when it is applied to real problems. The number of idle dimensions increases exponentially as the dimension of information expressed increases. For example, $2^{10} = 1024$-dimensional Clifford neuron is needed in order to deal with 513-dimensional information, and there are 1024 - 513 = 511 idle dimensions (note that $2^9 = 512 < 513$). On the other hand, 513-dimensional information can be dealt with the 513-dimensional vector neuron. All the dimensions are used to express information and there are no idle dimensions. Thus, there is no redundancy in the N-dimensional vector neuron in this sense.

There exist some neural network models that can solve the N-bit parity problem. The comparison between our result and the previous works is shown in Table 3.3. The number of neurons of the N-dimensional vector neuron and Aizenberg's model

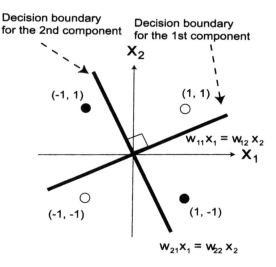

Figure 3.1   An example of the decision boundary in the input space of the 2-dimensional vector neuron (i.e., $N = 2$). The black circle means that the output in the parity problem is 1, and the white one 0.

is 1 constantly whereas those of the other models increase as N increases on the order N. The number of parameters of Lavretsky's model is the least, but the number of layers is $N - 1$, which increases as N increases. The number of parameters of the Stork and Allen's model is on the order of N, but the activation function of the hidden neurons is considerably complicated:

$$f(x) = \frac{1}{N} \left(x - \frac{\cos(\pi x)}{\alpha x} \right) \tag{3.34}$$

where α is a constant greater than 1.0. The number of parameters of the N-dimension al vector neuron is the least among the models on the order N^2. The number of layers of the N-dimensional vector neuron and Aizenberg's model is only 2, which is the least. As described above, the Aizenberg's model seems to be the best totally, but its activation function is somewhat special. Thus, we can conclude that the N-dimensional vector neuron proposed in this chapter is the best totally among the models with the traditional activation functions such as a step function. It should be emphasized here that the number of neurons needed is only one (i.e., a single neuron).

3.5   CONCLUSION

A solution to the N-bit parity problem with a single N-dimensional vector neuron suggests that making the dimensionality of neural networks high (for example, com-

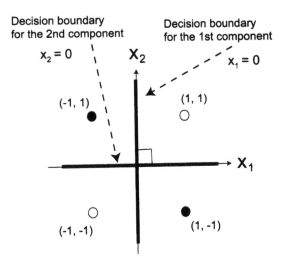

Figure 3.2   The decision boundary in the input space of the 2-dimensional vector neuron that solves the 2-parity problem (i.e., $N = 2$). The black circle means that the output in the parity problem is 1, and the white one is 0.

plex numbers and quaternions [5] is a new directionality for enhancing the ability of neural networks, and that it is worth researching the neural networks with high-dimensional parameters.

REFERENCES

1. N. N. Aizenberg, Yu. L. Ivaskiv, D. A. Pospelov, and G. F. Hudiakov. Multivalued threshold functions, Boolean complex-threshold functions and their generalization. *Kibernetika (Cybernetics)*, 4:44-51 (1971) (in Russian).

2. B. Widrow, J. McCool, and M. Ball. The complex LMS algorithm. *Proceedings of the IEEE*, 63:719-720 (1975).

3. A. Hirose, editor. *Complex-Valued Neural Networks*. World Scienific Publishing, Singapore, 2003.

4. A. Hirose, *Complex-Valued Neural Networks. Series on Studies in Computational Intelligence*, Vol. 32, Springer-Verlag, New York 2006.

5. T. Nitta, editor. *Complex-Valued Neural Networks: Utilizing High-Dimensional Parameters*. Information Science Reference, Hershey, PA, 2009.

6. T. Nitta. Solving the XOR problem and the detection of symmetry using a single complex-valued neuron. *Neural Networks*, 16:1101-1105, 2003.

7. T. Nitta. An analysis on fundamental structure of complex-valued neuron. *Neural Processing Letters*, 12:239-246, 2000.

Table 3.3 The comparison between our result and the previous works. *The number of layers* includes an input layer; it is 3 if the network has one hidden layer. *Direct link* means that there are at least one direct link between the input layer and the output layer in the neural network with at least one hidden layer. Note that the number of parameters in Aizenberg's work in the table is the estimated one by the author because Aizenberg et al. solved only the 3-, 8-, and 9-bit parity problems with a single complex-valued neuron.

	The number of neurons	The number of parameters	The number of layers	Direct link	Activation function
Ours	1	$\frac{N}{2}(N-1)$	2	No	Step function
Aizenberg et al. [34]	1	$2N+2$	2	No	Somewhat special
Setiono [35]	$\frac{3}{2}(N+1)$ or more	$\frac{N}{2}(N-1)$ $+2(N+1)$ or more	3	No	Sigmoidal function
Stork and Allen [36]	$N+3$	$2N+4$	3	No	Considerably complicated
Minor [37]	$\frac{1}{2}(3N+1)$ or more	$\frac{N}{2}(N-1)$ $+(N-1)$	3	Yes	Sigmoidal function
Lavretsky [38]	$N-1$	$2N-1$	$N-1$	Yes	Sigmoidal function
Liu et al. [39]	$\frac{1}{2}(3N+1)$ or more	$\frac{N}{2}(N+3)$ or more	3	Yes	Step function

8. M. L. Minsky and S. A. Papert. *Perceptrons*, MIT Press, Cambridge, MA, 1969.

9. T. Nitta. An extension of the back-propagation algorithm to complex numbers. *Neural Networks*, 10:1392-1415, 1997.

10. T. Nitta. Orthogonality of decision boundaries in complex-valued neural networks. *Neural Computation*, 16(1):73-97, 2004.

11. S. Buchholz, and G. Sommer. A hyperbolic multilayer perceptron. In *Proceedings of the International Joint Conference on Neural Networks*, IJCNN2000, Como, Italy, Vol. 2, 2000, pp. 129-133.

12. G. Sobczyk. The hyperbolic number plane. *The College Mathematics Journal*, 26(4):268-280, 1995.

13. T. Nitta, and S. Buchholz. On the decision boundaries of hyperbolic neurons. In *Proceedings of the International Joint Conference on Neural Networks*, IJCNN'08-Hong Kong, June 1-6, 2008, pp. 2973-2979.

14. T. Nitta, and H. D. Garis. A 3D vector version of the back-propagation algorithm. In *Proceedings of the IEEE/INNS International Joint Conference on Neural Networks*, Vol. 2, Beijing, 1992, pp. 511-516.

15. T. Nitta. Three-dimensional vector valued neural network and its generalization ability. *Neural Information Processing – Letters and Reviews*, 10(10):237-242, 2006.

16. T. Nitta. A back-propagation algorithm for neural networks based on 3D vector product. In *Proceedings of the IEEE/INNS International Joint Conference on Neural Networks*, IJCNN'93-Nagoya, Oct. 25-29, Vol. 1, 1993, pp. 589-592.

17. M. Kobayashi. Three-dimensional associative memory using exterior product. *IEE Transactions EIS*, 124(1):150-156 (2004) (In Japanese).

18. P. Arena, L. Fortuna, L. Occhipinti, and M. G. Xibilia. Neural networks for quaternion valued function approximation. In *Proceedings of the IEEE International Symposium on Circuit and Systems*, Vol. 6, pp. 307-310, 1994.

19. T. Nitta. A quaternary version of the back-propagation algorithm. In *Proceedings of the IEEE International Conference on Neural Networks*, 5:2753-2756, 1995.

20. H. -D. Ebbinghaus, et al., Editors. *Zahlen*, Springer-Verlag, Berlin, 1988 (in German).

21. M. Kobayashi and A. Nakajima. Twisted quaternary neural networks. *IEEJ Transactions on Electrical and Electronic Engineering*, 7(4):397-401, 2012.

22. T. Isokawa, H. Nishimura, and N. Matsui. Commutative quaternion and multistate hopfield neural networks. In *Proceedings of the IEEE World Congress on Computational Intelligence*, WCCI2010, pp. 1281-1286, Barcelona, Spain, July 18-23, 2010.

23. T. Nitta. A solution to the 4-bit parity problem with a single quaternary neuron. *Neural Information Processing – Letters and Reviews*, 5(2):33-39, 2005.

24. J. K. Pearson and D. L. Bisset. Back propagation in a Clifford algebra. In *Proceedings of the International Conference on Artificial Neural Networks*, Vol. 2, I. Aleksander and J. Taylor, Editors, 1992, pp. 413-416.

25. J. K. Pearson and D. L. Bisset. Neural networks in the Clifford domain. In *Proceedings of the IEEE World Congress on Computational Intelligence/IEEE International Conference on Neural Networks*, ICNN, Vol. 3, 1994, pp. 1465-1469.

26. S. Buchholz. A theory of neural computation with Clifford algebras. Ph.D. thesis, University of Kiel, 2005.

27. K. Gürlebeck, K. Habetha, and W. Spröβig, *Holomorphic Functions in the Plane and N-Dimensional Space*, Birkhäuser, Basel, 2008.

28. S. Buchholz and G. Sommer. On Clifford neurons and Clifford multi-layer perceptrons. *Neural Networks*, 21:925-935, 2008.

29. Y. Kuroe. Models of Clifford recurrent neural networks and their dynamics. In *Proceedings of the International Joint Conference on Neural Networks*, 2011, pp.1035-1041.

30. Y. Kuroe, S. Tanigawa, and H. Iima. Models of Hopfield-type Clifford neural networks and their energy functions - hyperbolic and dual valued networks -. In *Proceedings of the International Conference on Neural Information Processing*, Lecture Notes in Computer Science 7062, Springer, Belrin Heidelberg, 2011, pp. 560-569.

31. T. Nitta. N-dimensional vector neuron. In *Proceedings of the IJCAI-2007 Workshop on Complex-Valued Neural Networks and Neuro-Computing: Novel Methods, Applications and Implementations*, January 6-12, 2007, pp. 2-7.

32. D. E. Rumelhart, G. E. Hinton, and R. J. Williams. Learning representations by back-propagating erroes. *Nature*, 323:533-536, 1986.

33. D. E. Rumelhart, G. E. Hinton, and R. J. Williams, *Parallel Distributed Processing*, Vol. 1, MIT Press, Cambridge, 1986.

34. N. N. Aizenberg, I. N. Aizenberg, and G. A. Krivosheev. CNN based on universal binary neurons: learning algorithm with error-correction and application to impulsive-noise filtering on gray-scale images. In *Proceedings of the IEEE International Workshop on Cellular Neural Networks and their Applications*, Seville, Spain, pp. 309-314, 1996.

35. R. Setiono. On the solution of the parity problem by a single hidden layer feedforward neural network. *Neurocomputing*, 16:225-235, 1997.

36. D. G. Stork and J. D. Allen. How to solve the *N*-bit parity problem with two hidden units. *Neural Networks*, 5:923-926, 1992.

37. J. M. Minor. Parity with two layer feedforward nets. *Neural Networks*, 6:705-707, 1993.

38. E. Lavretsky. On the exact solution of the parity-*N* problem using ordered neural networks. *Neural Networks*, 13:643-649, 2000.

39. D. Liu, M. E. Hohil, and S. H. Smith. *N*-bit parity neural networks: new solutions based on linear programming. *Neurocomputing*, 48:477-488, 2002.

CHAPTER 4

LEARNING ALGORITHMS IN COMPLEX-VALUED NEURAL NETWORKS USING WIRTINGER CALCULUS

MD. FAIJUL AMIN[1,2] AND KAZUYUKI MURASE[1]

[1]University of Fukui, Fukui, Japan
[2]Khulna University of Engineering and Technology, Khulna, Bangladesh

Although complex-valued neural networks (CVNNs) have been proved much more efficient in processing complex-valued data than the real-valued neural networks (RVNNs), conventional derivation of the well-known learning algorithms employ real derivatives. Such derivations require reformulating the problem in the real domain by separating into real and imaginary parts; and consequently, it becomes tedious and awkward since the original problem is in the complex domain. Nevertheless, the main reason for the real-valued perspective is that the CVNNs bring in nonholomorphic functions quite naturally, for which the standard complex derivatives do not exist. There are two sources of non-holomorphism: (i) the real-valued loss functions and (ii) the nonholomorphic (nonanalytic) activation functions. The derivatives of such functions, however, are defined in Wirtinger calculus that generalizes the notion complex derivative, and the holomorphic function becomes a special case only. Most importantly, the Wirtinger calculus simplifies the derivative evaluation and enables us to remain in the complex domain.

This chapter provides a brief discussion on the Wirtinger calculus and derives several algorithms for the feedforward and recurrent CVNNs utilizing this calculus. A functional dependency graph among neurons helps evaluating the

Complex-Valued Neural Networks: Advances and Applications. Edited by Akira Hirose
Copyright © 2013 The Institute of Electrical and Electronics Engineers, Inc.

derivatives by visual inspection. For the feedforward networks, two algorithms are considered: the gradient descent (backpropagation) and the Levenberg–Marquardt (LM) algorithm. While deriving the LM algorithm, we encounter a least squares problem involving a complex vector and its conjugate, which is more general than the usual least squares problem in the complex domain. A solution with proof is given and used in the LM algorithm derivation. For the recurrent networks, we derive complex version of the real-time recurrent learning (RTRL) and the extended Kalman filter (EKF) algorithm. Computer simulation results are provided to illustrate each of the algorithms. The unified and systematic way of our derivations would enable the readers extending any algorithm in the RVNNs to the CVNN framework with least effort.

4.1 INTRODUCTION

The key features of complex-valued neural networks (CVNNs) are that the parameters are complex numbers and their computations utilize the complex algebraic rules. In order to get satisfactory performance from the networks, the parameters should be optimized through some optimization procedure commonly known as learning algorithm. Therefore, one of the most important matters in the CVNNs is to devise learning algorithms for them. The gradient- or partial-derivative-based algorithms are perhaps the most prevalent learning mechanisms in the neural networks. To this end, one encounters a problem because the standard complex derivative exists only for *analytic* or *holomorphic* functions, which entails a stringent condition in the complex domain.

The CVNNs bring in nonholomorphic functions in two ways: (i) with the loss function to be minimized over complex parameters and (ii) with the most widely used activation functions. The former is completely unavoidable as the loss function is necessarily real-valued and hence nonanalytic. The second source of nonholomorphism arises because boundedness and analiticity cannot be achieved at the same time in the complex domain, and it is the boundedness that is often preferred over analyticity for the activation functions [3, 23]. Although some researchers have proposed several holomorphic activation functions having singularities [15, 26], a general consideration would be that the activation functions can be nonholomorphic. In such a scenario, derivative-based optimization algorithms are unable to use standard complex derivatives since the derivatives do not exist (i.e., the *Cauchy–Riemann* equations do not hold). As an alternative, the conventional approach for algorithm derivation casts the optimization problem in the real domain by separating the real and imaginary components of a complex variable and then taking the real derivatives. This real-valued perspective treats a nondifferentiable mapping between $\mathbb{C}$ and $\mathbb{C}$ as a differentiable mapping between $\mathbb{R}^2$ and $\mathbb{R}^2$. Since the real-valued perspective arises within a complex variable framework, it is often awkward and tedious to reformulate the problem in the real domain [16].

An elegant approach that greatly simplifies derivations and can save computational labor in dealing with nonholomorphic functions is to use Wirtinger calculus [32]. The Wirtinger calculus can be considered as a generalization of complex derivative using conjugate coordinates where two derivatives $\frac{\partial f}{\partial z}$ and $\frac{\partial f}{\partial z^*}$ come in a pair. Here z^* denotes the complex conjugate of z. The derivatives are called $\mathbb{R}$-derivative and conjugate $\mathbb{R}$-derivative, respectively. The formal definitions and properties of the derivatives are discussed in Section 4.2.

A pioneering work that utilizes the concept of conjugate coordinates is by Brandwood [5]. The author formally defines complex gradient and the condition for stationary point. An application in adaptive array theory is also discussed in the paper. The work is further extended by van den Bos showing that the complex gradient and Hessian are related to their real counterparts by a simple linear transformation [28]. However, neither of the authors has cited the contribution of Wilhelm Wirtinger, an Austrian mathematician, who originally developed the concept of derivatives with respect to the conjugate coordinates. The reason might be due to the fact that the article was published in the German language. Today, the Wirtinger calculus is well-appreciated and has been fruitfully exploited by several recent works [4, 18].

Although Wirtinger calculus can be a useful tool in extending the well-known first- and second-order optimization algorithms used in the RVNNs to the CVNN framework, only few studies can be found in the literature (e.g., [17]). In [17], the Wirtinger calculus has been utilized to derive a gradient descent algorithm for a feedforward CVNN. The authors employ holomorphic activation functions and states that the derivation is simplified only because of the holomorphic functions. It is further stated that the evaluation of gradient in the nonholomorphic case has to be performed in the real domain as it is done traditionally. In this chapter, however, we show that the Wirtinger calculus can simplify the derivations with nonholomorphic activation functions too, which is the original motivation of Wirtinger calculus.

We derive several widely used learning algorithms for feedforward and recurrent CVNNs. Each algorithm is illustrated with computer simulation results. All computations are carried out in matrix–vector form so that it can be easily implemented in any computating environment where computations are optimized for matrix operations. An important aspect of our derivations is that we use functional dependency graph for a visual evaluation method of derivatives, which is particularly useful in multilayer CVNNs. Because the Wirtinger calculus essentially employs conjugate coordinates, a coordinate transformation matrix between the real and conjugate coordinate system plays an important role in the derivations. It turns out that the Wirtinger calculus, the coordinate transformation matrix, and the functional dependency graph are three useful tools for extending any derivative based optimization algorithm in the RVNNs to the CVNN framework.

In Section 4.3, we define complex gradient using the Wirtinger calculus. Our gradient evaluation is more general and the CVNN with holomorphic activation function becomes a special case only. Then a complex gradient descent algorithm is formulated for feedforward CVNNs in Section 4.4.1. We also derive a popular second-order learning method (in the sense, the Hessian matrix involving second-order derivatives is approximated by using Jacobian matrix), the Levenberg–Marquardt (LM) algorithm [10], for CVNN parameter optimization. The derivation is provided for feedforward CVNN in Section 4.4.2. We find that a key step of the LM algorithm is a solution to the least squares problem $\|\mathbf{b} - (\mathbf{Az} + \mathbf{Bz}^*)\|_{\min}$ in the complex domain, which is more general than the $\|\mathbf{b} - \mathbf{Az}\|_{\min}$. Here $\mathbf{z}^*$ denotes the conjugate of a column vector $\mathbf{z}$. A solution to the least squares problem has been given with a proof. Computer simulation results for the gradient descent and LM algorithm are presented in Section 4.4.3 in order to validate the derived algorithms. The results exhibit that as with the real-valued case, the complex LM algorithm provides much faster learning than the complex gradient descent algorithm. Although the LM algorithm is widely used in the RVNN training, no other study except ours has been done in the complex domain [1].

Section 4.5 derives two popular algorithms for recurrent CVNNs, namely complex real-time recurrent learning (CRTRL) and complex extended Kalman filter (CEKF) algorithms. It is well known that the recurrent neural networks are well suited for processing temporal or sequential information as they can have feedback connections in addition to the feedforward connections [30, 24]. Our derivations are based on the Wirtinger calculus and are more general (networks with any activation functions having the property of differentiable mapping from $\mathbb{R}^2$ to $\mathbb{R}^2$) than the derivations found in [8, 14, 9]. Both the CRTRL and CEKF are illustrated with computer simulations on a real-world wind prediction problem.

We summarize the key concepts of this chapter in Section 4.6.

4.2   DERIVATIVES IN WIRTINGER CALCULUS

This section briefly discusses the $\mathbb{R}$-derivative and the conjugate $\mathbb{R}$-derivative formally developed by the Austrian mathematician, Wilhelm Wirtinger [32]. The resulting calculus is therefore also known as Wirtinger calculus in the literature [7]. Rigorous descriptions with applications can be found in [22, 25, 5, 16].

Any function of a complex variable z can be defined as $f(z) = u(x, y) + jv(x, y)$, where $z = x + jy$. If all the partial derivatives u_x, u_y, v_x, and v_y exist, then the complex derivative of $f(z)$ is said to exist if the partial derivatives satisfy the Cauchy–Riemann equations, i.e., $u_x = v_y, \ v_x = -u_y$. In the complex domain, the functions satisfying the Cauchy–Riemann equations are called holomorphic functions. Otherwise, the functions are called nonholomorphic. As for instance, if a function $f(z)$ is real-valued, i.e., $v(x, y) = 0$, then it is nonholomorphic since the Cauchy–Riemann equations no longer hold. In other words, the Cauchy–Riemann equations are more stringent condition than the mere existence of real partial derivatives. Consequently, we do not have a definition of complex derivate for nonholomorphic functions.

Interestingly, any differentiable mapping, $f : \mathbb{R}^2 \to \mathbb{R}^2$ (or $\mathbb{R}$), can be treated in complex domain by introducing conjugate coordinates such that

$$\begin{pmatrix} z \\ z^* \end{pmatrix} = \begin{pmatrix} 1 & j \\ 1 & -j \end{pmatrix} \begin{pmatrix} x \\ y \end{pmatrix} \qquad (4.1)$$

This ingenious idea of Wirtinger allows us to deal with nonholomorphic functions in the complex domain. In other words, any nonholomorphic mapping $f : \mathbb{C} \to$

$\mathbb{C}$(or $\mathbb{R}$) is viewed from pseudo-real perspective in terms of conjugate coordinates. Note from Eq. (4.1) that the conjugate coordinates are related to the real coordinates by a simple coordinate transformation matrix. From the inverse relations, $x = (z + z^*)/2$ and $y = -j(z - z^*)/2$, Wirtinger defines the following pair of derivatives for a function $f(z, z^*)$:

$$\frac{\partial f}{\partial z} = \frac{1}{2}\left(\frac{\partial f}{\partial x} - j\frac{\partial f}{\partial y}\right), \quad \frac{\partial f}{\partial z^*} = \frac{1}{2}\left(\frac{\partial f}{\partial x} + j\frac{\partial f}{\partial y}\right) \qquad (4.2)$$

The derivatives are called $\mathbb{R}$-derivative and conjugate $\mathbb{R}$-derivative, respectively.

From the coordinate transformation viewpoint, one can take partial derivatives in either of the coordinate systems, whichever seems convenient. Then, if required, it is straightforward to switch to the other coordinate system by the simple linear transformation. When evaluating partial derivatives in the conjugate coordinate system, we take one of the variables, z and z^*, as constant. For example, in the evaluation of $\frac{\partial f}{\partial z}$, z^* is considered as constant; similarly in the evaluation of $\frac{\partial f}{\partial z^*}$, z is considered as a constant. An illustrative example is given below.

■ **EXAMPLE 4.1**

Suppose $g(z, z^*) = z^2 z^* = u + jv$, where $z = x + jy$, then

$$u(x, y) = x^3 + xy^2$$
$$v(x, y) = x^2 y + y^3$$

$$\begin{aligned}
\frac{\partial g}{\partial z} &= \frac{1}{2}\left(\frac{\partial}{\partial x} - j\frac{\partial}{\partial y}\right)(u + jv) \\
&= \frac{1}{2}\left((3x^2 + y^2 + j(2xy)) - j\left(2xy + j(x^2 + 3y^2)\right)\right) \\
&= 2(x^2 + y^2) \\
&= 2zz^*
\end{aligned}$$

$$\begin{aligned}
\frac{\partial g}{\partial z^*} &= \frac{1}{2}\left(\frac{\partial}{\partial x} + j\frac{\partial}{\partial y}\right)(u + jv) \\
&= \frac{1}{2}\left((3x^2 + y^2 + j(2xy)) + j\left(2xy + j(x^2 + 3y^2)\right)\right) \\
&= x^2 - y^2 + j2xy \\
&= z^2
\end{aligned}$$

Here the derivatives are computed in the real coordinate system defined in Eq. (4.2). However, one can get the similar results quickly if the derivatives are evaluated in the conjugate coordinate system. That is, $\dfrac{\partial(z^2 z^*)}{\partial z} = 2zz^*$ and $\dfrac{\partial(z^2 z^*)}{\partial z^*} = z^2$. ∎

Most importantly, the Wirtinger calculus generalizes the concept of derivatives in complex domain. It is easy to see from Eq. (4.1) that the Cauchy–Riemann equations are equivalent to $\frac{\partial f}{\partial z^*} = 0$. In other words, the holomorphic functions can be considered as functions of z only, not of z^*. This beautiful result is the key to deal with nonholomorphic functions in the gradient based optimization problems involving complex-valued parameters. There is no need to express or reformulate the optimization problem in the real domain by separating real and imaginary components which would be tedious and cumbersome.

The Wirtinger calculus enables us to perform all computations directly in the complex domain, and the derivatives obey all the rules of conventional calculus, including the chain rule, differentiation of products and quotients. Here are some useful identities that we use extensively in the derivation of learning algorithms throughout this chapter.

$$\left(\frac{\partial f}{\partial z}\right)^* = \frac{\partial f^*}{\partial z^*}; \quad \text{when } f \text{ is real } \left(\frac{\partial f}{\partial z}\right)^* = \frac{\partial f}{\partial z^*} \qquad \text{[Conjugation rule]} \quad (4.3)$$

$$\left(\frac{\partial f}{\partial z^*}\right)^* = \frac{\partial f^*}{\partial z}; \quad \text{when } f \text{ is real } \left(\frac{\partial f}{\partial z^*}\right)^* = \frac{\partial f}{\partial z} \qquad \text{[Conjugation rule]} \quad (4.4)$$

$$df = \frac{\partial f}{\partial z}dz + \frac{\partial f}{\partial z^*}dz^* \qquad \text{[Differential rule]} \qquad (4.5)$$

$$\frac{\partial h(g)}{\partial z} = \frac{\partial h}{\partial g}\frac{\partial g}{\partial z} + \frac{\partial h}{\partial g^*}\frac{\partial g^*}{\partial z} \qquad \text{[Chain rule]} \qquad (4.6)$$

$$\frac{\partial h(g)}{\partial z^*} = \frac{\partial h}{\partial g}\frac{\partial g}{\partial z^*} + \frac{\partial h}{\partial g^*}\frac{\partial g^*}{\partial z^*} \qquad \text{[Chain rule]} \qquad (4.7)$$

4.3 COMPLEX GRADIENT

The gradient of a real-valued scalar function of several complex variables can be evaluated in both real and conjugate coordinate systems. And there is a one-to-one correspondence between the coordinate systems. Let $\mathbf{z}$ be an n-dimensional column vector, i.e., $\mathbf{z} = (z_1, z_2, \ldots, z_n)^T \in \mathbb{C}^n$, where $z_i = x_i + jy_i$, $i = 1, 2, \ldots, n$. Then an isomorphism between the real and conjugate coordinate system is given by

$$\tilde{\mathbf{z}} \triangleq \begin{pmatrix} \mathbf{z} \\ \mathbf{z}^* \end{pmatrix} \Leftrightarrow \mathbf{r} \triangleq \begin{pmatrix} \mathbf{x} \\ \mathbf{y} \end{pmatrix} = \begin{pmatrix} \Re(\mathbf{z}) \\ \Im(\mathbf{z}) \end{pmatrix}$$

where $\Re(z)$ and $\Im(z)$ represent the real and imaginary parts of z, respectively. In the real-valued coordinates, the gradient is defined as

$$
\begin{aligned}
real\text{-}\nabla f &= \left(\frac{\partial f}{\partial x_1}, \frac{\partial f}{\partial x_2}, \ldots, \frac{\partial f}{\partial x_n}, \frac{\partial f}{\partial y_1}, \frac{\partial f}{\partial y_2}, \ldots, \frac{\partial f}{\partial y_n} \right)^T \\
&= \left(\frac{\partial f}{\mathbf{x}^T}, \frac{\partial f}{\mathbf{y}^T} \right)^T
\end{aligned}
\tag{4.8}
$$

where T denotes the transpose operator. Now if the real-valued partial derivatives are arranged according to the real and imaginary parts, component-wise, an intuitive definition of complex gradient could be

$$
\begin{aligned}
complex\text{-}\nabla f &= \left(\left\{ \frac{\partial f}{\partial x_1} + j\frac{\partial f}{\partial y_1} \right\}, \ldots, \left\{ \frac{\partial f}{\partial x_n} + j\frac{\partial f}{\partial y_n} \right\} \right)^T \\
&= \left(2\frac{\partial f}{\partial z_1^*}, \ldots, 2\frac{\partial f}{\partial z_n^*} \right)^T \\
&= 2\frac{\partial f}{\partial \mathbf{z}^*} \\
&\triangleq \nabla_{\mathbf{z}^*} f
\end{aligned}
\tag{4.9}
$$

The second line of Eq. (4.9) follows from Eq. (4.2). Note that this intuitive definition is valid only when f is a real-valued function. As will be shown next, a more formal derivation leads to the same definition of Eq. (4.9).

In the single complex variable case, the real and conjugate coordinates are related by the coordinate transformation matrix of Eq. (4.1). Similarly, the multivariable case can be written with a coordinate transformation matrix in the block matrix form

$$
\tilde{\mathbf{z}} = \begin{pmatrix} \mathbf{z} \\ \mathbf{z}^* \end{pmatrix} = \begin{pmatrix} \mathbf{I} & j\mathbf{I} \\ \mathbf{I} & -j\mathbf{I} \end{pmatrix} \begin{pmatrix} \mathbf{x} \\ \mathbf{y} \end{pmatrix} = \mathbf{M} \begin{pmatrix} \mathbf{x} \\ \mathbf{y} \end{pmatrix} = \mathbf{Mr}
\tag{4.10}
$$

where $\mathbf{I}$ is an identity matrix conforming to the size of $\mathbf{x}$ or $\mathbf{y}$. Note here that $\mathbf{M}^{-1} = \frac{1}{2}\mathbf{M}^H$, where H represents the Hermitian transpose operation. Since the coordinate transformation is a linear transformation it follows that for a real-valued scalar function, $f(\mathbf{z}, \mathbf{z}^*)$,

$$
\frac{\partial f}{\partial \mathbf{r}} = \frac{\partial \tilde{\mathbf{z}}^T}{\partial \mathbf{r}} \frac{\partial f}{\partial \tilde{\mathbf{z}}} = \mathbf{M}^T \frac{\partial f}{\partial \tilde{\mathbf{z}}}
$$

Since both f and $\mathbf{r}$ are real-valued

$$
\begin{aligned}
\left(\frac{\partial f}{\partial \mathbf{r}} \right) &= \left(\frac{\partial f}{\partial \mathbf{r}} \right)^* \\
&= \left(\mathbf{M}^T \frac{\partial f}{\partial \tilde{\mathbf{z}}} \right)^* \\
&= \mathbf{M}^H \frac{\partial f}{\partial \tilde{\mathbf{z}}^*} \qquad \text{[Eq. (4.3)]}
\end{aligned}
$$

The gradient descent update rule in the real-valued case is $\Delta \mathbf{r} = -\mu \dfrac{\partial f}{\partial \mathbf{r}}$, where μ is a small step size. Using the coordinate transformation of Eq. (4.10), we obtain

$$\Delta \widetilde{\mathbf{z}} = \mathbf{M} \Delta \mathbf{r} = -\mu \mathbf{M} \frac{\partial f}{\partial \mathbf{r}} = -\mu \mathbf{M} \mathbf{M}^H \frac{\partial f}{\partial \widetilde{\mathbf{z}}^*} = -2\mu \frac{\partial f}{\partial \widetilde{\mathbf{z}}^*} \qquad (4.11)$$

Because $\widetilde{\mathbf{z}}^* = \left(\mathbf{z}^H, \mathbf{z}^T \right)^T$, Eq. (4.11) can be written as

$$\Delta \widetilde{\mathbf{z}} = \begin{pmatrix} \Delta \mathbf{z} \\ \Delta \mathbf{z}^* \end{pmatrix} = -2\mu \begin{pmatrix} \dfrac{\partial f}{\partial \mathbf{z}^*} \\ \dfrac{\partial f}{\partial \mathbf{z}} \end{pmatrix} \Rightarrow \Delta \mathbf{z} = -2\mu \frac{\partial f}{\partial \mathbf{z}^*} \qquad (4.12)$$

Thus using the Wirtinger calculus, the complex gradient of a real-valued function with respect to a parameter vector $\mathbf{z}$ is evaluated as $\nabla_{\mathbf{z}^*} f = 2 \dfrac{\partial f}{\partial \mathbf{z}^*}$, but not $\dfrac{\partial f}{\partial \mathbf{z}}$! Note that this formal way of formulation conforms to our intuitive definition of Eq. (4.9). Although the multiplicative factor 2 appearing in the complex gradient may be ignored, we adhere to this as the exact relationship between the real gradient (had we solved the optimization problem in the real domain) and the complex gradient should include the factor. Thereby, one can verify the final result of derivation in the real domain with that in the complex domain and appreciate the simplicity obtained in the complex domain due to the Wirtinger calculus. No matter, whichever approach is followed the final result must be same, but the Wirtinger calculus is much more elegant and painless.

4.4   LEARNING ALGORITHMS FOR FEEDFORWARD CVNNS

4.4.1   Complex Gradient Descent Algorithm

Now that we have the notion for complex gradient, we are ready to derive the gradient descent learning algorithm for CVNNs. The derivation is carried out in matrix–vector form. As a result, the algorithm can be easily implemented in any computing environment where matrix computations are optimized. In the gradient descent algorithm, when applied in the supervised manner, the network is provided with a desired signal vector $\mathbf{d}$ from which an error signal can be computed as

$$\mathbf{e} = \mathbf{d} - \mathbf{y} \qquad (4.13)$$

where $\mathbf{y}$ denotes the network's output. Then the gradient descent algorithm minimizes a real-valued loss function

$$\xi(\mathbf{z}, \mathbf{z}^*) = \frac{1}{2} \sum_k e_k^* e_k = \frac{1}{2} \mathbf{e}^H \mathbf{e} \qquad (4.14)$$

where k stands for the kth element of network's output vector. For a given set of training examples, the loss function depends on the parameter vector $\mathbf{z}$ as well as on its conjugate $\mathbf{z}^*$ from the viewpoint of Wirtinger calculus. The parameter vector can be biases of the neurons in a particular layer, or the incident connection weights to a particular neuron, or even all the network parameters collected in a single column vector. During the learning process, the parameter vector $\mathbf{z}$ is iteratively updated along the opposite direction of gradient, i.e., to the negative of gradient. The negative of complex gradient as defined in Eq. (4.12) can be written as

$$-\nabla_{\mathbf{z}^*}\xi = -2\frac{\partial\xi}{\partial\mathbf{z}^*} = -2\left(\frac{\partial\xi}{\partial\mathbf{z}}\right)^* = -2\left(\frac{\partial\xi}{\partial\mathbf{z}^T}\right)^H \quad \text{[Eq. (4.3)]} \qquad (4.15)$$

We find that it is convenient to take derivative of a scalar or a column vector with respect to a row vector as it gives the Jacobian naturally. Now

$$-2\frac{\partial\xi}{\partial\mathbf{z}^T} = -\frac{\partial\left(\mathbf{e}^H\mathbf{e}\right)}{\partial\mathbf{e}^T}\frac{\partial\mathbf{e}}{\partial\mathbf{z}^T} - \frac{\partial\left(\mathbf{e}^H\mathbf{e}\right)}{\partial\left(\mathbf{e}^T\right)^*}\frac{\partial\mathbf{e}^*}{\partial\mathbf{z}^T} \quad \text{[Eq. (4.6) in matrix–vector form]}$$

$$= \mathbf{e}^H\mathbf{J}_{\mathbf{z}} + \mathbf{e}^T\left(\mathbf{J}_{\mathbf{z}^*}\right)^* \quad \text{[Eq. (4.4) in matrix–vector form]} \qquad (4.16)$$

Here, we define two Jacobian matrices, $\mathbf{J}_{\mathbf{z}} = \dfrac{\partial\mathbf{y}}{\partial\mathbf{z}^T}$ and $\mathbf{J}_{\mathbf{z}^*} = \dfrac{\partial\mathbf{y}}{\partial\mathbf{z}^H}$. Taking Hermitian conjugate transpose to both side of Eq. (4.16) yields the negative of complex gradient as

$$-\nabla_{\mathbf{z}^*}\xi = \mathbf{J}_{\mathbf{z}}^H\mathbf{e} + \left(\mathbf{J}_{\mathbf{z}^*}^H\mathbf{e}\right)^* \qquad (4.17)$$

It is clear from Eq. (4.17) that in order to evaluate complex gradient all we need is to compute a pair of Jacobians: $\mathbf{J}_{\mathbf{z}}$, the Jacobian of network output $\mathbf{y}$ w.r.t. the parameter vector $\mathbf{z}$; and $\mathbf{J}_{\mathbf{z}^*}$, the Jacobian of $\mathbf{y}$ w.r.t. $\mathbf{z}^*$. It should be noted that the Jacobians have the form of $\mathbf{P} - j\mathbf{Q}$ and $\mathbf{P} + j\mathbf{Q}$, respectively, because of the definition of derivatives in the Wirtinger calculus. Therefore, we can compute the other one while computing one of the Jacobians. It should be noted that $\mathbf{P}$ and $\mathbf{Q}$ are, in general, two different complex-valued matrices. Although our primary interest is on $-\nabla_{\mathbf{z}^*}\xi$, a convenient formulation may also include its conjugate term, so that the pair belongs to a point in the conjugate coordinate system. In that case, Eq. (4.17) can be extended as

$$\begin{pmatrix} -\nabla_{\mathbf{z}^*}\xi \\ -\nabla_{\mathbf{z}}\xi \end{pmatrix} = \begin{pmatrix} \mathbf{J}_{\mathbf{z}} & \mathbf{J}_{\mathbf{z}^*} \\ (\mathbf{J}_{\mathbf{z}^*})^* & (\mathbf{J}_{\mathbf{z}})^* \end{pmatrix}^H \begin{pmatrix} \mathbf{e} \\ \mathbf{e}^* \end{pmatrix} \qquad (4.18)$$

In the compact notation of conjugate coordinate system, an equivalent formulation is given by

$$-\nabla_{\tilde{\mathbf{z}}^*}\xi = \tilde{\mathbf{J}}_{\tilde{\mathbf{z}}}^H\tilde{\mathbf{e}} \qquad (4.19)$$

Note that Eq. (4.19) resembles the gradient descent algorithm formulation for RVNNs. This is intuitive because only the coordinate has been transformed from the real system to the conjugate system.

Let us now derive the gradient descent algorithm in explicit form for a multi-layer feedforward CVNN. To illustrate, we consider one hidden layer for the sake of notational convenience only. The method presented here, however, can be easily followed for any number of layers. The forward equations for signal passing through the network are given by

$$^{(1)}\mathbf{v} = {}^{(1)}\mathbf{W}\mathbf{x} + {}^{(1)}\mathbf{b}$$

$$^{(1)}\mathbf{y} = \phi({}^{(1)}\mathbf{v}) = \left(\phi_1({}^{(1)}v_1), \phi_2({}^{(1)}v_2), \ldots, \phi_m({}^{(1)}v_m)\right)^T$$

$$^{(2)}\mathbf{v} = {}^{(2)}\mathbf{W}{}^{(1)}\mathbf{y} + {}^{(2)}\mathbf{b}$$

$$\mathbf{y} = {}^{(2)}\mathbf{y} = \phi({}^{(2)}\mathbf{v}) = \left(\phi_1({}^{(2)}v_1), \phi_2({}^{(2)}v_2), \ldots, \phi_n({}^{(2)}v_n)\right)^T \qquad (4.20)$$

The notations for Eq. (4.20) are as follows. A left superscript indicates the layer number and the input layer is counted as 0-th layer. The vector $\mathbf{x}$ is the input signal; $^{(1)}\mathbf{y}$ and $\mathbf{y} = {}^{(2)}\mathbf{y}$ are the outputs at hidden and output layer, respectively; the weight matrix $^{(1)}\mathbf{W}$ connects the input units to the hidden units, while the matrix $^{(2)}\mathbf{W}$ connects the hidden units to the output units; the column vectors $^{(1)}\mathbf{b}$ and $^{(2)}\mathbf{b}$ are the biases to the hidden and output units, repectively; and $\phi_i(\cdot)$ is any activation function (*holomorphic* or *nonholomorphic*) having real partial derivatives.

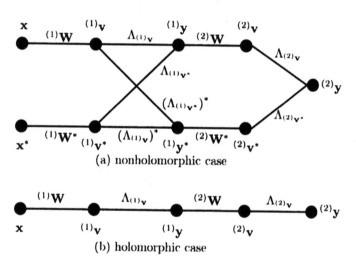

Figure 4.1   Functional dependency graph of a single hidden layer CVNN corresponding to Eq. (4.20). Each node represents a complex-vector-valued variable, and an edge connecting two nodes is labeled with the Jacobian of its right node with respect to its left node. (a) The general case, where activation functions are nonholomorphic; and (b) the special case, where activation functions are holomorphic. In the holomorphic case, conjugate Jacobians are the zero matrix. Thus, the graph of (a) reduces to the graph of (b).

Visual Evaluation of Jacobians in the Feedforward CVNN: In the feedforward CVNN, parameters are structured in layers. Therefore, it is very convenient to compute the Jacobians by visual inspection if we draw a functional dependency graph, which is a graphical representation of the chain rule in the differential calculus. Figure 4.1 depicts the functional dependency graph for a single hidden layer CVNN described by Eq. (4.20). In this figure, the dependency delegates from right to the left. Each edge is labeled with the Jacobian of its right node w.r.t. the left node. However, for any arbitrary vector $\mathbf{z}$, the Jacobians of interest are $\mathbf{J_z}$ and $\mathbf{J_{z^*}}$, i.e., the Jacobians of the rightmost node (labeled as $\mathbf{y}$ in Fig. (4.1)) w.r.t. to all other nodes appearing to its left at different depths.

To evaluate the Jacobian of the right most node (i.e., network's output) w.r.t. any other node to its left, we just need to follow the possible paths from the rightmost node to that node. Then the desired Jacobian is the sum of all possible paths, where for each path the labeled Jacobians are multiplied from the right to the left. For example, in Fig. 4.1

$$\mathbf{J}_{(1)\mathbf{v}} = \frac{\partial \mathbf{y}}{\partial^{(1)}\mathbf{v}^T}$$
$$= \Lambda_{(2)\mathbf{v}}{}^{(2)}\mathbf{W}\Lambda_{(1)\mathbf{v}} + \Lambda_{(2)\mathbf{v}^*}{}^{(2)}\mathbf{W}^* \left(\Lambda_{(1)\mathbf{v}^*}\right)^* \qquad (4.21)$$

where the Jacobians $\Lambda_{(1)\mathbf{v}}$, $\Lambda_{(1)\mathbf{v}^*}$, $\Lambda_{(2)\mathbf{v}}$, and $\Lambda_{(2)\mathbf{v}^*}$ are diagonal matrices consisting of the derivatives of activation function(s).

As an example, let $^{(1)}\mathbf{v} = \left(^{(1)}v_1, {}^{(1)}v_2, \ldots, {}^{(1)}v_m\right)^T$. Then

$$\Lambda_{(1)\mathbf{v}} = \begin{pmatrix} \frac{\partial \phi_1}{\partial^{(1)}v_1} & 0 & \cdots & 0 \\ 0 & \frac{\partial \phi_2}{\partial^{(1)}v_2} & \cdots & 0 \\ \vdots & \vdots & \ddots & \vdots \\ 0 & 0 & \cdots & \frac{\partial \phi_m}{\partial^{(1)}v_m} \end{pmatrix}$$

,

$$\Lambda_{(1)\mathbf{v}^*} = \begin{pmatrix} \frac{\partial \phi_1}{\partial^{(1)}v_1^*} & 0 & \cdots & 0 \\ 0 & \frac{\partial \phi_2}{\partial^{(1)}v_2^*} & \cdots & 0 \\ \vdots & \vdots & \ddots & \vdots \\ 0 & 0 & \cdots & \frac{\partial \phi_m}{\partial^{(1)}v_m^*} \end{pmatrix}$$

It may seem that the number of paths would increase in a multiplicative manner for many layers network, particularly when evaluating the Jacobian at a far node than the right most node. Here a trick is to reuse the computation (i.e., backpropagation). We only need to look for Jacobian to the immediate rightmost nodes, presumably the Jacobians are already computed there. Thus Eq. (4.21) can be alternatively computed as

$$\mathbf{J}_{(1)\mathbf{v}} = \mathbf{J}_{(1)\mathbf{y}}\Lambda_{(1)\mathbf{v}} + \mathbf{J}_{(1)\mathbf{y}^*} \left(\Lambda_{(1)\mathbf{v}^*}\right)^*$$

where $\mathbf{J}_{(1)\mathbf{y}} = \dfrac{\partial \mathbf{y}}{\partial^{(1)}\mathbf{y}^T}$ and $\mathbf{J}_{(1)\mathbf{y}^*} = \dfrac{\partial \mathbf{y}}{\partial^{(1)}\mathbf{y}^H}$.

It is now a simple task to find the update rule for the feedforward CVNN parameters. We note from Eq. (4.20) that $\mathbf{J}_{(1)\mathbf{b}} = \mathbf{J}_{(1)\mathbf{v}}$ and $\mathbf{J}_{(2)\mathbf{b}} = \mathbf{J}_{(2)\mathbf{v}}$. Thus update rules for the biases at hidden and output layer are

$$\Delta^{(1)}\mathbf{b} = \mu \left(\mathbf{J}_{(1)_\mathbf{b}}^H \mathbf{e} + \left(\mathbf{J}_{(1)_{\mathbf{b}^*}}^H \mathbf{e} \right)^* \right); \quad \Delta^{(2)}\mathbf{b} = \mu \left(\mathbf{J}_{(2)_\mathbf{b}}^H \mathbf{e} + \left(\mathbf{J}_{(2)_{\mathbf{b}^*}}^H \mathbf{e} \right)^* \right) \quad (4.22)$$

where μ is the learning rate. Extending the notation for vector gradient to matrix gradient of a real-valued scalar function [17] and using Eq. (4.20), the update rules for hidden and output layer weight matrices are given by

$$\Delta^{(1)}\mathbf{W} = \left(\Delta^{(1)}\mathbf{b} \right) \mathbf{x}^H; \quad \Delta^{(2)}\mathbf{W} = \left(\Delta^{(2)}\mathbf{b} \right) {}^{(1)}\mathbf{y}^H \quad (4.23)$$

This completes the derivation of the gradient descent learning algorithm in the feedforward CVNN. All computations are directly performed in the complex domain in matrix–vector form. As shown in Fig. 4.1 one can easily compute the required Jacobians by visual inspection from the functional dependency graph. Furthermore, if the activation function is holomorphic, the Jacobians corresponding to conjugate vector turns into zero. Consequently, Fig. 4.1(a) reduces to Fig. 4.1(b).

4.4.2 Complex Levenberg–Marquardt Algorithm

The naive gradient descent method presented above has a limitation in many practical applications of multilayer neural networks because of very slow training time and less accuracy in the network mapping function [2]. In order to overcome this problem, many algorithms have been applied in the neural networks, such as conjugate gradient, Newton's method, quasi-Newton method, Gauss–Newton method, and *Levenberg–Marquardt* (LM) algorithm. Among those, perhaps the LM algorithm is the most popular in the neural networks as it is computationally more efficient. In this section, we derive the LM algorithm for training feedforward CVNNs. The LM is basically a batch-mode fast learning algorithm with a modification to the Gauss–Newton algorithm. Therefore, the Gauss–Newton algorithm will be first derived in the complex domain.

The Gauss–Newton method iteratively *re-linearizes* the nonlinear model and update the current parameter set according to a least squares solution to the linearized model. In the CVNN, the linearized model of network output $\mathbf{g}(\mathbf{z}, \mathbf{z}^*)$ around $(\hat{\mathbf{z}}, \hat{\mathbf{z}}^*)$ is given by

$$\mathbf{y}(\hat{\mathbf{z}} + \Delta\mathbf{z}, \hat{\mathbf{z}}^* + \Delta\mathbf{z}^*) \approx \mathbf{y}(\hat{\mathbf{z}}, \hat{\mathbf{z}}^*) + \frac{\partial\mathbf{y}}{\partial\mathbf{z}^T}\bigg|_{\hat{\mathbf{z}}} \Delta\mathbf{z} + \frac{\partial\mathbf{y}}{\partial(\mathbf{z}^*)^T}\bigg|_{\hat{\mathbf{z}}^*} \Delta\mathbf{z}^*$$

$$= \hat{\mathbf{y}} + \mathbf{J}_\mathbf{z}\Delta\mathbf{z} + \mathbf{J}_{\mathbf{z}^*}\Delta\mathbf{z}^* \quad (4.24)$$

which follows from the differential rule of Eq. (4.5). The error associated with the linearized model is given by

$$\mathbf{e} = \hat{\mathbf{e}} - (\mathbf{J}_\mathbf{z}\Delta\mathbf{z} + \mathbf{J}_{\mathbf{z}^*}\Delta\mathbf{z}^*) \quad (4.25)$$

where $\hat{\mathbf{e}} = \mathbf{d} - \hat{\mathbf{y}}$ is error at the point $(\hat{\mathbf{z}}, \hat{\mathbf{z}}^*)$. Then the Gauss–Newton update rule is given by the least squares solution to $\|\hat{\mathbf{e}} - (\mathbf{J}_\mathbf{z}\Delta\mathbf{z} + \mathbf{J}_{\mathbf{z}^*}\Delta\mathbf{z}^*)\|$. So we encounter a more general least squares problem having the form of $\|\mathbf{b} - (\mathbf{Az} + \mathbf{Bz}^*)\|_{\min}$, as opposed to the well-known problem $\|\mathbf{b} - \mathbf{Az}\|_{\min}$. Although solving the problem $\|\mathbf{b} - \mathbf{Az}\|_{\min}$ is well known from the normal equation $\mathbf{A}^H\mathbf{b} = \mathbf{A}^H\mathbf{Az}$, it is not found in the literature (to the best of our knowledge) as to how to write the normal equation of $\|\mathbf{b} - (\mathbf{Az} + \mathbf{Bz}^*)\|_{\min}$. In the following, we solve the problem simply by using the coordinate transformation of Eq. (4.10) and the well-known real-valued normal equation.

Theorem 4.4.2. Let $\mathbf{A}$ and $\mathbf{B}$ be arbitrary complex matrices of same dimension. Then a solution to the least squares problem, $\|\mathbf{b} - (\mathbf{Az} + \mathbf{Bz}^*)\|_{\min}$, is given by the following normal equation:

$$\mathbf{C}^H\begin{pmatrix}\mathbf{b}\\\mathbf{b}^*\end{pmatrix} = \mathbf{C}^H\mathbf{C}\begin{pmatrix}\mathbf{z}\\\mathbf{z}^*\end{pmatrix}, \quad \text{where } \mathbf{C} = \begin{pmatrix}\mathbf{A} & \mathbf{B}\\\mathbf{B}^* & \mathbf{A}^*\end{pmatrix} \tag{4.26}$$

Proof: From Eq. (4.10), we know that the conjugate coordinates system is related to the real coordinate system by the transformation matrix $\mathbf{M}$, and $\mathbf{M}^{-1} = \frac{1}{2}\mathbf{M}^H$. The error equation and its complex conjugate associated to the least squares problem are

$$\mathbf{e} = \mathbf{b} - (\mathbf{Az} + \mathbf{Bz}^*), \tag{4.27}$$

$$\mathbf{e}^* = \mathbf{b}^* - (\mathbf{A}^*\mathbf{z}^* + \mathbf{B}^*\mathbf{z}) \tag{4.28}$$

Combining the above equations to form a single matrix equation and applying the coordinate transformation the problem can be transformed into real coordinate system, where the normal equation for least squares problem is well known. This gives the following equation

$$\mathbf{M}^H\begin{pmatrix}\mathbf{e}\\\mathbf{e}^*\end{pmatrix} = \mathbf{M}^H\begin{pmatrix}\mathbf{b}\\\mathbf{b}^*\end{pmatrix} - \mathbf{M}^H\mathbf{C}\left(\frac{1}{2}\mathbf{MM}^H\right)\begin{pmatrix}\mathbf{z}\\\mathbf{z}^*\end{pmatrix}; \quad \left[\frac{1}{2}\mathbf{MM}^H = \mathbf{I}\right]$$

$$= \mathbf{M}^H\begin{pmatrix}\mathbf{b}\\\mathbf{b}^*\end{pmatrix} - \frac{1}{2}\left(\mathbf{M}^H\mathbf{CM}\right)\mathbf{M}^H\begin{pmatrix}\mathbf{z}\\\mathbf{z}^*\end{pmatrix} \tag{4.29}$$

It can be shown that $\frac{1}{2}\mathbf{M}^H\mathbf{CM} = \mathbf{P}$ is a real-valued matrix. Consequently, Eq. (4.29) is real-valued matrix equation and can be rewritten as

$$\begin{pmatrix}\Re(\mathbf{e})\\\Im(\mathbf{e})\end{pmatrix} = \begin{pmatrix}\Re(\mathbf{b})\\\Im(\mathbf{b})\end{pmatrix} - \mathbf{P}\begin{pmatrix}\Re(\mathbf{z})\\\Im(\mathbf{z})\end{pmatrix}$$

$$= \mathbf{q} - \mathbf{Pr} \tag{4.30}$$

Because it is now completely in the real coordinate system, we can readily apply the normal equation $\mathbf{P}^T\mathbf{q} = \mathbf{P}^T\mathbf{Pr}$ for the least squares problem of Eq. (4.30). Noting that the ordinary transpose and Hermitian conjugate transpose is the same operation in the real-valued matrices, the real-valued normal equation, $\mathbf{P}^T\mathbf{q} = \mathbf{P}^T\mathbf{Pr}$, transforms to the following complex-valued normal equation (Eqs. (4.29) and (4.30) are equivalent):

$$\frac{1}{2}\mathbf{M}^H\mathbf{C}^H\mathbf{M}\mathbf{M}^H\begin{pmatrix}\mathbf{b}\\\mathbf{b}^*\end{pmatrix} = \frac{1}{2}\mathbf{M}^H\mathbf{C}^H\mathbf{M}\mathbf{M}^H\mathbf{C}\left(\frac{1}{2}\mathbf{M}\mathbf{M}^H\right)\begin{pmatrix}\mathbf{z}\\\mathbf{z}^*\end{pmatrix} \qquad (4.31)$$

Since $\frac{1}{2}\mathbf{M}\mathbf{M}^H = \mathbf{I}$ and $\mathbf{M}^H$ is invertible, Eq. (4.31) immediately yields the following normal equation in the complex form

$$\mathbf{C}^H\begin{pmatrix}\mathbf{b}\\\mathbf{b}^*\end{pmatrix} = \mathbf{C}^H\mathbf{C}\begin{pmatrix}\mathbf{z}\\\mathbf{z}^*\end{pmatrix}$$

as required.   ■

According to Theorem 4.4.2, the least squares solution to Eq. (4.25) gives the following Gauss–Newton update rule:

$$\begin{pmatrix}\Delta\mathbf{z}\\\Delta\mathbf{z}^*\end{pmatrix} = \mathbf{H}^{-1}\mathbf{G}^H\begin{pmatrix}\hat{\mathbf{e}}\\\hat{\mathbf{e}}^*\end{pmatrix} \qquad (4.32)$$

where $\mathbf{G} = \begin{pmatrix}\mathbf{J}_\mathbf{z} & \mathbf{J}_{\mathbf{z}^*}\\(\mathbf{J}_{\mathbf{z}^*})^* & (\mathbf{J}_\mathbf{z})^*\end{pmatrix}$ and $\mathbf{H} = \mathbf{G}^H\mathbf{G} = \begin{pmatrix}\mathbf{H}_{11} & \mathbf{H}_{12}\\\mathbf{H}_{21} & \mathbf{H}_{22}\end{pmatrix}$

The matrix $\mathbf{H}$ can be considered as an approximation to the Hessian matrix that would result from Newton method. Note that when $\mathbf{H} = \mathbf{I}$, the Gauss–Newton update rule reduces to the gradient descent algorithm. There is also a pseudo-Gauss–Newton algorithm, where the off-diagonal block matrices are $\mathbf{H}_{12} = \mathbf{H}_{12} = \mathbf{0}$ [16]. The pseudo-Gauss–Newton update rule then takes a simpler form:

$$\Delta\mathbf{z}^{pseudo-Gauss-Newton} = \mathbf{H}_{11}^{-1}\left(\mathbf{J}_\mathbf{z}^H\mathbf{e} + \left(\mathbf{J}_{\mathbf{z}^*}^H\mathbf{e}\right)^*\right) \qquad (4.33)$$

When the activation functions in the CVNN are holomorphic, the output function $\mathbf{g}(\mathbf{z})$ is also holomorphic. The Gauss–Newton update rule becomes very simple and resembles the real-valued case:

$$\Delta\mathbf{z}^{holomorphic} = \left(\mathbf{J}_\mathbf{z}^H\mathbf{J}_\mathbf{z}\right)^{-1}\mathbf{J}_\mathbf{z}^H\mathbf{e} \qquad (4.34)$$

It can be observed that all the computations use the Jacobian matrices extensively, which can be evaluated visually and efficiently from the functional dependency graph of Fig. 4.1. It thus shows the simplicity of our derivation using the Wirtinger calculus.

The LM algorithm makes a simple modification to the Gauss–Newton algorithm of Eq. (4.32) in the following way

$$\begin{pmatrix}\Delta\mathbf{z}\\\Delta\mathbf{z}^*\end{pmatrix} = \left(\mathbf{G}^H\mathbf{G} + \mu\mathbf{I}\right)^{-1}\mathbf{G}^H\begin{pmatrix}\hat{\mathbf{e}}\\\hat{\mathbf{e}}^*\end{pmatrix} \qquad (4.35)$$

The parameter μ is varied over the iterations. Whenever a step increases the error rather than decreasing, μ is multiplied by a factor of β. Otherwise, μ is divided by

β. A popular choice for the initial value of μ is 0.01 and $\beta = 10$. The LM is a batch-mode learning algorithm, and hence all the training examples are presented before a parameter update. Consequently, the Jacobians $\mathbf{J_z}$ and $\mathbf{J_{z^*}}$ become submatrices of two larger Jacobian matrices containing the derivatives for all examples. The following are the steps of the complex-LM algorithm:

1. Present all the input data to the CVNN and compute network outputs and error. Arrange error vectors for all the input patterns into a single column vector and compute the norm of the error vector.

2. Compute the Jacobian and conjugate Jacobian submatrices using Fig. 4.1 for all the patterns. Again arrange all the submatrices into two corresponding larger Jacobian matrices in such way that the patterns get augmented row-wise, the parameters column-wise.

3. Use Eq. (4.35) to obtain $\Delta \mathbf{z}$. Note that when the activation function is holomorphic or if the pseudo-Gauss-Newton is intended, update should be done according to Eqs. (4.34) or (4.33), respectively.

4. Recompute the norm of the error vector using $\mathbf{z} + \Delta \mathbf{z}$. If the new norm is smaller than the one computed in step 1, reduce μ by β and admit the update $\mathbf{z} = \mathbf{z} + \Delta \mathbf{z}$; and go back to step 1. If the error norm does not get reduced, then increase μ by β and go back to step 3.

5. The algorithm is stopped if some stopping criteria is met; for example, error goal is met or a given maximum number of iterations has been passed.

4.4.3 Computer Simulations

A computer experiment was performed in order to verify the algorithms presented in Section 4.4.1 and Section 4.4.2. The algorithms were implemented in the Matlab to utilize its matrix computing environment. We took the experimental data from [23], where the task is to learn the patterns shown in Table 4.1. We trained a 2-4-1 CVNN using the complex gradient descent learning algorithm and two variants of complex-LM algorithm. Note that the complex-LM algorithm uses the Gauss–Newton update rule as its basic constituent, which has a variant called the pseudo-Gauss–Newton method. Accordingly, two variants are called complex-LM and pseudo-complex-LM. In either case of the learning algorithms, the training was stopped when the error (mean squared error (MSE)) goal was met or a maximum number of iterations has been passed. The MSE goal was set to 0.0001 and the maximum number of iterations was set to 10 000. We used the same activation function of [23] in the hidden and output layers, which is nonholomorphic. The function has the following form:

$$f_{\mathbb{C}\to\mathbb{C}}(z) = f_R(\Re(z)) + jf_I(\Im(z)) \tag{4.36}$$

where $f_R(\cdot)$ and $f_I(\cdot)$ are real-valued log sigmoid functions.

Table 4.1   Learning patterns

Input 1	Input 2	Output
0	0	1
0	j	j
j	j	$1 + j$
j	1	j
1	1	$1 + j$
j	0	0
$1 + j$	$1 + j$	1
$1 + j$	j	j

$$j = \sqrt{-1}$$

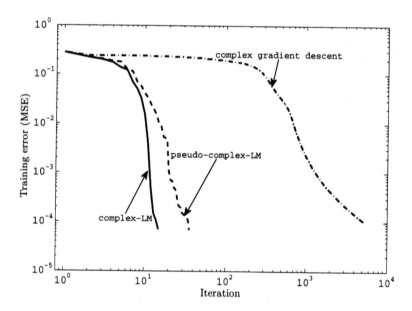

Figure 4.2   Learning curves of complex gradient descent, complex-LM, and pseudo-complex-LM algorithm.

The number of iterations required to meet error goal were only 15 and 36 for the complex-LM and the pseudo-complex-LM, respectively. The complex gradient descent, however, met the error goal at 5345-th iteration. Figure 4.2 shows the learning curves in log scale. It is clearly observed that the complex-LM and the pseudo-complex-LM algorithms converged very fast. Furthermore, the complex-LM is faster than the pseudo-complex-LM since the latter is an approximation to the former. Note that in the pseudo-complex-LM, approximation is done by block diagonal matrix to reduce the computations of matrix inversion (see Eq. (4.32)). As shown in Fig. 4.2, the convergence behavior of complex-LM and complex gradient descent algorithms resembles much like that in the RVNNs. Therefore, complex-LM learning in the CVNNs could be very useful in the CVNN applications very much like the LM algorithm in the RVNNs.

Similar to the RVNNs, the application of complex-LM algorithms in CVNNs is limited by the number of parameters of CVNNs, because it requires a matrix inversion computation in each iteration, whereby the matrix dimension is in the order of total number of learning parameters. Therefore, the complex-LM algorithms are applicable when faster and higher accuracy in the network mapping is required, such as system identification and time-series prediction in the complex domain.

4.5 LEARNING ALGORITHMS FOR RECURRENT CVNNS

The feedforward neural networks discussed in the previous section are often called static networks [6] since they have no feedback elements. On the other hand, recurrent networks having feedback connections can represent highly nonlinear dynamical systems [19]. These dynamic networks have capabilities superior to those of the feedforward networks with tapped delay line representations for processing temporal or sequential information. A number of learning algorithms exist for the real-valued recurrent neural networks, including real-time recurrent learning (RTRL) [31], backpropagation through time (BPTT) [29], and extended Kalman filter (EKF) [24].

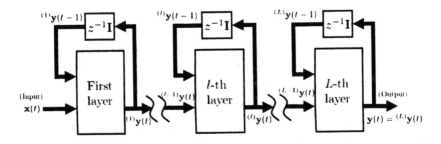

Figure 4.3   Block diagram of recurrent CVNN.

In this section, we utilize the Wirtinger calculus for deriving complex version of the RTRL and EKF algorithm, i.e., the CRTRL and the CEKF. A very general class of networks as shown in Fig. 4.3 is considered, which is referred to as recurrent multilayer perceptron (RMLP) in [24, 11]. The CRTRL has been derived in [8] for holomorphic activation function, while only the split-type sigmoid activation function has been considered in [14]. Both the works deal with a single-layered recurrent CVNN and reformulates the problem in real domain for computing real-valued gradient. In contrast, the derivations carried out here do not impose restrictions on the type of activation function and all computations are performed directly in the complex domain. We then derive CEKF and show how the augmented CEKF (ACEKF) of [9] naturally arises from the coordinate transformation viewpoint in the Wirtinger calculus. The CEKF employs the CRTRL algorithm for locally linearizing the recurrent CVNN model.

4.5.1   Complex Real-Time Recurrent Learning Algorithm

The network shown in Fig. 4.3 consists of one or more fully recurrent hidden layers. Feedback connections exist only in the same layer feeding its input by a unit time-delayed output. The network operates in discrete time steps, and at time instant t the output from lth layer is given by

$$^{(l)}\mathbf{y}(t) = \phi\left(^{(l)}\mathbf{v}(t)\right), \tag{4.37}$$

$$^{(l)}\mathbf{v}(t) = {}^{(l)}\overleftarrow{\mathbf{W}}{}^{(l)}\mathbf{y}(t-1) + {}^{(l)}\overrightarrow{\mathbf{W}}{}^{(l-1)}\mathbf{y}(t), \quad 1 \leq l \leq L \tag{4.38}$$

Here $\phi(\cdot)$ is any activation function having $\mathbb{R}^2 \to \mathbb{R}^2$ differentiable mapping property. The matrices $^{(l)}\overleftarrow{\mathbf{W}}$ and $^{(l)}\overrightarrow{\mathbf{W}}$ designate the feedback and feedforward connections, respectively. The biases are subsumed in the feedforward connections having a constant input.

The CRTRL is a gradient descent learning algorithm that computes derivatives through a recurrence relation. Figure 4.4 shows the functional dependency diagram of an output layer, l, along with its conjugate. The diagram has the similar role as of Fig. 4.1, i.e., to facilitate evaluating the Jacobians. However, because of the feedback connections, we define *dynamic Jacobian* in order to account for the indirect effects through time. The dynamic Jacobian matrix of lth layer output w.r.t. $^{(m)}\mathbf{w}_k$, the weight vector of kth neuron in mth layer ($m \leq l$), is as follows:

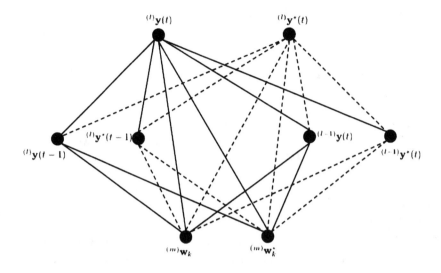

Figure 4.4   Functonal dependency graph for lth layer neurons. The dependency delegates from top to bottom.

$$
^{(l)}\mathbf{J}_{(m)\mathbf{w}_k}(t) = \overbrace{^{(l)}\mathbf{J}_{(l)\mathbf{y}(t-1)}}^{\text{Direct subpath}}\,{}^{(l)}\mathbf{J}_{(m)\mathbf{w}_k}(t-1) + \overbrace{^{(l)}\mathbf{J}_{(l)\mathbf{y}^*(t-1)}}^{\text{Direct subpath}}\underbrace{\left(^{(l)}\mathbf{J}_{(m)\mathbf{w}_k^*}\right)^*(t-1)}
$$

$$
\underbrace{\phantom{^{(l)}\mathbf{J}_{(l)\mathbf{y}(t-1)}\,{}^{(l)}\mathbf{J}_{(m)\mathbf{w}_k}(t-1) + ^{(l)}\mathbf{J}_{(l)\mathbf{y}^*(t-1)}\left(^{(l)}\mathbf{J}_{(m)\mathbf{w}_k^*}\right)^*(t-1)}}_{\text{Dynamic recurrent path}}
$$

$$
+ (1-\delta_{l,m})\left(\overbrace{^{(l)}\mathbf{J}_{(l-1)\mathbf{y}(t)}}^{\text{Direct subpath}}\,{}^{(l-1)}\mathbf{J}_{(m)\mathbf{w}_k}(t) + \overbrace{^{(l)}\mathbf{J}_{(l-1)\mathbf{y}^*(t-1)}}^{\text{Direct subpath}}\left(^{(l-1)}\mathbf{J}_{(m)\mathbf{w}_k^*}\right)^*(t)\right)
$$

$$
\underbrace{}_{\text{Dynamic forward path}}
$$

$$
+\quad \underbrace{\delta_{l,m}\,{}^{(l)}\mathbf{J}_{(m)\mathbf{w}_k}}_{\text{Direct recurrent and forward paths}} \qquad ,\ l \geq m \tag{4.39}
$$

where $\delta_{l,m}$ is the Kronecker delta. The direct path computations are as usual like the feedforward networks. The dynamic Jacobians are shown with the time step as their arguments forming the recurrence relation of Eq. (4.39). Initially all the derivatives are set to zero. Note that for $l < m$, the Jacobians are zero matrix as the output of a layer does not depend on the weights of succeeding layers. Now evaluating the direct path Jacobians yields the following expression:

$$^{(l)}\mathbf{J}_{(m)\mathbf{w}_k}(t) = \Lambda_{(l)\mathbf{v}(t)}{}^{(l)}\overleftarrow{\mathbf{W}}{}^{(l)}\mathbf{J}_{(m)\mathbf{w}_k}(t-1) + \Lambda_{(l)\mathbf{v}^*(t)}{}^{(l)}\overleftarrow{\mathbf{W}}{}^{*}\left(^{(l)}\mathbf{J}_{(m)\mathbf{w}_k^*}\right)^*(t-1)$$

$$+ (1-\delta_{l,m})\left(\Lambda_{(l)\mathbf{v}(t)}{}^{(l)}\overrightarrow{\mathbf{W}}{}^{(l-1)}\mathbf{J}_{(m)\mathbf{w}_k}(t) + \Lambda_{(l)\mathbf{v}^*(t)}{}^{(l)}\overrightarrow{\mathbf{W}}{}^{*}\left(^{(l-1)}\mathbf{J}_{(m)\mathbf{w}_k^*}\right)^*(t)\right)$$

$$+ \delta_{l,m}\Lambda_{(l)\mathbf{v}(t)}{}^{(l)}\mathbf{U}_k(t), \quad l \geq m \tag{4.40}$$

where $^{(l)}\mathbf{U}_k(t)$ is a matrix whose all rows except the kth one are zero since $^{(l)}\mathbf{w}_k$ has direct influence only to the kth neuron. The indirect influence, however, is already accounted in the dynamic Jacobians. The kth row consists of both the feedback and feedforward inputs to the lth layer, i.e., $\left(^{(l)}\mathbf{y}^T(t-1), {}^{(l-1)}\mathbf{y}^T(t)\right)$. It can be easily conceived from Eq. (4.39) that for a feedfoward CVNN, the recurrent path vanishes and the dynamic forward path simply reduces to direct forward path.

In the conjugate coordinate system, there are three additional Jacobian matrices: $^{(l)}\mathbf{J}_{(m)\mathbf{w}_k^*}(t)$, $\left(^{(l)}\mathbf{J}_{(m)\mathbf{w}_k}\right)^*(t)$, and $\left(^{(l)}\mathbf{J}_{(m)\mathbf{w}_k^*}\right)^*(t)$. Utilizing the dependency graph of Fig. 4.4 the complete Jacobian matrix in conjugate coordinate system can be written as

$$\begin{pmatrix} ^{(l)}\mathbf{J}_{(m)\mathbf{w}_k} & ^{(l)}\mathbf{J}_{(m)\mathbf{w}_k^*} \\ \left(^{(l)}\mathbf{J}_{(m)\mathbf{w}_k^*}\right)^* & \left(^{(l)}\mathbf{J}_{(m)\mathbf{w}_k}\right)^* \end{pmatrix}(t) = \begin{pmatrix} \Lambda_{(l)\mathbf{v}(t)} & \Lambda_{(l)\mathbf{v}^*(t)} \\ \left(\Lambda_{(l)\mathbf{v}^*(t)}\right)^* & \left(\Lambda_{(l)\mathbf{v}(t)}\right)^* \end{pmatrix}$$

$$\times \left[\begin{pmatrix} ^{(l)}\overleftarrow{\mathbf{W}} & 0 \\ 0 & ^{(l)}\overleftarrow{\mathbf{W}}{}^* \end{pmatrix} \begin{pmatrix} ^{(l)}\mathbf{J}_{(m)\mathbf{w}_k} & ^{(l)}\mathbf{J}_{(m)\mathbf{w}_k^*} \\ \left(^{(l)}\mathbf{J}_{(m)\mathbf{w}_k^*}\right)^* & \left(^{(l)}\mathbf{J}_{(m)\mathbf{w}_k}\right)^* \end{pmatrix}(t-1) \right.$$

$$+ (1-\delta_{l,m})\begin{pmatrix} ^{(l)}\overrightarrow{\mathbf{W}} & 0 \\ 0 & ^{(l)}\overrightarrow{\mathbf{W}}{}^* \end{pmatrix}\begin{pmatrix} ^{(l-1)}\mathbf{J}_{(m)\mathbf{w}_k} & ^{(l-1)}\mathbf{J}_{(m)\mathbf{w}_k^*} \\ \left(^{(l-1)}\mathbf{J}_{(m)\mathbf{w}_k^*}\right)^* & \left(^{(l-1)}\mathbf{J}_{(m)\mathbf{w}_k}\right)^* \end{pmatrix}(t)$$

$$\left. + \delta_{l,m}\begin{pmatrix} ^{(l)}\mathbf{U}_k & 0 \\ 0 & ^{(l)}\mathbf{U}_k^* \end{pmatrix}(t) \right], \quad l \geq m \tag{4.41}$$

A more compact form of Eq. (4.41) is shown below:

$$^{(l)}\widetilde{\mathbf{J}}_{(m)\widetilde{\mathbf{w}}_k}(t) = \widetilde{\Lambda}_{(l)\widetilde{\mathbf{v}}(t)}\left(^{(l)}\overleftarrow{\widetilde{\mathbf{W}}}{}^{(l)}\widetilde{\mathbf{J}}_{(m)\widetilde{\mathbf{w}}_k}(t-1) + \right.$$

$$\left. (1-\delta_{l,m})^{(l)}\overrightarrow{\widetilde{\mathbf{W}}}{}^{(l-1)}\widetilde{\mathbf{J}}_{(m)\widetilde{\mathbf{w}}_k}(t) + \delta_{l,m}\widetilde{\mathbf{U}}_k\right), \quad l \geq m \tag{4.42}$$

where a *tilde* over a complex vector and a Jacobian refers to their conjugate coordinate representations and over any other matrix, say $\widetilde{\mathbf{A}}$, denotes a block diagonal matrix composed of the original matrix and its conjugate, i.e., $\mathbf{A}$ and $\mathbf{A}^*$.

In the online training mode, weights are updated at discrete time steps according to the negative of gradient defined in Eq. (4.17):

$$^{(m)}\mathbf{w}_k(t+1) = {}^{(m)}\mathbf{w}_k(t) + \mu\left(^{(L)}\mathbf{J}_{(m)\mathbf{w}_k}^H(t)\mathbf{e}(t) + \left(^{(L)}\mathbf{J}_{(m)\mathbf{w}_k^*}^H(t)\mathbf{e}(t)\right)^*\right)$$

$$\tag{4.43}$$

where L denotes the output layer and μ is the learning rate. This completes our CRTRL algorithm derivation in matrix–vector form where all computations are carried out directly in the complex domain.

4.5.2 Complex Extended Kalman Filter Algorithm

The Kalman filter algorithm [13] provides an optimal solution to the linear Gaussian sequential state estimation problems. For nonlinear models such as neural networks, it is extended by linearizing the system locally at every update step of estimation, and hence it is called the extended Kalman filter (EKF). The algorithm often shows better performance than the gradient based algorithms especially when processing signals with rich dynamics [9]. One of the key features of the EKF algorithm is the use of second-order statistics such as covariance matrix. However, in the complex domain, random variables can be *proper* or *improper* [21]. The improper case is more general, and it is viewed from the real-valued perspective.

Let us consider a complex random vector $\mathbf{z} = \mathbf{x} + j\mathbf{y}$. Its real coordinate representation is $\mathbf{r} = (\mathbf{x}^T, \mathbf{y}^T)^T$ and the covariance in the real coordinate system is given by

$$
\begin{aligned}
\mathbf{P}_{\mathbf{rr}} &= \mathbb{E}\left(\mathbf{r}\mathbf{r}^T\right) \\
&= \mathbb{E}\left(\begin{pmatrix} \mathbf{x} \\ \mathbf{y} \end{pmatrix} \begin{pmatrix} \mathbf{x}^T & \mathbf{y}^T \end{pmatrix}\right) \\
&= \begin{pmatrix} \mathbf{P}_{\mathbf{xx}} & \mathbf{P}_{\mathbf{xy}} \\ \mathbf{P}_{\mathbf{xy}}^T & \mathbf{P}_{\mathbf{yy}} \end{pmatrix}
\end{aligned}
\tag{4.44}
$$

where $\mathbb{E}(\cdot)$ stands for the expectation operator. Under any coordinate transformation, say $\mathbf{M}$, of a random variable, the covariance matrix transforms into $\mathbf{MPM}^H$. Therefore, in the conjugate coordinate system, covariance matrix takes the following form:

$$
\begin{aligned}
\widetilde{\mathbf{P}}_{\widetilde{\mathbf{z}}} &= \begin{pmatrix} \mathbf{I} & j\mathbf{I} \\ \mathbf{I} & -j\mathbf{I} \end{pmatrix} \begin{pmatrix} \mathbf{P}_{\mathbf{xx}} & \mathbf{P}_{\mathbf{xy}} \\ \mathbf{P}_{\mathbf{xy}}^T & \mathbf{P}_{\mathbf{yy}} \end{pmatrix} \begin{pmatrix} \mathbf{I} & \mathbf{I} \\ -j\mathbf{I} & j\mathbf{I} \end{pmatrix} \\
&= \begin{pmatrix} \mathbf{P}_{\mathbf{zz}} & \mathbf{P}_{\mathbf{zz}^*} \\ (\mathbf{P}_{\mathbf{zz}^*})^* & (\mathbf{P}_{\mathbf{zz}})^* \end{pmatrix}
\end{aligned}
\tag{4.45}
$$

where

$$
\mathbf{P}_{\mathbf{zz}} = (\mathbf{P}_{\mathbf{xx}} + \mathbf{P}_{\mathbf{yy}}) - j\left(\mathbf{P}_{\mathbf{xy}} - \mathbf{P}_{\mathbf{xy}}^T\right)
$$
$$
\mathbf{P}_{\mathbf{zz}^*} = (\mathbf{P}_{\mathbf{xx}} - \mathbf{P}_{\mathbf{yy}}) + j\left(\mathbf{P}_{\mathbf{xy}} + \mathbf{P}_{\mathbf{xy}}^T\right)
$$

Note that $\widetilde{\mathbf{P}}_{\widetilde{\mathbf{z}}}$ has the following properties:

1. It is Hermitian and positive semidefinite, thus a valid covariance matrix.

2. It has the same structure of Jacobian matrix in the conjugate coordinate system discussed in the previous section (see Eqs. (4.18) and (4.19)), i.e., block

diagonal matrices as well as the block off-diagonal matrices are conjugate to each other. As we shall see later, this is an essential property for being a valid covariance matrix during the update process of CEKF algorithm.

A Similar covariance matrix is also described in [27] giving it the name *augmented covariance matrix*. However, we refer to it here as the covariance matrix in a conjugate coordinate system in order to adhere to the discussion in the previous sections, which allows a unified view of deriving learning algorithms for the CVNNs.

In order to find the equations for CEKF algorithm, we need to express the recurrent CVNN as a discrete time dynamical system with a state-space representation. The weight parameters are considered to be a *state* vector, network output has the role of an *observation* vector, and the error vector represents the *innovation*. Therefore, the dynamical behavior is given by

$$\mathbf{w}_t = \mathbf{w}_{t-1} + \omega_t, \tag{4.46}$$

$$\mathbf{y}_t = \mathbf{y}\left(\mathbf{w}_t, \mathbf{u}_t\right) + \nu_t \tag{4.47}$$

where ω_t and ν_t are complex Gaussian process noise and observation noise with the covariances, $\widetilde{\mathbf{Q}}_t$ and $\widetilde{\mathbf{R}}_t$, respectively. We indicate time step as a subscript for notational convenience. For the CEKF, a nonlinear CVNN model is linearized locally around the current estimate of weight parameters and is represented by the Jacobian matrix, $\widetilde{\mathbf{J}}_t$ which we evaluate by the CRTRL algorithm of previous section. We need another covariance matrix known as error covariance, $\widetilde{\mathbf{P}}_t$, associated with the state estimation. Now the update equations in conjugate coordinate system are as follows:

Prediction:

$$\widetilde{\mathbf{w}}_t^- = \widetilde{\mathbf{w}}_{t-1} \tag{4.48}$$

$$\widetilde{\mathbf{P}}_t^- = \widetilde{\mathbf{P}}_{t-1} + \widetilde{\mathbf{Q}}_t \tag{4.49}$$

Update:

$$\widetilde{\mathbf{G}}_t = \widetilde{\mathbf{P}}_t^- \widetilde{\mathbf{J}}_t^H \left(\widetilde{\mathbf{J}}_t \widetilde{\mathbf{P}}_t^- \widetilde{\mathbf{J}}_t^H + \widetilde{\mathbf{R}}_t\right)^{-1} \tag{4.50}$$

$$\widetilde{\mathbf{w}}_t = \widetilde{\mathbf{w}}_t^- + \widetilde{\mathbf{G}}_t \left(\widetilde{\mathbf{d}}_t - \widetilde{\mathbf{y}}_t\right) \tag{4.51}$$

$$\widetilde{\mathbf{P}}_t = \left(\mathbf{I} - \widetilde{\mathbf{G}}_t \widetilde{\mathbf{J}}_t^H\right) \widetilde{\mathbf{P}}_t^- + \widetilde{\mathbf{Q}}_t \tag{4.52}$$

It should be noted that any matrix having the conjugate coordinate structure, a property found in the Jacobian and covariance matrices, always preserves the same conjugate coordinate structure by its operation. Consequently, throughout the CEKF update equation, the covariance matrix $\widetilde{\mathbf{P}}_t$ always remains valid and the weight vector in conjugate coordinate form retains its similar structure.

4.5.3 Computer Simulations

In this section, we provide computer simulation results of CRTRL and CEKF on a real-world wind prediction problem. It is very important to predict wind speed and direction, especially for efficient wind power generation. Traditionally, wind modeling and forecasting are done by considering the speed and direction as independent variables. However, recent studies have shown a better modeling and forecasting of wind as a complex number field, noting the statistical dependence between the speed and direction [20].

We obtained real-world data from the Iowa (USA) Department of Transport at the location WASHINGTON (AWG). The data sampled for every 10 minutes was downloaded from the website[1] during the period between February 1, 2011 and February 28, 2011. Then the data were averaged over every 1-hour interval. In order to assess the performance of CRTRL and CEKF, a standard measure called prediction gain [12, 20] is evaluated. The prediction gain, R_p, defined as in [12] is given by

$$R_p \triangleq 10 \log_{10} \left(\frac{\sigma_x^2}{\sigma_e^2} \right) \quad \text{[dB]} \tag{4.53}$$

where σ_x^2 and σ_e^2 denote the mean squared value of input signal $\{x(k)\}$ and prediction error signal $\{e(k)\}$, respectively. A smaller prediction error would result in a larger prediction gain. Therefore, a better predictor would have a larger value of R_p.

A recurrent CVNN consisting one input unit, three fully recurrent hidden units, and one nonrecurrent output unit was trained with CRTRL and CEKF algorithms. The network weights and biases were initialized with random complex numbers taken uniformly within a small disc of radius 0.01. Figure 4.5 shows the actual and predicted wind speed by the CEKF and CRTRL. The activation function used here was split-type hyperbolic tangent function, $f(u + jv) = \tanh(u) + j \tanh(v)$. It can be observed that the CEKF predicted relatively better than the CRTRL algorithm. However, the CEKF requires additional computations due to Kalman filtering update equations.

Table 4.2   Prediction gain, R_p, for wind prediction problem. Averages taken over 20 independent runs.

Activation function	CRTRL	CEKF
split-tanh	11.19	12.27
tanh	9.59	11.60
tan	9.79	11.78
arctan	9.71	11.52

We also took simulation for three more activation functions which are holomorphic except at singular points. The functions are complex-valued version of hyperbolic tangent, circular tangent, and inverse circular tangent. They belong to the class of elementary transcendental functions [15]. Table 4.2 compares the prediction performance in terms of prediction gain, R_p, for different activation functions. The results are an average of 20 independent runs. In both CRTRL and CEKF, the

---

[1]http://mesonet.agron.iastate.edu/request/awos/1min.php

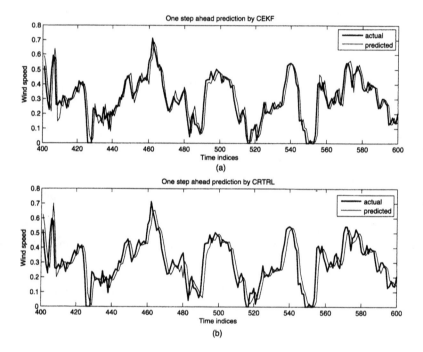

Figure 4.5   One step ahead prediction of wind speed: (a) CEKF algorithm and (b) CRTRL algorithm.

best prediction was obtained with the split-type hyperbolic tangent function. For all the activation functions, however, CEKF had better prediction performance than that of CRTRL. Furthermore, it can be observed that the performances of holomorphic functions were almost same within either of the CRTRL or CEKF algorithm. However, we noticed that some of the independent runs with holomorphic activation functions went out of bound due to the singular points. Those results were omitted in computing the averages in Table 4.2. Therefore, it seems that the boundedness is more important than the analyticity of complex activation functions in the multilayer recurrent CVNNs, unless we can ensure the avoidance of singularities.

4.6 CONCLUSION

In this chapter, first a brief discussion on Wirtinger calculus is presented. It is shown to be very useful in dealing with nonholomorphic functions that are obvious in the CVNNs. Most importantly, the well-known Cauchy–Riemann equations for holomorphic function becomes a special case of derivatives in the Wirtinger calculus. The derivative rules (e.g., product, quotient and chain rule) in the Wirtinger calculus comply with those in the ordinary calculus, thereby making it easier to use.

We have derived several learning algorithms for complex CVNNs, including complex gradient descent, complex-LM, CRTRL, and CEKF using the Wirtinger calculus, which enables performing all computations directly in the complex domain. The CRTRL and CEKF are particularly employed in the recurrent CVNNs. In the course of complex-LM derivation, we have encountered a general least squares problem in the complex domain. A solution with proof is presented and the result in utilized in the derivation. We point out that (i) the Wirtinger calculus, (ii) coordination transformation between the conjugate coordinate and the real coordinate system, and (iii) the functional dependency graph of Jacobians greatly simplifies the extension of the learning algorithms in the RVNNs to the CVNN framework. The approach is a unified and systematic way for the formulation of derivative based learning algorithms.

Computer simulation results are provided to verify the derivations. For feedforward CVNNs, it is shown that the complex-LM as well as its variant, the pseudo-complex-LM, have much faster learning convergence. This resembles the convergence behavior of LM algorithm in the RVNNs for which the LM is widely used in various RVNN applications. Therefore, as the application areas of CVNNs become wider, the complex-LM is expected to be very useful in those applications. For the recurrent CVNNs, computer simulation results show that the performance of the CEKF algorithm is superior to that of the CRTRL algorithm on a real-world wind prediction problem. Furthermore, the split-type hyperbolic tangent, a nonholomorphic activation function, seems to be a better choice than several holomorphic functions in the multilayer recurrent CVNNs.

Appendix

List of Notations

l	Layer number indicator
L	Total number of layers
t	Discrete time step
j	$\sqrt{-1}$
$(\cdot)^H$	Hermitian transpose operator
$(\cdot)^T$	Transpose operator without conjugation
$^{(l)}\mathbf{y}$	Outputs of lth layer neurons
$^{(l)}\mathbf{v}$	net-inputs of lth layer neurons
$\mathbf{x} = {}^{(0)}\mathbf{y}$	Inputs to the network
$\mathbf{y} = {}^{(L)}\mathbf{y}$	Outputs of the network
$^{(l)}\mathbf{w}_k$	Incident weight connections to kth neuron of lth layer
$^{(l)}\mathbf{b}$	Biases to lth layer neurons
$^{(l)}\mathbf{W}$	Incident weight connection matrix to lth layer neurons
$\mathbf{r} = \begin{pmatrix} \mathbf{x} \\ \mathbf{y} \end{pmatrix}$	Real coordinates representation of complex vector $\mathbf{z} = \mathbf{x} + i\mathbf{y}$
$\widetilde{\mathbf{z}} = \begin{pmatrix} \mathbf{z} \\ \mathbf{z}^* \end{pmatrix}$	Conjugate coordinates representation of complex vector $\mathbf{z}$
$\mathbf{M}$	Coordinate transformation matrix for real to conjugate coordinate transformation
$\mathbf{J_z}$	Jacobian matrix of output $\mathbf{y}$ with respect to (w.r.t.) $\mathbf{z}$
$\widetilde{\mathbf{J}}_{\widetilde{\mathbf{z}}}$	Jacobian matrix of output $\widetilde{\mathbf{y}}$ w.r.t. $\widetilde{\mathbf{z}}$
$\mathbf{P_{xx}}$	Auto covariance of random vector $\mathbf{x}$
$\mathbf{P_{xy}}$	Cross covariance of random vectors $\mathbf{x}$ and $\mathbf{y}$
$\widetilde{\mathbf{P}}_{\widetilde{\mathbf{z}}}$	Auto covariance of $\mathbf{z}$ in conjugate coordinate system
$\widetilde{\mathbf{P}}_t$	Error covariance matrix of state estimation in conjugate coordinate system
$\widetilde{\mathbf{Q}}_t$	Process noise covariance matrix in conjugate coordinate system
$\widetilde{\mathbf{R}}_t$	Measurement noise covariance matrix in conjugate coordinate system

REFERENCES

1. M. F. Amin, M. I. Amin, A. Al-Nuaimi, and K. Murase. Wirtinger calculus based gradient descent and Levenberg–Marquardt learning algorithms in complex-valued neural networks. In Proceedings of International Conference on Neural Information Processing, Shanghai, November 2011, pp. 550–559.

2. R. Battiti. First-and second-order methods for learning: between steepest descent and newton's method. *Neural Computation*, 4(2):141–166, 1992.

3. N. Benvenuto and F. Piazza. On the complex backpropagation algorithm. *IEEE Transactions on Signal Processing*, 40(4):967–969, 1992.

4. P. Bouboulis and S. Theodoridis. Extension of wirtinger's calculus to reproducing kernel Hilbert spaces and the complex kernel lms. *IEEE Transactions on Signal Processing*, 59(3):964–978, 2011.

5. D. H. Brandwood. A complex gradient operator and its application in adaptive array theory. *Microwaves, Optics and Antennas, IEE Proceedings H*, 130(1):11–16, 1983.

6. O. De Jesús and M. T. Hagan. Backpropagation algorithms for a broad class of dynamic networks. *IEEE Transactions on Neural Networks*, 18(1):14–27, 2007.

7. R. F. H. Fischer. *Precoding and Signal Shaping for Digital transmission*. Wiley Online Library, 2002.

8. S. L. Goh and D. P. Mandic. A complex-valued rtrl algorithm for recurrent neural networks. *Neural Computation*, 16(12):2699–2713, 2004.

9. S. L. Goh and D. P. Mandic. An augmented extended kalman filter algorithm for complex-valued recurrent neural networks. *Neural Computation*, 19(4):1039–1055, 2007.

10. M. T. Hagan and M. B. Menhaj. Training feedforward networks with the marquardt algorithm. *IEEE Transactions on Neural Networks*, 5(6):989–993, 1994.

11. S. Haykin et al. *Kalman Filtering and Neural Networks*. Wiley Online Library, 2001.

12. S. Haykin and L. Li. Nonlinear adaptive prediction of nonstationary signals. *IEEE Transactions on Signal Processing*, 43(2):526–535, 1995.

13. R. E. Kalman. A new approach to linear filtering and prediction problems. *Journal of basic Engineering*, 82(Series D):35–45, 1960.

14. G. Kechriotis and E. S. Manolakos. Training fully recurrent neural networks with complex weights. *IEEE Transactions on Circuits and Systems II: Analog and Digital Signal Processing*, 41(3):235–238, 1994.

15. T. Kim and T. Adali. Approximation by fully complex multilayer perceptrons. *Neural Computation*, 15(7):1641–1666, 2003.

16. K. Kreutz-Delgado. The complex gradient operator and the cr-calculus. *Arxiv preprint arXiv:0906.4835*, 2009.

17. H. Li and T. Adali. Complex-valued adaptive signal processing using nonlinear functions. *EURASIP Journal on Advances in Signal Processing*, 2008:122, 2008.

18. H. Li and T. Adali. Algorithms for complex ml ica and their stability analysis using wirtinger calculus. *IEEE Transactions on Signal Processing*, 58(12):6156–6167, 2010.

19. D. P. Mandic and J. A. Chambers. *Recurrent Neural Networks for Prediction: Learning Algorithms, architectures and stability*. Wiley, Hoboken, NJ, 2001.

20. D. P. Mandic, S. Javidi, S. L. Goh, A. Kuh, and K. Aihara. Complex-valued prediction of wind profile using augmented complex statistics. *Renewable Energy*, 34(1):196–201, 2009.

21. F. D. Neeser and J. L. Massey. Proper complex random processes with applications to information theory. *IEEE Transactions on Information Theory*, 39(4):1293–1302, 1993.

22. Z. Nehari. *Introduction to Complex Analysis*. Allyn and Bacon, 1961.

23. T. Nitta. An extension of the back-propagation algorithm to complex numbers. *Neural Networks*, 10(8):1391–1415, 1997.

24. G. V. Puskorius and L. A. Feldkamp. Neurocontrol of nonlinear dynamical systems with kalman filter trained recurrent networks. *IEEE Transactions on Neural Networks*, 5(2):279–297, 1994.

25. R. Remmert. *Theory of Complex Functions*, vol. 122. Springer, Berlin, 1991.

26. R. Savitha, S. Suresh, and N. Sundararajan. A fully complex-valued radial basis function network and its learning algorithm. *International Journal of Neural Systems*, 19(4):253–267, 2009.

27. P. J. Schreier and L. L. Scharf. Second-order analysis of improper complex random vectors and processes. *IEEE Transactions on Signal Processing*, 51(3):714–725, 2003.

28. A. Van Den Bos. Complex gradient and hessian. In *Vision, Image and Signal Processing, IEE Proceedings*, vol. 141, IET, 1994, pp. 380–383.

29. P. J. Werbos. Backpropagation through time: what it does and how to do it. *Proceedings of the IEEE*, 78(10):1550–1560, 1990.

30. R. J. Williams and D. Zipser. Experimental analysis of the real-time recurrent learning algorithm. *Connection Science*, 1(1):87–111, 1989.

31. R. J. Williams and D. Zipser. A learning algorithm for continually running fully recurrent neural networks. *Neural Computation*, 1(2):270–280, 1989.

32. W. Wirtinger. Zur formalen theorie der funktionen von mehr komplexen veränderlichen. *Mathematische Annalen*, 97(1):357–375, 1927.

CHAPTER 5

QUATERNIONIC NEURAL NETWORKS FOR ASSOCIATIVE MEMORIES

Teijiro Isokawa[1], Haruhiko Nishimura[2], and Nobuyuki Matsui[1]

[1]Graduate School of Engineering, University of Hyogo, Hyogo, Japan
[2]Graduate School of Applied Informatics, University of Hyogo, Hyogo, Japan

This chapter presents associative memories by Hopfield neural networks based on quaternion. Quaternion is a four-dimensional hypercomplex number system, which has been extensively employed in the fields of robotics, control of satellites, computer graphics, and so on. One of the benefits by quaternions is that affine transformations in three-dimensional space can be compactly described; thus neural networks based on quaternion are expected to process four or three-dimensional data efficiently.

There are several types of discrete-time driven quaternionic Hopfield neural networks, such as discrete state, continuous state, and multi-valued state for the representation of neuronal state. The stability of each network is theoretically proven by showing that the energy decreases monotonically with respect to the change in neuron states. Several schemes for embedding patterns onto the network are also presented. In addition to the quaternionic version of the Hebbian learning scheme, we describe (a) the Projection rule for embedding non-orthogonal patterns and (b) Local iterative learning, which is an implementation of the Projection rule.

Complex-Valued Neural Networks: Advances and Applications. Edited by Akira Hirose
Copyright © 2013 The Institute of Electrical and Electronics Engineers, Inc.

5.1 INTRODUCTION

Processing multi-dimensional data is an important problem for neural networks. Typically, a single neuron can take only one real value as its input; thus a network should be configured so that several neurons are used for accepting multi-dimensional data. This type of configuration is sometimes unnatural in applications of neural networks to engineering problem, such as processing of acoustic signals and coordinates in the plane. A series of acoustic signals has its amplitude and frequency that should not be operated separately, and a coordinate in two dimensional space has two parameters (x, y), only either of which is less significant for representing a coordinate. Thus, complex number systems have been utilized to represent two-dimensional data elements as a single entity. Application of complex numbers to neural networks have been extensively investigated [11, 12, 35].

Complex values can treat two-dimensional data elements as a single entity. But what about data with more than two elements? Obviously, this problem can be solved by applying several real-valued or complex-valued neurons. However, following the same reasoning as in the case of complex numbers, it would be useful to introduce a number system with higher dimensions, a so-called hypercomplex number system.

Quaternion is a four-dimensional hypercomplex number system introduced by Hamilton [8, 9]. This number system has been extensively employed in several fields, such as modern mathematics, physics, control of satellites, computer graphics, and so on [32, 24, 13]. One of the benefits provided by quaternions is that affine transformations of geometric figures in three-dimensional spaces, especially spatial rotations, can be represented compactly and efficiently. Applying quaternions to the field of neural networks has been recently explored in an effort to naturally represent high-dimensional information, such as color and three-dimensional body coordinates, by a quaternionic neuron, rather than by complex-valued or real-valued neurons.

In this respect, there has been a growing number of studies concerning the use of quaternions in neural networks. Multilayer perceptron (MLP) models have been developed [33, 2, 3, 30]. The use of quaternion in MLP models has been demonstrated in several applications such as control problems [2], color image compression [30], color night vision [25, 14], and prediction of chaos circuits and winds [29, 38]. Other types of network models has also been explored, such as the computational ability of a single quaternionic neuron [34] and the existence condition of an energy function in continuous-time and continuous-state recurrent networks [39].

In this chapter, we present and explore higher-dimensional associative memories based on quaternionic Hopfield neural networks, based on the Refs. [17, 19, 18, 20, 15, 16]. There are several types of discrete-time driven models, such as discrete state, continuous state, and multi-valued state used to represent the neuronal state. For these models, stability conditions are theoretically proven by showing that the energy with respect to the network state decreases monotonically when the state of a neuron changes.

Several schemes for embedding patterns in a network are also considered. In addition to the quaternionic equivalent of the traditional Hebbian learning scheme, the Projection rule for embedding non-orthogonal patterns and the Local iterative learning rule, an implementation of the Projection rule, are also introduced.

5.2 QUATERNIONIC ALGEBRA

5.2.1 Definition of Quaternion

Quaternions form a class of hypercomplex numbers consisting of a real number and three imaginary numbers – i, j, and k. Formally, a quaternion number is defined as a vector x in a four-dimensional vector space,

$$x = x^{(e)} + x^{(i)}i + x^{(j)}j + x^{(k)}k \tag{5.1}$$

where $x^{(e)}$, $x^{(i)}$, $x^{(j)}$, and $x^{(k)}$ are real numbers. The division ring of quaternions, H, constitutes the four-dimensional vector space over the real numbers with bases $1, i, j$, and k. Equation (5.1) can also be written using 4-tuple or 2-tuple notation as

$$x = (x^{(e)}, x^{(i)}, x^{(j)}, x^{(k)}) = (x^{(e)}, \vec{x}) \tag{5.2}$$

where $\vec{x} = (x^{(i)}, x^{(j)}, x^{(k)})$. In this representation, $x^{(e)}$ is the scalar part of x, and $\vec{x}$ forms the vector part. The quaternion conjugate is defined as

$$x^* = (x^{(e)}, -\vec{x}) = x^{(e)} - x^{(i)}i - x^{(j)}j - x^{(k)}k \tag{5.3}$$

Quaternion bases satisfy the following identities,

$$i^2 = j^2 = k^2 = ijk = -1, \tag{5.4}$$

$$ij = -ji = k, \; jk = -kj = i, \; ki = -ik = j \tag{5.5}$$

known as the Hamilton rule. From these rules, it follows immediately that multiplication of quaternions is not commutative.

Next, we define the operations between quaternions $p = (p^{(e)}, \vec{p}) = (p^{(e)}, p^{(i)}, p^{(j)}, p^{(k)})$ and $q = (q^{(e)}, \vec{q}) = (q^{(e)}, q^{(i)}, q^{(j)}, q^{(k)})$. The addition and subtraction of quaternions are defined in a similar manner as for complex-valued numbers or vectors, i.e.,

$$p \pm q = (p^{(e)} \pm q^{(e)}, \vec{p} \pm \vec{q}) \tag{5.6}$$

$$= (p^{(e)} \pm q^{(e)}, p^{(i)} \pm q^{(i)}, p^{(j)} \pm q^{(j)}, p^{(k)} \pm q^{(k)}) \tag{5.7}$$

The product of p and q is determined by Eq. (5.5) as

$$pq = (p^{(e)}q^{(e)} - \vec{p} \cdot \vec{q}, \; p^{(e)}\vec{q} + q^{(e)}\vec{p} + \vec{p} \times \vec{q}) \tag{5.8}$$

where $\vec{p} \cdot \vec{q}$ and $\vec{p} \times \vec{q}$ denote the dot and cross products, respectively, between three-dimensional vectors $\vec{p}$ and $\vec{q}$. The conjugate of the product is given as

$$(pq)^* = q^* p^* \tag{5.9}$$

The quaternion norm of x, denoted by $|x|$, is defined as

$$|x| = \sqrt{xx^*} = \sqrt{x^{(e)2} + x^{(i)2} + x^{(j)2} + x^{(k)2}} \tag{5.10}$$

5.2.2   Phase Representation of Quaternion

A quaternion x represented in Cartesian form can be transformed into polar form. Among the possible ways to define the polar representation of a quaternion, we adopt the representation defined in Refs. [4, 5]. In this polar form representation, the parameters required for expressing x are the amplitude $|x|$, and three phase angles $-\pi \leq \varphi < \pi$, $-\pi/2 \leq \theta < \pi/2$, and $-\pi/4 \leq \psi \leq \pi/4$. A quaternion x in polar form can be represented as

$$x = |x|e^{i\varphi}e^{k\psi}e^{j\theta} \tag{5.11}$$

where

$$
\begin{aligned}
e^{i\varphi} &= \cos\varphi + i\sin\varphi, \\
e^{j\theta} &= \cos\theta + j\sin\theta, \\
e^{k\psi} &= \cos\psi + k\sin\psi
\end{aligned}
$$

For details about representing these phase angles in the Cartesian system, refer to Chapter 2 of Ref. [4].

5.2.3   Quaternionic Analyticity

It is important to introduce an analytic function (or differentiable function) to serve as the activation function in the neural network. This section describes the required analyticity of the function in the quaternionic domain, in order to construct activation functions for quaternionic neural networks.

The condition for differentiability of the quaternionic function f is given by

$$\frac{\partial f(x)}{\partial x^{(e)}} = -i\frac{\partial f(x)}{\partial x^{(i)}} = -j\frac{\partial f(x)}{\partial x^{(j)}} = -k\frac{\partial f(x)}{\partial x^{(k)}} \tag{5.12}$$

The analytic condition for the quaternionic function, called the Cauchy–Riemann–Fueter (CRF) equation, yields:

$$\frac{\partial f(x)}{\partial x^{(e)}} + i\frac{\partial f(x)}{\partial x^{(i)}} + j\frac{\partial f(x)}{\partial x^{(j)}} + k\frac{\partial f(x)}{\partial x^{(k)}} = 0 \tag{5.13}$$

This is an extension of the Cauchy–Riemann (CR) equations defined for the complex domain. However, only linear functions and constants satisfy the CRF equation [27, 28, 38].

An alternative approach to assure analyticity in the quaternionic domain has been explored [27, 28, 37]. This approach is called *local analyticity* and is distinguished from the standard analyticity, i.e., global analyticity. Below, we briefly summarize the results on local analyticity presented in Ref. [37].

A quaternion x can be alternatively represented as:

$$x = x^{(e)} + u_x r, \tag{5.14}$$

$$r = \sqrt{x^{(i)^2} + x^{(j)^2} + x^{(k)^2}}, \tag{5.15}$$

$$u_x = \frac{x^{(i)}i + x^{(j)}j + x^{(k)}k}{r} \tag{5.16}$$

From the definition in Eq. (5.16), we deduce that $u_x^2 = -1$. Thus, a quaternion x can be treated as a complex value in the plane spanned by u_x, and it can be represented in the local coordinate system by u_x.

A quaternion $dx = (dx^{(e)}, dx^{(i)}, dx^{(j)}, dx^{(k)})$ can be decomposed by using

$$dx = dx_\| + dx_\perp \tag{5.17}$$

where

$$dx_\| = \frac{1}{2}(dx - u_x dx u_x), \quad dx_\perp = \frac{1}{2}(dx + u_x dx u_x)$$

Then, the following relations hold:

$$dx_\| x = x dx_\|, \quad dx_\perp x = x^* dx_\perp$$

$F(x + dx)$ can be expanded using the abovementioned representations as

$$F(x + dx) = F(x) + F^{(1)} + F^{(2)} + O(dx^3) \tag{5.18}$$

where

$$F^{(1)} = F'(x) dx_\| + \frac{F(x) - F(x^*)}{(x - x^*)} dx_\perp,$$

$$F^{(2)} = \frac{1}{2}F''(x) dx_\|^2 + \frac{F(x) - F(x^*)}{(x - x^*)^2}(dx_\perp dx_\| - dx dx_\perp)$$

$$+ \frac{F'(x)}{x - x^*} dx dx_\perp + \frac{F'(x^*)}{x^* - x} dx_\perp dx_\|$$

When we set $dx_\perp = 0$, i.e., $dx + u_r dx u_r = 0$, which results in $u_\alpha dx = dx u_\alpha$. This leads to $u_x \times d\vec{x} = 0$, because u_x is a quaternion without a real part. Thus, u_x and $d\vec{x}$ are parallel to each other. Then, $d\vec{x} = \delta u_x$ can be obtained. From Eq. (5.15), it follows that

$$r dr = x^{(i)} dx^{(i)} + x^{(j)} dx^{(j)} + x^{(k)} dx^{(k)}$$
$$= \vec{x} \cdot d\vec{x}$$
$$= u_x r \cdot u_x \delta$$
$$= r \delta u_x \cdot u_x$$
$$= r \delta$$

Hence, dx is represented as $dx = dx_\| = dx^{(e)} + dr u_x$. By introducing the local derivative operators

$$\frac{\partial}{\partial x_\|} = \frac{1}{2}\left(\frac{\partial}{\partial x^{(e)}} - u_x \frac{\partial}{\partial x^{(r)}}\right),$$

$$\frac{\partial}{\partial x_\|^*} = \frac{1}{2}\left(\frac{\partial}{\partial x^{(e)}} + u_x \frac{\partial}{\partial x^{(r)}}\right)$$

where

$$\frac{\partial}{\partial x^{(r)}} \equiv \frac{x^{(i)}}{r}\frac{\partial}{\partial x^{(i)}} + \frac{x^{(j)}}{r}\frac{\partial}{\partial x^{(j)}} + \frac{x^{(k)}}{r}\frac{\partial}{\partial x^{(k)}}$$

with the properties

$$\frac{\partial x}{\partial x_{\parallel}} = \frac{\partial x^*}{\partial x_{\parallel}^*} = 1 \quad \text{and} \quad \frac{\partial x^*}{\partial x_{\parallel}} = \frac{\partial x}{\partial x_{\parallel}^*} = 0$$

the local derivative of $F(x)$ is written as

$$F'(x) = \frac{\partial F(x)}{\partial x_{\parallel}}$$

and the local analytic condition for the function $F(x)$ is given by

$$\frac{\partial F(x)}{\partial x_{\parallel}^*} = 0 \quad \text{i.e.,} \quad \frac{\partial F}{\partial x^{(e)}} + u_x \frac{\partial F}{\partial x^{(r)}} = 0$$

in the corresponding local complex plane. This result corresponds to the one presented in Ref. [28], where $dx_{\perp} = 0$ always holds.

Moreover, if F is a function with the two arguments, x and x^*, it becomes

$$F(x + dx, x^* + dx^*)$$

$$= F(x, x^*) + \frac{\partial F}{\partial x_{\parallel}} dx_{\parallel} + \frac{\partial F}{\partial x_{\parallel}^*} dx_{\parallel}^* + \frac{1}{2}\left(\frac{\partial^2 F}{\partial x_{\parallel}^2} dx_{\parallel}^2 + \frac{\partial}{\partial x_{\parallel}^*}\left(\frac{\partial F}{\partial x_{\parallel}}\right) dx_{\parallel} dx_{\parallel}^*\right.$$

$$\left. + \frac{\partial}{\partial x_{\parallel}}\left(\frac{\partial F}{\partial x_{\parallel}^*}\right) dx_{\parallel}^* dx_{\parallel} + \frac{\partial^2 F}{\partial x_{\parallel}^{*2}} dx_{\parallel}^{*2}\right) + O(dx_{\parallel}^3) \tag{5.19}$$

with x and x^* being independent each other. As a result, complex-valued functions can be used as activation functions in quaternionic domains.

5.3 STABILITY OF QUATERNIONIC NEURAL NETWORKS

We present formalisms for neural networks whose variables are encoded by quaternion numbers. We start with the quaternion-valued neuron model with bipolar states. Next, this model is extended to include continuous states. Another type of neuron model, called multistate neuron model, is also presented. For each neuron model presented, networks are constructed and their stability properties are shown.

5.3.1 Network with Bipolar State Neurons

Neuron Model. The action potential and output state of neuron p are defined as follows:

$$s_p = \sum_q w_{pq} x_q - \theta_p, \tag{5.20}$$

$$y_p = f(s_p) \tag{5.21}$$

where x, w_{pq}, and θ are the input to the neuron, connection weight from neuron q to neuron p, and threshold, respectively [17, 19].

The activation function f determines the output of the neuron. For bipolar state neurons, we define this function as

$$f(s) = f^{(e)}(s^{(e)}) + f^{(i)}(s^{(i)})i + f^{(j)}(s^{(j)})j + f^{(k)}(s^{(k)})k \qquad (5.22)$$

and use the same signum function for each component of the quaternionic function:

$$f^{(e)}(s) = f^{(i)}(s) = f^{(j)}(s) = f^{(k)}(s) = \begin{cases} 1 & \text{for } s \geq 0 \\ -1 & \text{for } s < 0 \end{cases} \qquad (5.23)$$

Energy Function. The neurons are fully connected as in the case of real-valued Hopfield neural networks. We introduce the energy function for a network with N neurons:

$$E = -\frac{1}{2}\sum_{p=1}^{N}\sum_{q=1}^{N} x_p^* w_{pq} x_q + Re\left(\sum_{p=1}^{N} \theta_p^* x_p\right) \qquad (5.24)$$

When $w_{pq} = w_{qp}^*$, E always becomes a real-valued function. This can be checked by showing $E^* = E$ as follows:

$$\begin{aligned} E^* &= -\frac{1}{2}\sum_{p=1}^{N}\sum_{q=1}^{N} x_q^* w_{pq}^* x_p + Re\left(\sum_{p=1}^{N} x_p^* \theta_p\right) \\ &= -\frac{1}{2}\sum_{p=1}^{N}\sum_{q=1}^{N} x_q^* w_{qp} x_p + Re\left(\sum_{p=1}^{N} \theta_p^* x_p\right) \\ &= E \end{aligned}$$

This network allows self-connections whose values take real numbers, $w_{pp} = w_{pp}^* = (w_{pp}^{(e)}, \vec{0})$, and are set to non-negative values, $w_{pp}^{(e)} \geq 0$.

Network Stability. The stability of the network can be proved by showing that the energy E of the network never increases with time when there is a change in the state of a neuron, as in the case of real-valued Hopfield networks. Let $E_r(t)$ be the contribution of a neuron r to energy E at time t in the network, given as

$$
\begin{aligned}
E_r(t) &= -\frac{1}{2}\left\{\left(\sum_{p=1}^{N} x_p^*(t)w_{pr}\right)x_r(t) + x_r^*(t)\left(\sum_{q=1}^{N} w_{rq}x_q(t)\right) - x_r^*(t)w_{rr}x_r(t)\right\} \\
&\quad + Re\left(\theta_r^* x_r(t)\right) \\
&= -\frac{1}{2}\left\{\left(\sum_{p=1}^{N} w_{rp}x_p(t)\right)^* x_r(t) + x_r^*(t)\left(\sum_{q=1}^{N} w_{rq}x_q(t)\right) - x_r^*(t)w_{rr}x_r(t)\right\} \\
&\quad + \frac{1}{2}\left(\theta_r^* x_r + x_r^*\theta_r\right) \\
&= -\frac{1}{2}\left\{\left(\sum_{p=1}^{N} w_{rp}x_p(t) - \theta_r\right)^* x_r(t) + x_r^*(t)\left(\sum_{q=1}^{N} w_{rq}x_q(t) - \theta_r\right)\right. \\
&\quad \left. - x_r^*(t)w_{rr}x_r(t)\right\}
\end{aligned}
$$

By considering the relation

$$
\begin{aligned}
x_r^*(t)w_{rr}x_r(t) &= w_{rr}^{(e)} \cdot x_r^*(t)x_r(t) \\
&= w_{rr}^{(e)} \cdot |x_r(t)|^2 = 4\dot{w}_{rr}^{(e)}
\end{aligned}
$$

and the action potential of the neuron r (Eq. (5.20)),

$$
\begin{aligned}
E_r(t) &= -\frac{1}{2}\left\{s_r^*(t)x_r(t) + x_r^*(t)s_r(t) - 4w_{rr}^{(e)}\right\} \\
&= -Re\left\{x_r^*(t)s_r(t)\right\} + 2w_{rr}^{(e)} \tag{5.25}
\end{aligned}
$$

is obtained. Now, suppose that the state of neuron r is updated at time $(t + 1)$ according to Eq. (5.20). Its contribution to E, $E_r(t + 1)$, becomes

$$
\begin{aligned}
E_r(t + 1) &= -Re\left\{x_r^*(t + 1)s_r(t + 1)\right\} + 2w_{rr}^{(e)} \\
&= -Re\left\{x_r^*(t + 1)\left(s_r(t) - w_{rr}\left(x_r(t) - x_r(t + 1)\right)\right)\right\} + 2w_{rr}^{(e)} \\
&= -Re\left\{x_r^*(t + 1)s_r(t)\right\} + w_{rr}^{(e)} \cdot Re\left\{x_r^*(t + 1)\left(x_r(t) - x_r(t + 1)\right)\right\} \\
&\quad + 2w_{rr}^{(e)}
\end{aligned}
$$

The difference between the energies at time $t + 1$ and t, denoted by ΔE, becomes

$$
\begin{aligned}
\Delta E &= E_r(t + 1) - E_r(t) \\
&= -\left(Re\left\{x_r^*(t + 1)s_r(t)\right\} - Re\left\{x_r^*(t)s_r(t)\right\}\right) \\
&\quad + w_{rr}^{(e)} \cdot Re\left\{x_r^*(t + 1)\left(x_r(t) - x_r(t + 1)\right)\right\} \tag{5.26}
\end{aligned}
$$

The activation function $\boldsymbol{f}(\boldsymbol{s})$ can be represented by using Eqs. (5.22) and (5.23) as

$$\boldsymbol{f}(\boldsymbol{s}) = \frac{s^{(e)}}{|s^{(e)}|} + \frac{s^{(i)}}{|s^{(i)}|}\boldsymbol{i} + \frac{s^{(j)}}{|s^{(j)}|}\boldsymbol{j} + \frac{s^{(k)}}{|s^{(k)}|}\boldsymbol{k}$$

The first term in Eq. (5.26) is then reduced to

$$
\begin{aligned}
&Re\left\{\boldsymbol{x}_r^*(t+1)\boldsymbol{s}_r(t)\right\} \\
=\ &Re\left\{\left(\boldsymbol{f}\left(\boldsymbol{s}_r(t)\right)\right)^* \boldsymbol{s}_r(t)\right\} \\
=\ &Re\left\{\left(\frac{s_r^{(e)}(t)}{|s_r^{(e)}(t)|} + \frac{s_r^{(i)}(t)}{|s_r^{(i)}(t)|}\boldsymbol{i} + \frac{s_r^{(j)}(t)}{|s_r^{(j)}(t)|}\boldsymbol{j} + \frac{s_r^{(k)}(t)}{|s_r^{(k)}(t)|}\boldsymbol{k}\right)^* \boldsymbol{s}_r(t)\right\} \\
=\ &\sum_{\alpha=\{e,i,j,k\}} |s_r^{(\alpha)}|
\end{aligned}
$$

The state of neurons takes bipolar values, i.e., $x^{\{(e),(i),(j),(k)\}} \in \{1,-1\}$, the following inequality holds:

$$
\begin{aligned}
\sum_{\alpha=\{e,i,j,k\}} |s_r^{(\alpha)}| &\geq \sum_{\alpha=\{e,i,j,k\}} s_r^{(\alpha)}(t) \cdot x_r^{(\alpha)}(t) \\
&= Re\left\{\boldsymbol{x}_r^*(t)\boldsymbol{s}_r(t)\right\}
\end{aligned} \tag{5.27}
$$

By considering all updated cases of $(x_r^{(\alpha)}(t), x_r^{(\alpha)}(t+1)) = (\pm1,\pm1), (\pm1,\mp1)$,

$$
\begin{aligned}
&Re\left\{\boldsymbol{x}_r^*(t+1)\left(\boldsymbol{x}_r(t) - \boldsymbol{x}_r(t+1)\right)\right\} \\
=\ &\sum_{\alpha=\{e,i,j,k\}} x_r^{(\alpha)}(t+1) \cdot \left(x_r^{(\alpha)}(t) - x_r^{(\alpha)}(t+1)\right) \\
\leq\ &0
\end{aligned} \tag{5.28}
$$

holds. From $w_{rr}^{(e)} \geq 0$ and the relations of Eqs. (5.27) and (5.28), it is shown that the energy never increases, i.e., $\Delta E \leq 0$.

5.3.2 Network with Continuous State Neurons

The neuron model with bipolar state is extended to include continuous state, by introducing other types of activation functions [18]. This section describes the analysis of two types of activation functions.

Neuron Model and Activation Functions. The action potential and output state of neuron are determined by Eqs. (5.20) and (5.21).

Two types of quaternionic functions for $\boldsymbol{f}$ are presented in this section. The first function, $\boldsymbol{f}_1$, is designed so that each quaternionic component is updated independently, and is defined as

$$\boldsymbol{f}_1(\boldsymbol{s}) = f_1^{(e)}(s^{(e)}) + f_1^{(i)}(s^{(i)})\boldsymbol{i} + f_1^{(j)}(s^{(j)})\boldsymbol{j} + f_1^{(k)}(s^{(k)})\boldsymbol{k} \tag{5.29}$$

where each real-valued function $f_1^{(\alpha)}$ $(\alpha = \{e, i, j, k\})$ is set to an identical function:

$$f_1^{(e)}(s) = f_1^{(i)}(s) = f_1^{(j)}(s) = f_1^{(k)}(s) = \tanh(s/\eta) \tag{5.30}$$

where η is a positive constant and called steepness parameter. This is a straightforward extension of the conventional updating scheme for real-valued neurons, and it is often used in the quaternionic MLP models [33, 2, 30].

The second quaternionic function $\boldsymbol{f}_2$ is an extension of the activation function proposed in Ref. [7] for the complex domain to the quaternionic domain, and is defined as

$$\boldsymbol{f}_2(\boldsymbol{s}) = \frac{a\boldsymbol{s}}{1 + |\boldsymbol{s}|} \tag{5.31}$$

where a is a real-valued constant.

Energy Function. For a network with N neurons, we introduce the energy function

$$\begin{aligned}
\boldsymbol{E}(t) =&\ -\frac{1}{2}\sum_{p=1}^{N}\sum_{q=1}^{N}\boldsymbol{x}_p^*(t)\boldsymbol{w}_{pq}\boldsymbol{x}_q(t) + \frac{1}{2}\sum_{p=1}^{N}\left(\boldsymbol{\theta}_p^*\boldsymbol{x}_p(t) + \boldsymbol{x}_p\boldsymbol{\theta}_p^*(t)\right) \\
&\ + \sum_{p=1}^{N} G(\boldsymbol{x}_p(t))
\end{aligned} \tag{5.32}$$

where $G(\boldsymbol{x}(t))$ is a scalar function that satisfies

$$\frac{\partial G(\boldsymbol{x})}{\partial x^{(\alpha)}} = g^{(\alpha)}(x^{(e)}, x^{(i)}, x^{(j)}, x^{(k)}) \quad (\alpha = \{e, i, j, k\}) \tag{5.33}$$

$\boldsymbol{g}(\boldsymbol{x})$ is the inverse function of $\boldsymbol{f}(\boldsymbol{x})$ and is defined as

$$\begin{aligned}
\boldsymbol{g}(\boldsymbol{x}) =&\ \boldsymbol{f}^{-1}(\boldsymbol{x}) \\
=&\ g^{(e)}(x^{(e)}, x^{(i)}, x^{(j)}, x^{(k)}) + g^{(i)}(x^{(e)}, x^{(i)}, x^{(j)}, x^{(k)})\boldsymbol{i} \\
&\ + g^{(j)}(x^{(e)}, x^{(i)}, x^{(j)}, x^{(k)})\boldsymbol{j} + g^{(k)}(x^{(e)}, x^{(i)}, x^{(j)}, x^{(k)})\boldsymbol{k}
\end{aligned} \tag{5.34}$$

This definition and Eq. (5.20) lead to the following relation:

$$\boldsymbol{s}_p(t) = \boldsymbol{f}^{-1}(\boldsymbol{x}_p(t+1)) = \boldsymbol{g}(\boldsymbol{x}_p(t+1)) \tag{5.35}$$

When we impose $\boldsymbol{w}_{pq} = \boldsymbol{w}_{qp}^*$ as the constraint of connection weights, $\boldsymbol{E} = \boldsymbol{E}^*$ always holds, thus $\boldsymbol{E}$ is a real-valued function. This network allows self-connections and their values take real numbers, $\boldsymbol{w}_{pp} = \boldsymbol{w}_{pp}^* = (w_{pp}^{(e)}, \vec{0})$.

Stability Analysis. We also show that the energy E of this network never increases with time when the state of a neuron changes, as is the case of the neuron model with bipolar state. Let $E_r(t)$ be the contribution of a neuron r to energy E at time t. Then $E_r(t)$ is given as

$$
\begin{aligned}
E_r(t) &= -\frac{1}{2}\left\{ \left(\sum_{p=1}^{N} x_p^*(t)w_{pr} \right) x_r(t) + x_r^*(t)\left(\sum_{q=1}^{N} w_{rq}x_q(t) \right) \right.\\
&\quad \left. - x_r^*(t)w_{rr}x_r(t) \right\} + \frac{1}{2}\left(\theta_r^* x_r(t) + x_r^*\theta_r(t) \right) + G\left(x_r(t) \right)\\
&= -\frac{1}{2}\left\{ \left(\sum_{p=1}^{N} w_{rp}x_p(t) - \theta_r \right)^* x_r(t) \right.\\
&\quad \left. + x_r^*(t)\left(\sum_{q=1}^{N} w_{rq}x_q(t) - \theta_r \right) - x_r^*(t)w_{rr}x_r(t) \right\}\\
&\quad + G\left(x_r(t) \right)
\end{aligned}
$$

By taking into consideration Eq. (5.20), we obtain

$$
\begin{aligned}
E_r(t) &= -\frac{1}{2}\left\{ s_r^*(t)x_r(t) + x_r^*(t)s_r(t) - x_r^*(t)w_{rr}x_r(t) \right\} + G\left(x_r(t) \right)\\
&= -Re\left\{ x_r^*(t)s_r(t) \right\} + \frac{1}{2}w_{rr}^{(e)}x_r^*(t)x_r(t) + G\left(x_r(t) \right) \qquad (5.36)
\end{aligned}
$$

Suppose that only the state of neuron r is asynchronously updated at time $(t+1)$ according to Eq. (5.20). Then, its contribution to energy E becomes

$$
\begin{aligned}
E_r(t+1) &= -Re\left\{ x_r^*(t+1)s_r(t+1) \right\} + \frac{1}{2}w_{rr}^{(e)}x_r^*(t+1)x_r(t+1)\\
&\quad + G\left(x, (t+1) \right)\\
&= -Re\left\{ x_r^*(t+1)\left(s_r(t) + w_{rr}\Delta x_r \right) \right\}\\
&\quad + \frac{1}{2}w_{rr}^{(e)}x_r^*(t+1)x_r(t+1) + G\left(x_r(t+1) \right)
\end{aligned}
$$

where $\Delta x_r = x_r(t+1) - x_r(t)$. The difference of the energy between time $t+1$ and t, ΔE, becomes

$$
\begin{aligned}
\Delta E &= E_r(t+1) - E_r(t)\\
&= -Re\left(\Delta x_r^* s_r(t) \right) - w_{rr}^{(e)} \cdot Re\left\{ x_r^*(t+1)\Delta x_r \right\}\\
&\quad + \frac{1}{2}w_{rr}^{(e)}x_r^*(t+1)x_r(t+1) - \frac{1}{2}w_{rr}^{(e)}x_r^*(t)x_r(t)\\
&\quad + G(x_r(t+1)) - G(x_r(t))\\
&= -Re\left(\Delta x_r^* s_r(t) \right) - \frac{1}{2}w_{rr}^{(e)}\Delta x_r^*\Delta x_r + G(x_r(t+1)) - G(x_r(t))\\
&= -Re\left(\Delta x_r^* s_r(t) \right) - \frac{1}{2}w_{rr}^{(e)}|\Delta x_r|^2 + G(x_r(t+1)) - G(x_r(t))
\end{aligned}
$$

$$(5.37)$$

$G(x_r(t))$ can be expanded around $x_r(t+1)$ by using Taylor's theorem as

$$G(x_r(t)) \;=\; G(x_r(t+1)) - \sum_\alpha \Delta x_r^{(\alpha)} \frac{\partial G}{\partial x_r^{(\alpha)}} \bigg|_{x^{(\alpha)}=x_r^{(\alpha)}(t+1)}$$

$$+ \sum_{\alpha,\beta} \Delta x_r^{(\alpha)} \Delta x_r^{(\beta)} \frac{\partial^2 G}{\partial x_r^{(\alpha)} \partial x_r^{(\beta)}} \bigg|_{\substack{x^{(\alpha)}=\phi^{(\alpha)}, \\ x^{(\beta)}=\phi^{(\beta)}}}$$

where $\phi^{(\alpha)}$ exists between $x_r^{(\alpha)}(t)$ and $x_r^{(\alpha)}(t+1)$. Hence, the difference of the energy can be written as

$$\Delta E \;=\; -Re\Big(\Delta x_r^* s_r(t)\Big) - \frac{1}{2} w_{rr}^{(e)} |\Delta x_r|^2$$

$$+ \sum_\alpha \Delta x_r^{(\alpha)} \frac{\partial G}{\partial x_r^{(\alpha)}} \bigg|_{x^{(\alpha)}=x_r^{(\alpha)}(t+1)}$$

$$- \sum_{\alpha,\beta} \Delta x_r^{(\alpha)} \Delta x_r^{(\beta)} \frac{\partial^2 G}{\partial x_r^{(\alpha)} \partial x_r^{(\beta)}} \bigg|_{\substack{x^{(\alpha)}=\phi^{(\alpha)}, \\ x^{(\beta)}=\phi^{(\beta)}}}$$

Considering Eqs. (5.33) and (5.35), ΔE is reduced to

$$\Delta E \;=\; -\frac{1}{2} w_{rr}^{(e)} |\Delta x_r|^2 - \sum_{\alpha,\beta} \Delta x^{(\alpha)} \Delta x_r^{(\beta)} \frac{\partial g^{(\beta)}}{\partial x^{(\alpha)}} \bigg|_{\substack{x^{(\alpha)}=\phi^{(\alpha)}, \\ x^{(\beta)}=\phi^{(\beta)}}}, \qquad (5.38)$$

First let us consider the case that function f_1 (Eq. (5.29)) being used as an activation function of neurons. The inverse function of f_1, denoted by g_1, is calculated as

$$g_1(x) \;=\; g_1^{(e)}(x^{(e)}) + g_1^{(i)}(x^{(i)})i + g_1^{(j)}(x^{(j)})j + g_1^{(k)}(x^{(k)})k,$$

$$g_1^{(\alpha)}(x) \;=\; \tanh^{-1} x = \frac{\eta}{2} \ln \frac{1+x}{1-x}$$

Then, Eq. (5.38) becomes

$$\Delta E \;=\; -\frac{1}{2} w_{rr}^{(e)} |\Delta x_r|^2 - \sum_\alpha (\Delta x_r^{(\alpha)})^2 \frac{\partial g^{(\alpha)}}{\partial x^{(\alpha)}}$$

$$=\; -\frac{1}{2} w_{rr}^{(e)} |\Delta x_r|^2 - \sum_\alpha (\Delta x_r^{(\alpha)})^2 \cdot \frac{\eta}{(1+\phi^{(\alpha)})(1-\phi^{(\alpha)})}$$

because $\partial g^{(\beta)}/\partial x^{(\alpha)} = 0$ for $\alpha \neq \beta$ and $\partial g^{(\alpha)}/\partial x^{(\alpha)} = \eta/(1+x^{(\alpha)})(1-x^{(\alpha)})$. Furthermore, due to

$$\min \frac{\eta}{(1+\phi^{(\alpha)})(1-\phi^{(\alpha)})} = \eta \quad (\text{at } \phi^{(\alpha)} = 0)$$

the following inequality holds:

$$\Delta E \quad < \quad -\frac{1}{2}w_{rr}^{(e)}\left|\Delta x_r\right|^2 - \eta\sum_{\alpha}(\Delta x_r^{(\alpha)})^2$$

$$= \quad -\left(\frac{1}{2}w_{rr}^{(e)} + \eta\right)\left|\Delta x_r\right|^2 \tag{5.39}$$

In the case of $\boldsymbol{f}_1$ as an activation function, the energy never increases if $w_{rr}^{(e)} > -2\eta$.

Next, let us consider the case of using $\boldsymbol{f}_2$ (Eq. (5.31)) as the activation function. In this case, the inverse of $\boldsymbol{f}_2$ is

$$\boldsymbol{g}_2(\boldsymbol{x}) \quad = \quad \frac{\boldsymbol{x}}{a - |\boldsymbol{x}|}$$

$$= \quad g_2^{(e)}(\boldsymbol{x}) + g_2^{(i)}(\boldsymbol{x})\boldsymbol{i} + g_2^{(j)}(\boldsymbol{x})\boldsymbol{j} + g_2^{(k)}(\boldsymbol{x})\boldsymbol{k}$$

where

$$g_2^{(\alpha)}(\boldsymbol{x}) \quad = \quad \frac{x^{(\alpha)}}{a - |\boldsymbol{x}|}$$

The differential of $g_2^{(\beta)}(\boldsymbol{x})$ ($\beta = \{e, i, j, k\}$) with respect to $x^{(\alpha)}$ is calculated as

$$\frac{\partial g_2^{(\beta)}}{\partial x^{(\alpha)}} = \begin{cases} \dfrac{x^{(\alpha)}x^{(\beta)}}{(a - |\boldsymbol{x}|)^2|\boldsymbol{x}|} & (\alpha \neq \beta) \\[3mm] \dfrac{a|\boldsymbol{x}| - \sum_{\gamma \neq \beta}x^{(\gamma)^2}}{(a - |\boldsymbol{x}|)^2|\boldsymbol{x}|} & (\alpha = \beta) \end{cases}$$

Thus, the difference of the energy (Eq. (5.38)) becomes

$$\Delta E = -\frac{1}{2}w_{rr}^{(e)}|\Delta x_r|^2 - \sum_{\alpha}(\Delta x^{(\alpha)})^2 \frac{a}{(a - |\phi^{(\alpha)}|)^2} \tag{5.40}$$

where $-a < \phi^{(\alpha)} < a$. The energy never increases under the condition $a > 0$, when the state of the neuron changes.

5.3.3 Network with Continuous State Neurons Having Local Analytic Activation Function

In the previous section, we presented two types of activation functions. These functions, however, are not analytic functions, whereas in real-valued neurons analytic and bounded functions are often used. This section presents a quaternionic neuron with a local analytic function as an activation function [16].

Neuron Model and Activation Function. The action potential is determined by Eq. (5.20). We adopt the quaternionic function *tanh* as activation function, which has been explored for the complex-valued neural networks [22]. The output of the neuron is

$$x(t+1) = f(s(t)) = \tanh(s(t)) \qquad (5.41)$$

and $f(s)$ is locally analytic ($dx_\perp = 0$) satisfying

$$\frac{\partial f}{\partial s_\parallel^*} = 0$$

Hereinafter the symbol $\parallel$ will be omitted.

Energy Function. The energy function of a network with N neurons is defined as

$$
\begin{aligned}
E(t) &= -\frac{1}{2}\sum_{p=1}^{N}\sum_{q=1}^{N} x_p^*(t) w_{pq} x_q(t) + \frac{1}{2}\sum_{p=1}^{N}\left(\theta_p^* x_p(t) + x_p^*(t)\theta_p\right) \\
&\quad + Re\left(\sum_{p=1}^{N} G(x_p(t), x_p^*(t))\right)
\end{aligned} \qquad (5.42)
$$

where $G(x(t), x^*(t))$ is a function that satisfies

$$G(x_p(t), x_p^*(t)) = \int_0^{x_p(t)} g^*(v)\, dv \qquad (5.43)$$

Here, $g(v)$ is the inverse function of $f(v)$, i.e. $g(v) = f^{-1}(v)$, and thus, using Eq. (5.41), the following relation holds:

$$s_p(t) = f^{-1}(x_p(t+1)) = g(x_p(t+1)) \qquad (5.44)$$

When tanh is used as the activation function, i.e., $f(s) = \tanh(s)$, the inverse function $g(x)$ is

$$g(x) = \frac{1}{2}\ln\frac{1+x}{1-x} \qquad (5.45)$$

Note that this function satisfies $g^*(x) = g(x^*)$.

It is always satisfied that E should be a real-valued function ($E = E^*$), by the condition imposed on the connection weight, $w_{pq} = w_{qp}^*$. This network allows self-connections whose values take real numbers, $w_{pp} = w_{pp}^* = (w_{pp}^{(e)}, \vec{0})$.

Stability Analysis. The difference of the energy between time $t+1$ and t, ΔE, can be deduced in a similar way to the one presented in the previous section, i.e.,

$$
\begin{aligned}
\Delta E &= E_r(t+1) - E_r(t) \\
&= -Re\left(\Delta x_r^* s_r(t)\right) - \frac{1}{2}w_{rr}^{(e)}|\Delta x_r|^2 \\
&\quad + Re(G(x_r(t+1), x_r^*(t+1))) - Re(G(x_r(t), x_r^*(t))) \qquad (5.46)
\end{aligned}
$$

$G(x_r(t), x_r^*(t))$ can be expanded around $(x_r(t+1), x_r^*(t+1))$ as

$$
\begin{aligned}
G(x_r&(t), x_r^*(t)) \\
&= G(x_r(t+1) - \Delta x_r, x_r^*(t+1) - \Delta x_r^*) \\
&= G(x_r(t+1), x_r^*(t+1)) + \frac{\partial G}{\partial x}(-\Delta x_r) + \frac{\partial G}{\partial x^*}(-\Delta x_r^*) \\
&+ \frac{1}{2}\left\{ \frac{\partial^2 G}{\partial x^2}(-\Delta x_r)^2 + \frac{\partial}{\partial x^*}\left(\frac{\partial G}{\partial x}\right)(-\Delta x_r)(-\Delta x_r^*) \right. \\
&\left. + \frac{\partial}{\partial x}\left(\frac{\partial G}{\partial x^*}\right)(-\Delta x_r^*)(-\Delta x_r) + \frac{\partial^2 G}{\partial x^{*2}}(-\Delta x_r^*)^2 \right\}
\end{aligned}
\tag{5.47}
$$

From Eqs. (5.44) and (5.45), the derivatives of G are

$$
\begin{aligned}
\frac{\partial G}{\partial x}\bigg|_{x=x_r(t+1)} &= g^*(x(t+1)) \\
&= g(x_r^*(t+1)) \\
&= s_r^*(t),
\end{aligned}
$$

$$
\frac{\partial G}{\partial x^*} = 0, \quad \frac{\partial}{\partial x}\left(\frac{\partial G}{\partial x^*}\right) = 0, \quad \frac{\partial^2 G}{\partial x^{*2}} = 0,
$$

$$
\frac{\partial}{\partial x^*}\left(\frac{\partial G}{\partial x}\right) = \frac{\partial s^*}{\partial x^*}, \quad \frac{\partial^2 G}{\partial x^2} = \frac{\partial s^*}{\partial x} = 0
$$

By substituting Eq. (5.47) into Eq. (5.46) with the above derivatives, we obtain

$$
\begin{aligned}
\Delta E &= -\frac{1}{2}w_{rr}^{(e)}|\Delta x_r|^2 - Re\left(\Delta x_r^* s_r(t)\right) + Re\left(s_r^*(t)\Delta x_r\right) \\
&- Re\left(\frac{1}{2}\frac{\partial s^*}{\partial x^*}\Delta x_r \Delta x_r^*\right)
\end{aligned}
$$

The second and third terms of this equation vanishes, and when the relation $\Delta x = \partial x/\partial s \cdot \Delta s$, where $\Delta s_r = s_r(t) - s_r(t-1)$, is considered, ΔE becomes:

$$
\Delta E = -\frac{1}{2}w_{rr}^{(e)}|\Delta x_r|^2 - \frac{1}{2}Re\left(\frac{\partial x}{\partial s}\right)|\Delta s_r|^2
\tag{5.48}
$$

The term $\partial x/\partial s$ is calculated with $s_r = s_r^{(e)} + r_s u_s$ as follows:

$$
\frac{\partial x}{\partial s} = \frac{1}{2}\left(\frac{\partial x}{\partial s^{(e)}} - \frac{\partial x}{\partial s^{(r)}}u_s\right)
\tag{5.49}
$$

By considering the condition of the CR equations due to the local analyticity, the following relation holds:

$$
\frac{\partial x}{\partial s^*} = \frac{1}{2}\left(\frac{\partial x}{\partial s^{(e)}} + \frac{\partial x}{\partial s^{(r)}}u_s\right)
$$

which leads to

$$\frac{\partial x}{\partial s^{(e)}} = -\frac{\partial x}{\partial s^{(r)}} u_s$$

Substituting this equation to Eq. (5.49), we obtain

$$\frac{\partial x}{\partial s} = \frac{\partial x}{\partial s^{(e)}}$$

When $x = x^{(e)} + x^{(i)}i + x^{(j)}j + x^{(k)}k$, the real part of $\partial x/\partial s$ becomes

$$
\begin{aligned}
Re\left(\frac{\partial x}{\partial s}\right) &= Re\left(\frac{\partial x}{\partial s^{(e)}}\right) \\
&= Re\left(\frac{\partial x^{(e)}}{\partial s^{(e)}} + \frac{\partial x^{(i)}}{\partial s^{(e)}}i + \frac{\partial x^{(j)}}{\partial s^{(e)}}j + \frac{\partial x^{(k)}}{\partial s^{(e)}}k\right) \\
&= \frac{\partial x^{(e)}}{\partial s^{(e)}}
\end{aligned}
$$

Finally, ΔE is reduced to

$$\Delta E = -\frac{1}{2}w_{rr}^{(e)}|\Delta x_r|^2 - \frac{\partial x^{(e)}}{\partial s^{(e)}}|\Delta s_r|^2 \qquad (5.50)$$

The *tanh* function with the argument s can be described by

$$\tanh(s) = \frac{\sinh(2s^{(e)})}{\cosh(2s^{(e)}) + \cos(2r_s)} + u_s\frac{\sinh(2r_s)}{\cosh(2s^{(e)}) + \cos(2r_s)}$$

then

$$\frac{\partial x^{(e)}}{\partial s^{(e)}} = \frac{d}{ds^{(e)}}\left(\frac{\sinh(2s^{(e)})}{\cosh(2s^{(e)}) + \cos(2r_s)}\right) = 2\frac{1 + \cosh(2s^{(e)})\cos(2r_s)}{(\cosh(2s^{(e)}) + \cos(2r_s))^2}$$

is obtained. The first and second terms of Eq. (5.50) take non-positive values under the conditions of $w_{rr}^{(e)} > 0$ and $-\pi/4 \leq r_s \leq \pi/4$, respectively. Thus these conditions are the stability conditions, i.e. $\Delta E \leq 0$.

5.3.4   Network with Multistate Neurons

This section describes another type of neuron models, called the phaser or multistate model. This type of neuron models has been extensively explored in the field of complex-valued neural networks [1, 10, 21, 31]. In these models, the phases and amplitudes of states in complex-valued neurons are utilized. Quaternionic multistate neuron model is an extension of the complex-valued ones [20], which also utilizes the phase and amplitude of a quaternion as its state.

Neuron Model.   In the multistate neuron, the state of a neuron p is represented in polar form with $|u_p| = 1$, i.e.,

$$
\begin{aligned}
u_p &= e^{i\varphi_p} e^{k\psi_p} e^{j\theta_p} \\
&= q^{(\varphi_p)} q^{(\psi_p)} q^{(\theta_p)}
\end{aligned}
\tag{5.51}
$$

where $q^{(\varphi)} = e^{i\varphi}$, $q^{(\psi)} = e^{k\psi}$, and $q^{(\theta)} = e^{j\theta}$. The action potential of neuron p at time t, $h_p(t)$, is defined as

$$
\begin{aligned}
h_p(t) &= \sum_q w_{pq} u_q(t) \\
&= \sum_q w_{pq} e^{i\varphi_q(t)} e^{k\psi_q(t)} e^{j\theta_q(t)} \\
&= \sum_q w_{pq} q^{(\varphi_q)}(t) q^{(\psi_q)}(t) q^{(\theta_q)}(t)
\end{aligned}
\tag{5.52}
$$

where $w_{pq} \in H$ denotes the connection weight from neuron q to neuron p.

As an activation function of a neuron, we employ the complex-valued multistate signum function introduced in [21], and extend it to the quaternionic domain. The state of neuron p at $(t + 1)$ is defined as

$$
u_p(t + 1) = qsign(h_p(t))
\tag{5.53}
$$

where

$$
qsign(u) = csign_A(q^{(\varphi)}) csign_B(q^{(\psi)}) csign_C(q^{(\theta)})
\tag{5.54}
$$

The update is conducted for each of components in u, i.e., $q^{(\varphi)}$, $q^{(\psi)}$, and $q^{(\theta)}$. Function $csign_A(\,\cdot\,)$ used for updating $q^{(\varphi)}$, is defined as

$$
csign_A(q^{(\varphi)}) \equiv
\begin{cases}
e^{i(-\pi + 0 \cdot \varphi_0)} = -e^0 \\
\quad \text{for } -\pi \le \arg q^{(\varphi)} < -\pi + \varphi_0 \\
-e^{i\varphi_0} \\
\quad \text{for } -\pi + \varphi_0 \le \arg q^{(\varphi)} < -\pi + 2\varphi_0 \\
-e^{i2\varphi_0} \\
\quad \text{for } -\pi + 2\varphi_0 \le \arg q^{(\varphi)} < -\pi + 3\varphi_0 \\
\quad \vdots \\
-e^{i(A-1)\varphi_0} \\
\quad \text{for } -\pi + (A - 1)\varphi_0 \le \arg q^{(\varphi)} < -\pi + A\varphi_0
\end{cases}
\tag{5.55}
$$

where φ_0 defines a quantized unit $\varphi_0 = 2\pi/A$. Thus the state of a neuron takes the quantized levels of A. The quaternionic signum functions $csign_B(\,\cdot\,)$ for $q^{(\psi)}$ and $csign_C(\,\cdot\,)$ for $q^{(\theta)}$ can be defined in a similar way, with considering the domains of

ψ and θ. They are defined as

$$
csign_B(q^{(\psi)}) \equiv
\begin{cases}
e^{k(-\frac{\pi}{4}+0\cdot\psi_0)} \\
\quad \text{for } -\frac{\pi}{4} \leq \arg q^{(\varphi)} < -\frac{\pi}{4} + \psi_0 \\
\quad \vdots \\
e^{k(-\frac{\pi}{4}+(B-1)\cdot\psi_0)} \\
\quad \text{for } -\frac{\pi}{4} + (B-1)\psi_0 \leq \arg q^{(\varphi)} \leq -\frac{\pi}{4} + B\psi_0
\end{cases}
\tag{5.56}
$$

and

$$
csign_C(q^{(\theta)}) \equiv
\begin{cases}
e^{j(-\frac{\pi}{2}+0\cdot\theta_0)} \\
\quad \text{for } -\frac{\pi}{2} \leq \arg q^{(\theta)} < -\frac{\pi}{2} + \theta_0 \\
\quad \vdots \\
e^{j(-\frac{\pi}{2}+(C-1)\cdot\theta_0)} \\
\quad \text{for } -\frac{\pi}{2} + (C-1)\theta_0 \leq \arg q^{(\theta)} < -\frac{\pi}{2} + C\theta_0
\end{cases}
\tag{5.57}
$$

where B and C are integers, and $\psi_0 = \pi/(2B)$ and $\theta_0 = \pi/C$ determine quantized levels.

Neurons are updated in an asynchronous manner with the condition that the components $q^{(\varphi)}$, $q^{(\psi)}$, and $q^{(\theta)}$ of a neuron are never updated simultaneously. The mechanism for updating the state of the r-th neuron in the network, at time t, is defined as

$$
u_p(t+1) =
\begin{cases}
q^{(\varphi_p)}(t)q^{(\psi_p)}(t)q^{(\theta_p)}(t) = u_p(t) & \text{for } p \neq r \\
q^{(\varphi_p)}(t)q^{(\psi_p)}(t+1)q^{(\theta_p)}(t+1) \\
\qquad\qquad \text{or} & \text{for } p = r \\
q^{(\varphi_p)}(t+1)q^{(\psi_p)}(t+1)q^{(\theta_p)}(t)
\end{cases}
\tag{5.58}
$$

Energy Function and Stability Analysis. The stability of the network can be investigated by introducing the energy function and by showing that the energy never increases when the state of the network changes, as shown in the previous sections. The energy function of a network consisting of N neurons is defined as

$$
E(t) = -\frac{1}{2}\sum_{p=1}^{N}\sum_{q=1}^{N} u_p^*(t) w_{pq} u_q(t)
\tag{5.59}
$$

When the connection weight $w_{pq} = w_{qp}^*$ is satisfied, E becomes a real-valued function ($E = E^*$). This network allows self-connections whose values take real numbers, $w_{pp} = w_{pp}^* = (w_{pp}^{(e)}, \vec{0})$, and are set to non-negative values, $w_{pp}^{(e)} \geq 0$.

Let $E_r(t)$ be the contribution of a given neuron r to energy E at time t. Thus, $E_r(t)$ is written as

$$
\begin{aligned}
E_r(t) &= -\frac{1}{2}\left\{\left(\sum_{p=1}^{N} u_p^*(t)w_{pr}\right) u_r(t) + u_r^*(t)\left(\sum_{q=1}^{N} w_{rq}u_q(t)\right)\right.\\
&\qquad \left. - u_r^*(t)w_{rr}u_r(t)\right\}\\
&= -\frac{1}{2}\left\{\left(\sum_{p=1}^{N} w_{rp}u_p(t)\right)^* u_r(t) + u_r^*(t)\left(\sum_{q=1}^{N} w_{rq}u_q(t)\right)\right.\\
&\qquad \left. - u_r^*(t)w_{rr}u_r(t)\right\}
\end{aligned}
\tag{5.60}
$$

By considering the relation in Eq. (5.52), along with

$$
\begin{aligned}
u_r^*(t)w_{rr}u_r(t) &= w_{rr}^{(e)} \cdot u_r^*(t)u_r(t)\\
&= w_{rr}^{(e)} \cdot |u_r(t)|^2 = w_{rr}^{(e)}
\end{aligned}
$$

we obtain

$$
\begin{aligned}
E_r(t) &= -\frac{1}{2}\left\{h_r^*(t)u_r(t) + u_r^*(t)h_r(t) - w_{rr}^{(e)}\right\}\\
&= -Re\left\{u_r^*(t)h_r(t)\right\} + \frac{1}{2}w_{rr}^{(e)}
\end{aligned}
\tag{5.61}
$$

Suppose that the state of the neuron r is updated at time $(t+1)$ according to Eq. (5.52). Its contribution to E changes to

$$
\begin{aligned}
E_r(t+1) &= -Re\left\{u_r^*(t+1)h_r(t+1)\right\} + \frac{1}{2}w_{rr}^{(e)}\\
&= -Re\left\{u_r^*(t+1)\right.\\
&\qquad \left.\left(h_r(t) - w_{rr}\left(u_r(t) - u_r(t+1)\right)\right)\right\} + \frac{1}{2}w_{rr}^{(e)}\\
&= -Re\left\{u_r^*(t+1)h_r(t)\right\}\\
&\qquad +w_{rr}^{(e)} \cdot Re\left\{u_r^*(t+1)\left(u_r(t) - u_r(t+1)\right)\right\} + \frac{1}{2}w_{rr}^{(e)}
\end{aligned}
$$

The difference between energies at time $t+1$ and t, ΔE, becomes

$$
\begin{aligned}
\Delta E &= E_r(t+1) - E_r(t)\\
&= -\left(Re\left\{u_r^*(t+1)h_r(t)\right\} - Re\left\{u_r^*(t)h_r(t)\right\}\right)\\
&\qquad +w_{rr}^{(e)} \cdot Re\left\{u_r^*(t+1)\left(u_r(t) - u_r(t+1)\right)\right\}\\
&= -(X_1 - X_2) + w_{rr}^{(e)} \cdot (X_3 - 1)
\end{aligned}
\tag{5.62}
$$

where

$$X_1 = Re\{u_r^*(t+1)h_r(t)\},$$
$$X_2 = Re\{u_r^*(t)h_r(t)\},$$
$$X_3 = Re\{u_r^*(t+1)u_r(t)\}$$

In order to decompose X_1, X_2, and X_3, we first investigate the relation between u_r and h_r. The state of neuron r at time $(t+1)$ is described as

$$u_r(t+1) = q^{(\varphi_r)}(t+1)q^{(\psi_r)}(t+1)q^{(\theta_r)}(t+1)$$
$$= e^{ia\varphi_0}q^{(\varphi_r)}(t)e^{kb\psi_0}q^{(\psi_r)}(t)e^{jc\theta_0}q^{(\theta_r)}(t) \quad (5.63)$$

where a, b, and c are integers, and $a = 0$ or $c = 0$, due to the scheme of updating the neuron state (Eq. (5.58)). Let $\Delta\varphi$, $\Delta\psi$, and $\Delta\theta$ be the phase shifts of components φ, ψ, and θ, respectively, the action potential of neuron r at time t can be calculated from the neuron state at time $(t+1)$ as

$$h_r(t) = |h_r(t)|e^{i\Delta\varphi}q^{(\varphi_r)}(t+1)e^{k\Delta\psi}q^{(\psi_r)}(t+1)e^{j\Delta\theta}q^{(\theta_r)}(t+1)$$
$$= |h_r(t)|e^{i(a\varphi_0+\Delta\varphi)}q^{(\varphi_r)}(t)e^{k(a\psi_0+\Delta\psi)}q^{(\psi_r)}(t)e^{j(a\theta_0+\Delta\theta)}q^{(\theta_r)}(t)$$
$$(5.64)$$

Here we introduce the assumption that the phase shifts are not large enough to surpass a sector of a unit circle, i.e., $|\Delta\varphi| < \varphi_0$, $|\Delta\psi| < \psi_0$, and $|\Delta\theta| < \theta_0$.

Let us consider to extract the term X_3:

$$u_r^*(t+1)u_r(t) = \left(e^{ia\varphi_0}q^{(\varphi_r)}(t)e^{kb\psi_0}q^{(\psi_r)}(t)e^{jc\theta_0}q^{(\theta_r)}(t)\right)^*$$
$$q^{(\varphi_r)}(t)q^{(\psi_r)}(t)q^{(\theta_r)}(t)$$
$$= e^{-i(c\theta_0+\theta_r)}e^{-kb\psi_0}e^{-k\psi_r}e^{-ia\varphi_0}e^{k\psi_r}e^{j\theta_r}$$

By the relation $e^{-k\psi}e^{i\varphi}e^{k\psi} = \cos\varphi + e^{-k2\psi}i\sin\varphi$, the right-hand side of this equation can be decomposed as

$$e^{-i(c\theta_0+\theta_r)}e^{-kb\psi_0}e^{-k\psi_r}e^{-ia\varphi_0}e^{k\psi_r}e^{j\theta_r}$$
$$= \cos(-a\varphi_0)e^{-j(c\theta_0+\theta_r)}e^{-kb\psi_0}e^{j\theta_r}$$
$$+e^{-j(c\theta_0+\theta_r)}e^{-k(b\psi_0+2\psi_r)}e^{-j}(-i\sin(-a\varphi_0))$$

Thus X_3 becomes

$$X_3 = \cos(c\theta_0)\cos(b\psi_0)\cos(a\varphi_0) - \sin(c\theta_0)\sin(b\psi_0+2\psi_r)\sin(a\varphi_0) \quad (5.65)$$

The second term on the right-hand side of Eq. (5.65) can be omitted when either $a = 0$ or $c = 0$, due to the updating scheme of the state of the neurons (see Eq. (5.63)). Thus, we obtain $X_3 = \cos(c\theta_0)\cos(b\psi_0) \le 1$ for $a = 0$, or $X_3 = \cos(b\psi_0)\cos(a\varphi_0) \le 1$.

Next, let us consider to extract X_1 and X_2. These terms can be decomposed in a similar way to decompose X_3:

$$
\begin{aligned}
X_1 &= Re\{u_r^*(t+1)h_r(t)\} \\
&= Re\Big\{e^{-\boldsymbol{j}(c\theta_0+\theta_r)}e^{-\boldsymbol{k}(b\psi_0+\psi_r)}e^{-\boldsymbol{i}(a\varphi_0+\varphi_r)} \\
&\quad \cdot |h_r(t)| \cdot e^{\boldsymbol{i}(a\varphi_0+\varphi_r+\Delta\varphi)}e^{\boldsymbol{k}(b\psi_0+\psi_r+\Delta\psi)}e^{\boldsymbol{j}(c\theta_0+\theta_r+\Delta\theta)}\Big\} \quad (5.66)
\end{aligned}
$$

$$
\begin{aligned}
&= \cos(\Delta\theta)\cos(\Delta\psi)\cos(\Delta\varphi) \\
&\quad - \sin(\Delta\theta)\sin(2b\psi_0+2\psi_r+\Delta\psi)\cdot\sin(\Delta\varphi), \quad\quad\quad (5.67)
\end{aligned}
$$

$$
\begin{aligned}
X_2 &= \cos(c\theta_0+\Delta\theta)\cos(b\psi_0+\Delta\psi)\cos(a\varphi_0+\Delta\varphi) \\
&\quad - \sin(c\theta_0+\Delta\theta)\sin(b\psi_0+2\psi_r+\Delta\psi)\sin(a\varphi_0+\Delta\varphi) \quad (5.68)
\end{aligned}
$$

The second term on the right-hand side of these equations can be omitted when $a = 0$ or $c = 0$, because $\Delta\varphi = 0$ (or $\Delta\theta = 0$) means that the component φ (or θ, resp.) of the state of the neuron has not been updated. Finally, $X_1 - X_2$ becomes

$$
\begin{aligned}
&X_1 - X_2 \\
&= \begin{cases} \cos(\Delta\theta)\cos(\Delta\varphi) - \cos(c\theta_0+\Delta\theta)\cos(b\psi_0+\Delta\psi) & (\text{for } a=0, \Delta\varphi=0) \\[2mm] \cos(\Delta\psi)\cos(\Delta\varphi) - \cos(b\psi_0+\Delta\psi)\cos(b\varphi_0+\Delta\varphi) & (\text{for } c=0, \Delta\theta=0) \end{cases}
\end{aligned}
$$
$$(5.69)$$

$X_1 - X_2$ becomes positive or zero in either case when $|\Delta\varphi| < \varphi_0$, $|\Delta\psi| < \psi_0$, and $|\Delta\theta| < \theta_0$ hold.

Let us recall the difference of the energy caused by the change of the state of neuron r. The first term of Eq. (5.62) becomes negative or zero, due to $(X_1 - X_2) \le 0$. The second term of this equation also takes a negative or zero value when we set $w^{(e)} \ge 0$. As a result we obtain $\Delta E \le 0$, indicating that the energy of the network never increases when the state of the network changes, thus proving the stability of the network.

Condition for Embedding Patterns.   This section describes the required condition for each desired memory pattern to be a stable point in this network. A quaternionic pattern vector is set to

$$
\epsilon_p^\mu = |\epsilon_p^\mu|e^{\boldsymbol{i}\xi_{\varphi_p}^\mu}e^{\boldsymbol{k}\xi_{\psi_p}^\mu}e^{\boldsymbol{j}\xi_{\theta_p}^\mu}
$$

where $\xi_{\varphi_p}^\mu$, $\xi_{\psi_p}^\mu$, and $\xi_{\theta_p}^\mu$ are

$$
\begin{aligned}
\xi_{\varphi_p}^\mu &\in \{0, \dots, A-1\}, \\
\xi_{\psi_p}^\mu &\in \{0, \dots, B-1\}, \\
\xi_{\theta_p}^\mu &\in \{0, \dots, C-1\}
\end{aligned}
\quad (5.70)
$$

A pattern ϵ_p^μ represents a stable configuration of the network, if the relation

$$u_p(t+1) = u_p(t) = \epsilon_p^\mu \tag{5.71}$$

holds for every neuron p. This condition can be described by the phase relations as follows:

$$
\begin{aligned}
\xi_{\varphi_p}^\mu \varphi_0 &\leq \arg(h^{(\varphi_p)}) + \tfrac{\varphi_0}{2} < \xi_{\varphi_p}^\mu \varphi_0 + \varphi_0, \\
\xi_{\psi_p}^\mu \psi_0 &\leq \arg(h^{(\psi_p)}) + \tfrac{\psi_0}{2} < \xi_{\psi_p}^\mu \psi_0 + \psi_0, \\
\xi_{\theta_p}^\mu \theta_0 &\leq \arg(h^{(\theta_p)}) + \tfrac{\theta_0}{2} < \xi_{\theta_p}^\mu \theta_0 + \theta_0
\end{aligned}
\tag{5.72}
$$

where h_p is represented as $h_p = |h_p| e^{i\varphi^{(h)}} e^{i\psi^{(h)}} e^{i\theta^{(h)}} = |h_p| h^{(\varphi_p)} h^{(\psi_p)} h^{(\theta_p)}$. Thus, the relations of Eq. (5.72) become

$$
\begin{aligned}
|\arg(h^{(\varphi_p)}) - \xi_{\varphi_p}^\mu \varphi_0| &< \tfrac{\varphi_0}{2}, \\
|\arg(h^{(\psi_p)}) - \xi_{\psi_p}^\mu \psi_0| &< \tfrac{\psi_0}{2}, \\
|\arg(h^{(\theta_p)}) - \xi_{\theta_p}^\mu \theta_0| &< \tfrac{\theta_0}{2}
\end{aligned}
\tag{5.73}
$$

Furthermore, in the case of multistate networks, greater stability can be achieved by introducing the threshold parameters κ_φ, κ_ψ, and κ_θ such that

$$
\begin{aligned}
|\arg(h^{(\varphi_p)}) - \xi_{\varphi_p}^\mu \varphi_0| &< \kappa_\varphi < \tfrac{\varphi_0}{2}, \\
|\arg(h^{(\psi_p)}) - \xi_{\psi_p}^\mu \psi_0| &< \kappa_\psi < \tfrac{\psi_0}{2}, \\
|\arg(h^{(\theta_p)}) - \xi_{\theta_p}^\mu \theta_0| &< \kappa_\theta < \tfrac{\theta_0}{2}
\end{aligned}
\tag{5.74}
$$

5.4 LEARNING SCHEMES FOR EMBEDDING PATTERNS

5.4.1 Hebbian Rule

We introduce a quaternion equivalent of the Hebbian rule for embedding patterns in the network [17, 18, 15]. The Hebbian rule is defined as

$$w_{pq} = \frac{1}{4N} \sum_{\mu=1}^{n_p} \epsilon_p^\mu \epsilon_q^{\mu*} \tag{5.75}$$

where ϵ_p^μ represents the pattern vector for neuron p in the μ-th pattern and n_p is the number of stored patterns. This form satisfies the conditions $w_{pq} = w_{qp}^*$ and $w_{pp} \geq 0$ as shown below:

$$w_{qp}^* = \frac{1}{4N} \sum_{\mu=1}^{n_p} \left(\epsilon_q^\mu \epsilon_p^{\mu*} \right)^* = \frac{1}{4N} \sum_{\mu=1}^{n_p} \epsilon_p^\mu \epsilon_q^{\mu*} = w_{pq}$$

and

$$w_{pp} = \frac{1}{4N} \sum_{\mu=1}^{n_p} \epsilon_p^\mu \epsilon_p^{\mu*} = \frac{1}{4N} \sum_{\mu=1}^{n_p} |\epsilon_p^\mu|^2 = \frac{n_p}{N} > 0$$

Using the weight matrix of Eq. (5.75), each ϵ_μ is a fixed point when orthogonality among the patterns ϵ_μ is satisfied, i.e., for $\mu, \nu = 1, \dots, n_p$,

$$\sum_{q=1}^{N} \epsilon_q^{\mu *} \epsilon_q^{\nu} = 4N\delta_{\mu,\nu} = 4N(\delta_{\mu,\nu}^{(e)}, \vec{0}), \tag{5.76}$$

where $\delta_{\mu,\nu}^{(e)}$ denotes the Kronecker delta. This property can be verified by applying a stored pattern ϵ^ν as the input to the network. For neuron p, the action potential s_p is calculated as

$$
\begin{aligned}
s_p &= \sum_{q=1}^{N} w_{pq} \epsilon_q^{\nu} \\
&= \frac{1}{4N} \sum_{q=1}^{N} \left(\sum_{\mu=1}^{n_p} \epsilon_p^{\mu} \epsilon_q^{\mu *} \right) \epsilon_q^{\nu} \\
&= \frac{1}{4N} \sum_{\mu=1}^{n_p} \epsilon_p^{\mu} \sum_{q=1}^{N} \epsilon_q^{\mu *} \epsilon_q^{\nu} \\
&= \frac{1}{4N} \sum_{\mu=1}^{n_p} \epsilon_p^{\mu} 4N\delta_{\mu,\nu} \\
&= \epsilon_p^{\nu}
\end{aligned}
$$

The output of this neuron is obtained by applying the activation function,

$$x_p = f(s_p) = f(\epsilon_p^{\nu}) = \epsilon_p^{\nu}$$

5.4.2 Projection Rule

A major limitation of the Hebbian rule is that it works only when patterns ϵ satisfy the condition described in Eq. (5.76). This means that the patterns to be embedded in the network must be orthogonal to each other. However, the patterns provided in most cases are non-orthogonal.

The Projection rule [23, 36, 26] is a learning scheme that can embed non-orthogonal patterns in a network. The key idea of the Projection rule is that non-orthogonal patterns are first projected onto orthogonal ones, and then the Hebbian rule is applied to the projected patterns [15]. Projection is conducted by introducing the matrix $\{Q_{\mu\nu}\}$, defined as

$$Q_{\mu\nu} = \frac{1}{N} \sum_{p} \epsilon_p^{\mu *} \epsilon_p^{\nu} \tag{5.77}$$

The weight matrix of the network, $\tilde{w}$, is calculated by

$$\tilde{w}_{pq} = \frac{1}{N} \sum_{\mu,\nu} \epsilon_p^{\mu} \left(Q^{-1} \right) \epsilon_q^{\nu *} \tag{5.78}$$

where Q^{-1} is the pseudo inverse matrix of Q.

Patterns embedded by this scheme become stable points in the network, as in the case of the Hebbian rule. This can be checked by calculating the action potential of a neuron by applying an embedded pattern as the input to the network, as

$$
\begin{aligned}
\tilde{s}_p &= \sum_{q=1}^{N} \tilde{w}_{pq} \epsilon_q^\sigma \\
&= \frac{1}{N} \sum_{\mu,\nu} \epsilon_p^\mu \left(Q^{-1}\right)_{\mu\nu} \sum_q \epsilon^{\nu*} \epsilon_q^\sigma \\
&= \sum_{\mu,\nu} \epsilon_p^\mu \left(Q^{-1}\right)_{\mu\nu} Q_{\nu\sigma} \\
&= \sum_\mu \epsilon_p^\mu \left(Q^{-1}Q\right)_{\mu\sigma} \\
&= \sum_\mu \epsilon_p^\mu \delta_{\mu\sigma} \\
&= \epsilon_p^\sigma
\end{aligned}
\tag{5.79}
$$

5.4.3   Iterative Learning for Quaternionic Multistate Neural Network

A Local iterative learning scheme [6] is an implementation of the projection rule. The connection weights of the network in this scheme are formed by iteratively presenting the desired memory patterns. This scheme allows easy implementation of pattern storage and to control the depth of basins for each local minimum.

The quaternionic version of the iterative learning scheme [15] are formulated in the multistate networks:

$$
\begin{aligned}
w_{pq}^{new} &= w_{pq}^{old} + \delta w_{pq}, \tag{5.80} \\
\delta w_{pq} &= \frac{1}{N} \epsilon_p^\mu \epsilon_q^{\mu*} \tag{5.81}
\end{aligned}
$$

After the update, the action potential is described as

$$
\begin{aligned}
h_p^{new} &= \sum_q w_{pq}^{new} u_q \\
&= \sum_q \left(w_{pq}^{old} + \delta w_{pq}\right) u_q \\
&= h_p^{old} + \sum_q \delta w_{pq} u_q \tag{5.82}
\end{aligned}
$$

In the above equation, when $u_q = \epsilon_q^\mu$, we obtain

$$
h_p^{new} = h_p^{old} + \epsilon_p^\mu \tag{5.83}
$$

After $(L+1)$ updates, Eq. (5.83) takes the form

$$h_p^{(L+1)} = h_p^0 + (L+1)\epsilon_p^\mu \tag{5.84}$$

This equation can be expressed as

$$|h_p^{(L+1)}|e^{i(\varphi^{(L+1)})}e^{k(\psi^{(L+1)})}e^{j(\theta^{(L+1)})}$$
$$= |h_p^0|e^{i\varphi^0}e^{k\psi^0}e^{j\theta^0} + (L+1)|\epsilon_p^\mu|e^{i\xi_{\varphi_p}^\mu \varphi_0}e^{k\xi_{\psi_p}^\mu \psi_0}e^{j\xi_{\theta_p}^\mu \theta_0}$$

Note that the definitions of ξ^μs are in Eq. (5.70). By multiplying $e^{-i\xi_{\varphi_p}^\mu \varphi_0}$ on the left-hand side and $e^{-j\xi_{\theta_p}^\mu \theta_0}e^{-k\xi_{\psi_p}^\mu \psi_0}$ on the right-hand side, we obtain

$$|h_p^{(L+1)}|e^{i(\varphi^{(L+1)}-\xi_{\varphi_p}^\mu \varphi_0)}e^{k(\psi^{(L+1)}-\xi_{\psi_p}^\mu \psi_0)}e^{j(\theta^{(L+1)}-\xi_{\theta_p}^\mu \theta_0)}$$
$$-|h_p^{(L+1)}|e^{i(\varphi^{(L+1)}-\xi_{\varphi_p}^\mu \varphi_0)}e^{k\psi^{(L+1)}}2i\sin\left(\theta^{(L+1)}-\xi_{\theta_p}^\mu \theta_0\right)\sin\left(\xi_{\psi_p}^\mu \psi_0\right)$$
$$= |h_p^0|e^{i(\varphi^0-\xi_{\varphi_p}^\mu \varphi_0)}e^{k(\psi^0-\xi_{\psi_p}^\mu \psi_0)}e^{j(\theta^0-\xi_{\theta_p}^\mu \theta_0)}$$
$$-|h_p^0|e^{i(\varphi^0-\xi_{\varphi_p}^\mu \varphi_0)}e^{k\psi^0}2i\sin\left(\theta^0-\xi_{\theta_p}^\mu \theta_0\right)\sin\left(\xi_{\psi_p}^\mu \psi_0\right) + (L+1)|\epsilon_p^\mu|$$

Note that, due to the noncommutability of $e^{k\varphi}$ and $e^{j\theta}$, an additional term appears in this equation, which never appears in the complex-valued multistate networks. From the real part of the left-hand side of Eq. (5.85), we obtain

$$|h_p^{(L+1)}|\left(\cos(\varphi_p^{(L+1)}-\xi_{\varphi_p}^\mu \varphi_0)\cdot\cos(\psi_p^{(L+1)}-\xi_{\psi_p}^\mu \psi_0)\right.$$
$$\cdot\cos(\theta_p^{(L+1)}-\xi_{\theta_p}^\mu \theta_0)+\sin(\varphi_p^{(L+1)}-\xi_{\varphi_p}^\mu \varphi_0)$$
$$\cdot\sin(\psi_p^{(L+1)}-\xi_{\psi_p}^\mu \psi_0)\cdot\sin(\theta_p^{(L+1)}-\xi_{\theta_p}^\mu \theta_0)$$
$$+2\sin(\varphi_p^{(L+1)}-\xi_{\varphi_p}^\mu \varphi_0)\cdot\cos(\psi_p^{(L+1)})$$
$$\left.\cdot\sin(\theta_p^{(L+1)}-\xi_{\theta_p}^\mu \theta_0)\cdot\sin(\xi_{\psi_p}^\mu \psi_0)\right)$$
$$= |h_p^{(L+1)}|X_1$$

Similarly, from the right-hand side of Eq. (5.85), we obtain

$$|h_p^0|\left(\cos(\varphi_p^0-\xi_{\varphi_p}^\mu \varphi_0)\cdot\cos(\psi_p^0-\xi_{\psi_p}^\mu \psi_0)\right.$$
$$\cdot\cos(\theta_p^0-\xi_{\theta_p}^\mu \theta_0)+\sin(\varphi_p^0-\xi_{\varphi_p}^\mu \varphi_0)\cdot\sin(\psi_p^0-\xi_{\psi_p}^\mu \psi_0)$$
$$\cdot\sin(\theta_p^0-\xi_{\theta_p}^\mu \theta_0)+\sin(\varphi_p^0-\xi_{\varphi_p}^\mu \varphi_0)\cdot\cos(\psi_p^0)$$
$$\left.\cdot 2\sin(\theta_p^0-\xi_{\theta_p}^\mu \theta_0)\cdot\sin(\xi_{\psi_p}^\mu \psi_0)\right) + (L+1)|\epsilon_p^\mu|$$
$$= |h_p^0|X_2 + (L+1)|\epsilon_p^\mu|$$

Due to $|h_p^{(L+1)}|X_1 = |h_p^0|X_2 + (L+1)|\epsilon_p^\mu|$, the following relation holds:

$$X_1 = \frac{|h_p^0|X_2 + (L+1)|\epsilon_p^\mu|}{|h_p^{(L+1)}|} \tag{5.85}$$

When

$$\left||h_p^0| - (L+1)|\epsilon_p^\mu|\right| < |h_p^{L+1}| < |h_p^0| + (L+1)|\epsilon_p^\mu| \tag{5.86}$$

holds, Eq. (5.85) satisfies the relation

$$\frac{|h_p^0|X_2 + (L+1)|\epsilon_p^\mu|}{\left||h_p^0| - (L+1)|\epsilon_p^\mu|\right|} > X_1 > \frac{|h_p^0|X_2 + (L+1)|\epsilon_p^\mu|}{|h_p^0| + (L+1)|\epsilon_p^\mu|} \tag{5.87}$$

For large values of L,

$$\frac{|h_p^0|X_2 + (L+1)|\epsilon_p^\mu|}{\left||h_p^0| - (L+1)|\epsilon_p^\mu|\right|} \simeq \frac{(L+1)|\epsilon_p^\mu|}{(L+1)|\epsilon_p^\mu|} = 1,$$

$$\frac{|h_p^0|X_2 + (L+1)|\epsilon_p^\mu|}{|h_p^0| + (L+1)|\epsilon_p^\mu|} \simeq \frac{(L+1)|\epsilon_p^\mu|}{(L+1)|\epsilon_p^\mu|} = 1$$

Thus, from Eq. (5.87), it can be found that $X_1 \approx 1$ for large values of L. The case $X_1 = 1$ is obtained when the following relations hold:

$$\cos(\varphi_p^{(L+1)} - \xi_{\varphi_p}^\mu \varphi_0) = 1 \quad (\sin(\varphi_p^{(L+1)} - \xi_{\varphi_p}^\mu \varphi_0) = 0),$$

$$\cos(\psi_p^{(L+1)} - \xi_{\psi_p}^\mu \psi_0) = 1 \quad (\sin(\psi_p^{(L+1)} - \xi_{\psi_p}^\mu \psi_0) = 0),$$

$$\cos(\theta_p^{(L+1)} - \xi_{\theta_p}^\mu \theta_0) = 1 \quad (\sin(\theta_p^{(L+1)} - \xi_{\theta_p}^\mu \theta_0) = 0)$$

Thus, we obtain

$$\left|\arg(h^{(\varphi_p)\,L+1}) - \xi_{\varphi_p}^\mu \varphi_0\right| < \left|\arg(h^{(\varphi_p)\,0}) - \xi_{\varphi_p}^\mu \varphi_0\right|,$$

$$\left|\arg(h^{(\psi_p)\,L+1}) - \xi_{\psi_p}^\mu \psi_0\right| < \left|\arg(h^{(\psi_p)\,0}) - \xi_{\psi_p}^\mu \psi_0\right|,$$

$$\left|\arg(h^{(\theta_p)\,L+1}) - \xi_{\theta_p}^\mu \theta_0\right| < \left|\arg(h^{\theta_p\,0}) - \xi_{\theta_p}^\mu \theta_0\right| \tag{5.88}$$

In the case of multistate networks, it can be shown that the desired patterns in the network become stable when the condition in Eq. (5.74) is satisfied by iteratively updating the connection weights.

5.5 CONCLUSION

This chapter describes three quaternionic neural networks that are Hopfield-type recurrent neural networks, whose parameters are encoded by quaternions.

As in the case of complex-valued neuron models, two types of neuron models exist. One model uses a quaternion for a neuron state. The bipolar-state and continuous-state neurons in this chapter adopt this type of neuron model. The other model, termed multistate neuron, utilizes a phaser representation of quaternions. A quaternion is represented by three kinds of phases and an amplitude. Thus, the multistate quaternionic neuron presented in this chapter attains three degrees of freedom.

All networks in this chapter are shown to work as associative memories, i.e., the network state eventually reaches an embedded state. We prove this by defining energy functions with respect to the neuron states and connection weights and by showing that these energies, under certain conditions, decrease when the state of the neurons change.

Schemes for embedding patterns in the networks are also presented. Specifically, the quaternionic equivalents of the Hebbian rule, Projection rule, and Local iterative learning rule are discussed in detail. The Hebbian rule is limited by the constraint that embedded patterns must be orthogonal to each other. The Projection rule can overcome this limitation by projecting non-orthogonal patterns to orthogonal ones. However, this scheme is computationally expensive because the projection operation requires the calculation of a pseudo-inverse matrix. Local iterative learning is an implementation of the Projection rule. The weight matrix is gradually modified by iteratively applying embedded patterns, such as the backpropagation learning scheme for MLP models.

REFERENCES

1. I. N. Aizenberg, N. N. Aizenberg, and J. Vandewalle. *Multi-Valued and Universal Binary Neurons – Theory, Learning and Applications –*. Kluwer Academic Publishers, Boston/Dordrecht/London, 2000.

2. P. Arena, L. Fortuna, G. Muscato, and M.G. Xibilia. Multilayer Perceptrons to Approximate Quaternion Valued Functions. *Neural Networks*, 10(2):335–342, 1997.

3. S. Buchholz and G. Sommer. Quaternionic spinor MLP. In *8th European Symposium on Artificial Neural Networks (ESANN 2000)*, pages 377–382, 2000.

4. T. Bülow. *Hypercomplex Spectral Signal Representations for the Processing and Analysis of Images*. PhD thesis, Christian-Albrechts-Universität zu Kiel, 1999.

5. T. Bülow and G. Sommer. Hypercomplex Signals—A Novel Extension of the Analytic Signal to the Multidimensional Case. *IEEE Transactions on Signal Processing*, 49(11):2844–2852, 2001.

6. S. Diederich and M. Opper. Learning of Correlated Patterns in Spin-Glass Networks by Local Learning Rules. *Phys. Rev. Lett.*, 58:949–952, 1987.

7. G. M. Georgiou and C. Koutsougeras. Complex domain backpropagation. *IEEE Transactions on Circuits and Systems II*, 39(5):330–334, 1992.

8. W. R. Hamilton. *Lectures on Quaternions*. Hodges and Smith, Dublin, 1853.

9. T. L. Hankins. *Sir William Rowan Hamilton*. Johns Hopkins University Press, Baltimore and London, 1980.

10. A. Hirose. Dynamics of fully complex-valued neural networks. *Electronics Letters*, 28(16):1492–1494, 1992.

11. A. Hirose, editor. *Complex-Valued Neural Networks: Theories and Application*, volume 5 of *Innovative Intelligence*. World Scientific Publishing, Singapore, 2003.

12. A. Hirose. *Complex-Valued Neural Networks*, volume 32 of *Studies in Computational Intelligence*. Springer-Verlag, Berlin, Heidelberg, 2006.

13. S. G. Hoggar. *Mathematics for Computer Graphics*. Cambridge University Press, Cambridge, 1992.

14. T. Isokawa, N. Matsui, and H. Nishimura. Quaternionic Neural Networks: Fundamental Properties and Applications. In T. Nitta, editor, *Complex-Valued Neural Networks: Utilizing High-Dimensional Parameters*, chapter XVI, pages 411–439. Information Science Reference, Hershey, New York, 2009.

15. T. Isokawa, H. Nishimura, and N. Matsui. An Iterative Learning Scheme for Multistate Complex-Valued and Quaternionic Hopfield Neural Networks. In *Proceedings of International Joint Conference on Neural Networks (IJCNN2009)*, pages 1365–1371, 2009.

16. T. Isokawa, H. Nishimura, and N. Matsui. On the Fundamental Properties of Fully Quaternionic Hopfield Network. In *Proceedings of IEEE World Congress on Computational Intelligence (WCCI2012)*, 2012 (to appear).

17. T. Isokawa, H. Nishimura, N.Kamiura, and N.Matsui. Fundamental Properties of Quaternionic Hopfield Neural Network. In *Proceedings of 2006 International Joint Conference on Neural Networks*, pages 610–615, 2006.

18. T. Isokawa, H. Nishimura, N.Kamiura, and N.Matsui. Dynamics of Discrete-Time Quaternionic Hopfield Neural Networks. In *Proceedings of 17th International Conference on Artificial Neural Networks*, pages 848–857, 2007.

19. T. Isokawa, H. Nishimura, N.Kamiura, and N.Matsui. Associative Memory in Quaternionic Hopfield Neural Network. *International Journal of Neural Systems*, 18(2):135–145, 2008.

20. T. Isokawa, H. Nishimura, A. Saitoh, N. Kamiura, and N. Matsui. On the Scheme of Quaternionic Multistate Hopfield Neural Network. In *Proceedings of Joint 4th International Conference on Soft Computing and Intelligent Systems and 9th International Symposium on advanced Intelligent Systems (SCIS & ISIS 2008)*, pages 809–813, 2008.

21. S. Jankowski, A. Lozowski, and J. M. Zurada. Complex-Valued Multistate Neural Associative Memory. *IEEE Transactions on Neural Networks*, 7(6):1491–1496, 1996.

22. T. Kim and T. Adalı. Approximation by Fully Complex Multilayer Perceptrons. *Neural Computation*, 15:1641–1666, 2003.

23. T. Kohonen. *Self-Organization and Associative Memory*. Springer, Berlin, Heidelberg, 1984.

24. J. B. Kuipers. *Quaternions and Rotation Sequences: A Primer With Applications to Orbits, Aerospace and Virtual Reality*. Princeton Univ Press, Princeton, 1998.

25. H. Kusamichi, T. Isokawa, N. Matsui, Y. Ogawa, and K. Maeda. A New Scheme for Color Night Vision by Quaternion Neural Network. In *Proceedings of the 2nd International Conference on Autonomous Robots and Agents (ICARA2004)*, pages 101–106, 2004.

26. D.-L. Lee. Improvements of complex-valued hopfield associative memory by using generalized projection rules. *IEEE Transaction on Neural Networks*, 17(5):1341–1347, 2006.

27. S. D. Leo and P. P. Rotelli. Local Hypercomplex Analyticity. In *eprint arXiv:funct-an/9703002*, 1997.

28. S. D. Leo and P. P. Rotelli. Quaternonic analyticity. *Applied Mathematics Letters*, 16(7):1077–1081, 2003.

29. D. P. Mandic, C. Jahanchahi, and C. C. Took. A Quaternion Gradient Operator and Its Applications. *IEEE Signal Processing Letters*, 18(1):47–50, 2011.

30. N. Matsui, T. Isokawa, H. Kusamichi, F. Peper, and H. Nishimura. Quaternion Neural Network with Geometrical Operators. *Journal of Intelligent & Fuzzy Systems*, 15(3–4):149–164, 2004.

31. M. K. Müezzinoğlu, C. Güzeliş, and J. M. Zurada. A New Design Method for the Complex-Valued Multistate Hopfield Associative Memory. *IEEE Transactions on Neural Networks*, 14(4):891–899, 2003.

32. R. Mukundan. Quaternions: From Classical Mechanics to Computer Graphics, and Beyond. In *Proceedings of the 7th Asian Technology Conference in Mathematics*, pages 97–105, 2002.

33. T. Nitta. An Extension of the Back-propagation Algorithm to Quaternions. In *Proceedings of International Conference on Neural Information Processing (ICONIP'96)*, volume 1, pages 247–250, 1996.

34. T. Nitta. A Solution to the 4-bit Parity Problem with a Single Quaternary Neuron. *Neural Information Processing - Letters and Reviews*, 5(2):33–39, 2004.

35. T. Nitta, editor. *Complex-Valued Neural Networks: Utilizing High-Dimensional Parameters*. Information Science Reference, Hershey, New York, 2009.

36. L. Personnaz, I. Guyon, and G. Dreyfus. Collective Computational Properties of Neural Networks: New Learning Mechanisms. *Phys. Rev. A*, 34:4217–4228, 1986.

37. C. Schwartz. Calculus with a quaternionic variable. *Journal of Mathematical Physics*, 50(1):013523, 2009.

38. B. C. Ujang, C. C. Took, and D. P. Mandic. Quaternion-Valued Nonlinear Adaptive Filtering. *IEEE Transactions on Neural Networks*, 22(8):1193–1206, 2011.

39. M. Yoshida, Y. Kuroe, and T. Mori. Models of Hopfield-type Quaternion Neural Networks and Their Energy Functions. *International Journal of Neural Systems*, 15(1–2):129–135, 2005.

MODELS OF RECURRENT CLIFFORD NEURAL NETWORKS AND THEIR DYNAMICS

Yasuaki Kuroe

Kyoto Institute of Technology, Kyoto, Japan

Recently, models of neural networks in the real-number domain have been extended into the high-dimensional domain such as the complex- and quaternion-number domains, and several high-dimensional models have been proposed. These extensions are generalized by introducing Clifford algebra (geometric algebra). In this chapter we extend conventional real-valued models of recurrent neural networks into the domain defined by Clifford algebra and discuss their dynamics. Since geometric product is noncommutative, some different models can be considered. We present three models of fully connected recurrent neural networks, which are extensions of the real-valued Hopfield type neural networks to the domain defined by Clifford algebra. We study dynamics of the proposed models from the point view of existence conditions of an energy function. We derive existence conditions of an energy function for two classes of the Hopfield type Clifford neural networks.

6.1 INTRODUCTION

In recent years, there have been increasing research interests of artificial neural networks and many efforts have been made on applications of neural networks to various fields. As applications of the neural networks spread more widely, developing neural network models which can directly deal with complex numbers is desired in various fields. Several models of complex-valued neural networks have been proposed and their abilities of information processing have been investigated [1, 2]. Moreover, those studies are extended into the quaternion-number domain, and models of quaternion neural networks are proposed and actively studied [2, 11]. These extensions are generalized by introducing Clifford algebra (geometric algebra). Recently, Clifford algebra has been recognized to be powerful and practical framework for the representation and solutions of geometrical problems. It has been applied to various problems in science and engineering [12, 13]. Neural computation with Clifford algebra is, therefore, expected to possess superior ability of information processing and to realize superior computational intelligence.

In this chapter we extend conventional real-valued models of recurrent neural networks into the domain defined by Clifford algebra and discuss their dynamics. Since geometric product is noncommutative, some different models can be considered. We present three models of fully connected recurrent neural networks, which are extensions of the real-valued Hopfield-type neural networks to the domain defined by Clifford algebra. We also discuss dynamics of those models from the viewpoint of existence of an energy function. We have already derived existence conditions and proposed energy functions for Hopfield-type complex and quaternion- valued neural networks [9, 10, 11]. Those results can be revisited from the point of view of Clifford algebra models. Based on the those results, we discuss existence conditions of an energy function for two classes of the Hopfield-type Clifford neural networks.

6.2 CLIFFORD ALGEBRA

We consider the finite-dimensional Clifford algebra defined over the real field $\mathbb{R}$. Its outline is given in this section. See Refs. 4 and 5 for details.

6.2.1 Definition

Let $\mathbb{R}^{p,q,r}$ denote a $(p + q + r)$-dimensional vector space over the real field $\mathbb{R}$. Let a commutative scalar product be defined as $* : \mathbb{R}^{p,q,r} \times \mathbb{R}^{p,q,r} \to \mathbb{R}$. That is,

$$a * b = b * a \in \mathbb{R} \text{ for } a, b \in \mathbb{R}^{p,q,r}.$$

For $\mathbb{R}^{p,q,r}$, the canonical basis, denoted by $\overline{\mathbb{R}}^{p,q,r}$, is defined as totally ordered set

$$\overline{\mathbb{R}}^{p,q,r} := \{e_1, \ldots, e_p, e_{p+1}, \ldots, e_{p+q}, e_{p+q+1}, \ldots, e_{p+q+r}\} \subset \mathbb{R}^{p,q,r} \quad (6.1)$$

where the $\{e_i\}$ have the property

$$e_i * e_j = \begin{cases} +1, & 1 \leq i = j \leq p, \\ -1, & p < i = j \leq p+q, \\ 0, & p+q < i = j \leq p+q+r, \\ 0, & i \neq j \end{cases} \tag{6.2}$$

The combination of a vector space with a scalar product is called a quadratic space denoted by $(\mathbb{R}^{p,q,r}, *)$. Note that $e_i * e_i$ takes not only the value 1 but also the values -1 and 0. Clifford algebra is defined over the quadratic space $(\mathbb{R}^{p,q,r}, *)$ by introducing so-called Clifford product (geometric product) denoted by $\circ$. The Clifford algebra over $(\mathbb{R}^{p,q,r}, *)$ is denoted by $\mathbb{G}(\mathbb{R}^{p,q,r})$ or simply $\mathbb{G}_{p,q,r}$.

Definition of Clifford Algebra $\mathbb{G}_{p,q,r}$. Let $\mathbb{G}_{p,q,r}$ denote the associative algebra over the quadratic space $(\mathbb{R}^{p,q,r}, *)$ and let $\circ$ denote the product. The $\mathbb{G}_{p,q,r}$ is said to be Clifford algebra if the following are satisfied.

- $\mathbb{G}_{p,q,r}$ contains the field $\mathbb{R}$ and the vector space $\mathbb{R}^{p,q,r}$ as distinct subspaces.

- $\mathbb{G}_{p,q,r}$ is a vector space equipped with vector addition $+$ and multiplication with scalar ($\alpha \in \mathbb{R}$).

- There exists the product $\circ$ which satisfies the following properties.

    1. The algebra is closed under the product $\circ$, that is,

    $$a \circ b \in \mathbb{G}_{p,q,r} \text{ for all } a, b \in \mathbb{G}_{p,q,r}.$$

    2. Associativity:

    $$(a \circ b) \circ c = a \circ (b \circ c) \text{ for all } a, b, c \in \mathbb{G}_{p,q,r}$$

    3. Distributivity:

    $$a \circ (b + c) = a \circ b + a \circ c \text{ for all } a, b, c \in \mathbb{G}_{p,q,r}$$

    and

    $$(b + c) \circ a = b \circ a + c \circ a \text{ for all } a, b, c \in \mathbb{G}_{p,q,r}.$$

    4. Scalar multiplication:

    $$\alpha \circ a = a \circ \alpha = \alpha a, \text{ for all } a \in \mathbb{G}_{p,q,r}, \alpha \in \mathbb{R}.$$

    5. Let $a \in \mathbb{R}^{p,q,r} \subset \mathbb{G}_{p,q,r}$; then

    $$a \circ a = a * a \in \mathbb{R} \tag{6.3}$$

Note that item 5 implies that the Clifford product of any vector in the vector space $\mathbb{R}^{p,q,r}$ with itself equals their inner product, which links the vector space to the Clifford algebra. Note also that the commutativity is not imposed on the Clifford product $\circ$; that is, it is in general noncommutative.

6.2.2   Basic Properties and Algebraic Basis

The elements of Clifford algebra $\mathbb{G}_{p,q,r}$ are called multivectors whereas the elements of $\mathbb{R}^{p,q,r}$ are called vectors. For multivectors $a, b \in \mathbb{G}_{p,q,r}$, the Clifford product $a \circ b$ is expressed as a sum of its symmetric and antisymmetric parts:

$$a \circ b = \frac{1}{2}(a \circ b + b \circ a) + \frac{1}{2}(a \circ b - b \circ a).$$

If a and b are vectors, that is, $a, b \in \mathbb{R}^{p,q,r}$, the following relation holds.

$$(a + b) \circ (a + b) = (a + b) * (a + b)$$

$$\Leftrightarrow a \circ a + a \circ b + b \circ a + b \circ b = a * a + 2a * b + b * b$$

$$\Leftrightarrow \frac{1}{2}(a \circ b + b \circ a) = a * b$$

Let us express the antisymmetric part as

$$a \wedge b := \frac{1}{2}(a \circ b - b \circ a),$$

then

$$a \circ b = a * b + a \wedge b.$$

The product $\wedge$ is called the outer or wedge product. In particular, for basis vectors e_i, e_j in $\mathbb{R}^{p,q,r}$,

$$e_i \circ e_j = e_i \wedge e_j$$

since $e_i * e_j = 0$ $(i \neq j)$ from (6.2), which implies

$$e_i \circ e_j = -e_j \circ e_i. \tag{6.4}$$

We are now in the position to construct a basis of the Clifford algebra $\mathbb{G}_{p,q,r}$, which is called an algebraic basis of $\mathbb{G}_{p,q,r}$. ¿From now on, the Clifford product will be denoted by juxtaposition of symbols. For example, $a \circ b$ is now written as ab. Since the Clifford product is associative, $(a \circ b) \circ c$ or $a \circ (b \circ c)$ is written as abc. Also, the product operator $\prod$ refers to the Clifford product of the operands, for example, $\prod_{i=1}^{3} a_i = a_1 a_2 a_3$.

Consider the Clifford product of a number of different elements of the canonical basis $\overline{\mathbb{R}}^{p,q,r}$ of $\mathbb{R}^{p,q,r}$, called a basis blade, which plays an important role to construct a basis of the Clifford algebra $\mathbb{G}_{p,q,r}$.

Let $\mathbb{A}$ be an ordered set and let $\mathbb{A}[i]$ denote the ith elements of $\mathbb{A}$. That is, if $\mathbb{A} = \{2, 3, 1\}$, then $\mathbb{A}[2] = 3$. A basis blade in $\mathbb{G}_{p,q,r}$ denoted by $e_{\mathbb{A}}$ is defined; let $\mathbb{A} \subset \{1, 2, \dots, p+q+r\}$, then

$$e_{\mathbb{A}} = \prod_{i=1}^{|\mathbb{A}|} \overline{\mathbb{R}}^{p,q,r}[\mathbb{A}[i]]. \tag{6.5}$$

where $|\mathbb{A}|$ denotes the number of elements of the set $\mathbb{A}$. The number of the factors under the Clifford products in each basis blade $e_{\mathbb{A}}$, that is, $|\mathbb{A}|$ is called grade. For example, if $\mathbb{A} = \{2, 3, 1\}$, then $e_{\mathbb{A}} = e_2 e_3 e_1$ and its grade is 3.

Given a vector space $\mathbb{R}^{p,q,r}$ with a canonical basis $\overline{\mathbb{R}}^{p,q,r}$ in (6.1), there are 2^{p+q+r} ways to combine the $\{e_i\}$ with the Clifford product such that no two of these products are linearly independent, that is, there exist 2^{p+q+r} linearly independent basis blades. The collection of 2^{p+q+r} linearly independent basis blades forms an algebraic basis of $\mathbb{G}_{p,q,r}$. The choice of basis is arbitrary, however, it is useful to choose an ordered basis, called the canonical algebraic basis, defined as follows. Let $\mathbb{I} = \{1, 2, \cdots, p + q + r\}$, its power set is denoted by $\mathcal{P}[\mathbb{I}]$ and its ordered power set is denoted by $\mathcal{P}_O[\mathbb{I}]$. For example, if $\mathbb{I} = \{1, 2, 3\}$, then

$$\mathcal{P}_O[\mathbb{I}] = \{\{\emptyset\}, \{1\}, \{2\}, \{3\}, \{1, 2\}, \{1, 3\}, \{2, 3\}, \{1, 2, 3\}\}$$

where $\emptyset$ is the empty set. The canonical algebraic basis of $\mathbb{G}_{p,q,r}$, denoted by $\overline{\mathbb{G}}_{p,q,r}$ is defined:

$$\overline{\mathbb{G}}_{p,q,r} := \{e_{\mathbb{A}} : \mathbb{A} \in \mathcal{P}_O[\mathbb{I}]\}$$

where we let $e_{\emptyset} = 1 \in \mathbb{R}$. For example, let $p + q + r = 3$ and consider $\mathbb{R}^3 := \mathbb{R}^{p,q,r}$ with a canonical basis $\overline{\mathbb{R}}^3 = \{e_1, e_2, e_3\}$. The canonical algebraic basis $\overline{\mathbb{G}}_3$ of $\mathbb{G}_3$ is then given by

$$\overline{\mathbb{G}}_3 = \{1, e_1, e_2, e_3, e_1 e_2, e_1 e_3, e_2 e_3, e_1 e_2 e_3\}$$

A general multivector of $\mathbb{G}_{p,q,r}$ is written as a linear combination of the elements of the canonical algebraic basis $\overline{\mathbb{G}}_{p,q,r}$ thus defined, that is, $a \in \mathbb{G}_{p,q,r}$ is written as

$$a = \sum_{i=1}^{2^{p+q+r}} a^{(i)} \overline{\mathbb{G}}_{p,q,r}[i] \tag{6.6}$$

where $a^{(i)} \in \mathbb{R}$. Recall that $\overline{\mathbb{G}}_{p,q,r}[i]$ denotes the ith element of $\overline{\mathbb{G}}_{p,q,r}$.

The absolute value (modulus) of $a \in \mathbb{G}_{p,q,r}$, denoted by $|a|$, is defined as

$$|a| = \left(\sum_{i=1}^{2^{p+q+r}} a^{(i)^2} \right)^{1/2}.$$

6.3 HOPFIELD-TYPE NEURAL NETWORKS AND THEIR ENERGY FUNCTIONS

It is well known that one of the pioneering works that triggered the research interests of neural networks in the last two decades is the proposal of models for neural networks by J. J. Hopfield [6, 7], which are fully connected recurrent neural networks. He introduced the idea of an energy function to formulate a way of understanding the computation performed by dynamics of fully connected neural networks and showed that a combinatorial optimization problem can be solved by the neural networks. The neural network models proposed by Hopfield are called Hopfield-type neural networks; and by using concept of energy functions, they have been applied to various problems such as qualitative analysis of neural networks, synthesis of associative memories, optimization problems, etc., ever since. It is, therefore, of great interest to develop models of Clifford algebraic neural networks of Hopfield-type and to investigate their dynamics. In this section we review the model of the Hopfield-type neural networks and its energy function.

J. J. Hopfield proposed both discrete-time and continuous-time models of fully connected recurrent neural networks and introduced the idea of energy functions. We consider the continuous-time Hopfield-type neural network, which is implemented by an electric circuit shown in Fig. 6.1 [6, 7]. The circuit consists of n nonlinear

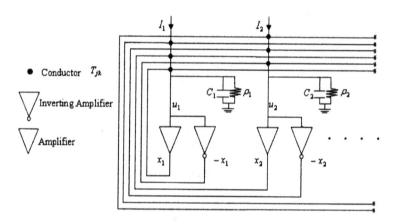

Figure 6.1 Hopfield-type neural network.

amplifiers interconnected by an RC network, and conductances and ideal current sources. Each amplifier provide an output voltage x_j given by $f(u_j)$, where u_j is the input voltage and f is a nonlinear activation function. For each amplifier, it contains an inverting amplifier whose output is $-x_j$ which permits a choice of the sign of the amplifier and the outputs x_j and $-x_j$ are usually provided by two output terminals of the same operational amplifier circuit. The pair of nonlinear amplifiers with an RC network is refereed to as a "neuron" and the RC network partially define the time constant of the neuron and provide for integrative analog summation of the synaptic input currents from other neurons in the network. A synapse between two neurons is defined by a conductance T_{jk} which connects one of the two outputs (x_k or $-x_k$) of amplifier k to the input of amplifier j, and this connection is made with a resistor of value $R_{jk} = 1/|T_{jk}|$. As shown in Fig. 6.1, the circuit included an externally supplied input current I_j for each neuron, which represents an external input signal (or bias) to neuron j.

Writing the Kirchhoff's current law at the input node of amplifier j, we obtain

$$C_j \frac{d}{dt} u_j = -\frac{1}{R_i} u_j + \sum_{k=1}^{n} T_{jk} x_j + I_j \quad j = 1, 2, \ldots, n \qquad (6.7)$$
$$x_j = f(u_j)$$

where

$$\frac{1}{R_j} = \frac{1}{\rho_j} + \sum_{k=1}^{n} \frac{1}{R_{jk}}.$$

In order to analyze dynamics of the neural network, the following function has been defined as an energy function of the network [6].

$$E(x) = -\frac{1}{2} \sum_{j=1}^{n} \sum_{k=1}^{n} T_{jk} x_j x_k - \sum_{j=1}^{n} I_j x_j + \sum_{j=1}^{n} \frac{1}{R_j} \int_{0}^{x_j} f^{-1}(\sigma) d\sigma \qquad (6.8)$$

By using the energy function J. J. Hopfield showed that if the activation function is bounded, continuously differentiable and monotonically increasing, and $T_{jk} = T_{kj}$, then the time evolution of the network is a motion in state space that seeks out the minima of E and comes to a stop such points and E is a Liapunov function of the network. Moreover, any optimization problem that is mapped to the energy function Eq. (6.8) can be solved by this neural network.

Letting $\tau_j := R_j C_j$, $w_{jk} := R_j T_{jk}$ and $b_j := R_j I_j$, we can rewrite (6.7) as

$$\tau_j \frac{du_j}{dt} = -u_j + \sum_{k=1}^{n} w_{jk} x_k + b_j \quad j = 1, 2, \ldots, n \qquad (6.9)$$
$$x_j = f(u_j)$$

6.4 MODELS OF HOPFIELD-TYPE CLIFFORD NEURAL NETWORKS

In this section we present models of fully connected recurrent neural networks, which are extensions of the real-valued Hopfield neural networks into the domain of the Clifford algebra presented in the previous section. Since geometric product is non-commutative, different models can be developed. We will show three models of Hopfield-type Clifford neural networks. In Section 6.2 we write the multivectors, that is, elements of the Clifford algebra, in boldface like $a \in \mathbb{G}_{p,q,r}$. ¿From now on, we write them in normal face like $a \in \mathbb{G}_{p,q,r}$ for simplicity.

The first model is a direct extension of the Hopfield neural networks, described by differential equations of the same form as (6.9)

$$\tau_i \frac{du_i}{dt} = -u_i + \sum_{j=1}^{n} w_{ij} v_j + b_i \quad i = 1, 2, \ldots, n \qquad (6.10)$$
$$v_i = f(u_i)$$

where n is the number of neurons, τ_i is the time constant of the ith neuron, u_i and v_i are the state and the output of the ith neuron at time t, respectively, b_i is the threshold value, w_{ij} is the connection weight coefficient from the jth neuron to the ith one and $f(\cdot)$ is the activation function of the neurons. In the model u_i, v_i, b_i and w_{ij} are multivectors, that is, the elements of the Clifford algebra $\mathbb{G}_{p,q,r}$: $u_i \in \mathbb{G}_{p,q,r}$, $v_i \in \mathbb{G}_{p,q,r}$, $b_i \in \mathbb{G}_{p,q,r}$, $w_{ij} \in \mathbb{G}_{p,q,r}$. The time constant τ_i is a positive real number: $\tau_i \in \mathbb{R}, \tau_i > 0$. $w_{ij}v_j$ is the Clifford product of w_{ij} and v_j in $\mathbb{G}_{p,q,r}$: $w_{ij} \circ v_j$. The activation function $f(\cdot)$ is a nonlinear function which maps from a multivector to a multivector: $f : \mathbb{G}_{p,q,r} \to \mathbb{G}_{p,q,r}$. For a multivector $\boldsymbol{u}(t) = \sum_{i=1}^{2^{p+q+r}} u^{(i)}(t)\overline{\mathbb{G}}_{p,q,r}[i]$, its time derivative is defined by

$$\frac{d}{dt}u_i(t) := \sum_{i=1}^{2^{p+q+r}} \frac{d}{dt}u^{(i)}(t)\overline{\mathbb{G}}_{p,q,r}[i].$$

Since in $\mathbb{G}_{p,q,r}$, the Clifford product is non-commutative, the model in which the product $w_{ij}v_j$ in the model (6.10) is replaced by v_jw_{ij} is a different model. As the second model we consider the model which is described by differential equations of the form:

$$\tau_i \frac{du_i}{dt} = -u_i + \sum_{j=1}^{n} v_jw_{ij} + b_i \qquad i = 1, 2, \ldots, n \qquad (6.11)$$
$$v_i = f(u_i)$$

where the definitions of all the symbols are same as those in (6.10).

The third one is the model in which $w_{ij}v_j$ in the model (6.10) is replaced by $w_{ij}^* v_j w_{ij}$ [1], which is described by differential equations of the form:

$$\tau_i \frac{du_i}{dt} = -u_i + \sum_{j=1}^{n} w_{ij}^* v_j w_{ij} + b_i \qquad i = 1, 2, \ldots, n. \qquad (6.12)$$
$$v_i = f(u_i)$$

where the definitions of all the symbols are same as those in (6.10). The connection weight coefficient w_{ij}^* could generally be any multivecter in $\mathbb{G}_{p,q,r}$ different from w_{ij}. It is useful in the Clifford algebra to let * be an involution operator. An involution is an operation that maps an operand to itself when applied twice: $(w^*)^* = w$. Examples of involution in the Clifford algebra are inversion, reversion and conjugation.

6.5 DEFINITION OF ENERGY FUNCTIONS

As stated in Section 6.3, J. J. Hopfield introduced the idea of an energy function to formulate a way of understanding the computation performed by fully connected

---

[1]In Clifford algebra the a geometric transformation such as a rotation is expressed in the form of a sandwiching product with an element like this.

recurrent neural networks and showed that a combinatorial optimization problem can be solved by them. The energy functions have been applied to various problems such as qualitative analysis of neural networks, synthesis of associative memories, optimization problems etc. ever since. It is, therefore, of great interest to investigate existence conditions of energy functions and to obtain energy functions for the neural networks (6.10), (6.11), and (6.12). In this section we give the definition of energy functions for the models of Hopfield-type Clifford neural networks (6.10), (6.11), and (6.12).

If the neural network (6.10) is real-valued, that is, u_i, v_i, b_i, and w_{ij} are all real, $u_i \in \mathbb{R}$, $v_i \in \mathbb{R}$, $b_i \in \mathbb{R}$, $w_{ij} \in \mathbb{R}$ and the activation function is a real nonlinear function $f : \mathbb{R} \to \mathbb{R}$, the network (6.10) is equivalent to the Hopfeild neural network (6.9). The following function can be an energy function for the network (6.10), which is corresponding to the energy function given by (6.8) for the network (6.7).

$$E(v) = -\frac{1}{2}\sum_{i=1}^{n}\sum_{j=1}^{n} w_{ij}v_iv_j - \sum_{i=1}^{n} b_iv_i + \sum_{i=1}^{n}\int_0^{v_i} f^{-1}(\rho)d\rho \quad (6.13)$$

where $v = [v_1, v_2, \cdots, v_n] \in \mathbb{R}^n$ and $f^{-1}(\cdot)$ is the inverse function of $f(\cdot)$. The function $E(v)$ is a mapping $E : \mathbb{R}^n \to \mathbb{R}$ and has the following property.

Let $\left.\frac{dE(v)}{dt}\right|_{(6.10)}$ be the time derivative of $E(v)$ along the trajectories of (6.10). If the weight coefficients satisfy

$$w_{ji} = w_{ij} \quad (i, j = 1, 2, \ldots, n) \quad (6.14)$$

and the nonlinear function $f(\cdot)$ is continuously differentiable, bounded, and monotonically increasing, then

$$\left.\frac{dE(v)}{dt}\right|_{(6.10)} \leq 0$$

and furthermore

$$\left.\frac{dE(v)}{dt}\right|_{(6.10)} = 0 \text{ if and only if } \frac{dv}{dt} = 0.$$

It is still an open question what properties should be demanded as energy functions and how to define and construct them. As the first step to the problem, we define an energy function for the Clifford neural networks (6.10), (6.11), and (6.12) by the analogy to that for Hopfield-type real-valued neural networks as follows.

Definition 1 *Consider the Clifford neural network* $(\mathcal{N})$ *where* $\mathcal{N}$ *is the equation number* 6.10, 6.11, *or* 6.12. *E is an energy function of the Clifford neural network* $(\mathcal{N})$, *if the following conditions are satisfied.*

(i) *$E(\cdot)$ is a mapping $E : \mathbb{G}_{p,q,r} \to \mathbb{R}$ and bounded from below.*

(ii) *The derivative of E along the trajectories of the network* $(\mathcal{N})$, *denoted by* $\left.\frac{dE}{dt}\right|_{(\mathcal{N})}$, *satisfies*

$$\left.\frac{dE}{dt}\right|_{(\mathcal{N})} \leq 0.$$

Furthermore,

$$\left.\frac{dE}{dt}\right|_{(\mathcal{N})} = 0 \quad \textit{if and only if} \quad \frac{dv_i}{dt} = 0 \ (\, i = 1, 2, \ldots, n \,).$$

Based on the definition we will discuss existence conditions of an energy function for two classes of the Clifford neural networks, $\mathbb{G}_{0,2,0}$ and $\mathbb{G}_{0,1,0}$ in the following section.

6.6 EXISTENCE CONDITIONS OF ENERGY FUNCTIONS

We have already derived existence conditions and proposed energy functions for Hopfield-type complex and quaternion-valued neural networks. Based on those results we discuss existing conditions of an energy function for the corresponding classes of Hopfield-type Clifford neural networks described by (6.10), (6.11), and (6.12).

6.6.1 Assumptions on Clifford Activation Functions

One of the important factors to characterize dynamics of recurrent neural networks is their activation functions which are nonlinear functions. It is therefore, important to discuss which type of nonlinear functions is chosen as activation functions for Clifford neural networks (6.10), (6.11), and (6.12). In the real-valued neural networks, the activation is usually chosen to be a smooth and bounded function such as a sigmoidal function. Recall that, in the complex-valued domain, Liouville's theorem says that if $f(\cdot)$ is analytic at all points of the complex plane and bounded, then $f(\cdot)$ is constant. Since a suitable $f(\cdot)$ should be bounded, it follows from the theorem that if we choose an analytic function for $f(\cdot)$, it is constant over the entire complex plain, which is clearly not suitable. In the complex-valued neural networks in Ref. 9, in place of analytic function, a function whose real and imaginary parts are continuously differentiable with respect to the real and imaginary variables of its argument, respectively, is chosen for the activation function and the existence conditions of an energy function are derived [9]. In this paper we extend these conditions on the activation functions to those of the Clifford neural networks (6.10), (6.11), and (6.12).

Letting $f^{(i)}$, $i = 1, 2, \ldots, 2^{p+q+r}$ be real value functions: $f^{(i)} : \mathbb{R}^{2^{p+q+r}} \to \mathbb{R}$, the nonlinear function on the Clifford algebra $f(u) : \mathbb{G}_{p,q,r} \to \mathbb{G}_{p,q,r}$ is described as follows:

$$f(u) = \sum_{i=1}^{2^{p+q+r}} f^{(i)}(u^{(1)}, u^{(2)}, \cdots, u^{(2^{p+q+r})}) \overline{\mathbb{G}}_{p,q,r}[i] \tag{6.15}$$

where

$$u = \sum_{i=1}^{2^{p+q+r}} u^{(i)} \overline{\mathbb{G}}_{p,q,r}[i]. \tag{6.16}$$

For example, in the Clifford algebra $\mathbb{G}_2 := \mathbb{G}_{p,q,r}$ where we let $p + q + r = 2$, its canonical basis is described by

$$\overline{\mathbb{G}}_2 = \{1, e_1, e_2, e_1 e_2\}$$

and the nonlinear function $f(u) : \mathbb{G}_2 \to \mathbb{G}_2$ is described as

$$
\begin{aligned}
f(u) \;=\; & f^{(0)}(u^{(0)}, u^{(1)}, u^{(2)}, u^{(3)}) \\
& + f^{(1)}(u^{(0)}, u^{(1)}, u^{(2)}, u^{(3)}) e_1 \\
& + f^{(2)}(u^{(0)}, u^{(1)}, u^{(2)}, u^{(3)}) e_2 \\
& + f^{(3)}(u^{(0)}, u^{(1)}, u^{(2)}, u^{(3)}) e_1 e_2
\end{aligned}
\tag{6.17}
$$

We assume the following conditions on the activation function $f(u) : \mathbb{G}_{p,q,r} \to \mathbb{G}_{p,q,r}$ of the neural networks (6.10), (6.11) and (6.12).

(i) $f^{(l)}(\,\cdot\,), (l = 0, 1, \ldots, 2^{p+q+r})$ are continuously differentiable with respect to $u^{(m)}, (m = 0, 1, \ldots, 2^{p+q+r})$.

(ii) $f(\,\cdot\,)$ is a bounded function, that is, there exists some $M > 0$ such that $|f(\,\cdot\,)| \le M$.

¿From this assumption, we can define the Jacobian matrix of the activation function f at a point u, denoted by $\boldsymbol{J}_f(u) = \{\alpha_{lm}(u)\} \in \mathbb{R}^{2^{p+q+r} \times 2^{p+q+r}}$ where

$$\alpha_{lm}(u) = \left. \frac{\partial f^{(l)}}{\partial u^{(m)}} \right|_u .
\tag{6.18}$$

6.6.2 Existence Conditions for Clifford Neural Networks of Class $\mathbb{G}_{0,2,0}$

The canonical basis of the Clifford algebra $\mathbb{G}_{0,2,0}$ is given by

$$\overline{\mathbb{G}}_{0,2,0} = \{1, e_1, e_2, e_1 e_2\}$$

and an element of $\mathbb{G}_{0,2,0}$, $x \in \mathbb{G}_{0,2,0}$, is described as follows.

$$x = x^{(0)} + x^{(1)} e_1 + x^{(2)} e_2 + x^{(3)} e_1 e_2
\tag{6.19}$$

The multiplication table of $\mathbb{G}_{0,2,0}$ is obtained as shown in Table 6.1.

It can be seen that the Clifford algebra $\mathbb{G}_{0,2,0}$ is isomorphic to the quaternion numbers $\mathbb{H}$. A quaternion number is defined by

$$x = x^{(0)} + i x^{(1)} + j x^{(2)} + k x^{(3)}
\tag{6.20}$$

where $x^{(0)}, x^{(1)}, x^{(2)}$, and $x^{(3)}$ are real numbers, $\{i, j, k\}$ are imaginary units for which the following relations hold.

$$
\begin{aligned}
i^2 = -1, \qquad & j^2 = -1, \qquad k^2 = -1, \\
ij = -ji = k, \qquad & jk = -kj = i, \qquad ki = -ik = j.
\end{aligned}
\tag{6.21}
$$

Table 6.1   Multiplication table for geometric algebra $\mathbb{G}_{0,2,0}$

$\parallel$	1	e_1	e_2	e_1e_2
1	1	e_1	e_2	e_1e_2
e_1	e_1	-1	e_1e_2	$-e_2$
e_2	e_2	$-e_1e_2$	-1	e_1
e_1e_2	e_1e_2	e_2	$-e_1$	-1

The multiplications of the quaternion numbers are performed according to the above relations. Note that quaternion numbers are noncommutative on multiplication, that is $xy \neq yx$ where x and y are quaternion numbers. It can be seen that, identifying e_1, e_2 and e_1e_2 in $\mathbb{G}_{0,2,0}$ with the imaginary units i, j and k in the quaternion numbers, respectively, the Clifford algebra $\mathbb{G}_{0,2,0}$ is isomorphic to the quaternion numbers $\mathbb{H}$.

Here we discuss the existence conditions of energy functions for the Clifford neural networks of the class $\mathbb{G}_{0,2,0}$ described by (6.10), (6.11), and (6.12). In model (6.12), we let the involution operator $*$ be the conjugation defined as follows. For $w \in \mathbb{G}_{0,2,0}$ described as

$$w = w^{(0)} + w^{(1)}e_1 + w^{(2)}e_2 + w^{(3)}e_1e_2,$$

w^* is defined as follows.

$$w^* = w^{(0)} - w^{(1)}e_1 - w^{(2)}e_2 - w^{(3)}e_1e_2. \tag{6.22}$$

Furthermore for $x \in \mathbb{G}_{0,2,0}$, $Sc(\,\cdot\,)$ is defined as

$$Sc(x) = x^{(0)}.$$

This implies that $Sc(\,\cdot\,)$ corresponds to the operator which picks up the real part $x^{(0)}$ of x in the case of quaternion numbers.

We need the following assumptions on the weight coefficients and the activation functions of (6.10), (6.11), and (6.12).

Assumption 1 *The weight coefficients of the Clifford neural networks of the class* $\mathbb{G}_{0,2,0}$ *(6.10), (6.11) and (6.12) satisfy*

$$w_{ji} = w_{ij}^* \quad (i, j = 1, 2, \ldots, n) \tag{6.23}$$

Note that the involution operator $*$ is defined in (6.22).

Assumption 2 *The activation function f of the Clifford neural networks (6.10), (6.11), and (6.12) of the class* $\mathbb{G}_{0,2,0}$ *satisfies*

(i) f is an injective function,

(ii)   The Jacobian matrix $\mathbf{J}_f(u)$ is a symmetric matrix for all $u \in \mathbb{G}_{0,2,0}$,

(iii) The Jacobian matrix $\mathbf{J}_f(u)$ is positive definite for all $u \in \mathbb{G}_{0,2,0}$.

Because of the condition (i) of Assumption 2 and boundedness of f, there exists the inverse function of f, denoted by $g = f^{-1} : \mathbb{G}_{0,2,0} \to \mathbb{G}_{0,2,0}$. We express g as $u = g(v)$:

$$
\begin{aligned}
g(v) \;=\; & g^{(0)}(v^{(0)}, v^{(1)}, v^{(2)}, v^{(3)}) \\
& + g^{(1)}(v^{(0)}, v^{(1)}, v^{(2)}, v^{(3)})e_1 \\
& + g^{(2)}(v^{(0)}, v^{(1)}, v^{(2)}, v^{(3)})e_2 \\
& + g^{(3)}(v^{(0)}, v^{(1)}, v^{(2)}, v^{(3)})e_1 e_2
\end{aligned}
\tag{6.24}
$$

where $g^{(l)}(\,\cdot\,) : \mathbb{R}^4 \to \mathbb{R}$ $(l = 0, 1, 2, 3)$. Then, the following lemma holds.

Lemma 1 *If f satisfies Assumption 2, there exists a scalar function $G(\,\cdot\,) : \mathbb{G}_{0,2,0}^n \to \mathbb{R}$, such that*

$$
\frac{\partial G}{\partial v^{(l)}} = g^{(l)}(v^{(0)}, v^{(1)}, v^{(2)}, v^{(3)}) \qquad (l = 0, 1, 2, 3).
\tag{6.25}
$$

This lemma can be proved by defining the function $G(v)$ as

$$
\begin{aligned}
G(v) \;:=\; & \int_0^{v^{(0)}} g^{(0)}(\rho, 0, 0, 0)d\rho \\
& + \int_0^{v^{(1)}} g^{(1)}(v^{(0)}, \rho, 0, 0)d\rho \\
& + \int_0^{v^{(2)}} g^{(2)}(v^{(0)}, v^{(1)}, \rho, 0)d\rho \\
& + \int_0^{v^{(3)}} g^{(3)}(v^{(0)}, v^{(1)}, v^{(2)}, \rho)d\rho.
\end{aligned}
\tag{6.26}
$$

We now propose candidates of the energy functions for the Clifford neural networks (6.10), (6.11), and (6.12) of the class $\mathbb{G}_{0,2,0}$ as follows. For the network (6.10),

$$
E_{(6.10)}(v) \;=\; -\sum_{i=1}^{n}\sum_{j=1}^{n} \frac{1}{2} Sc\,(v_i^* w_{ij} v_j + 2b_i^* v_i) - G(v_i)
\tag{6.27}
$$

where $v = [v_1, v_2, \ldots, v_n]^T \in \mathbb{G}_{0,2,0}^n$. For the network (6.11)

$$
E_{(6.11)}(v) \;=\; -\sum_{i=1}^{n}\sum_{j=1}^{n} \frac{1}{2} Sc\,(v_i^* v_j w_{ij} + 2b_i^* v_i) - G(v_i).
\tag{6.28}
$$

For the network (6.12)

$$E_{(6.12)}(\boldsymbol{v}) = -\sum_{i=1}^{n}\sum_{j=1}^{n}\frac{1}{2}Sc\left(v_i^* w_{ij}^* v_j w_{ij} + 2b_i^* v_i\right) - G(v_i). \quad (6.29)$$

We now obtain the following theorem:

Theorem 6.1 *If the Clifford neural networks* (6.10), (6.11), *and* (6.12) *of the class* $\mathbb{G}_{0,2,0}$ *satisfy Assumptions 1 and 2, then there exists an energy function which satisfies Definition 1.*

This theorem can be proved as follows. Calculating the time derivatives of the functions (6.27), (6.28), and (6.29) along the trajectories of the networks (6.10), (6.11) and (6.12), respectively, by using Lemma 1, we can show the conditions of Definition 1 of energy functions holds.

The existing conditions of energy functions thus obtained are ones on the connection weight coefficients w_{ij} and the activation function $f(\cdot)$. As examples of the functions which satisfy Assumption 2,

$$f(u) = \frac{u}{1+|u|} \quad (6.30)$$

$$\begin{aligned} f(u) = \ & \tanh(u^{(0)}) + \tanh(u^{(1)})e_1 \\ & + \tanh(u^{(2)})e_2 + \tanh(u^{(3)})e_1e_2 \end{aligned} \quad (6.31)$$

can be considered. Equation (6.30) has the same form as that of the complex-valued function which is often used in the complex-valued neural networks [9]. The function (6.31) is a split activation function, that is, each component of its argument is transformed separately.

6.6.3   Existence Conditions for Clifford Neural Networks of Class $\mathbb{G}_{0,1,0}$

The canonical basis of the Clifford algebra $\mathbb{G}_{0,1,0}$ is given by

$$\overline{\mathbb{G}}_{0,1,0} = \{1, e_1\}.$$

An elemet of $\mathbb{G}_{0,1,0}$, $x \in \mathbb{G}_{0,1,0}$, is described as follows.

$$x = x^{(0)} + x^{(1)}e_1. \quad (6.32)$$

Because $e_1e_1 = -1$, identifying e_1 with the imaginary unit i of the complex numbers, the Clifford algebra $\mathbb{G}_{0,1,0}$ is isomorphic to the complex numbers $\mathbb{C}$. Since the Clifford product in $\mathbb{G}_{0,1,0}$ is commutative the models (6.10), (6.11), and (6.12) are essentially equivalent. Here we discuss existence conditions of energy function for the neural network (6.10) of the class $\mathbb{G}_{0,1,0}$.

We need the following assumptions on the weight coefficients and the activation functions of (6.10).

Assumption 3 *The weight coefficients of the Clifford neural networks* (6.10) *of the class* $\mathbb{G}_{0,1,0}$ *satisfy*

$$w_{ji} = w_{ij}^* \quad (i,j = 1,2,\ldots,n) \tag{6.33}$$

where $*$ *is defined: for* $w = x^{(0)} + x^{(1)}e_1 \in \mathbb{G}_{0,1,0}$, $w^* = x^{(0)} - x^{(1)}e_1$.

The activation function (6.10) in the Clifford algebra $\mathbb{G}_{0,1,0}$ is described by

$$f(u) = f^{(0)}(u^{(0)}, u^{(1)}) + f^{(1)}(u^{(0)}, u^{(1)})e_1$$

where $u = u^{(0)} + u^{(1)}e_1$.

Assumption 4 *The activation function* f *of the Clifford neural networks* (6.10) *of the class* $\mathbb{G}_{0,1,0}$ *is an injective function and satisfies*

$$
\begin{aligned}
&\text{(i)} \quad \frac{\partial f^{(0)}}{\partial u^{(0)}} > 0, \\
&\text{(ii)} \quad \frac{\partial f^{(0)}}{\partial u^{(1)}} = \frac{\partial f^{(1)}}{\partial u^{(0)}}, \\
&\text{(iii)} \quad \frac{\partial f^{(0)}}{\partial u^{(0)}} \frac{\partial f^{(1)}}{\partial u^{(1)}} - \frac{\partial f^{(0)}}{\partial u^{(1)}} \frac{\partial f^{(1)}}{\partial u^{(0)}} > 0
\end{aligned}
\tag{6.34}
$$

for all $u \in \mathbb{G}_{0,1,0}$.

Note that the conditions (6.34) are equivalent to the condition that the Jacobian matrix $\boldsymbol{J}_f(u)$ of f is symmetric and positive definite for all $u \in \mathbb{G}_{0,1,0}$. Therefore Assumption 2 on the activation function in $\mathbb{G}_{0,2,0}$ and Assumption 4 on the activation function in $\mathbb{G}_{0,1,0}$ are the same. Because of the injectivity and boundedness of f, there exists the inverse function of f, denoted by $g = f^{-1} : \mathbb{G}_{0,1,0} \to \mathbb{G}_{0,1,0}$. We express g as $u = g(v)$:

$$g(v) = g^{(0)}(v^{(0)}, v^{(0)}) + g^{(1)}(v^{(0)}, v^{(1)})e_1 \tag{6.35}$$

The following lemma holds.

Lemma 2 *If* f *satisfies Assumption 4, there exists a scalar function* $G(\cdot) : \mathbb{G}_{0,1,0}^n \to \mathbb{R}$, *such that*

$$
\begin{aligned}
\frac{\partial G}{\partial v^{(0)}} &= g^{(0)}(v^{(0)}, v^{(1)}) \\
\frac{\partial G}{\partial v^{(1)}} &= g^{(1)}(v^{(0)}, v^{(1)})
\end{aligned}
\tag{6.36}
$$

This lemma can be proved by defining the function $G(v)$ as

$$G(v) := \int_0^{v^{(0)}} g^{(0)}(\rho, 0)d\rho + \int_0^{v^{(1)}} g^{(0)}(v^{(0)}, \rho)d\rho \tag{6.37}$$

We now propose candidates of the energy functions for the Clifford neural networks (6.10) of the class $\mathbb{G}_{0,1,0}$ as follows.

$$E(v) \;=\; -\sum_{i=1}^{n}\sum_{j=1}^{n}\frac{1}{2}Sc\left(v_i^* w_{ij} v_j + 2b_i^* v_i\right) - G(v_i) \qquad (6.38)$$

where $v = [v_1, v_2, \ldots, v_n]^T \in \mathbb{G}_{0,1,0}^n$ and $Sc(\,\cdot\,)$ is defined; $Sc(x) = x^{(0)}$ for $x \in \mathbb{G}_{0,1,0}$.

The following theorem is obtained.

Theorem 6.2 *If the Clifford neural networks* (6.10) *of the class* $\mathbb{G}_{0,1,0}$ *satisfy Assumptions 3 and 4, then there exists an energy function which satisfies Definition 1.*

This theorem can be proved in the similar manner to that of 6.1 as follows. Calculating the time derivatives of the function (6.38) along the trajectories of the networks (6.10) by using Lemma 2, we can show the conditions of Definition 1 of energy functions hold.

The existence conditions of energy functions thus obtained are ones on the connection weight coefficients w_{ij} and the activation function $f(\,\cdot\,)$. It is important to note that the existence conditions of energy functions for the Clifford neural networks of the class $\mathbb{G}_{0,2,0}$ and $\mathbb{G}_{0,1,0}$ are the same in the sense: the involution self-equality on the connection weight coefficients $w_{ji} = w_{ij}^*$ and the symmetry and positive definiteness of the Jacobian matrix of the activation functions.

Further investigation on the existence conditions on the activation function in $\mathbb{G}_{0,1,0}$ can be carried out [10]. We consider two restricted classes of nonlinear functions in $\mathbb{G}_{0,1,0}$: $f : \mathbb{G}_{0,1,0} \to \mathbb{G}_{0,1,0}$.

The functions of the first class are

$$f(u) = f^{(0)}(u^{(0)}) + i f^{(1)}(u^{(1)}). \qquad (6.39)$$

Let us represent $f : \mathbb{G}_{0,1,0} \to \mathbb{G}_{0,1,0}$ in the polar representation by letting $u = r\exp(e_1\theta)$, $r = \sqrt{u^{(0)^2} + u^{(1)^2}}$, $\theta = \tan^{-1}(u^{(1)}/u^{(0)})$ as follows.

$$f(u) = \psi(r,\theta)\exp\left(e_1\phi(r,\theta)\right).$$

The functions of the second class are

$$f(u) = \psi(r)\exp\left(e_1\phi(\theta)\right). \qquad (6.40)$$

The existence conditions of energy functions for the activation functions of the first class (6.39) is immediately obtained from Theorem 6.2 and the conditions of Assumption 4.

Theorem 6.3 *The activation functions of the first class (6.39) satisfy the conditions of Assumption 4 if and only if*

$$\frac{\partial f^{(0)}}{\partial u^{(0)}} > 0 \ \text{ and } \ \frac{\partial f^{(1)}}{\partial u^{(1)}} > 0$$

for all $u \in \mathbb{G}_{0,1,0}$.

For the activation functions of the second class (6.40) the following theorem is obtained.

Theorem 6.4 *The activation functions of the second class (6.40) satisfy the conditions of Assumption 4 if and only if*

$$\frac{d\psi(r)}{dr} \ > \ 0 \ \text{ for all } \ r \geq 0, \quad \lim_{r \to 0} \frac{\psi(r)}{r} > 0 \tag{6.41}$$

and

$$\phi(\theta) \ = \ \theta + n\pi \tag{6.42}$$

where n is an integer.

It is seen from the theorem that the activation (6.40) must take the form

$$f(u) = \psi(r)e^{i\theta}$$

for satisfying the conditions of Assumption 4 because $\phi(\theta) = \theta + n\pi$.

It is seen from Theorem 6.3 that, for the activation functions of the first class (6.39) in $\mathbb{G}_{n,1,0}$, the existence condition is a direct extension of that of the real valued Hopfield-type neural networks. On the other hand, for the activation functions of the second class (6.40) in $\mathbb{G}_{0,1,0}$, only the condition on the modulus r is similar to that of the real-valued networks. Note that, the activation function of the second type satisfying the existence condition does not vary the phase θ of an input.

6.7 CONCLUSION

Recently, models of neural networks in the real-number domain have been extended into the high dimensional domain such as the complex- and quaternion-number domain. These extensions are generalized by introducing Clifford algebra (geometric algebra). In this chapter we extend conventional real-valued models of recurrent neural networks into the domain defined by Clifford algebra and discuss their dynamics. Since geometric product is noncommutative, some different models can be developed. Three models of fully connected recurrent Clifford neural networks, which are extensions of the real-valued Hopfield-type neural networks to the domain defined by Clifford algebra, were presented. We studied dynamics of the proposed models from the point view of existence conditions of an energy function. The existence conditions were discussed for two classes of Hopfield-type Clifford neural networks: the neural networks of the class $\mathbb{G}_{0,1,0}$ and $\mathbb{G}_{0,2,0}$.

The contribution of this chapter is based on the study [14]. The existence conditions for the Hopfield type Clifford neural networks of the class $\mathbb{G}_{1,0,0}$ and $\mathbb{G}_{0,0,1}$ are discussed in [15]. The Clifford algebras $\mathbb{G}_{1,0,0}$ and $\mathbb{G}_{0,0,1}$ are isomorphic to the hyperbolic number and the dual number, respectively [16]. Further work is underway in deriving the existence conditions for more general classes of Hopfield-type Clifford neural networks.

REFERENCES

1. A. Hirose (editor), *Complex-Valued Neural Networks Theoris and Applications*, World Scientific, Singapore, 2003.

2. T. Nitta (editor), *Complex-Valued Neural Networks Utilizing High-Dimensional Parameters*, IGI Global, 2009.

3. S. Buchholz, *A Theory of Neural Computation with Clifford Algebra*, Ph.D. Thesis, University of Kiel, 2005.

4. P. Lounesto, *Clifford Algebras and Spinors*, 2nd edition, Cambrige University Press, 2001.

5. Christian Perwass, *Geometric Algebra with Applications in Engineering*, Springer-Verlag 2009.

6. J. J. Hopfield, Neurons with graded response have collective computational properties like those of two-state neurons, *Proceedings of National Academy of Science USA*, vol.81, pp.3088–3092, 1984.

7. J. J. Hopfield and D. W. Tank. Neural' computation of decisions in optimization problems; *Biological Cybernetics*, vol.52, pp.141–152, 1985.

8. D. W. Tank and J. J. Hopfield, "Simple 'neural' optimization networks: an A/D converter, signal decision circuit, and a linear programming circuit," *IEEE Transactions on Circuits and Systems*, vol.33, pp.533–541, 1986.

9. N. Hashimoto, Y. Kuroe, and T. Mori, On energy function for complex-valued neural networks, *Trans. of the Institute of System, Control and Information Engineers*, vol.15, no.10, pp.559-565, 2002 (in Japanese).

10. Y. Kuroe, M. Yoshida, and T. Mori, On activation functions for complex-valued neural networks - existence of energy functions -, *Artificial Neural Networks and Neural Information Processing - ICANN/ICONIP 2003, Okyay Kaynak et. al. (editors), Lecture Notes in Computer Science* 2714, pp.985-992, Springer-Verlag, Berlin, 2003.

11. M. Yoshida, Y. Kuroe, and T. Mori, Models of Hopfield-type quaternion neural networks and their energy functions, *International Journal of Neural Systems*, Vol.15, Nos.1 & 2, pp.129-135, 2005.

12. L. Dorst, D. Fontijne and S. Mann, *Geometric Algebra for Computer Science An object-oriented Approach to Geometry*, Morgan Kaufmann Publisher, San Francisco, 2007.

13. E. Bayro-Corrochano and G. Scheuermann (Editors.), *Geometric Algebra Computing in Engineering and Computer Science*, Springer-Verlag, Berlin, 2010.

14. Y. Kuroe, Models of Clifford recurrent neural networks and their dynamics, *Proceedings of 2011 International Joint Conference on Neural Networks*, pp.1035-1041, 2011.

15. Y. Kuroe, S. Tanigawa, and H. Iima, Models of Hopfield-type Clifford neural networks and their energy functions - hyperbolic and dual valued networks -, Proceedings of ICONIP 2011, Lecture Notes in Computer Science 7062, pp.560–569, Springer-Verlag, Berlin, 2011.

16. S. G. Gal, *Introduction to Geometric Function Theory of Hypercomplex Variables*, Nova Science Publishers, New York, 2004.

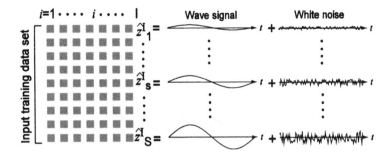

Figure 1.5   A set of teacher signals [35] (See Page 16).

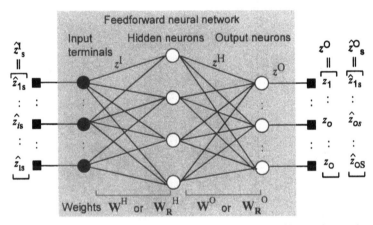

Figure 1.6   Basic construction of the complex- and real-valued feedforward neural networks [35] (See Page 17).

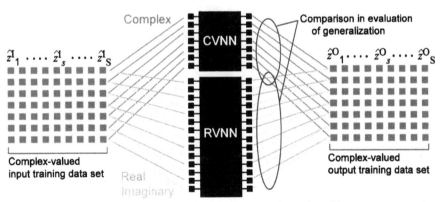

Figure 1.7   Schematic diagram of the learning process for pairs of input-output teachers [35] (See Page 18).

Complex-Valued Neural Networks: Advances and Applications. Edited by Akira Hirose

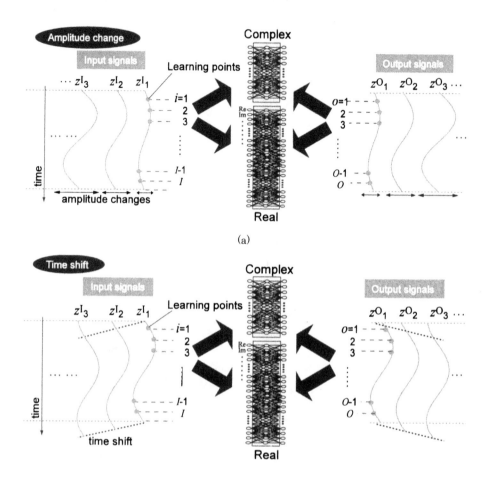

Figure 1.8 Schematic diagrams showing how to feed signals to observe (a) time-shift and (b) amplitude-change generalization [35] (See Page 22).

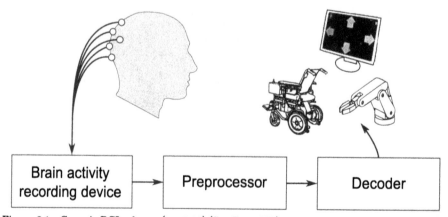

Figure 8.1 Generic BCI scheme (see text) (See Page 187).

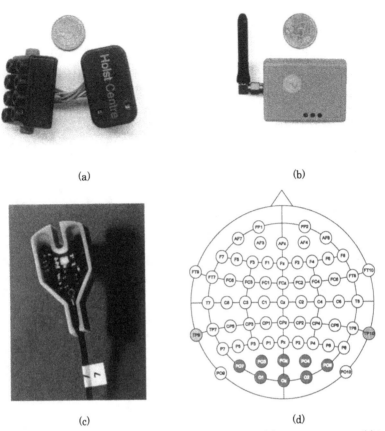

(a)

(b)

(c)

(d)

Figure 8.4 (a) Wireless eight-channel amplifier/transmitter. (b) Receiver station. (c)Active electrode (Brain Products Acticap2) used for EEG acquisition. (d)Locations of the electrodes on the scalp: the recording electrodes are shaded in dark blue, the reference electrode is shaded in light green, and the ground electrode has gray background (See Page 193).

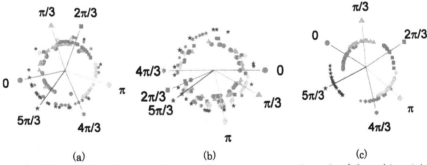

(a)

(b)

(c)

Figure 8.6 Distribution of estimated phases (expressed as angular values) for subject 1 in the experiment described in Section 8.3.2 for channels Oz (left), POz-Oz (central) and POz-O2 (right). Each dot corresponds to the phase estimated from a one second interval recorded when the subject was observing a particular phase-shifted stimulus. Colors represent target-classes (with the stimulus shifted by $\Delta\phi_{mc} = m_c \pi / 3$, where m_c is the class index). Radial lines correspond to the circular means for each class. For the sake of visualization, each class is drawn on a circle with a different radius. (See Page 195).

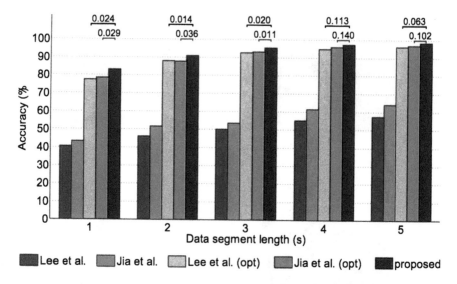

Figure 8.10 Average (among all subjects) discrimination accuracy as a function of the EEG segment length for Lee et al's method [27] using channel Oz referenced to the mastoid (blue), Jia et al.'s method [24] using the bipolar POz - Oz channel (light-blue), Lee et al.'s method [27] for the optimal channel (green), Jia et al.'s method [24] for the optimal channel (orange), and the proposed multichannel method based on MLMVN and feature selection (brown). The numbers above the horizontal braces (at the top of the chart) are the repeated-measures ANOVA p -values for the differences between the results of the proposed method and the optimal channel version methods (See Page 202).

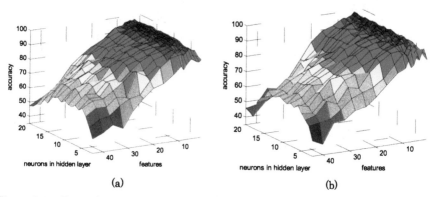

(a)   (b)

Figure 8.11 Dependency of the averaged accuracy in a five-fold cross-validation test of the MLMVN classifier on the number of neurons N_h in the hidden layer and the number $\bar{d}$ of best features used. The best features were estimated according to a feature selection based on standard deviation (left) and based on a Watson--Williams test (right). Results are presented for subject 1 while using five seconds of EEG recording for classifying six phase-shifted targets flickering at 10Hz on the 60-Hz LCD screen (See Page 202).

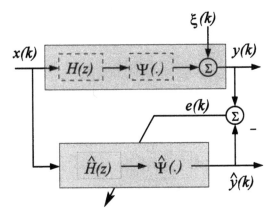

Figure 9.1   Schematic of Wiener system identification (See Page 215).

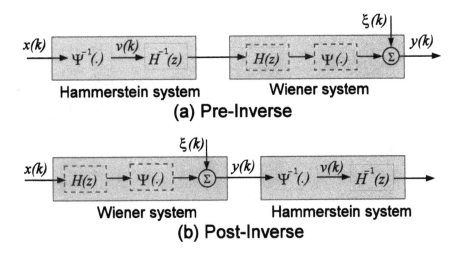

Figure 9.2   Schematic of inverse for a Wiener system (See Page 220).

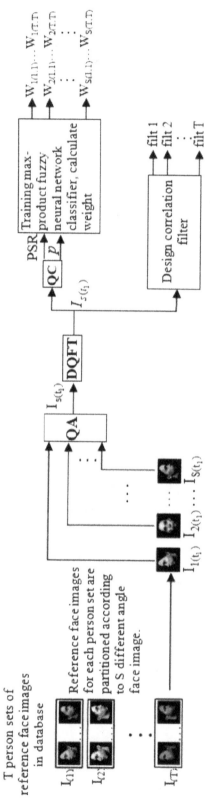

Figure 10.2 Schematic of the enrollment stage (See Page 256).

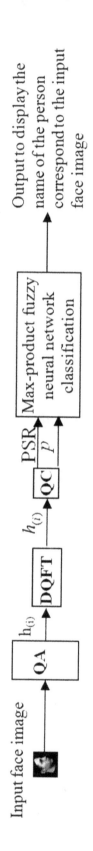

Figure 10.4 Schematic of recognition stage (See Page 260).

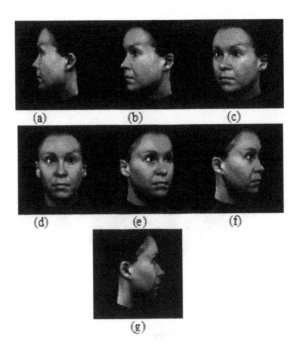

Figure 10.7   An example of a person set with view-invariant face images (a) facing 90° to left, (b) facing 60° to left, (c) facing 30° to left, (d) facing 0° in-front, (e) facing 30° to right, (f) facing 60° to right, and (g) facing 90° to right (See Page 267).

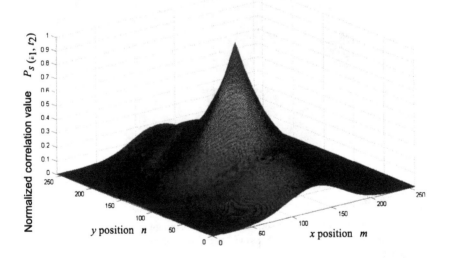

Figure 10.8   Sample correlation plane for input face image matching with the exact reference face image of the same person class in the database (authentic case) (See Page 268).

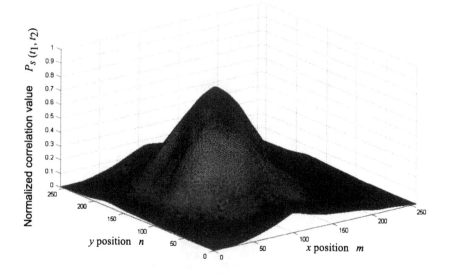

Figure 10.9 Sample correlation plane for input face image matching with one of the reference face image of different person in the database (See Page 269).

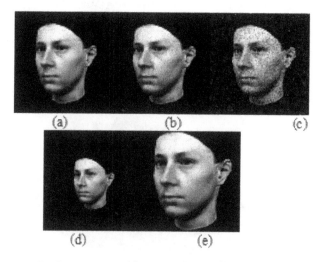

Figure 10.12 An example of a person set (a) original image (b) embedded with mild salt and pepper noise, (c) embedded with heavy salt and pepper noise, (d) shrink (e) dilation (See Page 272).

CHAPTER 7

META-COGNITIVE COMPLEX-VALUED RELAXATION NETWORK AND ITS SEQUENTIAL LEARNING ALGORITHM

RAMASAMY SAVITHA,[1] SUNDARAM SURESH,[1] AND NARASIMHAN SUNDARARA

[1]School of Computer Engineering, Nanyang Technological University, Singapore
[2]Visiting Research Professor, Sri Jaya Chamarajendra College of Engineering (SJCE), Mysore, India

This chapter presents a meta-cognitive learning algorithm for a single hidden layer complex-valued neural network called "Meta-cognitive Fully Complex-valued Relaxation Network (McFCRN) ". McFCRN has two components: a cognitive component and a meta-cognitive component. A fully complex-valued relaxation network (FCRN) with a fully complex-valued Gaussian like activation function ($sech$) in the hidden layer and an exponential activation function in the output layer forms the cognitive component. The meta-cognitive component contains a self-regulatory learning mechanism which controls the learning ability of FCRN by deciding *what to learn*, *when to learn* and *how to learn* from a sequence of training data. The input parameters of cognitive components are chosen randomly, and the output parameters are estimated by minimizing a logarithmic error function. The problem of explicit minimization of magnitude and phase errors in the logarithmic error function is converted to system of linear equations and output parameters of FCRN are computed analytically. McFCRN starts with zero hidden neuron and builds the number of neurons required to approximate the target function. The meta-cognitive component selects the best learning strategy for FCRN to acquire the knowledge from training data and also adapts the learning strategies to implement best human learning components.

Performance studies on a function approximation and real-valued classification problems show that proposed McFCRN performs better than the existing results reported in the literature.

7.1 META-COGNITION IN MACHINE LEARNING

Meta-cognition means knowledge about knowledge and includes knowledge about when and how to use particular strategies for learning or for problem solving. It involves several separate but related cognitive processes and knowledge structures, which share the self as the referent as the common theme [7]. Metacognition research includes the studies regarding reasoning about one's own thinking, memory and executive processes that control the strategy selection and processing allocation, where the self is the referent [34]. In this section, we shall briefly discuss the various models of meta-cognition and describe the various meta-cognitive neural networks that are developed in the literature.

7.1.1 Models of Meta-cognition

Machine self-knowledge and introspective capabilities are two important issues of machine learning that are of concern for the machine learning community. Minsky and McCarthy were the pioneers to delve deep into these issues. Minsky [17] proposed the idea that for a machine to answer adequately about the world, including questions about itself in the world, it has to have an executable model of itself. Minsky stated that an intelligent machine should have a computational model of the outside world so that it can answer questions about actions in the world without actually performing the action, through simulated execution. Minsky's idea was reaffirmed by McCarthy, who stated that a machine that is required to act intelligently should declaratively represent its knowledge [16]. Ever since then, the formal definition of meta-cognition has been refined to include meta-reasoning, meta-knowledge, and control: [7] presents a detailed survey of these definitions.

Although many researchers in the artificial intelligence community have recognized the necessity of reasoning about one's own beliefs, few have both modeled and represented the processes that generate beliefs and made them available to the reasoner itself. There are two kinds of systems in the category of meta-cognition: (a) systems that reason forward to decide what action to perform or what computation to execute (viz., forward strategic control) and (b) systems that reason backward to explain a failure or to learn (viz., backward meta-cognitive monitoring). Systems with forward strategic control attempt to choose a reasoning action based on some knowledge of the mental actions at the disposal of the system. For example, probabilistic estimations and decision theory have been used to select a computation that has the most expected utility [10]. Decision-analytic methods [12] have been used to weigh the trade-off between deliberation cost, execution cost, and goal value when choosing a goal toward which to direct attention and when deciding which action to take to attain a chosen goal. Systems with backward meta-cognitive monitoring represents feedback from the reasoning process. This feedback can be used for learning in tasks such as explanation and interpretive understanding. For example, a computational model of introspection and failure driven learning [6], [8] have been built.

Nelson and Narens proposed a model of human meta-cognition that combines both forward strategic control and backward meta-cognitive monitoring [18]. According to the Nelson and Narens model of meta-cognition, there are two components, namely, a cognitive component and a meta-cognitive component, as shown in Fig. 7.1. The cognitive component represents the knowledge and the meta-cognitive component has a dynamic model of the cognitive component (a mental simulation of the cognitive component). The information flow from the cognitive component to the meta-cognitive component is considered as a monitory signal, while the information flow in the reverse direction is considered as a control signal. In particular, the information flowing from the meta-cognitive component to the cognitive component (control) either changes the state of the cognitive component or changes the cognitive component itself. As a result, one of the following three actions could occur at the cognitive component: (a) initiate an action, (b) continue an action, or (c) terminate an action. However, as the control signal does not yield any information from the cognitive component, a monitory signal is needed. The basic notion of monitoring is that the meta-cognitive component is informed about the cognitive component. This changes the state of the meta-cognitive component's model of the cognitive component, including "no change in state ". It must be noted that the monitory signal is logically independent of the control signal.

Recently, a class of machine learning algorithms have been developed based on the Nelson and Narens model of meta-cognition. In the next section, we briefly discuss the network architecture and explain the analogy between these learning systems and the model of meta-cognition proposed by Nelson and Narens.

7.1.2 Meta cognitive Neural Networks

Similar to the Nelson and Narens model of meta-cognition, a Meta-cognitive Neural Network (McNN) also has two components, namely, a cognitive component and meta-cognitive component, as shown in Fig. 7.1. A multilayer perceptron network is the cognitive component of McNN and a self-regulatory learning mechanism is its meta-cognitive component. The meta-cognitive component has a dynamic model of the cognitive component and *controls* its learning ability by selecting suitable strategies for each sample in the training data set. Thus, for a given training data set, it decides *what to learn*, *when to learn*, and *how to learn* in a meta-cognitive framework. As a result, when a training sample is presented, one of the following actions occur in the cognitive component: (a) sample deletion, (b) sample learning, or (c) sample skip. Thus, during the entire training process, the self-regulatory learning mechanism controls the learning process of cognitive component by enabling the samples with higher information content to be learnt first and samples with lower information content to be learnt during the later stages of the training process. Samples with similar information content are deleted during the training process. Thus, the meta-cognitive component prevents learning similar samples in every epoch of the batch learning process, thereby avoiding overtraining and improving the gener-

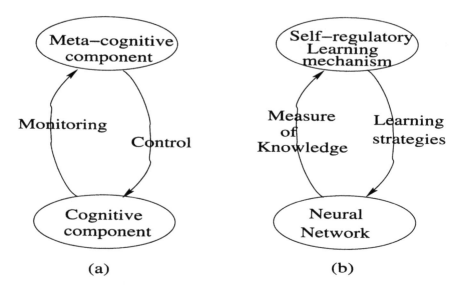

Figure 7.1   Analogy between Nelson and Narens model of meta-cognition and meta-cognitive neural networks. (a) Nelson and Narens model of meta-cognition. (b) Meta-cognitive neural networks.

alization performance of the cognitive network. The cognitive component *monitors* the meta-cognitive component by updating its relative knowledge with respect to the knowledge contained in the training data set.

A self-regulatory resource allocation network [29], and the meta-cognitive neural network [3] are the real-valued meta-cognitive networks available in the literature. Recently, the principles of meta-cognition has also been extended to neuro-fuzzy inference system [32].

The principles of meta-cognition have also been extended to the complex domain and we have developed a few meta-cognitive fully complex-valued neural networks and their learning algorithms. In the next section, we briefly discuss these networks and their learning algorithms.

7.2 META-COGNITION IN COMPLEX-VALUED NEURAL NETWORKS

The fully complex-valued neural networks developed based on the principles of meta-cognition include the Meta-cognitive Fully Complex-valued Radial Basis Function Network (Mc-FCRBF) [24] and the Complex-valued Self-regulatory Resource Allocation Network (CSRAN) [31]. In this section, we briefly discuss these networks and their learning algorithms.

7.2.1 Problem Definition

Given a training data set $\{(\mathbf{z}^1, \mathbf{y}^1), \ldots, (\mathbf{z}^t, \mathbf{y}^t), \ldots, (\mathbf{z}^N, \mathbf{y}^N)\}$, where, N is the total number of training samples with $\mathbf{z}^t = [z_1^t, \ldots, z_m^t]^T \in \mathbb{C}^m$ as the complex-valued inputs, and $\mathbf{y}^t = [y_1^t, \ldots, y_n^t]^T \in \mathbb{C}^n$ as the complex-valued target outputs. The aim of a fully complex-valued neural network is to approximate the relationship between the inputs and their respective target values. In a function approximation problem, $\mathbf{z}^t \in \mathbb{C}^m$ is the m-dimensional complex-valued input vector and $\mathbf{y}^t \in \mathbb{C}^n$ is its desired target (i.e., functional value for the given input $\mathbf{z}^t$). In classification problems, the ($\mathbf{z}^t \in \mathbb{C}^m$) is the m-dimensional transformed complex-valued input feature vector and the target $\mathbf{y}^t \in \mathbb{C}^n$ is the n-dimensional complex-valued coded class label obtained from the actual class label (c^t) using

$$y_j^t = \begin{cases} 1 + i1 & \text{if } c^t = j \\ -1 - i1 & \text{otherwise} \end{cases} \quad j = 1, \ldots, n; \ t = 1, \ldots, N \qquad (7.1)$$

where n is the total number of classes, and i is the Complex operator.

7.2.2 Meta-cognitive Fully Complex-valued Radial Basis Function Network

Mc-FCRBF is a meta-cognitive fully complex-valued radial basis function network. A Fully Complex-valued Radial Basis Function (FC-RBF) network [21] is the cognitive component of Mc-FCRBF and a self-regulatory learning mechanism is its meta-cognitive component.

Cognitive component: An FCRBF is a three-layered fully complex-valued network with a linear input layer, a nonlinear hidden layer and a linear output layer. The neurons at the hidden layer of FC-RBF employ the fully complex-valued $sech$ activation function. Thus, the response of the kth hidden neuron (h_k^t) with the $sech$ activation function for an input $\mathbf{z}^t \in \mathbb{C}^m$ is given by

$$h_k^t = sech\left[\mathbf{v}_k^T(\mathbf{z}^t - \mathbf{u}_k)\right]; \ k = 1, 2, \ldots, K \qquad (7.2)$$

where $\mathbf{u}_k = [u_k^1, \ldots, u_k^m]^T \in \mathbb{C}^m$ is the center of the kth hidden neuron, $\mathbf{v}_k = [v_k^1, \ldots, v_k^m]^T \in \mathbb{C}^m$ is the scaling factor of the kth hidden neuron, and the superscript T is the transpose operator.

The predicted output of the jth output neuron ($\hat{y}_j^t$) for an input $\mathbf{z}^t$ is given by:

$$\hat{y}_j^t = \sum_{k=1}^{K} w_{jk} h_k^t; \ j = 1, 2, \ldots, n \qquad (7.3)$$

The residual error ($\mathbf{e}^t$) of the network is given by

$$\mathbf{e}^t = \mathbf{y}^t - \hat{\mathbf{y}}^t \qquad (7.4)$$

and the mean squared error function (E) is given by

$$E = \frac{1}{2} \mathbf{e}^t \mathbf{e}^{t^H} \qquad (7.5)$$

where the superscript H represents the Complex Hermitian operator.

The objective of Mc-FCRBF learning algorithm is to estimate the following network parameters: the hidden neuron centers $(\mathbf{u}_k)$, the scaling factor of the hidden neurons $(\mathbf{v}_k)$ and the output weights $(\mathbf{w}_k)$, such that the error function (Eq. (7.5)) is minimized for all the training samples. The fully complex-valued learning algorithm of this network has been derived and the parameter update rules for the free parameters of the network [21] are given by

$$\Delta \mathbf{w}_k = \eta_w \bar{h}_k \, e^t; \quad k = 1, 2, \ldots, K \tag{7.6}$$

$$\Delta \mathbf{v}_k = \eta_v \overline{\mathbf{w}}_k^T \, e^t \, \bar{f}' \left(\mathbf{v}_k^T (\mathbf{z}^t - \mathbf{u}_k) \right) \left(\overline{\mathbf{z}^t - \mathbf{u}_k} \right) \tag{7.7}$$

$$\Delta \mathbf{c}_k = -\eta_c \overline{\mathbf{w}}_k^T \, e^t \, \bar{f}' \left(\mathbf{v}_k^T (\mathbf{z}^t - \mathbf{u}_k) \right) \overline{\mathbf{v}}_k \tag{7.8}$$

Meta-cognitive component: A self-regulatory learning mechanism is the meta-cognitive component of Mc-FCRBF. When a new sample is presented to the network, the meta-cognitive component *controls* the learning ability of FC-RBF by choosing one of the following strategies:

Action (a) *Sample Deletion:* Delete those samples from the training data set that contain information similar to that already learnt by the network. This action addresses the *what-to-learn* component of the meta-cognition.

Action (b) *Sample Learning:* Use the sample to update the network parameters in the current epoch. This represents *how-to-learn* the sample in the meta-cognitive framework .

Action (c) *Sample Skip:* Skip the sample from learning in the current epoch and retain the sample in the training data set, thereby, deciding *when-to-learn* the sample in the context of meta-cognition.

The cognitive component *monitors* the meta-cognitive component and updates the meta-cognitive component's dynamic model of the cognitive component using the instantaneous magnitude and phase errors based on the residual error of FC-RBF $(e^t = [e_1^t, \ldots, e_k^t, \ldots, e_n^t]^T)$ defined as:

$$e_k^t = y_k^t - \hat{y}_k^t; \quad k = 1, \ldots, n; \ t = 1, \ldots, N \tag{7.9}$$

Based on the residual error, the monitory signals of Mc-FCRBF are defined by

- The instantaneous magnitude error:

$$M_t^e = \frac{1}{n} \sqrt{e^{tH} . e^t} \tag{7.10}$$

- The instantaneous phase error:

$$\phi_t^e = \frac{1}{n} \sum_{k=1}^{n} \left| arg(y_k^t . \overline{(\hat{y}_k^t)}) \right| \tag{7.11}$$

where $\overline{(\hat{y}_k^t)}$ refers to the conjugate of the predicted output $\hat{y}_k^t$ and the function $arg(.)$ returns the phase of a complex-valued number in $[-\pi, \pi]$ and is given by

$$arg(z) = atan\left(\frac{imag(z)}{real(z)}\right) \tag{7.12}$$

Use these monitory signals, the three actions of the meta-cognitive learning are described in detail below:

- **Sample Deletion:** If $M_t^e < E_d^M$ and $\phi_t^e < E_d^\phi$, where E_d^M is the delete magnitude threshold and E_d^ϕ is the delete phase threshold, then the sample t is deleted from the training data set. The thresholds E_d^M and E_d^ϕ are chosen based on the desired accuracy.

- **Sample Learning:** If the sample learning condition given by

$$\text{If} \quad M_t^e \geq E_l^M \quad \text{or} \quad \phi_t^e \geq E_l^\phi \tag{7.13}$$

is satisfied in the current epoch, then the parameters of the network are updated using the gradient descent based parameter update rules (given in Eq. (7.7), Eq. (7.8), Eq. (7.6)) in the current epoch only. Here, E_l^M is the parameter update magnitude threshold and E_l^ϕ is the parameter update phase threshold. It must be noted that the parameter update magnitude threshold (E_l^M) and parameter update phase threshold (E_l^ϕ) are not fixed. They are self-regulated based on the residual error of the sample in the current epoch, according to the following conditions:

$$\text{If } M_t^e \geq E_l^M, \text{ then } E_l^M := \delta E_l^M - (1-\delta)M_t^e \tag{7.14}$$

$$\text{If } \phi_t^e \geq E_l^\phi, \text{ then } E_l^\phi := \delta E_l^\phi - (1-\delta)\phi_t^e \tag{7.15}$$

where δ is the slope at which the thresholds are self-regulated. Larger value of δ results in a slow decay of the thresholds from their initial values. This helps fewer samples with significant information to be learnt first, and samples containing less significant information to be learnt last. Therefore, larger values of δ ensures that the meta-cognitive principles are emulated efficiently. Usually, δ is set close to 1.

- **Sample Skip:** If a sample does not satisfy the sample deletion or sample learning condition in the current epoch, then the sample is skipped in the current epoch and is retained in the training data set as such. Due to the self-regulating nature of the parameter update thresholds, the sample might be used in learning in subsequent epochs.

Thus, Mc-FCRBF is a batch learning meta-cognitive fully complex-valued network. Hence it requires the complete training data set before training. Moreover, it also requires that the number of hidden neurons are fixed a priori. However, in real-world applications like the medical diagnosis, the complete training data set is not available a priori. Hence, it is desirable to derive sequential learning algorithms that learn the training samples one-by-one and discard them after learning. In such a sequential learning algorithm, the network begins with zero hidden neurons and adds and deletes neurons during the training process to achieve a parsimonious network structure. In the next section, we briefly explain a sequential learning algorithm for a complex-valued self-regulatory resource allocation network.

7.2.3 Complex-Valued Self-Regulatory Resource Allocation Network

CSRAN is a fully complex-valued sequential learning algorithm that approximates a given function using the principles of meta-cognition. The basic building block of the CSRAN is a fully complex-valued radial basis function network. As CSRAN is a sequential learning algorithm, it starts with no hidden neuron and builds the necessary number of hidden neurons based on the information contained in the current sample. CSRAN has a self-regulating scheme which controls the learning process by proper selection of the training samples.

Without loss of generality, we assume that after sequentially learning $t-1$ observations, CSRAN has built a network with K hidden neurons. For a given input, the predicted output $(\hat{\mathbf{y}}_t = [\hat{y}_t^1, \ldots, \hat{y}_t^n]^T \in \mathbb{C}^n)$ of the CSRAN with K hidden neurons is given by

$$\hat{y}_j^t = \sum_{k=1}^{K} w_{jk} h_k^t; \; j = 1, \ldots, n \tag{7.16}$$

$$h_k^t = sech\left[\mathbf{v}_k^T(\mathbf{z}^t - \mathbf{u}_k)\right]; \; k = 1, \ldots, K$$

where $w_{jk} \in \mathbb{C}$ is the complex-valued weight connecting the kth hidden neuron to the jth output neuron, $\mathbf{v}_k = [v_{k1}, \ldots, v_{km}]^T \in \mathbb{C}^m$ is the complex-valued scaling factor of the kth hidden neuron, $\mathbf{u}_k = [c_{k1}, \ldots, c_{km}]^T \in \mathbb{C}^m$ is the center of the kth hidden neuron, the superscript T denotes the transpose operator and $sech(z) = 2/(e^z + e^{-z})$.

The residual error $(\mathbf{e}^t)$ of the CSRAN for the current observation $(\mathbf{x}^t, \mathbf{y}^t)$ is defined as

$$\mathbf{e}^t = \mathbf{y}^t - \hat{\mathbf{y}}^t \tag{7.17}$$

Using the residual error, we estimate the instantaneous magnitude error (M_t^e) and the normalized absolute phase error (ϕ_t^e) as defined in Eqs. (7.10) and (7.11).

In a sequential learning framework, the observation data/samples arrive one-by-one and one at a time. CSRAN algorithm regulates the sequential learning process by selecting appropriate samples for learning. The schematic diagram of the self-regulating scheme is shown in Fig. 7.2. The basic working principles of the self-regulating scheme are explained in the following paragraph.

Based on the instantaneous magnitude (M_t^e) and absolute phase error (ϕ_t^e) of each sample in the training sequence, the self-regulating scheme performs one of the following three actions:

Action (a) *Sample Deletion*: Samples are deleted without being used in the learning process.

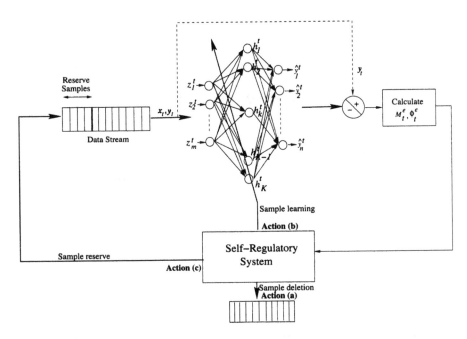

Figure 7.2   Schematic diagram of CSRAN and its self-regulatory learning scheme.

Action (b) *Sample Learning*: Learning includes growing/pruning the hidden neuron or updating the network parameters.

Action (c) *Sample Reserve*: The samples are pushed to the rear end of the training sequence and can be used at a later stage.

The concept behind these actions representing each block of Fig. 7.2 are described in detail below:

Action (a) Sample Deletion: When both the instantaneous magnitude error (M_t^e) (given in Eq. (7.10)) and the absolute phase error (ϕ_t^e) (given in Eq. (7.11)) of a sample are less than their fixed delete thresholds, the self-regulating scheme deletes the sample without using it in the learning process. The sample deletion criterion is given by

$$M_t^e \leq E_d^M \quad and \quad \phi_t^e \leq E_d^\phi \tag{7.18}$$

where E_d^M is the sample delete magnitude threshold and E_d^ϕ is the sample delete phase threshold. The 'sample deletion' criterion removes similar samples from the training sequence. Hence, it avoids over-training and reduces the computational effort.

Action (b) Sample Learning: In a self-regulating scheme, the learning process involves the allocation of new hidden neurons ('growing'), updating of network parameters ('update') and removing redundant neurons ('pruning').

Neuron Growing Criterion: As the training samples arrive sequentially, some of the selected samples will be used to 'add' new hidden neurons based on the following criterion

$$M_t^e \geq E_a^M \quad or \quad \phi_t^e \geq E_a^\phi \tag{7.19}$$

where E_a^M is the neuron growing magnitude threshold and E_a^ϕ is the neuron growing phase threshold.

It should be pointed out here that the neuron growing thresholds (E_a^M, E_a^ϕ) are not kept constant. They are adaptively varied based on the current residual error as given below:

$$
\begin{aligned}
\text{If} \quad M_t^e &\geq E_a^M, \quad \text{then} \quad E_a^M := \delta E_a^M - (1 - \delta) M_t^e \\
\text{If} \quad \phi_t^e &\geq E_a^\phi, \quad \text{then} \quad E_a^\phi := \delta E_a^\phi - (1 - \delta) \phi_t^e
\end{aligned}
\tag{7.20}
$$

where the slope parameter (δ) controls the rate at which the neuron growing thresholds (E_a^M, E_a^ϕ) are regulated and hence influence the neuron growth. In general, the slope parameter is initialized close to 1.

When a new hidden neuron ($K + 1$) is added to the network, the parameters associated with it are initialized as

$$\mathbf{w}_{K+1} = \mathbf{e}_t; \quad \mathbf{c}_{K+1} = \mathbf{x}_t; \quad \mathbf{v}_{K+1} = \kappa(\mathbf{x}_t - \mathbf{c}_{nr}) \tag{7.21}$$

where nr is the nearest neuron, defined as that neuron with the smallest Euclidean distance from the current sample. The scaling factor κ determines the overlap between the samples in the input space. As κ increases, the overlap between the responses of the hidden neurons also increases.

Network Parameter Update Criterion: If a new observation ($\mathbf{x}_t, \mathbf{y}_t$) arrives and the parameter update criterion is satisfied then the parameters of the network are updated using a C-EKF [13]. The parameter update criterion is given by

$$M_t^e \geq E_l^M \quad or \quad \phi_t^e \geq E_l^\phi \tag{7.22}$$

where E_l^M is the parameter update magnitude threshold and E_l^ϕ is the parameter update phase threshold. The parameter update thresholds (E_l^M, E_l^ϕ) are also adapted based on the residual error of the current sample as given below

$$
\begin{aligned}
\text{If} \quad M_t^e &\geq E_l^M, \quad \text{then} \quad E_l^M := \delta E_l^M - (1 - \delta) M_t^e \\
\text{If} \quad \phi_t^e &\geq E_l^\phi, \quad \text{then} \quad E_l^\phi := \delta E_l^\phi - (1 - \delta) \phi_t^e
\end{aligned}
\tag{7.23}
$$

where δ is a slope that controls the rate of self-adaptation of the parameter update magnitude and phase thresholds. Usually, δ is set close to 1.

The main advantage of the self-regulating thresholds is that it helps in selecting appropriate samples to add neuron or update the network parameters, i.e., the CSRAN algorithm uses sample with higher error to either add a new hidden neuron or update the network parameters first and the remaining samples for fine tuning the network parameters.

The network parameters ($\boldsymbol{\alpha}^t = [\mathbf{u}_1, \ldots, \mathbf{u}_K, \mathbf{v}_1, \ldots, \mathbf{v}_K, \mathbf{w}_1, \ldots, \mathbf{w}_K]^T$) are updated for the current sample (t) as

$$\boldsymbol{\alpha}^t = \boldsymbol{\alpha}^{t-1} + G^t \mathbf{e}^t \tag{7.24}$$

where $\mathbf{e}^t$ is the residual error and G^t is complex-valued Kalman gain matrix given by

$$G^t = P^{t-1}\mathbf{a}^t \left[R + \mathbf{a}^{t^H} P^{t-1} \mathbf{a}^t \right]^{-1} \qquad (7.25)$$

where $\mathbf{a}^t$ is the complex-valued gradient vector, $R = r_0 I_{n \times n}$ is the variance of the measurement noise and P^t is the error covariance matrix.

The gradient vector $(\mathbf{a}^t)$ (set of partial derivatives of output with respect to α_t) is defined as

$$\mathbf{a}^t = \begin{bmatrix} \frac{\partial \widehat{y}_1^t}{\partial u_{11}} & \cdots & \frac{\partial \widehat{y}_1^t}{\partial u_{Km}} & \frac{\partial \widehat{y}_1^t}{\partial v_{11}} & \cdots & \frac{\partial \widehat{y}_1^t}{\partial v_{Km}} & \frac{\partial \widehat{y}_1^t}{\partial w_{11}} & \cdots & \frac{\partial \widehat{y}_1^t}{\partial w_{nK}} \\ \vdots & & \vdots & \vdots & & \vdots & \vdots & & \vdots \\ \frac{\partial \widehat{y}_n^t}{\partial u_{11}} & \cdots & \frac{\partial \widehat{y}_n^t}{\partial u_{Km}} & \frac{\partial \widehat{y}_n^t}{\partial v_{11}} & \cdots & \frac{\partial \widehat{y}_n^t}{\partial v_{Km}} & \frac{\partial \widehat{y}_n^t}{\partial w_{11}} & \cdots & \frac{\partial \widehat{y}_n^t}{\partial w_{nK}} \end{bmatrix}^T$$

where, the gradients for the free parameters w_{lk}, $\mathbf{v}_k$ and $\mathbf{u}_k$ are given by Eqs. (7.6), (7.7), and (7.8), respectively.

The error covariance matrix is updated as

$$P^t = \left[I - G^t \mathbf{a}^{t^H} \right] P^{t-1} + qI \qquad (7.26)$$

where q is a process noise covariance usually set close to 0 and I is an identity matrix of dimension $K(2m + n) \times K(2m + n)$.

Neuron Pruning Criterion: CSRAN algorithm uses the contribution of the hidden neuron to delete the superfluous neuron. The contribution of the kth hidden neuron is defined as

$$r_k = \frac{h_k^t}{\max_j h_j^t} \qquad (7.27)$$

If $\|r_k\| < E_p$ AND $arg(r_k) < E_p$ for N_w consecutive samples, then the kth neuron is superfluous and is removed from the network. Here, E_p is the neuron pruning threshold. If the neuron pruning threshold (E_p) is set at a lower value, then pruning seldom occurs and all the added neurons will remain in the network irrespective of their contribution to the network output. On the other hand, higher value of E_p results in frequent pruning, resulting in oscillations and insufficient neurons to approximate the function.

When a neuron is added to the network, the error covariance matrix (P_t) is updated as

$$P^t = \begin{bmatrix} P^{t-1} & 0 \\ 0 & p^0 I_{(2m+n) \times (2m+n)} \end{bmatrix} \qquad (7.28)$$

where p^0 is the estimated uncertainty of initial parameters. On the other hand, when a neuron (say, kth neuron) is removed from the network, the dimensionality of the error covariance matrix is reduced by removing the respective rows and columns of the P_t matrix, i.e. remove $(i - 1)(2m + n) + 1$ to $i(2m + n)$ rows and columns of the P_t matrix. For initialization of the C-EKF parameters, p_0, q and r_0, one should refer to Ref. (13).

Action (c) Sample Reserve: If the current observation $(\mathbf{z}^t, \mathbf{y}^t)$ does not satisfy the sample deletion criterion or the neuron growing criterion or the parameter update criterion, then the sample is pushed to the rear end of the data stream. Due to the self-adaptive nature of the thresholds, these reserve samples may also contain some useful information and will be used later in the learning process.

These three actions of self-regulating learning are repeated for all the samples in the training sequence.

7.2.4   Issues in Mc-FCRBF and CSRAN

Although Mc-FCRBF and CSRAN are meta-cognitive in nature, they suffer from the following drawbacks:

Mc-FCRBF is a gradient descent based batch learning algorithm derived by minimizing the mean squared error function. However, the mean squared error function is an explicit representation of only the magnitude of error and does not represent the phase of the error explicitly. Hence, Mc-FCRBF might not approximate the phase of the complex-valued function accurately. As CSRAN also uses the gradients derived from the mean squared error function, it might not also approximate the phase of the complex-valued function accurately. Moreover, Mc-FCRBF is a batch learning algorithm that learns the given training samples over a number of epochs, and hence, requires large computational effort to learn the training samples. CSRAN also uses the C-EKF to update the network parameters and hence, requires considerable computational effort.

To overcome these issues of Mc-FCRBF and CSRAN, in the following sections, we introduce a more accurate, fast learning fully complex-valued meta-cognitive neural network namely, 'Meta-cognitive Fully Complex-valued Relaxation Network (McFCRN)' and its sequential learning algorithm. We also study the performance of McFCRN on a synthetic complex-valued function approximation problem and a set of real-valued benchmark classification problems.

7.3   META-COGNITIVE FULLY COMPLEX-VALUED RELAXATION NETWORK

In this section, we present the description of "Meta-cognitive Fully Complex-valued Relaxation Network (McFCRN)" [23]. We first describe the architecture and learning algorithm of FCRN that is the cognitive component of McFCRN. Then, we present in detail the meta-cognitive component of McFCRN and its various control strategies.

7.3.1   Cognitive Component: A Fully Complex-valued Relaxation Network (FCRN)

We describe the fully complex-valued relaxation network and its projection-based learning algorithm in detail in this section. Fully Complex-valued Relaxation Network (FCRN) is a single hidden layer feed forward network. FCRN uses a projection based learning algorithm that does not require the number of hidden neurons to be fixed a priori. Instead, it begins with zero hidden neurons and builds a minimal network architecture to approximate the function defined by the training data set.

Without loss of generality, let us assume that K neurons are added to the network after learning $t - 1$ samples. The architecture of FCRN with K hidden neurons is presented in Fig. 7.3.

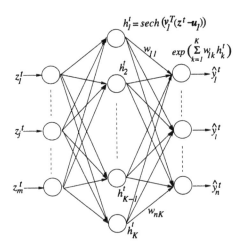

Figure 7.3   The architecture of FCRN.

The neurons in the hidden layer of the network employ the fully complex-valued activation function of the type of hyperbolic secant [21] ($sech(z) = 2/(e^z + e^{-z})$) to map the input features to a hyper-dimensional Complex plane, i.e., $\mathbf{C}^m \to \mathbf{C}^K$. Thus, the response of the jth hidden neuron for a given input $\mathbf{z}^t \in \mathbf{C}^m$ is given by

$$h_j^t = sech\left[\mathbf{v}_j^T\left(\mathbf{z}^t - \mathbf{u}_j\right)\right], \; j = 1, \ldots, K \tag{7.29}$$

where $\mathbf{v}_j \in \mathbf{C}^m$ is the complex-valued scaling factor and $\mathbf{u}_j \in \mathbf{C}^m$ is the complex-valued center of the hidden neurons.

The neurons in the output layer of FCRN employ an 'exp' activation function and the predicted output ($\widehat{\mathbf{y}}^t$) of FCRN with K hidden neurons is given by

$$\widehat{y}_k^t = exp\left(\sum_{j=1}^{K} w_{kj} h_j^t\right), \; k = 1, \ldots, n \tag{7.30}$$

where w_{kj} is the output weight connecting the jth hidden neuron and the kth output neuron.

The essential properties for a fully complex-valued activation function require that it has to be nonlinear, analytic and bounded *almost everywhere* (*a.e.*) [14]. Both the activation functions, '$sech$' and 'exp' functions, employed in the hidden and output layers of FCRN satisfy these essential properties as shown in [21] and [28], respectively. Hence, when operated in the bounded region of the Complex plane [14], FCRN with at most K hidden neurons is capable of learning N distinct samples with random and constant hidden layer parameters ($\mathbf{u}_j$ and $\mathbf{v}_j$).

FCRN network is a complex-valued network that is used to approximate both the magnitude and phase of the complex-valued signals accurately. Hence, the error function should be an explicit representation of both the magnitude and the phase of the complex-valued error, of the form:

$$J \;=\; g(\mathbf{y}^t, \widehat{\mathbf{y}}^t) \tag{7.31}$$
$$\text{where } \mathbf{y}^t \;=\; M^t.exp(\phi^t); \ \widehat{\mathbf{y}}^t = \widehat{M}^t.exp(\widehat{\phi}^t)$$

where M^t and ϕ^t are the true/target magnitude and phase of the tth sample and $\widehat{M}^t_k$ and $\widehat{\phi}^t_k$ are the predicted magnitude and phase of the tth sample.

One possible choice of the error function J that is an explicit representation of both magnitude and phase can be taken as

$$J \;=\; \left[ln\left(\frac{M^t}{\widehat{M}^t}\right)^2 + \left(\phi^t - \widehat{\phi}^t\right)^2 \right] \tag{7.32}$$

which can be equivalently written as

$$J \;=\; \left[ln\left(\frac{\mathbf{y}^t}{\widehat{\mathbf{y}}^t}\right) \overline{ln\left(\frac{\mathbf{y}^t}{\widehat{\mathbf{y}}^t}\right)} \right] \tag{7.33}$$

where $\widehat{\mathbf{y}}^t$ is the predicted output of the network as defined in Eq. (7.30) and $\overline{ln\left(\frac{\mathbf{y}^t}{\widehat{\mathbf{y}}^t}\right)}$ is the complex conjugate of $ln\left(\frac{\mathbf{y}^t}{\widehat{\mathbf{y}}^t}\right)$.

Given the training data set $\{(\mathbf{z}^1, \mathbf{y}^1), \ldots, (\mathbf{z}^t, \mathbf{y}^t), \ldots, (\mathbf{z}^N, \mathbf{y}^N)\}$, the objective is to estimate the output weights w_{kj} with h^t_j obtained using randomly chosen hidden layer parameters such that the minimum energy state of Eq. (7.33) is estimated, or

$$W^* \;=\; arg\min_W \ J(W) \tag{7.34}$$

where the arg in the above equation represents the function argument. Estimation of the minimum energy state of Eq. (7.34) yields the optimum output weight (W^*) for the selected random hidden layer parameters. The complex-valued neural network used to determine this minimum energy state for a given training data set is called a "fully complex-valued relaxation network."

Substituting for $\widehat{\mathbf{y}}_t$ from Eq. (7.30) in Eq. (7.33), we have

$$J \;=\; \frac{1}{2} \sum_{t=1}^{N} \sum_{k=1}^{C} \left(ln\left(y^t_k\right) - \left(\sum_{j=1}^{K} w_{kj} h^t_j\right) \right)$$
$$\cdot \left(\overline{ln\left(y^t_k\right)} - \left(\overline{\sum_{j=1}^{K} w_{kj} h^t_j}\right) \right) \tag{7.35}$$

where h_j^t is the response of the jth hidden neuron for the tth sample and y_k^t is target to the kth output neuron of the tth sample.

Using the definition of the partial derivatives of a real-valued function of complex-valued variables, the derivative of the error function J (Eq. (7.35)) with respect to the output weights w_{kj} is

$$\frac{\partial J}{\partial w_{kj}} = \sum_{t=1}^{N} h_j^t \left[ln\left(\overline{y}_k^t\right) - \sum_{p=1}^{K} \overline{w}_{kp}\, \overline{h}_p^t \right] \tag{7.36}$$

The minimum energy state of the error function J is obtained by equating its first order derivative to 0, *i.e.*,

$$\frac{\partial J}{\partial w_{kj}} = \sum_{t=1}^{N} h_j^t \left[ln\left(\overline{y}_k^t\right) - \sum_{p=1}^{K} \overline{w}_{kp}\, \overline{h}_p^t \right] = 0 \tag{7.37}$$

Rearranging the above equation, we can obtain

$$\sum_{p=1}^{K} \overline{w}_{kp} \sum_{t=1}^{N} h_j^t\, \overline{h}_p^t = \sum_{t=1}^{N} ln\left(\overline{y}_k^t\right) h_j^t \tag{7.38}$$

Eq. (7.38) is reduced to

$$\sum_{p=1}^{K} \overline{w}_{kp} A_{jp} = B_{jk} \tag{7.39}$$

The above equation can be represented in matrix form as

$$\overline{\mathbf{W}} \mathbf{A} = \mathbf{B} \tag{7.40}$$

where $\mathbf{A} \in \mathbf{C}^{K \times K}$ is the projection matrix given by

$$A_{jp} = \sum_{t=1}^{N} h_j^t \overline{h}_p^t; \ j, p = 1, \ldots, K \tag{7.41}$$

and $\mathbf{B} \in \mathbf{C}^{C \times K}$ is the output matrix given by

$$B_{jk} = \sum_{t=1}^{N} ln\left(\overline{y}_{kt}\right) h_j^t; \ j = 1, \ldots, K, k = 1, \ldots, n \tag{7.42}$$

Equation (7.40) is a system of linear equations and can be easily solved by the inversion of the matrix $\mathbf{A}$. It can be observed from the definition of the projection matrix in Eq. (7.41) that the matrix $\mathbf{A}$ is a Hermitian square matrix. The matrix $\mathbf{A}$ is non-singular, and is hence, invertible [30].

Hence, the unique and optimum output weights of FCRN network can be estimated as:

$$\mathbf{W}^* = \overline{\mathbf{B}}\,\overline{\mathbf{A}}^{-1} \qquad (7.43)$$

Equation (7.43) is the linear least square solution to the set of linear equations given by Eq. (7.38). The output weights given in Eq. (7.43) are the optimal weights for a given random hidden layer parameters. Thus, FCRN estimates the minimum energy state of the error function defined in Eq. (7.32) and is computationally less intensive.

7.3.2   Meta-cognitive Component: A Self-regulatory Learning Mechanism

In this section, we describe the working principles of the meta-cognitive component of McFCRN that controls the learning process of FCRN (cognitive component) by selecting suitable learning strategies for each sample (control signal) in the training data set.

The self-regulatory learning mechanism uses these errors to measure the relative knowledge of the cognitive component (FCRN) in comparison to the knowledge contained in the training data set. Based on these measures of relative knowledge, the meta-cognitive component *controls* the learning process of FCRN by selecting one of the following strategies:

Strategy (a): Sample Deletion Samples that contain knowledge already learnt by FCRN are deleted.

Strategy (b): Sample Learning Samples with relatively new knowledge are used to add a new hidden neuron or update the output weights of existing neurons

Strategy (c): Sample Reserve Samples that satisfy neither of the above conditions are pushed to the rear end of the stack for future use.

We explain each of these strategies in detail next:

- **Strategy (a): Sample Deletion** If the sample delete criteria given by:

$$M_t^e < E_d^M \ and \ \phi_t^e < E_d^\phi \qquad (7.44)$$

is satisfied, then the sample is deleted from the training data set. Here, E_d^M and E_d^ϕ are the magnitude and phase delete thresholds, respectively. They are usually set based on the desired accuracy.

- **Strategy (b): Sample Learning** Samples are used to either add a new hidden neuron or to update the parameters of the network. Thus, sample learning strategy comprises of the neuron addition strategy and the parameter update strategy.

  - *Neuron addition strategy:* As the training samples arrive sequentially, some of the selected samples will be used to 'add' new hidden neurons based on the following criterion

$$M_t^e \geq E_a^M \ or \ \phi_t^e \geq E_a^\phi \qquad (7.45)$$

where E_a^M is the neuron growing magnitude threshold and E_a^ϕ is the neuron growing phase threshold. These thresholds are not constants, but are self-regulated such that samples with higher error are learnt first, followed by samples with lower error. The self-regulation occurs according to:

$$\begin{aligned} \text{If } M_t^e &\geq E_a^M, \; E_a^M &= \delta E_a^M - (1-\delta)M_t^e \\ \text{If } \phi_t^e &\geq E_a^\phi, \; E_a^\phi &= \delta E_a^\phi - (1-\delta)\phi_t^e \end{aligned} \tag{7.46}$$

where δ is the slope at which the thresholds are self-regulated. Larger value of δ results in a slow decay of the thresholds from their initial values. This helps fewer samples with significant information to be learnt first, and samples containing less significant information to be learnt last. Thus, larger values of δ ensures that the meta-cognitive principles are emulated efficiently. Usually, δ is set close to 1. When a new neuron is added to FCRN, the input parameters ($\mathbf{u}_K$ and $\mathbf{v}_K$) of the new neuron are initialized randomly and the optimal output weights are computed using the projection based learning algorithm. Accordingly, the following sequence of operations are carried out:

$$\mathbf{A}_{(K+1)\times(K+1)} = \left[\begin{array}{c|c} \mathbf{A}_{K\times K} & \overline{\mathbf{a}_{K+1}} \\ \hline \mathbf{a}_{K+1}^T & a_{K+1,K+1} \end{array} \right] \tag{7.47}$$

where matrix $\mathbf{A}_{K\times K} \in \mathbf{C}^{K\times K}$ is updated as

$$A_{kp} = A_{kp} + \overline{h_k^t}h_p^t; \; k,p = 1,\dots,K \tag{7.48}$$

where h_k^t is the response of the kth hidden neuron to the tth sample being used to add the neuron.

The $\mathbf{C}^{K\times 1}$ vector $\mathbf{a}_{K+1} = [a_{1,K+1},\dots a_{p,K+1},\dots,a_{K,K+1}]$ is given by

$$a_{p,K+1} = \sum_{l=1}^{t} h_{K+1}^l \overline{h}_p^l; p = 1,\dots,K \tag{7.49}$$

and the complex-valued scalar $a_{(K+1)(K+1)}$ is given by

$$a_{(K+1)(K+1)} = \sum_{l=1}^{t} h_{K+1}^l \overline{h}_{K+1}^l \tag{7.50}$$

Similarly, the dimensionality of the $\mathbf{B}$ matrix is also increased from $K \times n$ to $(K+1) \times n$ according to

$$\mathbf{B} = \left[\begin{array}{c} \mathbf{B}_{K\times n} \\ \mathbf{b}_{1\times n} \end{array} \right] \tag{7.51}$$

where the $K \times n$ matrix is updated with the current sample t according to:

$$\mathbf{B} = \sum_{l=1}^{t} ln\left(\bar{y}_k^t\right) h_j^t; \; j = 1, \ldots, K, k = 1, \ldots, n \quad (7.52)$$

and the output matrix $\mathbf{B}$ is appended with $1 \times n$ elements corresponding to the $K + 1$-th neuron as:

$$\mathbf{b} = \sum_{l=1}^{t} ln\left(\bar{y}_k^l\right) h_{K+1}^l; \; k = 1, \ldots, n \quad (7.53)$$

Finally, the output weights are estimated as

$$\begin{bmatrix} \mathbf{w}_K \\ \mathbf{w}_{K+1} \end{bmatrix} = \begin{bmatrix} \mathbf{B}_{K \times n} \\ \mathbf{b}_{1 \times n} \end{bmatrix} \begin{bmatrix} \mathbf{A}_{K \times K} & \overline{\mathbf{a}_{K+1}} \\ \hline \mathbf{a}_{K+1}^T & a_{K+1,K+1} \end{bmatrix}^{-1} \quad (7.54)$$

- *Parameter update strategy:* When a sample contains significant information that is not novel, but is less familiar to FCRN, the output weights of the network are updated according to Eq. (7.43). The parameter update criterion is given by

$$M_t^e \geq E_l^M \; \textbf{OR} \; \phi_t^e \geq E_l^\phi \quad (7.55)$$

where E_l^M and E_l^ϕ are the parameter update magnitude and phase thresholds, respectively. Similar to the neuron addition thresholds, the parameter update thresholds are also self-regulated according to

$$\begin{aligned} \text{If } M_t^e \geq E_l^M, \; E_l^M &= \delta E_l^M - (1 - \delta) M_t^e \\ \text{If } \phi_t^e \geq E_l^\phi, \; E_l^\phi &= \delta E_l^\phi - (1 - \delta) \phi_t^e \end{aligned} \quad (7.56)$$

It is intuitive that the initial values of the self-regulating parameter update thresholds are lesser than their respective neuron add thresholds. It is usually set at a value smaller than the smallest value the neuron addition thresholds can achieve after self-regulation. For a complete guideline on the initialization of the various self-regulating thresholds of the meta-cognitive component, one must refer to Ref. (31).

- **Strategy (b): Sample Reserve Strategy** If the current observation $(\mathbf{z}^t, \mathbf{y}^t)$ does not satisfy the sample deletion criterion or the neuron growing criterion or the parameter update criterion, then the sample is pushed to the rear end of the data stream. Due to the self-adaptive nature of the thresholds, these reserve samples may also contain some useful information and will be used later in the learning process.

These three control strategies of the meta-cognitive component are repeated for all the samples in the training process and help to improve the generalization performance of FCRN as will be shown in Section 7.4 and Section 7.5.

The learning algorithm of McFCRN is summarized in Pseudocode 1.

Pseudocode 1 Pseudo code for McFCRN algorithm

```
Given the training data set:
        (z¹,y¹),...(zᵗ,yᵗ), ..., (zᴺ,yᴺ)
```
$$(\mathbf{z}^1,\mathbf{y}^1),...(\mathbf{z}^t,\mathbf{y}^t), ..., (\mathbf{z}^N,\mathbf{y}^N)$$
```
    START
        For each input,
        Compute the network output (ŷᵗ) using Eq. (7.30).
        Compute Mᵗᵉ and φᵗᵉ using Eqs. (7.10) and (7.11),
        respectively.
        If Mᵗᵉ < E_d^M AND φᵗᵉ < E_d^φ
          Delete the sample.
        Else if Mᵗᵉ ≥ E_a^M OR φᵗᵉ ≥ E_a^φ
          Add a neuron. K = K+1;
          Choose the center and scaling factor of the
          K-th neuron (v_K and u_K) randomly.
          Compute the hidden layer responses (hⱼᵗ) using
                                          Eq.(7.29).
          Compute the projection matrix (A) according to
                                          Eq. (7.41).
          Compute the matrix B using Eq. (7.42).
          Estimate the optimum output weights (w_K)
          using Eq. (7.43).
        Else if Mᵗᵉ ≥ E_l^M OR φᵗᵉ ≥ E_l^φ
          Update the optimum output weight of the
          network using Eq. (7.43).
        Else
          Reserve the sample for future use.
    END
```

7.4 PERFORMANCE EVALUATION OF MCFCRN: SYNTHETIC COMPLEX-VALUED FUNCTION APPROXIMATION PROBLEM

In this section, we evaluate the complex-valued function approximation performance of McFCRN in comparison to other complex-valued networks available in the literature. The approximation ability of McFCRN is studied using a synthetic complex-valued function approximation problem [28]. The synthetic complex-valued function approximation problem is defined in Ref. 28) as

$$f(\mathbf{z}) = \frac{1}{1.5}\left(z_3 + 10z_1 z_4 + \frac{z_2^2}{z_1}\right) \tag{7.57}$$

where $\mathbf{z}$ is a 4-dimensional complex-valued vector, z_1, z_2, z_3 and z_4 are complex-valued variables of magnitude less than 2. The study was conducted with a training set with 3000 samples and a testing set with 1000 samples. The root mean squared magnitude error (J_{Me}) (Eq. (7.58)) and the average absolute phase error (Φ_e) (eq. (7.59)), as defined in Ref. 28) , are used as the performance measures for the complex-valued function approximation problems.

$$J_{Me} = \sqrt{\frac{1}{N \times n}\sum_{t=1}^{N}\left[\sum_{l=1}^{n}(e_l^t \cdot \bar{e}_l^t)\right]} \tag{7.58}$$

$$\Phi_e = \frac{1}{N \times n}\sum_{t=1}^{N}\left[\sum_{k=1}^{n} \mid arg\left(y_k^t \overline{\hat{y}_k^t}\right)\mid\right] \times \frac{180}{\pi} \tag{7.59}$$

Performance of McFCRN is compared against the best performing results of other complex-valued learning algorithms available in the literature. The algorithms used for comparison are: Fully Complex-valued Multi-layer Perceptron (FC-MLP) [14], Complex-valued Extreme Learning Machine (C-ELM) [15], Complex-valued Radial Basis Function network (CRBF) [5], the Complex-valued Minimal Resource Allocation Network [9], Fully Complex-valued Radial Basis Function network (FC-RBF) [21] and Fully Complex-valued Relaxation Network (FCRN) [30]. For FC-MLP network, *asinh* activation function is used at the hidden layer. The Gaussian activation function is used at the hidden layer of C-ELM, CRBF and CMRAN learning algorithms. For FC-RBF, FCRN, and McFCRN the 'sech' activation function is used at the hidden layer. The number of neurons used for approximation, the training time, the root mean squared magnitude error and the average absolute phase error of McFCRN in comparison with the other learning algorithms is presented in Table 7.1.

Comparing the training and testing performances of the various complex-valued learning algorithms presented in Table 7.1, McFCRN has the lowest generalization magnitude and phase errors. It can also be observed that McFCRN requires only 10 neurons to approximate the function. Although FCRN also requires only 10 neurons, its testing magnitude and phase errors are slightly greater than those of McFCRN. This is because the meta-cognitive component of McFCRN helps to delete similar samples, thereby, improving its generalization performance.

7.5 PERFORMANCE EVALUATION OF MCFCRN: REAL-VALUED CLASSIFICATION PROBLEMS

Recent research studies have shown that the complex-valued neurons have better computational power than the real-valued neurons [19] and that the complex-valued

Table 7.1   Performance comparison for the function approximation problem

Algorithm	K	Train time (s)	Training error		Testing error	
			J_{Me}	Φ_e	J_{Me}	Φ_e
FC-MLP	15	1857	0.029	15.74	0.054	15.6
C-ELM	15	0.2	0.192	90	0.23	88.2
CMRAN	14	52	0.026	2.23	0.48	18.7
C-RBF	15	9686	0.15	51	0.18	52
FC-RBF	20	1910	0.02	15.9	0.05	15.8
FCRN	10	0.42	0.03	1.38	0.06	3.22
McFCRN	10	10.5	0.04	1.5	0.041	2.98

neural networks are better decision makers than the real-valued networks. The better decision making ability of complex-valued neural networks is attributed to the presence of two decision boundaries that are orthogonal to each other as shown by Ref. 20). In this section, we evaluate the classification performance of McFCRN using a set of benchmark real-valued classification problems from the UCI machine learning repository [4] and a practical mammogram classification for breast cancer detection [11].

7.5.1   Real-valued Classification Problem in the Complex Domain

Consider $\{(\mathbf{x}^1, c^1), \ldots (\mathbf{x}^t, c^t), \ldots, (\mathbf{x}^N, c^N)\}$, where $\mathbf{x}^t = [x_1^t \ldots x_j^t \ldots x_m^t]^T \in \Re^m$ are a set of N observations belonging to n distinct classes, where $\mathbf{x}^t$ is the m-dimensional real-valued input features of tth observation and $c^t \in \{1, 2, \ldots, n\}$ is its class label.

Solving the real-valued classification problem in the Complex domain requires that the real-valued input features be mapped onto the Complex space ($\Re^m \rightarrow \mathbb{C}^m$) and the class labels are coded in the Complex domain. In a Multi-Layered network with Multi-Valued Neuron (MLMVN) [1], a multiple-valued threshold logic to map the complex-valued input to n discrete outputs using a piecewise continuous activation function (n is the total number of classes). Thus, the transformation does not perform one-to-one mapping of the real-valued input features to the Complex domain, and might cause misclassification. In a Phase-Encoded Complex-Valued Neural Network (PE-CVNN) [2], the complex-valued input features are obtained by phase encoding the real-valued input features between $[0, \pi]$ using the transformation $z^t = exp(i\pi x^t)$, where x^t are the real-valued input features normalized in $[0,1]$. Recently, a fully complex-valued radial basis function (FC-RBF) classifier [27] and a fast learning phase encoded complex-valued extreme learning machine (PE-CELM) classifier [25, 26] have been developed using the phase encoded transformation to convert the real-valued input features to the Complex domain. However, the phase encoded transformation maps the real-valued input features onto the unit circle in the I and II quadrants of the Complex plane, completely ignoring the other two quadrants and other regions in the I and II quadrants. Therefore, the transformation used in the PE-CVNN does not completely exploit the advantages of the orthogonal decision boundaries.

To overcome the issues due to the transformation, a nonlinear transformation using $asinh$ function has been proposed in Ref. (22). Although this transformation also maps the real-valued features to the I and II quadrants, the region of the Complex-valued input space is not restricted to the unit circle. However, this transformation also ignores the other two quadrants of the Complex plane and does not effectively use the advantages of the orthogonal decision boundaries. In this paper, the complex-valued input features ($\mathbf{z}^t = [z_1^t \dots z_j^t \dots z_m^t]^T$) are obtained by using a circular transformation. The circular transformation for the jth feature of the tth sample is given by:

$$z_j^t = sin(ax_j^t + bx_j^t + \alpha_j); \ j = 1, \dots, m \tag{7.60}$$

where a, $b \in [0, 1]$ are randomly chosen scaling constants and $\alpha_j \in [0, 2\pi]$ is used to shift the origin to enable effective usage of the four quadrants of the Complex plane. As the circular transformation performs one-to-one mapping of the real-valued input features to the Complex domain, it uses all the four quadrants of the Complex domain effectively and overcomes the issues due to transformation in the existing complex-valued classifiers.

The coded class label in the Complex domain $\mathbf{y}^t = [y_1^t \dots y_l^t \dots y_n^t]^T \in \mathbb{C}^n$ is given by

$$y_l^t = \begin{cases} 1 + 1i & \text{if } c^t = l \\ -1 - 1i & \text{otherwise} \end{cases} \ l = 1, \dots, n; \tag{7.61}$$

The classification problem in the Complex domain is defined as: Given the training data set, $\{(\mathbf{z}^1, \mathbf{y}^1), \dots (\mathbf{z}^t, \mathbf{y}^t), \dots, (\mathbf{z}^N, \mathbf{y}^N)\}$, estimate the decision function ($F : \mathbb{C}^m \rightarrow \mathbb{C}^n$) to enable an accurate prediction of the class labels of unseen samples. The predicted class label of the tth sample ($\hat{c}^t$) is obtained from the predicted output of the network ($\hat{\mathbf{y}}^t$) as

$$\hat{c}^t = \max_{l=1,2,\dots,n} \text{Re}\left(\hat{y}_l^t\right) \tag{7.62}$$

7.5.2 Data Sets

The decision-making performance of McFCRN is evaluated using a set of benchmark classification problems from the UCI machine learning repository [4]. Table 7.2 presents the details of the various benchmark data sets including the number of features, and number of samples used in training/testing data sets used in the study. The availability of small number of samples, the sampling bias, and the overlap between classes introduce additional complexity in the classification and may affect the classification performance of the classifier [33]. To study the effect of these factors, we also consider the Imbalance Factor ($I.F.$) of the training and testing data sets, defined as

$$I.F. \; = \; 1 - \frac{n}{N} \min_{l=1,\dots,n} N_l \tag{7.63}$$

where N_l is the number of samples belonging to a class l. Note that $N \; = \; \sum_{l=1}^{n} N_l$. The imbalance factor gives a measure of the sample imbalance in the various classes of the training data set, and the imbalance factor of each data set considered in this study is also presented in Table 7.2. The training data set of the image segmentation problem is a balanced data set, while the remaining data sets are unbalanced in nature. As it can be observed from the table, the imbalance factors of the training data sets vary widely in the range from 0.1 to 0.68.

Table 7.2 Description of the various real-valued classification problems used in the performance study

Type of data set	Prob.	No. of features	No. of classes	No. of samples		I.F.	
				Train	Test	Train	Test
Multi-category	Image segmentation	19	7	210	2,100	0	0
	Vehicle classification	18	4	424	422	0.1	0.12
	Glass identification	9	6	109	105	0.68	0.73
Binary	Liver disease	6	2	200	145	0.17	0.145
	PIMA data	8	2	400	368	0.225	0.39
	Breast cancer	9	2	300	383	0.26	0.33
	Heart disease	14	2	70	200	0.14	0.1

7.5.3 Modifications in McFCRN Learning Algorithm to Solve Real-Valued Classification Problems

The learning algorithm of McFCRN described in Section 7.3 has been developed to solve complex-valued function approximation problems. Although they can also be used to approximate the decision surface to solve real-valued classification problems, the classification performance is affected by the definition of error and the sample learn criteria. Hence, we modify the meta-cognitive component to improve the classification performance of McFCRN. In this respect, the predicted output in Eq. (7.30) is replaced to accommodate the hinge loss function and the criteria for neuron addition/parameter update is modified to incorporate a classification measure also.

Hinge loss error function: Recently, it was shown in Ref. β5) and Ref. β3) that in real-valued classifiers, the hinge loss function helps the classifier to estimate the posterior probability more accurately than the mean squared error function. Hence, in this paper, we modify the error function defined in Eq. (7.33) as

$$
J = \begin{cases} 0, & \text{if } \text{Real}(y_l^t \widehat{y}_l^t) \geq 1 \\ ln\left(\frac{\mathbf{y}^t}{\widehat{\mathbf{y}}^t}\right) ln\left(\frac{\mathbf{y}^t}{\widehat{\mathbf{y}}^t}\right), & \text{otherwise} \end{cases} \quad l = 1, \ldots, n \quad (7.64)
$$

Criteria for learning: While solving real-valued classification problems in the Complex domain, it is mandatory that the class labels are predicted accurately. Hence, we have modified the neuron addition and parameter update criteria are modified to ensure accurate prediction of the class labels. Accordingly, the neuron addition criteria is modified as

$$
\text{If } \widehat{c}^t \neq c^t \text{ or } \left(M_t^e \geq E_a^M \text{ and } \phi_t^e \geq E_a^\phi\right) \quad (7.65)
$$

Add a neuron to the network. Choose the neuron center ($\mathbf{u}_K$) and the scaling factor ($\mathbf{v}_K$) randomly and compute the optimum output weights according to Eq. (7.43). Here, the predicted class labels are estimated using Eq. (7.62).

The parameter update criteria is modified as

$$
\text{If } \widehat{c}^t \neq c^t \text{ or } \left(M_t^e \geq E_l^M \text{ and } \phi_t^e \geq E_l^\phi\right) \quad (7.66)
$$

Then, update the output weight according to Eq. (7.43).

7.5.4 Performance Measures

The following performance measures are used to evaluate the classification performance of FCRN in comparison to other complex-valued learning algorithms on the problems presented in Table 7.2.

Average classification efficiency: The average classification efficiency (η_a) is defined as the average ratio of number of correctly classified samples in each class, to the total number of samples in each class.

$$
\eta_a = \frac{1}{n} \sum_{l=1}^{n} \frac{q_{ll}}{N_l} \times 100\% \quad (7.67)
$$

where q_{ll} is the total number of correctly classified samples in the training/testing data set.

Overall classification efficiency: The overall classification efficiency (η_o) is defined as the ratio of total number of correctly classified samples to the total number of samples available in the training/testing data set.

$$\eta_o = \frac{\sum_{l=1}^{n} q_{ll}}{N} \times 100\% \tag{7.68}$$

In the next section, we evaluate the classification performance of McFCRN with the above modifications, on a set of benchmark and practical classification problems and verify the improved performance due to the meta-cognitive component and orthogonal decision boundaries of McFCRN.

7.5.5 Multi-category Benchmark Classification Problems

First, to study the effect of meta-cognition on a simple problem, we studied the performance of McFCRN on the IRIS classification problem. In the IRIS classification problem, 4 input features are used to classify the samples into one of the 3 classes. McFCRN achieves an overall testing classification efficiency of 98.1% with 7 hidden neurons. Also, it is observed during the training process that of the total 45 training samples, 7 samples are used to add a neuron and the remaining 38 samples are deleted during the training process. On the other hand, SVM classifier uses all the training samples and 25 neurons to achieve an overall testing efficiency of 96.19%. Thus, the effect of meta-cognition is clearly evident in the IRIS classification problem.

Next, the performance results of McFCRN is studied in comparison with other complex-valued classifiers and a few best performing real-valued classifiers on the three multi-category benchmark classification problems. Support Vector Machines and Self-adaptive Resource Allocation Network (SRAN) [29] are the two real-valued classifiers used for comparison. The complex-valued classifiers used in comparison are: Phase Encoded Complex valued Extreme Learning Machine (PE-CELM), Bi-linear Branch-cut Complex-valued Extreme Learning Machine (BB-CELM) [25], FC-RBF [27], Mc-FCRBF [24], CSRAN [31] and FCRN [30]. The results for SVM and SRAN classifiers are reproduced from Ref. 29). The performance results for PE-CELM, and BB-CELM are reproduced from Ref. 25), those of FC-RBF classifier from Ref. 27) and those of Mc-FCRBF classifier from Ref. 24). The number of neurons used in the classification, and the testing classification accuracies of McFCRN in comparison with the aforementioned classifiers for the multi-category benchmark classification problems are presented in Table 7.3.

From the table, it can be observed that the generalized performance of McFCRN is better than other real-valued and complex-valued classifiers available in the literature. Also, the computational effort required to train McFCRN is significantly less. McFCRN evidently outperforms the real-valued classifiers used in comparison, especially in the unbalanced vehicle classification and the glass identification data sets. The following observations are notable from the performance results on the multi-category benchmark data sets presented in Table 7.3:

- **Balanced data set-Image segmentation problem:** McFCRN uses only 194 samples of the total 210 samples from the training data set to learn the decision surface described by the image segmentation problem. Moreover, it requires only a fewer neurons and a slightly improved generalization performance.

- **Unbalanced data set-Vehicle classification problem:** The meta-cognitive component of McFCRN uses only 572 of the total 620 samples to approximate the decision surface represented by the vehicle classification data set. It is observable from the table that the meta-cognitive component improves the generalization ability of FCRN by at least 1%.

- **Unbalanced data set-Glass identification problem:** In the glass identification problem with highly unbalanced data set, McFCRN deleted 18 samples of the total 336 training samples during the training process. Of the remaining 318 samples, 80 samples are used to add neurons, and 238 samples are used in parameter update. It can also be observed from Table 7.3 that the meta-cognitive component improves the generalization ability of FCRN at least by 3%.

7.5.6 Binary Classification Problems

We study the classification performance of McFCRN classifier using the benchmark binary classification problems described in Table 7.2. The performance of McFCRN is compared with the real-valued SVM, ELM, SRAN [29] PE-CELM, BB-CELM [25], FC-RBF [27], Mc-FCRBF [24], CSRAN [31] and FCRN [30]. The results for SVM and SRAN classifiers are reproduced from Ref. (29), those of PE-CELM, and BB-CELM are reproduced from Ref. (25). The classification results of FC-RBF and Mc-FCRBF classifiers are reproduced from Ref. (27) and Ref. (24), respectively. The performance results of McFCRN classifier on the binary classification problems in comparison to these classifiers are presented in Table 7.4.

From the table, it can be observed that McFCRN classifier outperforms all the other real-valued/complex-valued classifiers used in this study. Although FC-RBF is also a fully complex-valued classifier with the *sech* activation function in the hidden layer, the energy function used in McFCRN helps it to perform better than FC-RBF classifier. Moreover, the meta-cognitive component of McFCRN improves the generalization ability of FCRN classifier.

7.6 CONCLUSION

In this chapter, we have discussed the various meta-cognitive fully complex-valued learning algorithms available in the literature. We have also presented a Meta-cognitive Fully Complex-valued Relaxation Network (McFCRN). McFCRN has two components, namely, the cognitive and meta-cognitive component. FCRN is the cognitive component of McFCRN and a self-regulatory learning mechanism is the meta-cognitive component of McFCRN. FCRN, which is the cognitive component of McFCRN, uses a logarithmic error function that is an explicit representation of

Table 7.3   Performance comparison for the multi-category classification problems.

Problem	Classifier domain	Learning model	No. of neurons	Training time (sec.)	Testing η	
					η_o	η_a
Image segmentation	Real-valued	SVM	127	721	91.38	91.38
		ELM	49	0.25	90.23	90.23
		SRAN	48	22	93	93
	Complex-valued	FC-RBF	38	421	92.33	92.33
		Mc-FCRBF	36	362	92.9	92.9
		CSRAN	54	339	88	88
		BB-CELM	65	0.03	92.5	92.5
		PE-CELM	75	0.03	92.1	92.1
		FCRN	70	0.4	93.3	93.3
		McFCRN	60	14.23	93.8	93.8
Vehicle classification	Real-valued	SVM	340	550	70.62	68.51
		ELM	150	0.4	77.01	77.59
		SRAN	113	55	75.12	76.86
	Complex-valued	FC-RBF	70	678	77.01	77.46
		Mc-FCRBF	90	638	79.38	78.25
		CSRAN	80	352	79.15	79.16
		BB-CELM	100	0.11	80.3	80.4
		PE-CELM	100	0.11	80.8	81.1
		FCRN	90	0.8	82.62	82.46
		McFCRN	90	19.8	83.2	83.4
Glass identification	Real-valued	SVM	183	320	70.4	75.61
		ELM	80	0.05	81.31	87.43
		SRAN	59	28	86.2	80.95
	Complex-valued	FC-RBF	90	452	83.76	80.95
		Mc-FCRBF	90	364	84.75	83.33
		CSRAN	80	452	83.5	78.09
		BB-CELM	70	0.08	88.16	81
		PE-CELM	70	0.08	86.35	80
		FCRN	80	0.25	94.5	88.3
		McFCRN	80	16.22	97.7	92.2

both magnitude and phase of the complex-valued errors to enable accurate approximations. For random constant input and hidden layer parameters, FCRN estimates the unique and optimum output weights corresponding to the minimum energy point of the logarithmic error function using a projection based batch learning algorithm. The projection based learning algorithm of FCRN begins with zero hidden neurons

Table 7.4   Performance comparison on benchmark binary classification problems.

Problem	Classifier domain	Classifier	K	Training time (s)	Testing efficiency (η_o)
Liver		SVM	141	0.0972	71.03
	Real-valued	ELM	100	0.1685	72.41
disorders		SRAN	91	3.38	66.9
	Complex-valued	FC-RBF	20	133	74.46
		Mc-FCRBF	20	112	76.6
		CSRAN	20	38	67.59
		BB-CELM	15	0.06	75.17
		PE-CELM	10	0.05	75.86
		FCRN	10	0.05	75.86
		McFCRN	10	1.3	76.55
PIMA		SVM	221	0.205	77.45
	Real-valued	ELM	100	0.2942	76.63
data		SRAN	97	12.24	78.53
	Complex-valued	FC-RBF	20	130.3	78.53
		Mc-FCRBF	20	103	79.89
		CSRAN	20	64	77.99
		BB-CELM	10	0.15	78.8
		PE-CELM	5	0.08	78.53
		FCRN	15	0.125	80.71
		McFCRN	15	1.46	81.82
Breast		SVM	24	0.1118	96.6
	Real-valued	ELM	66	0.1442	96.35
cline3-6 cancer		SRAN	7	0.17	96.87
	Complex-valued	FC-RBF	10	158.3	97.12
		Mc-FCRBF	10	125	97.4
		CSRAN	20	60	96.08
		BB-CELM	15	0.06	92.69
		PE-CELM	15	0.09	97.13
cline3-6		FCRN	15	0.16	97.4
		McFCRN	15	1.23	97.65
Heart		SVM	42	0.038	75.5
	Real-valued	ELM	36	0.15	76.5
Disease		SRAN	28	0.534	78.5
	Complex-valued	FC-RBF	20	45.6	78
		Mc-FCRBF	20	32.8	79.5
		CSRAN	20	26	76.5
cline3-6		BB-CELM	5	0.03	83
		PE-CELM	5	0.02	83.5
		FCRN	10	0.03	84.5
		McFCRN	10	0.16	85.5

and builds a minimal network architecture to approximate the function defined by the training data set. Thus FCRN requires lesser computational effort as the weights are learnt directly by inversion of a nonsingular matrix. The self-regulatory learning mechanism of McFCRN decides *what-to-learn*, *when-to-learn* and *how-to-learn* in a meta-cognitive framework by choosing suitable learning strategies for each sample in the training data set. The two components of McFCRN and their learning algorithm are explained in detail. Performance study on a function approximation problem and a set of real-valued classification problems show the superior performance and computational abilities of McFCRN.

Acknowledgment

The first and second authors would like to thank the Nanyang Technological University-Ministry of Defence (NTU-MINDEF), Singapore, for the financial support (Grant number: MINDEF-NTU-JPP/11/02/05) to conduct this study.

REFERENCES

1. I. Aizenberg and C. Moraga. Multilayer feedforward neural network based on multi-valued neurons (MLMVN) and a backpropagation learning algorithm. *Soft Computing*, 11(2):169–183, 2007.

2. M. F. Amin and K. Murase. Single-layered complex-valued neural network for real-valued classification problems. *Neurocomputing*, 72(4-6):945–955, 2009.

3. G. Sateesh Babu and S. Suresh. Meta-cognitive neural network for classification problems in a sequential learning framework. *Neurocomputing*, 81:86–96, 2012.

4. C. Blake and C. Merz. UCI repository of machine learning databases. *Department of Information and Computer Sciences, University of California, Irvine*, 1998.

5. S. Chen, S. McLaughlin, and B. Mulgrew. Complex valued radial basis function network,part I: Network architecture and learning algorithms. *EURASIP Signal Processing Journal*, 35(1):19–31, 1994.

6. M. T. Cox. *Introspective multistrategy learning: Constructing a learning strategy under reasoning failure*. Technical Report, GIT-CC-96-06. Ph.D. dissertation, College of Computing, Georgia Institute of Technology, Atlanta, 1996.

7. M. T. Cox. Metacognition in computation: A selected research review. *Artificial Intelligence*, 169(2):104–141, 2005.

8. M. T. Cox and A. Ram. Introspective multistrategy learning: On the construction of learning strategies. *Artificial Intelligence*, 112:1–55, 1999.

9. J. P. Deng, N. Sundararajan, and P. Saratchandran. Communication channel equalization using complex-valued minimal radial basis function neural networks. *IEEE Transactions on Neural Networks*, 13(3):687–696, 2002.

10. J. Doyle. *A model for deliberation, action, and introspection*. Technical Report, TR-581. Ph.D. dissertation, Department of Computer Science, Massachusetts Institute of Technology, Cambridge, USA, 1980.

11. J. Suckling et al. The mammographic image analysis society digital mammogram database. *Exerpta Medica International Congress Series*, 1069:375–378, 1994.

12. O. Etzioni. Embedding decision-analytic control in a learning architecture. *Artificial Intelligence*, 49:129–159, 1991.

13. S. L. Goh and D. P. Mandic. An augmented extended kalman filter algorithm for complex-valued recurrent neural networks. *Neural Computation*, 19(4):1039–1055, 2007.

14. T. Kim and T. Adali. Fully complex multi-layer perceptron network for nonlinear signal processing. *Journal of VLSI Signal Processing Systems for Signal, Image, and Video Technology*, 32(1/2):29–43, 2002.

15. M. B. Li, G.-B. Huang, P.Saratchandran, and N.Sundararajan. Fully complex extreme learning machine. *Neurocomputing*, 68(1–4):306–314, 2005.

16. J. McCarthy. *Programs with Common Sense*, M. L. Minsky editor Semantic Information Processing, MIT Press, Cambridge, MA, USA, 1968, pp. 403–418.

17. M. L. Minsky. *Matter, mind and models*, M. L. Minsky editor Semantic Information Processing, MIT Press, Cambridge, MA, USA, 1968, pp. 727–738.

18. T. O. Nelson and L. Narens. Metamemory: A theoretical framework and new findings. pp. 9–24, 1992.

19. T. Nitta. The computational power of complex-valued neuron. *Artificial Neural Networks and Neural Information Processing ICANN/ICONIP. Lecture Notes in Computer Science*, 2714:993–1000, 2003.

20. T. Nitta. Orthogonality of decision boundaries of complex-valued neural networks. *Neural Computation*, 16(1):73–97, 2004.

21. R. Savitha, S. Suresh, and N. Sundararajan. A fully complex-valued radial basis function network and its learning algorithm. *International Journal of Neural Systems*, 19(4):253–267, 2009.

22. R. Savitha, S. Suresh, and N. Sundararajan. A fast learning complex-valued neural classifier for real-valued classification problems. *International Joint Conference on Neural Networks (IJCNN 2011)*, pp. 2243–2249, 2011.

23. R. Savitha, S. Suresh, and N. Sundararajan. A meta-cognitive learning algorithm for a fully complex-valued relaxation network. *Neural Networks*, 32:209–218, 2012.

24. R. Savitha, S. Suresh, and N. Sundararajan. Meta-cognitive learning in fully complex-valued radial basis function network. *Neural Computation*, 24(5):1297–1328, 2012.

25. R. Savitha, S. Suresh, N. Sundararajan, and H. J. Kim. Fast learning fully complex-valued classifiers for real-valued classification problems. *D. Liu et al. (Editors): ISNN 2011, Part I, Lecture Notes in Computer Science (LNCS)*, 6675:602–609, 2011.

26. R. Savitha, S. Suresh, N. Sundararajan, and H. J. Kim. Fast learning complex-valued classifiers for real-valued classification problems. *International Journal of Machine Learning and Cybernetics (DOI: 10.1007/s13042-012-0112-x)*, 2012.

27. R. Savitha, S. Suresh, N. Sundararajan, and H. J. Kim. A fully complex-valued radial basis function classifier for real-valued classification. *Neurocomputing*, 78(1):104–110, 2012.

28. R. Savitha, S. Suresh, N. Sundararajan, and P. Saratchandran. A new learning algorithm with logarithmic performance index for complex-valued neural networks. *Neurocomputing*, 72(16-18):3771–3781, 2009.

29. S. Suresh, K. Dong, and H. J. Kim. A sequential learning algorithm for self-adaptive resource allocation network classifier. *Neurocomputing*, 73(16–18):3012–3019, 2010.

30. S. Suresh, R. Savitha, and N. Sundararajan. A fast learning fully complex-valued relaxation network (FCRN). *IEEE International Joint Conference on Neural Networks, 2011. (IJCNN 2011)*, pp. 1372–1377, 2011.

31. S. Suresh, R. Savitha, and N. Sundararajan. A sequential learning algorithm for complex-valued resource allocation network-CSRAN. *IEEE Transactions on Neural Networks*, 22(7):1061–1072, 2011.

32. S. Suresh and K. Subramanian. A sequential learning algorithm for meta-cognitive neuro-fuzzy inference system for classification problems. *IEEE International Joint Conference on Neural Networks, 2011. (IJCNN 2011)*, pp. 2507–2512, 2011.

33. S. Suresh, N. Sundararajan, and P. Saratchandran. Risk-sensitive loss functions for sparse multi-category classification problems. *Information Sciences*, 178(12):2621 – 2638, 2008.

34. H. M. Wellman. Metamemory revisited. *In M. T. H. Chi (editors), Contributions to Human Development (Trends in Memory Development Research)*, 9:31–51, 1983.

35. T. Zhang. Statistical behavior and consistency of classification methods based on convex risk minimization. *Annals of Statistics*, 32(1):56–85, 2003.

CHAPTER 8

MULTILAYER FEEDFORWARD NEURAL NETWORK WITH MULTI-VALUED NEURONS FOR BRAIN–COMPUTER INTERFACING

Nikolay V. Manyakov,[1] Igor Aizenberg,[2] Nikolay Chumerin,[1] and Marc M. Van Hulle[1]

[1]Laboratory for Neuro- & Psychophysiology, KU Leuven, Leuven, Belgium
[2]Computational Intelligence Laboratory, Texas A&M University-Texarkana, Texarkana, Texas, USA

In this chapter, we describe a multilayer feedforward neural network equipped with multi-valued neurons and its application to the domain of brain–computer interfacing (BCI). A new methodology for electroencephalogram (EEG)-based BCI is developed with which subjects can issue commands by looking at the corresponding targets that are flickering at the same frequency but with different initial phase. Two filter-based feature selection procedures are discussed for extracting relevant information from the phases estimated from the recorded EEGs. The proposed multichannel methodology is compared with existing single channel approaches and the results show that the former performs better in terms of accuracy and length of EEG interval considered for phase estimation.

8.1 BRAIN–COMPUTER INTERFACE (BCI)

Ever since it was acknowledged that the brain controls our intentions, motivations, decisions, muscles, and so on, theories were developed and experiments set up to better understand its neural origin. These efforts also led to the challenge to mimic the brain by constructing artificial ones or to incorporate some of its traits into intelligent systems. One example is the artificial neural networks. They show the kind of adaptive behavior, learning capacity, and pattern recognition capabilities which we generally attribute to the brain. They also were the first to generate these capabilities by modifying synaptic connections between the artificial neurons, which is considered to be one of the ways our brain stores memories and displays adaptive behavior. Besides understanding the brain by developing models and theories, one also started to record and monitor brain activity directly, as well as to decode it in terms of the underlying sensory, cognitive and motor processes.

Soon after Hans Berger performed his first electroencephalography (EEG) recordings back in 1928, scientists started to analyze change in the electrical activity recorded over the subject's scalp in response to external stimuli or changes in the subject's mental or cognitive state. They found correlates providing, albeit indirectly, important insights into how the evoked EEG changes could be turned into command(s) for controlling a computer. This is in fact the principle behind the Brain–Computer Interfaces (BCIs).[2] It records brain activity, decodes it, and issues commands, all with the aim to enable the subject, from whom the recording are made, to interact with the external world, by controlling a computer program (e.g., a game), a robot actuator, and so on, bypassing the need for muscular activity. While this was first demonstrated in the early 1970's [51], BCIs received widespread attention only recently with the advent of EEG devices and computer technology that made it possible to perform on-line monitoring and decoding. BCI research is now widely considered as one of the most successful applications of the neuroscience as it can provide an outlook for immediately improving the quality of life of patients suffering from severe communication and motor disabilities such as in the case of (terminal stage) amyotrophic lateral sclerosis, stroke, traumatic brain or spinal cord injury, cerebral palsy, muscular dystrophy etc. For example, with the use of a BCI, a locked-in syndrome patient (re)gains the ability to communicate his/her intentions, desired motor actions, emotions, etc. [32, 37].

Any BCI system (see Fig. 8.1) consists of the following components: a recording device, a preprocessor, a decoder, and an external device, such as a robot actuator or a computer display where the result of the issued commands are shown to the subject. Brain activity is either recorded inside (*invasively*) or outside the brain (*noninvasively*), e.g., on the scalp. Apart from EEG, noninvasive BCIs [10, 15, 11] have been described that employ magnetoencephalography (MEG) and functional magnetic resonance imaging (fMRI). Invasive BCIs are based on electrode arrays implanted in brain tissue [50, 38, 39] or just above it as in the case of the electrocorticograms (ECoG) [28]. Preprocessing is done with the spatial and temporal filtering (for example, the notch filter to remove power line interference) of the recorded signals, along with the selection and construction of signal features that detect information relevant for the considered decoding task. The decoder performs the classification or regression of the preprocessed signal into the control signal of the external

---

[2]Sometimes the term Brain–Machine Interfaces (BMIs) is used, generalizing the type of controllable device.

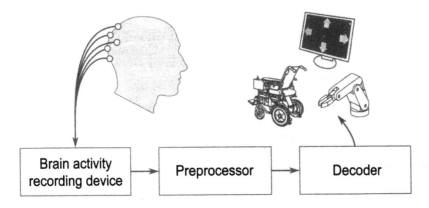

Figure 8.1   Generic BCI scheme (see text). (See color insert.)

device. The feedback provided to the subject, of the outcome of the decoder, is an important aspect of the BCI system as it enables one to detect mistakes and motivates in this way the subject to better modulate his/her brain activity, when adhering to a so-called neurofeedback principle, or to improve the preprocessor and the decoder, or both. Thus, when the feedback is used to improve the outcome, the BCI can be viewed as a closed-loop system.

8.1.1   Invasive BCI

The origin of invasive BCI's can be traced back to 1999 when, for the first time, it was shown that ensembles of cortical neurons could directly control a robotic manipula tor [13]. Since then a steady increase in the number of publications can be observed. Invasive BCIs can be divided according to the type of signal used. They can rely on *action potentials* (*spikes*), which is a short-lasting event with a rapid, stereotypical change in the membrane potential. Spike trains are extracted by high-pass filtering the extracellular recordings (above 500 Hz). For BCI purposes, recordings are made from either a single cortical area (for example, the primary motor cortical area, M1) or from multiple ones, thereby taking advantage of the distributed processing of information in the brain. For decoding purposes, either spike trains from a few neurons, with prominent tuning properties [46, 47], or from a large ensemble of neurons (hundreds of cells) [38, 12, 54] are considered. If the low-frequency component (below 300 Hz) of the extracellular recording is used, then we are dealing with *local field potentials* (LFPs). LFPs represent the composite extracellular potentials from hundreds or thousands of neurons around the electrode tip. They are more stable than spikes as they can be recorded for longer period of time, which makes them attractive for BCI applications [39, 40, 44]. All invasive BCIs require brain surgery; and, as a consequence, much of the research is done on animal such as monkeys [46, 47, 26], rather than directly on humans [25, 23]. Spike- or LFP-based BCIs are primary developed for motor control, for example, of an arm actuator [26, 46, 47, 54], where for decoding a linear regression of the spike firing rate into the position and velocity of the limb is usually considered. For a review of invasive BCI, we refer to Ref. 26.

8.1.2   Noninvasive BCI

Noninvasive BCI mostly rely on *electroencephalogram* (EEG) recordings, which measure cumulative simultaneous synchronous activity of thousands or millions of pyramidal neurons mainly in close proximity of the scalp. Since such recordings do not require any surgery, and therefore can be performed on human subjects directly, they have attracted more attention in the scientific community than their invasive counterparts. Noninvasive BCI can be divided according to the brain signal paradigm used. We can distinguish BCIs based on *event-related potentials* (ERPs) [19, 17, 16], which are stereotyped electrophysiological responses to time- and phase-locked internal or external stimuli [30]. In order to detect the ERP component in the signal, one trial is usually not enough and several trials should be averaged to reduce additive noise and other irrelevant activity in the recorded signals. The most-known BCI of this type is the one based on the *cognitive* P300 ('oddball') component of ERP in the parietal cortex, which is evoked in response to an infrequent preferred stimulus but not to a frequent, nonpreferred stimulus. The aim of the decoder is then to detect an enhanced positive-going signal component with a latency of about 300 ms when observing the rare stimulus [43]. It has been widely used to achieve a letter spelling or other type of communication system operating in visual, auditory, or tactile mode [19, 15, 49]. Besides cognitive, also early *sensory* components of the ERP have been used, — for example, the *visually evoked potential* (VEP) [51].

Whereas BCIs based on ERPs deal with information encoded in the temporal domain (the averaged ERP waveform), another BCI detects changes in the power of a particular frequency band ("rhythm") evoked by some voluntary acts, for example, the imagination of right/left-hand movements. Since those events in EEG recordings are not phase locked to the onset of the voluntary acts, an averaging method is of no use here. The relevant information is primarily encoded in the frequency domain. By monitoring *event-related desynchronization* (ERD) and *event-related synchronization* (ERS) in the mu- and beta-bands, in response to the imagined movement, one can construct different types of BCI applications [56, 42]. The detection of other mental tasks (e.g., imagined cube rotation, number subtraction, word association [41]) also belong to this category.

8.2   BCI BASED ON STEADY-STATE VISUAL EVOKED POTENTIALS

In this chapter we focus on a particular type of VEP-based BCI, namely one based on the *Steady-State Visual Evoked Potential* (SSVEP). It relies on the psychophysiological properties of EEG responses recorded from the occipital pole during the periodic presentation of identical visual stimuli (i.e., flickering stimuli). When the periodic presentation is at a sufficiently high rate (above 6 Hz), the individual transient vi-

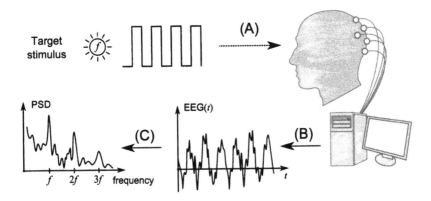

Figure 8.2 Schematic overview of the SSVEP decoding approach: (A) the subject looks at the Target stimulus, flickering at frequency f, (B) noisy EEG-signals are recorded, (C) the power spectral density plot of the EEG signal (estimated over a sufficiently large time window) shows dominant peaks at f, $2f$, and $3f$.

sual responses overlap, leading to a *steady-state* signal: the signal resonates at the stimulus rate and its multipliers [30]. This means that, when the subject is looking at stimuli flickering at frequency f, the frequency f and its harmonics $2f$, $3f$, ... are salient in the Fourier transform of the EEG signal, as schematically illustrated in Figure 8.2. However, as the amplitude of a typical EEG signal decreases as $1/f$ in the spectral domain [8], the power of f decreases with increasing frequency (as is the case with the harmonics as well).

As the SSVEP is embedded in other ongoing brain activity and (recording) noise; hence, when considering a too small recording window, the flickering frequency f could not be detected or erroneously detected. To overcome this problem, averaging over several time intervals [14], recording over longer time intervals [53] and/or preliminary training [18, 31, 34] are often used for increasing the *signal-to-noise ratio* (SNR) and the detectability of the responses.

An SSVEP-based BCI can be considered as a dependent one according to the classification proposed in Ref. 57. The dependent BCI does not use the brain's normal output pathways (for example, the brain's activation of muscles for typing a letter) to carry the message, but activity in these pathways (e.g., muscles) is needed to generate the brain activity (e.g., EEG) that does carry it. In the case of SSVEP BCI, the brain's output channel is EEG, but the generation of the EEG signal depends on the gaze direction (subject should look at flickering stimulus) and therefore on extraocular muscles and the cranial nerves that activate them. A dependent BCI is essentially an alternative method for detecting/decoding of the messages carried by the brain's normal output pathways. It has the advantages of a high information transfer rate (the amount of information communicated per unit time) [9] and little (or no) user training [53].

As a stimulation device for SSVEP BCI, either light-emitting diodes (LEDs) or computer screens (LCD or CRT monitors) are used [59]. While the LEDs can evoke

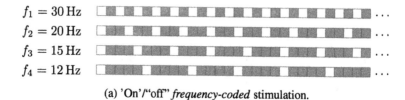

(a) 'On'/"off" *frequency-coded* stimulation.

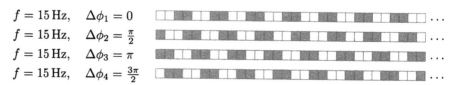

(b) 'On'/"off" (50 % duty cycle) *phase-coded* stimulation.

Figure 8.3   Examples of frame-based ("on/off") stimulation patterns for frequency-coded (a) and phase-coded (b) SSVEP BCIs. The white-shaded squares indicate the "on" frames, while the dark-shaded squares are the "off" frames. Only 30 frames corresponding to 500 ms of stimulation (on a 60-Hz screen) are shown.

more prominent SSVEP responses [59], they still require additional equipment (considering that the feedback is presented on a computer screen). Therefore, SSVEP-based BCI systems mostly rely on computer screens for visual stimulation in order to combine stimulation and feedback presentation devices. However, the latter also have their disadvantages as the stimulation frequencies need to be related to the refresh rate of the computer screen [52] (see Section 8.2.1), whereas LEDs can be stimulated at any desirable frequency. In any case, the flickering frequency needs to be restricted to specific (subject-dependent) frequency bands to obtain good responses [34].

8.2.1   Frequency-Coded SSVEP BCI

The stimulation sequence is constructed in the follwoing way: an intense ("on") stimulus is shown for q frames, and a less intense ("off") stimulus for the next w frames. Hence, the flickering period of the stimulus is $q + w$ frames and the corresponding stimulus frequency is $f_{scr}/(q + w)$, where f_{scr} is the refresh rate of the computer screen used for stimulation. An example of an "on/off" stimulations pattern (based on $q = 1$ "on" frames, indicated by the white-shaded squares) for 20, 15, 12, and 10 Hz constructed for an $f_{scr} = 60$ Hz is shown in Fig. 8.3(a). The whole subset of SSVEP stimulation frequencies for a 60-Hz screen consists of the following frequencies: 30, 20, 15, 12, 10, 8.57, 7.5, 6.66, and 6 Hz.

Frequency-coded SSVEP BCIs rely on the detection of the SSVEP induced by one of several ($f_1, \ldots, f_N$) stimulation frequencies, one for each selectable target. Thus, the information is encoded into the frequency domain. The detection is usually based on monitoring of an increase (with respect to the normal resting condition) in the *power spectral density* (*psd*) of one of the stimulation frequencies (i.e., $f_1, \ldots, f_N$ and their subharmonics) during the time the subject is gazing at the corresponding target [21]. After detecting the increase, e.g., at frequency f, the BCI system produces an output (command) associated with that target.

The number of encodable targets in frequency-coded SSVEP-based BCI is factually even lower than the dividers of the screen's refresh rate as it is not desirable to take frequencies that are dividers of one another [52]. To clarify this, consider again the previously mentioned nine frequencies for a 60-Hz screen. Assume we have 10 Hz and 20 Hz flickering frequencies. In this case, when the subject is gazing at the 10-Hz target, we have an increase in the *psd* at 10 Hz and consequent subharmonics, which are 20 Hz, 30 Hz, and so on. While powers in those subharmonics are decreasing with frequency, there is still a significant peak at 20 Hz, i.e., the 10-Hz stimulation produces also an increase in *psd* amplitude at 20 Hz. Thus, it is likely to make a mistake by erroneously interpreting the 20-Hz frequency based on EEG recordings. Due to this fact, we have to further limit the number of possible frequencies simultaneously used for stimulation.

8.2.2 Phase-Coded SSVEP BCI

In order to increase the number of encodable targets in SSVEP-based BCI, the phase has been proposed in addition (or as an alternative) to the frequency [24, 27, 33]: even a single frequency could be used with different phase lags for encoding different targets. For example, assume we have an $f = 15$-Hz stimulation, on a 60-Hz monitor, which is constructed by repeating one stimulation period (with length $T_{fr} = 4$ frames) of $q = 1$ intense frames followed by $w = 3$ "off" frames. This leads to the stimulation profile $\alpha(k)$ (where k is the video frame index) as visualized in Fig. 8.3(b). Let us consider a phase lag $\Delta\phi$. One period of stimulation takes T_{fr} frames and corresponds to 2π, thus, the phase lag $\Delta\phi$ produces a corresponding stimulation delay of $\Delta k = T_{fr}\Delta\phi/2\pi = 2\Delta\phi/\pi$ frames. Note, that Δk must be an integer, which is the case when $\frac{2\pi}{\Delta\phi} \in \mathbb{Z}$. For example, with a phase lag $\Delta\phi = \frac{\pi}{2}$, the corresponding frame lag is $\Delta k = 1$ and the corresponding stimulation profiles for targets 2, 3, and 4 are constructed by shifting in time the profile $\alpha(k)$, by 1, 2, and 3 frames (into the future), respectively, as depicted in Fig. 8.3(b). By design, the resulting set of stimuli is circular (i.e., target 3 could be received from target 1 by shifting on π in either direction). The phases estimated from the EEG responses on the phase-coded stimulation also demonstrate a similar property (of being circular). When the subject is presented with such phase-coded stimulations, by extracting phase information from the Fourier transform of the EEG signal at $f = 15$ Hz and by comparing it to the phase of some reference signal (for example, the phase of the EEG response for a stimulus with zero phase lag [27]), one can detect the target the subject is looking at. The comparison to the reference phase is one of the simplest solutions to the more general problem of constructing a mapping of circular data (estimated phases from EEG data may be represented on the unit circle in the complex plane) onto circular target-classes [35, 36]. By combining the frequency- and phase-based approaches, one can increase the number of encoded targets [24].

8.3   EEG SIGNAL PREPROCESSING

8.3.1   EEG Data Acquisition

We made recordings with a *wireless* EEG system consisting of two parts: an amplifier coupled with a wireless transmitter and a USB receiver (Fig. 8.4(a), 8.4(b)). The wireless EEG system was developed by *Holst Centre*[3] and built around their ultra-low power eight-channel EEG amplifier chip. Each EEG channel is sampled with a resolution of 12 bit per sample at 1024 Hz. We use an EEG-cap with large filling holes and sockets for active Ag/AgCl electrodes (ActiCap, Brain Products, Fig. 8.4(c)). The recordings are made with eight electrodes located primarily on the occipital pole, namely at positions PO7, PO3, POz, PO4, PO8, O1, Oz, O2 according to the international 10–10 system (Fig. 8.4(d)). The reference and ground electrodes are placed on the right and left mastoids, respectively, mainly for comparing our results to those of [27], in which case the recordings were done with a single Oz electrode referenced to the right mastoid. For further analysis we additionally considered EEGs from the mentioned electrodes with respect to *common average reference* (CAR)[4] and all possible bipolar combinations,[5] thus leading to 44 channels $s_d(t)$. The phases were extracted as

$$\varphi_d = \arg\left(\sum_t s_d(t) \cos(2\pi n_h f t) + i \sum_t s_d(t) \sin(2\pi n_h f t) \right) \qquad (8.1)$$

where $i = \sqrt{-1}$, f is the stimulus frequency, and n_h indicates the considered (sub)-harmonic(s). We used segments $s_d(t)$ of length T ($T = 1, \ldots, 5$ seconds) cropped from the stimulation stage recordings. We further restrict ourselves to only the principal harmonic, thus considering only $n_h = 1$, leading to 44-dimensional feature space of phases φ_d. Note the difference in notations: we use $\Delta\phi$ to denote the phase shifts in the visual stimulation, while φ is used for the phases extracted from the recorded EEG data.

8.3.2   Experiment Description

Seven subjects (all male, aged 23–35, average 28.3 years) participated in the experiment. The subjects were sitting about 60 cm from a notebook's LCD screen (with refresh rate $f_{scr} = 60$ Hz) on which the stimuli of size 6×6 cm were shown. A set of $N = 6$ stimuli flickering at $f = 10$ Hz with phase lags of $\Delta\phi = \pi/3$ were simultaneously presented using the stimulation profiles shown in Fig. 8.5. The stimulus had a 50% duty cycle ($\frac{q}{q+w} \cdot 100\%$) as this was reported to produce better detectable

---

[3] *http://www.holstcentre.com/*
[4] The CAR signal is a difference between the EEG from the current electrode and the average ones from all electrodes used in the recordings.
[5] The resulting signal is the difference between the EEG from the current electrode and other preselected one.

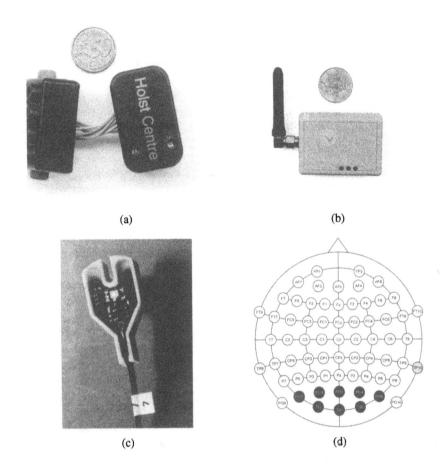

Figure 8.4   (a) Wireless eight-channel amplifier/transmitter.   (b) Receiver station. (c) Active electrode (Brain Products Acticap2) used for EEG acquisition. (d) Locations of the electrodes on the scalp: the recording electrodes are shaded in dark blue, the reference electrode is shaded in light green, and the ground electrode has gray background. (See color insert.)

SSVEP responses for mostly all frequencies and for $f = 10$ Hz in particular [48]. The stimuli were arranged in two rows and three columns, separated 7.5 cm horizontally and 7.75 cm vertically. The fixation point marker was placed for five seconds on each stimulus followed by a one second interval allowing the gaze to shift to the next stimulus (during this time no stimuli were shown). Each stimulus was attended by the subject $L = 20$ times. In total, we acquired $6 \times 20 = 120$ five-second-long EEG intervals.

8.3.3 Feature Selection

We wish to decode N different phase shifted stimuli (in our case $N = 6$) based on K (in our case $K = 44$) phase features. Since both the input features (extracted phases) and the output classes are circular, our classifier should be able to map the K-dimensional torus into a circle. To achieve this, we firstly reduce the number of features K through a filter-based (thus, not considering the classifier output) feature selection procedure. As it was pointed out in Ref. 22, the objective of feature selection is threefold:

1. To improve the prediction performance of the classifier (by avoiding undesirable input variables that can make the classifier's learning process to adjust to inseparable data).

2. To provide low computationally complex classifiers that are also more cost-effective (by reducing the number of input channels/variables of the classifier).

3. To yield a better understanding of the underlying process that generated the data.

To understand the necessity of selecting appropriate channels, let us consider Fig. 8.6, where phases extracted from EEG recordings are represented by shaped and colored symbols (each shape and color correspond to a particular phase shifted target in a particular round of the experiment, where the subject was asked to gaze at a particular flickering stimulus for $T = 1$ second) for three different channels: Oz referenced to the mastoid (as it was considered in Ref. 27), bipolar Oz–POz (as it was considered in Ref. 24) and the best channel according to the standard deviation selection procedure described below. It is clearly seen that the latter yields the best separability of the classes. The feature selection procedure should be applied to training data, with further restriction to selected channels for new data coming for classification.

The feature selection procedure has to take into account the circular nature of the data. Thus, when calculating estimates, we have to rely on circular statistics [20]. In

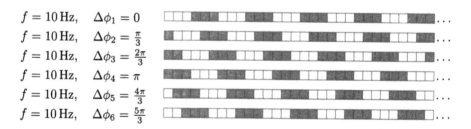

$f = 10\,\text{Hz}, \quad \Delta\phi_1 = 0$

$f = 10\,\text{Hz}, \quad \Delta\phi_2 = \frac{\pi}{3}$

$f = 10\,\text{Hz}, \quad \Delta\phi_3 = \frac{2\pi}{3}$

$f = 10\,\text{Hz}, \quad \Delta\phi_4 = \pi$

$f = 10\,\text{Hz}, \quad \Delta\phi_5 = \frac{4\pi}{3}$

$f = 10\,\text{Hz}, \quad \Delta\phi_6 = \frac{5\pi}{3}$

Figure 8.5   Phase-coded "on/off" stimulation patterns for 10-Hz stimulation on a 60-Hz screen. As in Fig. 8.3, the white-shaded squares indicate the intensified ("on") frames, and the dark-shaded ones indicate the "off" frames. Each row corresponds to one target stimulation profile.

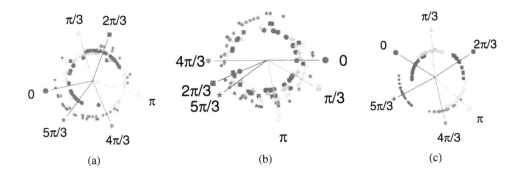

Figure 8.6   Distribution of estimated phases (expressed as angular values) for subject 1 in the experiment described in Section 8.3.2 for channels Oz (left), POz–Oz (central) and POz–O2 (right). Each dot corresponds to the phase estimated from a one second interval recorded when the subject was observing a particular phase-shifted stimulus. Colors represent target-classes (with the stimulus shifted by $\Delta\phi_{m_c} = m_c\pi/3$, where m_c is the class index). Radial lines correspond to the circular means for each class. For the sake of visualization, each class is drawn on a circle with a different radius. (See color insert.)

this case, the mean value for a set of phases $\varphi_d^1, \varphi_d^2, \ldots, \varphi_d^L$ is estimated as

$$\arg\left(\sum_{l=1}^{L} e^{i\varphi_d^l}\right) \tag{8.2}$$

where i is the imaginary unit, d is feature index and l is the trial index ($l = 1, \ldots, L$). The mean values are, for the data of each class, drawn as radial lines in Fig. 8.6. The proposed estimation of the mean value by converting the phases into a complex number $e^{i\varphi_d^l}$ on a unit circle is a convenient way to visualize the data and the classifier output. Additionally to this, the unique correspondence between phases and unit length complex numbers can be further exploited when constructing our classifier.

If we take into account not only the argument but also the length R_d of the sum vector $\sum_l e^{i\varphi_d^l}$, we can estimate the circular standard deviation according to

$$\sqrt{2(1 - R_d)} \tag{8.3}$$

Those standard deviations are in turn used as the basis of the following heuristic feature selection method. If we look into the distribution of our data (see Fig. 8.6), we may find that channels with a good separability between classes also possess the property that the standard deviation (scatterness of the data) within each class is minimized. Indeed, if we look, for example, into the "black" class (stars) in Fig. 8.6, we observe a decrease in the standard deviation of the right (better separable) channel compared to the channels visualized left from it. Thus, the maximal standard deviation between all encoded classes can serve as a way to arrange the channels in increasing order. By taking the first channels in this ranking, we factually perform a filter feature selection.

As another more rigorous feature selection procedure, we can rely on a statistical test for testing differences between mean values of paired classes. First of all, we assume that the data from each class m_c ($m_c = 1, \ldots, N$) and each feature d ($d = 1, \ldots, K$) are taken from the von Mises distribution

$$p_d^{m_c}(\varphi|\mu_d^{m_c}, \kappa_d^{m_c}) = \exp(\kappa_d^{m_c} \cdot \cos(\varphi - \mu_d^{m_c}))/(2\pi I_0(\kappa_d^{m_c})) \qquad (8.4)$$

where I_0 is the modified Bessel function of order zero, and $\kappa_d^{m_c}$ and $\mu_d^{m_c}$ are the parameters responsible for the circular variance and the circular mean. By considering this assumption and the equalities of κ's, we can perform pairwise (each class *vs.* each class for every channel) Watson–Williams tests, which is the circular analogue of the one-factor ANOVA. Assigning to each channel the maximal p-value between all pairwise tests, we can rank them in ascending order. And, as in the previously described feature selection procedure, we perform a filter feature selection procedure by taking the first channels in this ranking. Albeit we rely here on the assumption of a von Mises distribution with equal concentration parameter κ, it was shown that the Watson–Williams test is robust against deviations from this assumption [58].

8.4 DECODING BASED ON MLMVN FOR PHASE-CODED SSVEP BCI

8.4.1 Multi-Valued Neuron

The discrete *multi-valued neuron* (MVN) was introduced in Ref. 6 as a neural element based on the principles of multiple-valued threshold logic over the field of complex numbers. These principles have been initially formulated in Ref. 7 and then presented in Ref. 5. The concept of multiple-valued threshold logic over the field of complex numbers was recently comprehensively covered in Ref. 1.

The discrete MVN performs a mapping between n inputs and a single output. This mapping is described by a multiple-valued (k-valued) function of n variables $f(z_1, x_2, \ldots, x_n)$, which is a function of k-valued logic over the field of complex numbers [1]. For simplicity, we will omit in what follows "over the field of complex numbers" but keeping it in mind. The values of the k-valued logic are encoded by the kth roots of unity $\varepsilon^j = e^{i2\pi j/k}$, $j \in 0, 1, \ldots, k-1$ (i is an imaginary unity), not by integers $0, 1, \ldots, k-1$ as in the classical k-valued logic. A k-valued function, which can be learned by a single MVN, is called a multiple-valued (k-valued) threshold function or a threshold function of k-valued logic. A k-valued threshold function can be represented using $n+1$ complex-valued weights as follows [5, 1]:

$$f(x_1, x_2, \ldots, x_n) = P(w_0 + w_1 x_1 + \cdots + w_n x_n) \qquad (8.5)$$

where $x_1, x_2, \ldots, x_n$ are the variables on which this function depends (neuron inputs), and $w_0, w_1, \ldots, w_n$ are the weights. The values of the function and of the variables are complex. They are the kth roots of unity: $\varepsilon^j = e^{i2\pi j/k}$, $j \in 0, 1, \ldots, k-1$,

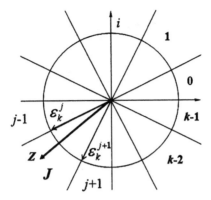

Figure 8.7 Geometrical interpretation of the discrete MVN activation function $P(z) = e^{i2\pi j/k}$.

i is an imaginary unity. P is the activation function of the neuron:

$$P(z) = e^{i2\pi j/k}, \text{ if } 2\pi j/k \leq \arg z < 2\pi(j+1)/k \qquad (8.6)$$

where $j = 0, 1, \ldots, k-1$ are values of k-valued logic, $z = w_0 + w_1 x_1 + \cdots + w_n x_n$ is the weighted sum, and $\arg z$ is the argument of the complex number z. The activation function is illustrated in Fig. 8.7. This activation function (8.6) divides the complex plane into k equal sectors with the angular size $2\pi/k$. If the weighted sum falls into the sector number $j \in 0, 1, \ldots, k-1$, then according to (8.6) the neuron's output is equal to ε^j. Thus, the neuron's output is completely determined by the argument (phase) of the weighted sum and does not depend on its magnitude. This circularity of the MVN activation function is very important for solving those problems, which we consider in this chapter.

The continuous MVN has been proposed in Ref. 3. Its inputs and output are located on the unit circle and they can be arbitrary points. The continuous MVN activation function is

$$P(z) = e^{i\mathrm{Arg}\,z} = z/|z| \qquad (8.7)$$

where $z = w_0 + w_1 x_1 + \cdots + w_n x_n$ is the weighted sum, and $\mathrm{Arg}\,z$ is the main value of the argument of the complex number z. Thus, for the continuous MVN, its output is the projection of the weighted sum on the unit circle, as it is determined by the activation function (8.7) (see Fig. 8.8).

MVN learning is detailed in Ref. 1. The most efficient MVN learning algorithm is based on the error-correction rule. The one for the discrete MVN was proposed in Ref. 5, which was then generalized in Ref. 2 for the continuous MVN. The convergence of the learning algorithm for the discrete MVN is proven in Refs. 5 and 1. It is shown in Ref. 4 that for the continuous MVN the learning process is reduced to that of the discrete MVN with $k \to \infty$ in (8.6) and it converges as well. The error-correction learning rule for both the discrete and the continuous MVN is as follows.

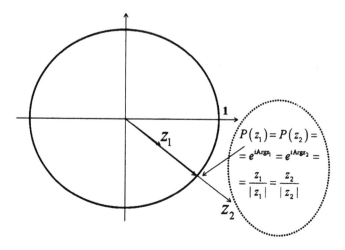

Figure 8.8   Geometrical interpretation of the continuous MVN activation function.

Let D and Y be, respectively, the desired and actual outputs of the MVN. Then, the weights adjustment is performed according to the rule

$$W_{r+1} = W_r + \frac{\alpha_r}{n+1}(D-Y)\bar{X} \tag{8.8}$$

where $\bar{X}$ is the neuron's input vector with complex-conjugated components, r is the number of the current weighting vector, n is the number of neuron inputs (the length of the input vector), W_r and W_{r+1} are the weighting vectors, before and after correction, respectively, α_r is the learning rate (it should always be equal to 1). The training of the neuron using this rule is performed without requiring differentiability of the activation function (actually, both activation functions (8.6) and (8.7) are not differentiable being functions of a complex variable). In Ref. 2, the following modification of the learning rule (8.8) was suggested:

$$W_{r+1} = W_r + \frac{\alpha_r}{(n+1)|z_r|}(D-Y)\bar{X} \tag{8.9}$$

where $|z_r|$ is the absolute value of the current weighted sum. The learning rule (8.9) works better for those input/output mappings that have many irregular jumps. The factor $1/|z_r|$ in (8.9) is *de facto* a self-adaptive learning rate. Geometrically, learning rules (8.8) and (8.9) are reduced to a movement along the unit circle in the shortest possible way from the "incorrect" actual output to the "correct" desired output, which is determined by the error (see Fig. 8.9).

8.4.2   Multilayer Feedforward Neural Network with Multi-Valued Neurons (MLMVN)

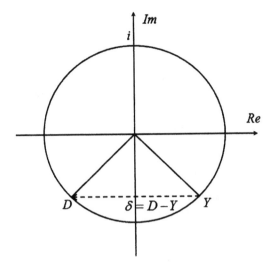

Figure 8.9 Geometrical interpretation of the MVN learning rule.

Multilayer Feedforward Neural Network with Multi-Valued Neurons (MLMVN) is a neural network with a standard feedforward topology [45]. This is a multilayer neural network for which all neurons from a given layer receive input from the neurons from the preceding layer. However, the use of MVN as a basic neuron for MLMVN has some important differences and advantages compared to a standard multilayer feedforward neural network (MLFBP) based on sigmoidal neurons (the latter is often referred to as a multilayer perceptron, i.e., MLP). The most important difference is with the way the backpropagation learning process is organized.

As shown in Refs. 2, 4, and 1, the MLMVN learning algorithm is based on the same error-correction learning rule as in the case of a single MVN. Let us consider how the MLMVN learning algorithm is organized.

Let us consider a MLMVN consisting of $m-1$ hidden layers and one output layer. For the output layer (the mth layer) the weights for the kth neuron of this (mth) layer have to be adjusted according to the following rule:

$$\tilde{w}_l^{km} = w_l^{km} + \frac{\alpha_{km}}{N_{m-1}+1}\delta_{km}\tilde{\tilde{Y}}_{l,m-1}, \quad l = 1, \ldots, N_m - 1,$$
$$\tilde{w}_0^{km} = w_0^{km} + \frac{\alpha_{km}}{N_{m-1}+1}\delta_{km} \tag{8.10}$$

where $\tilde{w}$ represents the corrected weight, N_{m-1} the number of neurons in the ($m - 1$)st layer (the last hidden layer preceding the output layer; evidently, this is also the number of inputs of all neurons in the mth layer), α_{km} the learning rate (it should always be equal to 1), $Y_{l,m-1}$ the actual output of the ith neuron of the ($m - 1$)st layer, which is corrected when it has the tilde ($\tilde{\ }$) supersign and conjugated when it has the bar ($\bar{\ }$) supersign, and $\delta_{km} = \frac{1}{N_{m-1}+1}\delta_{km}^*$ the error of the kth neuron of the mth (output) layer which is obtained from the global network error taken from the same neuron:

$$\delta_{km}^* = D_{km} - Y_{km} \tag{8.11}$$

where D_{km} and Y_{km} are, respectively, the desired and actual outputs of the kth neuron from the mth layer.

For the hidden layers neurons, except for the first one, the error is calculated by backpropagating it from the next layer followed by the weight adjustment:

$$
\begin{aligned}
\delta_{kj} &= \frac{1}{N_{j-1}+1} \sum_{i=1}^{N_{j+1}} \delta_{i,j+1} (w_k^{ij+1})^{-1}, \\
\bar{w}_l^{kj} &= w_l^{kj} + \frac{\alpha_{kj}}{(N_{j-1}+1)|z_{kj}|} \delta_{kj} \bar{Y}_{l,j-1}, \quad l = 1, \ldots, N_j - 1, \\
\bar{w}_0^{kj} &= w_0^{kj} + \frac{\alpha_{kj}}{(N_{j-1}+1)|z_{kj}|} \delta_{kj}
\end{aligned}
\tag{8.12}
$$

where the indexes kj stand for the kth neuron from the jth layer, whose weights are adjusted, $|z_{kj}|$ the absolute value of the current weighted sum of this neuron, N_{j-1} the number of neurons in the $(j-1)$st layer (this is also the number of inputs of all neurons in the jth layer), α_{kj} the learning rate (it should always be equal to 1), $Y_{l,j-1}$ the actual output of the lth neuron of the $(j-1)$st layer, which is corrected when it has the ˜ supersign and conjugated when it has the ⁻ supersign, and δ_{kj} the error of the kth neuron of the jth layer. Finally, for the first hidden layer, the error is backpropagated from the second one after which the weights are adjusted as follows:

$$
\begin{aligned}
\delta_{k1} &= \sum_{i=1}^{N_2} \delta_{i2} (w_k^{i2})^{-1}, \\
\bar{w}_l^{k1} &= w_l^{k1} + \frac{\alpha_{k1}}{(n+1)|z_{k1}|} \delta_{kj} \bar{x}_l, \quad l = 1, \ldots, n, \\
\bar{w}_0^{k1} &= w_0^{k1} + \frac{\alpha_{k1}}{(n+1)|z_{k1}|} \delta_{k1}
\end{aligned}
\tag{8.13}
$$

where the indexes $k1$ stand for the kth neuron of the 1st layer, $\bar{x}_l$ the lth input component complex conjugated, n the number of network inputs (it is also the number of inputs of all 1st hidden layer neurons), α_{k1} the learning rate (it should always be equal to 1), and δ_{k1} the error of the kth neuron of the 1st layer. The convergence of the learning process based on the learning rules (8.10)–(8.13) is proven in Ref. 1.

The MLMVN has shown very nice results for a number of benchmark problems [2] and real-world problems such as the identification of the type of blur and its parameters in image restoration [4], time-series prediction, among others [1]. It was shown that the MLMVN outperforms a standard MLFBP and many other kernel-based and neuro-fuzzy techniques in terms of the classification/prediction rate. It also employs fewer parameters to solve a particular problem.

8.4.3   MLMVN for Phase-Coded SSVEP BCI

For our phase-coded SSVEP BCI system, we want to perform mapping from the phases, estimated from the EEG recordings, onto the target-class indicators. Since both input and output are circular, we can represent them as complex numbers with unit length. For doing so, we convert all preselected phases φ_d (according to the feature selection algorithm described in Section 8.3.3) into complex numbers $e^{i\varphi_d}$. Those numbers will be used as an input into our MLMVN. During training, for the training samples of class m_c ($m_c = 1, \ldots, N$, where N is the number of target classes) we used as the network's desired output value $D_{m_c} = \exp(i2\pi(m_c - \frac{1}{2})/N)$. Then, after the training, from the output Y_{1m} of the network ($k = 1$, since we have a network with a single output), the resulting class index $\tilde{m}$ is deduced as an integer satisfying two conditions: $2\pi(\tilde{m} - 1)/N \leq \arg Y_{1m} < 2\pi\tilde{m}/N$ and $1 \leq \tilde{m} \leq N$.

During training we kept track of an angular variant of the root mean square error (RMSE) [1]. The training was stopped when the RMSE got lower than a predefined threshold which, in our experiments, was set to 0.1 radian.

For our experiments, we used an MLMVN with a single hidden layer. This choice was motivated by the next observations. The use of a single multi-valued neuron for our problem did not allow us to achieve a proper separability between the classes, since the training did not decrease below a predefined training error value due to the more complex, nonlinear nature of the separation problem. This calls for a MLMVN. Since we did not observe any significant improvement in performance when increasing the number of hidden layers, but only an increase in training time, we stick to the minimal number of hidden layers, i.e., one.

8.5   SYSTEM VALIDATION

Figure 8.10 shows the result of a five-fold cross-validation performed on the methods of Refs. 27 and 24 and the proposed one using a MLMVN classifier, for different EEG interval lengths T used for phase estimation. It is clear that the results obtained with the MLMVN significantly outperform those of the other considered methods, according to a repeated-measures ANOVA ($p < 0.01$), at least for the tested subjects. By applying the single-channel methods from Refs. 24 and 27 to the optimal channel (obtained via a wrapper like exhaustive search through all channels s_d on the training data), we also observe the superiority of the proposed multichannel classifier (see p-values in Fig. 8.10).

We have also verified the number of neurons in the hidden layer N_h (considering range from 2 to 20) of the MLMVN and the number of best features required for obtaining a satisfactory decoding accuracy. The best features were selected according to the two proposed in Section 8.3.3 methods namely, a feature selection based on the circular standard deviation and on the Watson–Williams test. As it can be seen from Fig. 8.11, both feature selection methods perform quite equally in terms of achieved accuracy.

We also see that selecting more features actually decreases the classification performance. For the comparison described above we considered the four best separating features according to our heuristic method based on the standard deviation. As to the number of neurons in the hidden layer (N_h), we observed for the optimal number of selected channels, in the case of a good separability between classes, only a slight increase in accuracy for N_h from two to six (see Fig. 8.11). For all other cases, we observe that the accuracy increases for N_h increasing until about 10 and further decreases (see Fig. 8.11). Based on this, we decided to use $N_h = 10$ for the comparison reported above.

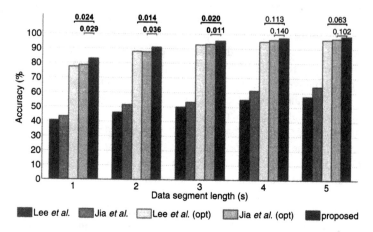

Figure 8.10 Average (among all subjects) discrimination accuracy as a function of the EEG segment length for Lee et al.'s method [27] using channel Oz referenced to the mastoid (blue), Jia et al.'s method [24] using the bipolar POz–Oz channel (light-blue), Lee et al.'s method [27] for the optimal channel (green), Jia et al.'s method [24] for the optimal channel (orange), and the proposed multichannel method based on MLMVN and feature selection (brown). The numbers above the horizontal braces (at the top of the chart) are the repeated-measures ANOVA p-values for the differences between the results of the proposed method and the optimal channel version methods. (See color insert.)

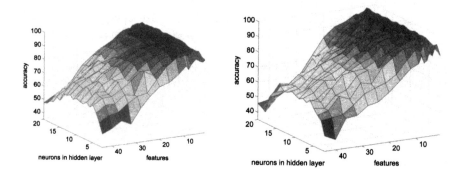

Figure 8.11 Dependency of the averaged accuracy in a five-fold cross-validation test of the MLMVN classifier on the number of neurons N_h in the hidden layer and the number $\bar{d}$ of best features used. The best features were estimated according to a feature selection based on standard deviation (left) and based on a Watson–Williams test (right). Results are presented for subject 1 while using five seconds of EEG recording for classifying six phase-shifted targets flickering at 10 Hz on the 60-Hz LCD screen. (See color insert.)

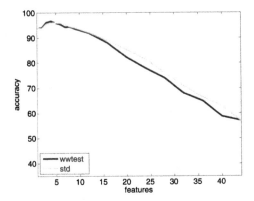

Figure 8.12   Averaged accuracy plotted as a function of the number of best features selected by the method based on the standard deviation (std) and the Watson–Williams test (ww-test). The plots were generated with the data shown in Fig. 8.11. (See color insert.)

8.6 DISCUSSION

As it can be seen from Fig. 8.6, the channel combination and the referencing method influence the separability of the classes. Thus, a proper selection of the channels should always be verified, which was also indicated in Ref. 24. But as they only considered one channel and did not provide a discriminative way to select it, our results for the multichannel combination and automatic feature selection can be viewed as an improvement (and also a generalization). Additionally to this, it is clear that only some channels combinations provide a good separability. This calls for a search for an appropriate spatial filtering approach for weighting the channels in such a way that the best separability is obtained. As a step in this direction, in Ref. 29 a canonical correlation analysis is used to incorporate all recorded EEG channels into one weighted sum.

In Ref. 24 the authors considered for their decoder one optimal channel, while we used a classifier that incorporates several best channels. Here the question arises: do we actually gain anything by considering several optimal channels? As one can see from Fig. 8.12, the classification accuracy rises up to its maximum at about 4–5 best features. This tells us that the combination of several best channels outperforms the case of only one optimal channel. This confirms the use of multichannel classifiers (as, for example, the MLMVN used in this study) and underlines their benefit with respect to the single channel decoders as the one of Refs. 24 and 27.

In Ref. 24 the authors analyzed the dependency of the decoding performance on the number of harmonics considered. And they found that the considering harmonics in the decoding improves the result. In this study we have restricted ourselves to only the fundamental frequency ($n_h = 1$). But we have to say that the proposed decoding algorithm is also able to incorporate any other features (as, for example, harmonics). This could, probably, lead to even better results.

One way to assess any new BCI system is by estimating the *information transfer rate* (ITR) [55] which favors more accurate, faster systems with more encoded targets. In our design we did not aim to increase the ITR, but rather to prove the introduced concept of multichannel detection based on MLMVN. In order to increase the ITR, we can incorporate more phase-shifted targets, choose another frequency with more space for encoding such targets. Or we can even consider phase shift and frequency combinations, as it was shown in Ref. 24.

Appendix: Decoding Methods

A.1 METHOD OF JIA AND CO-WORKERS

In Ref. 24, the following method was proposed. Based on the training data, the reference phases $\phi^{\text{ref}}_{m_c, f}$ are estimated by averaging, over the whole training set, the Fourier coefficients (obtained by using FFT) at the stimulation frequency f of each target class $m_c = 1, \ldots, N$ (see Eq. (8.2)). Here, only one optimal electrode (according to Ref. 24) or Oz–POz bipolar combination is considered. When decoding new data (thus, the test set), the Fourier coefficients at stimulation frequency f are estimated from the same, previously selected optimal electrode. This coefficient is projected onto all reference $\phi^{\text{ref}}_{m_c, f}$ phases and the resulting target class $\tilde{m}$ is selected as the one with the maximal projected value $\rho_{\tilde{m}}$. If we consider not only the fundamental frequency f, but also its harmonics, then we compute the lengths of the coefficient projections not only for the fundamental frequency, but also for its harmonics, on the respective reference phases, and sum up the resulting lengths for each target class separately, and then take the $\arg\max$ of the resulting sums to infer the index of the target class.

A.2 METHOD OF LEE AND CO-WORKERS

In Ref. 27, the following method was proposed. The EEG signals recorded from Oz channel referenced to the mastoid were band pass filtered in the range $[f - 2, f + 2]$ Hz, where f is the stimulation frequency. Based on the training data (1 min of recordings on a subject observing a flickering stimulus with "zero" phase lag), an SSVEP$_{\text{ref}}$ is generated by averaging all epochs (EEG recordings corresponding to one period of stimulation, from one channel). The reference value t_{ref} is defined from the obtained SSVEP$_{\text{ref}}$ as the latency of the maximum amplitude peak. In the decoding stage, the phase lag between SSVEP$_{\text{ref}}$ and SSVEP$_{\text{gaze}}$ is evaluated to infer the target class. This was done by cutting the SSVEP$_{\text{gaze}}$ signal into one-period-long segments, and take the average, and determine in this average the latency of the maximum amplitude peak, called t_{peak}. Next, the difference $\Delta t = t_{\text{ref}} - t_{\text{peak}}$ is transformed into a phase difference $\theta = 2\pi\Delta t f$. This phase difference θ is then wrapped to the interval $[0, 2\pi)$ by adding or subtracting (if necessary) 2π. The achieved phase distance θ is compared to the expected phase delays $\theta_{m_c} = 2\pi(m_c - 1)/N$ $(m_c = 1, \ldots, N)$ through an estimation of the angular distance as $D_{m_c} = |\theta_{m_c} - \theta|$. The resulting target class is then derived as $\arg\min_{m_c} D_{m_c}$.

REFERENCES

1. I. Aizenberg. *Complex-Valued Neural Networks with Multi-Valued Neurons*, Vol. 353. Springer Verlag, Berlin, 2011.

2. I. Aizenberg and C. Moraga. Multilayer feedforward neural network based on multi-valued neurons (MLMVN) and a backpropagation learning algorithm. *Soft Computing*, 11:169–183, 2007.

3. I. Aizenberg, C. Moraga, and D. Paliy. A feedforward neural network based on multi-valued neurons. In *Computational Intelligence, Theory and Aplications*, Advances in Soft Computing, B. Reusch, editor, Springer, Berlin, 2005.

4. I. Aizenberg, D. Paliy, J. M. Zurada, and J. Astola. Blur identification by multilayer neural network based on multi-valued neurons. *IEEE Transactions on Neural Networks*, 19(5):883–898, 2008.

5. I. N. Aizenberg, N. N. Aizenberg, and J. Vandewalle. *Multi-Valued and Universal Binary Neurons: Theory, Learning, and Applications.* Kluwer Academic Publisher, Dordecht, 2000.

6. N. N. Aizenberg and I. N. Aizenberg. CNN based on multi-valued neuron as a model of associative memory for grey scale images. In *Cellular Neural Networks and their Applications, 1992. Second International Workshop on. CNNA-92 Proceedings.* IEEE, New York, 1992, pp. 36–41.

7. N. N. Aizenberg and Yu. L. Ivaskiv. *Multiple-Valued Threshold Logic.* Naukova Dumka Publisher House, Kiev, 1977.

8. P. Allegrini, D. Menicucci, R. Bedini, L. Fronzoni, A. Gemignani, P. Grigolini, B. J. West, and P. Paradisi. Spontaneous brain activity as a source of ideal 1/f noise. *Physical Review E*, 80(6):061914, 2009.

9. B. Allison, T. Luth, D. Valbuena, A. Teymourian, I. Volosyak, and A. Gräser. BCI demographics: How many (and what kinds of) people can use an SSVEP BCI? *IEEE Transactions on Neural Systems and Rehabilitation Engineering*, 18(2):107–116, 2010.

10. N. Birbaumer, A. Kübler, N. Ghanayim, T. Hinterberger, J. Perelmouter, J. Kaiser, I. Iversen, B. Kotchoubey, N. Neumann, and H. Flor. The thought translation device (TTD) for completely paralyzed patients. *IEEE Transactions on Rehabilitation Engineering*, 8(2):190–193, 2000.

11. B. Blankertz, G. Dornhege, M. Krauledat, K. R. Müller, and G. Curio. The non-invasive Berlin brain–computer interface: Fast acquisition of effective performance in untrained subjects. *NeuroImage*, 37(2):539–550, 2007.

12. J. M. Carmena, M. A. Lebedev, C. S. Henriquez, and M. A. L. Nicolelis. Stable ensemble performance with singleneuron variability during reaching movements in primates. *Journal of Neuroscience*, 25(46):10712–10716, 2005.

13. J. K. Chapin, K. A. Moxon, R. S. Markowitz, and M. A. L. Nicolelis. Real-time control of a robot arm using simultaneously recorded neurons in the motor cortex. *Nature Neuroscience*, 2:664–670, 1999.

14. M. Cheng, X. Gao, S. Gao, and D. Xu. Design and implementation of a brain–computer interface with high transfer rates. *IEEE Transactions on Biomedical Engineering*, 49(10):1181–1186, 2002.

15. N. Chumerin, N. Manyakov, A. Combaz, J. Suykens, R. Yazicioglu, T. Torfs, P. Merken, H. Neves, C. Van Hoof, and M. Van Hulle. P300 detection based on feature extraction in on-line brain–computer interface. In *Lecture Notes in Computer Science: Vol. 5803/2009. 32nd Annual Conference on Artificial Intelligence. Paderborn, Germany*, Springer, Berlin, 2009, pp. 339–346.

16. A. Combaz, N. Chumerin, N. V. Manyakov, A. Robben, J. A. K. Suykens, and M. M. Van Hulle. Towards the detection of error-related potentials and its integration in the context of a P300 speller brain–computer interface. *Neurocomputing*, 80:73–82, 2012.

17. A. Combaz, N. V. Manyakov, N. Chumerin, J. A. K. Suykens, and M. M. Van Hulle. Feature extraction and classification of EEG signals for rapid P300 mind spelling. In *International Conference on Machine Learning and Applications*, Miami Beach, Florida, December 2009, pp. 386–391.

18. R. G. de Peralta Menendez, J. M. M. Dias, J. A. Soares, H. A. Prado, and S. G. Andino. Multiclass brain computer interface based on visual attention. In *ESANN2009 proceedings, European Symposium on Artificial Neural Networks*, Bruges, Belgium, 2009, pp. 437–442.

19. L. A. Farwell and E. Donchin. Talking off the top of your head: Toward a mental prosthesis utilizing event-related brain potentials. *Electroencephalography and Clinical Neurophysiology*, 70(6):510–523, 1988.

20. N. I. Fisher. *Statistical Analysis of Circular Data*. Cambridge University Press, New York, 1996.

21. O. Friman, I. Volosyak, and A. Graser. Multiple channel detection of steady-state visual evoked potentials for brain–computer interfaces. *IEEE Transactions on Biomedical Engineering*, 54(4):742–750, 2007.

22. I. Guyon and A. Elisseeff. An introduction to variable and feature selection. *The Journal of Machine Learning Research*, 3:1157–1182, 2003.

23. L. R. Hochberg, M. D. Serruya, G. M. Friehs, J. A. Mukand, M. Saleh, A. H. Caplan, A. Branner, D. Chen, R. D. Penn, and J. P. Donoghue. Neural ensemble control of prosthetic devices by human with tetraplegia. *Nature*, 442:164–171, 2006.

24. C. Jia, X. Gao, B. Hong, and S. Gao. Frequency and phase mixed coding in SSVEP-based brain–computer interface. *IEEE Transaction on Biomedical Engineering*, 58(1):200–206, 2011.

25. P. R. Kennedy and R. A. E. Bakay. Restoration of neural output from a paralyzed patient by a direct brain connection. *Neuroreport*, 9(8):1707, 1998.

26. M. A. Lebedev and M. A. L. Nicolelis. Brain–machine interface: Past, present and future. *Trends in Neuroscience*, 29(9):536–546, 2005.

27. P-L. Lee, J-J. Sie, Y-J. Liu, C-H. Wu, M-H. Lee, C-H. Shu, P-H. Li, C-W. Sun, and K-K. Shyu. An SSVEP-actuated brain computer interface using phase-tagged flickering sequences: A cursor system. *Annals of Biomedical Engineering*, 38(7):2383–2397, 2010.

28. E. C. Leuthardt, G. Schalk, J. R. Wolpaw, J. G. Ojemann, and D. W. Moran. A brain–computer interface using electrocorticographic signals in humans. *Journal of Neural Engineering*, 1:63, 2004.

29. Y. Li, G. Bin, X. Gao, B. Hong, and S. Gao. Analysis of phase coding SSVEP based on canonical correlation analysis (CCA). In *5th International IEEE EMBS Conference on NeuralEngineering*, IEEE, New York, 2011, pp. 368–371.

30. S. J. Luck. *An Introduction to the Event-Related Potential Technique*. MIT Press, Cambridge, MA, 2005.

31. A. Luo and T. J. Sullivan. A user-friendly SSVEP-based brain–computer interface using a time-domain classifier. *Journal of Neural Engineering*, 7:026010, 2010.

32. J. N. Mak and J. R. Wolpaw. Clinical applications of brain–computer interfaces: Current state and future prospects. *IEEE Reviews in Biomedical Engineering*, 2:187–199, 2009.

33. N. V. Manyakov, N. Chumerin, A. Combaz, A. Robben, and M. M. Van Hulle. Multichannel decoding for phase-coded SSVEP brain–computer interface. *International Journal of Neural Systems*, 22(5):1250022, 2012.

34. N. V. Manyakov, N. Chumerin, A. Combaz, A. Robben, and M. M. Van Hulle. Decoding SSVEP responses using time domain classification. In *Proceedings of the International Conference on Fuzzy Computation and 2nd International Conference on Neural Computation*, 2010, pp. 376–380.

35. N. V. Manyakov, N. Chumerin, A. Combaz, A. Robben, M. van Vliet, and M. M. Van Hulle. Decoding phase-based information from SSVEP recordings: A comparative study. In *Machine Learning for Signal Processing, IEEE Workshop on*, Beijing, China, September 2011, pp. 1–6.

36. N. V. Manyakov, N. Chumerin, A. Combaz, A. Robben, M. van Vliet, and M. M. Van Hulle. Decoding phase-based information from SSVEP recordings with use of complex-valued neural network. In *The 12th International Conference on Intelligent Data Engineering and Automated Learning*, Norwich, UK, September 2011, pp. 135–143.

37. N. V. Manyakov, N. Chumerin, A. Combaz, and M. Van Hulle. Comparison of classification methods for P300 brain-computer interface on disabled subjects. *Computational Intelligence and Neuroscience*, 2011(519868):1–12, 2011.

38. N. V. Manyakov and M. M. Van Hulle. Decoding grating orientation from microelectrode array recordings in monkey cortical area V4. *International Journal of Neural Systems*, 20(2):95–108, 2010.

39. N. V. Manyakov, R. Vogels, and M. M. Van Hulle. Decoding stimulus-reward pairing from local field potentials recorded from monkey visual cortex. *IEEE Transactions on Neural Networks*, 21(12):1892–1902, 2010.

40. C. Mehring, J. Rickert, E. Vaadia, S. C. de Oliveira, A. Aertsen, and S. Rotter. Inference of hand movements from local field potentials in monkey motor cortex. *Nature Neuroscience*, 6(12):1253–1254, 2003.

41. J. del R. Millán, F. Renkens, J. Mouriño, and W. Gerstner. Noninvasive brain-actuated control of a mobile robot by human EEG. *IEEE Transactions on Biomedical Engineering*, 51(6):1026–1033, 2004.

42. G. Pfurtscheller, C. Guger, G. Müller, G. Krausz, and C. Neuper. Brain oscillations control hand orthosis in a tetraplegic. *Neuroscience Letters*, 292(3):211–214, 2000.

43. W. S. Pritchard. Psychophysiology of P300. *Psychological Bulletin*, 89(3):506–540, 1981.

44. J. Rickert, S. C. de Oliveira, E. Vaadia, A. Aertsen, S. Rotter, and C. Mehring. Encoding of movement direction in different frequency ranges of motor cortical local field potentials. *Journal of Neuroscience*, 25(39):8815–8824, 2005.

45. D. E. Rumelhart and J. L. McClelland. *Parallel Distributed Processing: Explorations in the Microstructure of Cognition*. MIT Press, Cambridge, MA, 1986.

46. M. Serruya, N. G. Hatsopoulos, L. Paninski, M. R. Fellows, and J. P. Donoghue. Instant neural control of a movement signal. *Nature*, 416:141–142, 2002.

47. D. M. Taylor, S. I. H. Tillery, and A. B. Schwartz. Direct cortical control of 3D neuroprosthetic devices. *Science*, 296(5574):1829–1832, 2002.

48. F. Teng, Y. Chen, A. M. Choong, S. Gustafson, C. Reichley, P. Lawhead, and D. Waddell. Square or sine: Finding a waveform with high success rate of eliciting SSVEP. *Computational Intelligence and Neuroscience*, 2011(364385), 2011.

49. M. Thulasidas, C. Guan, and J. Wu. Robust classification of EEG signal for brain-computer interface. *IEEE Transaction on Neural Systems and Rehabilitation Engineering*, 14(1):24–29, 2006.

50. M. Velliste, S. Perel, M. C. Spalding, A. S. Whitford, and A. B. Schwartz. Cortical control of a prosthetic arm for self-feeding. *Nature*, 453(7198):1098–1101, 2008.

51. J. J. Vidal. Toward direct brain–computer communication. *Annual Review of Biophysics and Bioengineering*, 2:157–180, 1973.

52. I. Volosyak, H. Cecotti, and A. Gräser. Impact of frequency selection on LCD screens for SSVEP based brain–computer interface. In *Proceedings of IWANN, Part I, LNCS 5517*, 2009, pp. 706–713.

53. Y. Wang, R. Wang, X. Gao, B. Hong, and S. Gao. A practical VEP-based brain–computer interface. *IEEE Transactions on Neural Systems and Rehabilitation Engineering*, 14(2):234–240, 2006.

54. J. Wessberg, C. R. Stambaugh, J. D. Kralik, P. D. Beck, M. Laubach, J. K. Chapin, J. Kim, S. J. Biggs, M. A. Srinivasan, and M. A. L. Nicolelis. Real-time prediction of hand trajectory by ensembles of cortical neurons in primates. *Nature*, 408:361–365, 2000.

55. J. R. Wolpaw, N. Birbaumer, W. J. Heetderks, D. J. McFarland, P. H. Peckham, G. Schalk, E. Donchin, L. A. Quatrano, C. J. Robinson, and T. M. Vaughan. Brain–computer interface technology: A review of the first international meeting. *IEEE Transactions on Rehabilitation Engineering*, 8(2):164–173, June 2000.

56. J. R. Wolpaw, D. J. McFarland, and T. M. Vaughan. Brain–computer interface research at the Wadsworth Center. *IEEE Transactions on Rehabilitation Engineering*, 8(2):222–226, 2000.

57. J. R. Wolpaw, N. Birbaumer, D. J. McFarland, G. Pfurtscheller, and T. M. Vaughan. Brain-computer interfaces for communication and control. *Clinical Neurophysiology*, 113:767–791, 2002.

58. J. H. Zar. *Biostatistical Analysis*. Prentice Hall, Upper Saddle River, NJ, 1999.

59. D. Zhu, J. Bieger, G. G. Molina, and R. M. Aarts. A survey of stimulation methods used in SSVEP-based BCIs. *Computational Intelligence and Neuroscience*, 2010:1–12, 2010.

CHAPTER 9

COMPLEX-VALUED B-SPLINE NEURAL NETWORKS FOR MODELING AND INVERSE OF WIENER SYSTEMS

XIA HONG[1], SHENG CHEN[2,3] AND CHRIS J. HARRIS[2]

[1] University of Reading, Reading UK
[2] University of Southampton, Southampton, UK
[3] King Abdulaziz University, Jeddah, Saudi Arabia

Many communication signal processing applications manifest as the problem of modeling and inverse of complex-valued (CV) Wiener systems. This contribution develops a CV B-spline neural network approach for efficient identification of the CV Wiener system as well as effective inverse of the estimated CV Wiener model. Specifically, the CV nonlinear static function in the Wiener system is represented using the tensor product from two univariate B-spline neural networks. Following the use of a simple least squares parameter initialization, the Gauss–Newton algorithm is applied for estimating the model parameters that include the CV linear dynamic model coefficients and B-spline neural network weights. The identification algorithm naturally incorporates the efficient De Boor algorithm with both the B-spline curve and first-order derivative recursions. Moreover, an accurate inverse of the CV Wiener system can readily be obtained using the estimated model. In particular, the inverse of the CV nonlinear static function in the Wiener system can be calculated effectively using the Gauss–Newton algorithm based on the estimated B-spline neural network model with the aid of the inverse of De Boor algorithm. The effectiveness of our approach is demonstrated using the application of digital predistorter design for high-power amplifiers with memory.

Complex-Valued Neural Networks: Advances and Applications. Edited by Akira Hirose
Copyright © 2013 The Institute of Electrical and Electronics Engineers, Inc.

9.1   INTRODUCTION

Communication signal processing applications often involve complex-valued (CV) functional representations for signals and systems. CV artificial neural networks have been studied theoretically and applied widely in nonlinear signal and data processing [1, 2, 3, 4, 5, 6, 7, 8, 9, 10, 11]. Note that most artificial neural networks cannot be automatically extended from the real-valued (RV) domain to the CV domain because the resulting model would in general violate Cauchy–Riemann conditions, and this means that the training algorithms become unusable. A number of analytic functions were introduced for the fully CV multilayer perceptrons (MLP) [4]. A fully CV radial basis function (RBF) nework was introduced in Ref. [8] for regression and classification applications. Alternatively, the problem can be avoided by using two RV artificial neural networks, one processing the real part and the other processing the imaginary part of the CV signal/system. An even more challenging problem is the inverse of a CV nonlinear system, which is typically found in practical applications. This is an under-researched area, and a few existing methods, such as the algorithm proposed in Ref. [10], are not very effective in tackling practical CV signal processing problems. In order to develop an efficient approach for modeling and inverse of CV Wiener systems, we have turned to the RV signal processing field for motivations and inspirations.

A popular approach to nonlinear systems identification in the RV domain is to use block-oriented nonlinear models which comprise the linear dynamic models and static or memoryless nonlinear functions [12, 13, 14, 15, 16, 17]. Specifically, the Wiener model, which comprises a linear dynamical model followed by a nonlinear static transformation, offers a reasonable model for linear systems with a nonlinear measurement device that are widely found in industrial and biological systems [18, 19, 20, 21, 22, 23]. The model representation of the unknown nonlinear static function in the Wiener model is fundamental to its identification, control and/or other applications. Various approaches have been developed in order to capture the *a priori* unknown nonlinearity in the Wiener system, including the nonparametric method [24], subspace model identification methods [22], fuzzy modeling [25] and the parametric method [13, 20, 21]. With its best conditioning property, the B-spline curve has been widely used in computer graphics and computer aided geometric design [26]. The B-spline curves consist of many polynomial pieces, offering versatility. In particular, the De Boor algorithm [27], which uses numerically stable recurrence relations, offers a highly efficient means of constructing B-spline curve. The B-spline basis functions for RV nonlinear systems modeling have been widely applied [28, 29, 30, 31].

Many practical communication applications involve propagating complex-valued signals through CV nonlinear dynamic systems that can be represent by the Wiener model. For example, at the transmitter of broadband communication systems, the transmitted signal is distorted by the high-power amplifier (HPA) with memory that can be characterized by the CV Wiener model [32, 33]. Also some nonlinear communication channels can usually be represented by a finite duration impulse response (FIR) filter followed by a CV static nonlinear function, namely, a CV Wiener model.

Accurate identification of a CV Wiener model is often the first successful step in these applications. Moreover, an accurate inverse of the estimated CV Wiener model is required, such as in digital predistorter design for compensating the distortions of the Wiener HPA at the transmitter [34, 35, 36, 37, 38, 39] and deconvolution or equalization at the receiver [2, 3]. Our previous work [40] has developed an efficient B-spline neural network approach for general modeling of CV Wiener systems, which represents the CV nonlinear static function in the Wiener system using the tensor product from two univariate B-spline neural networks. This novel approach is different from the existing CV neural network based on spline functions [3, 41, 42], in both model representation and identification algorithms [40]. By minimizing the mean square error (MSE) between the model output and the system output, the Gauss–Newton algorithm, coupled with a simple least squares (LS) parameter initialization, is readily applicable for the parameter estimation in the proposed CV model, which naturally incorporates the De Boor recursions for both the B-spline curves and first-order derivatives.

The significance of the proposed method [40] is twofold. Firstly, it extends the B-spline model to accommodate general CV Wiener systems. Secondly, the proposed model based on B-spline functions has a significant advantage over many other modelling paradigms in that it enables stable and efficient evaluations of functional and derivative values, as required in the Gauss–Newton optimization algorithm. The additional contribution of our current work is to develop an effective inverse of the CV Wiener system so as to complete the whole task for identification and inverse of the generic Wiener system. We demonstrate that the B-spline neural network scheme for modeling of CV Wiener systems proposed in Ref. [40] has a further advantage in that an accurate inverse of the CV Wiener system can directly be achieved from the estimated Wiener model in a very efficient way. In particular, the inverse of the CV nonlinear static function in the Wiener model is calculated effectively using the Gauss–Newton algorithm based on the inverse of De Boor algorithm, which again utilizes naturally the B-spline curve and first order derivative recursions. The effectiveness of the proposed approach for identification and inverse of CV Wiener systems is illustrated using the application of digital predistorter design for broadband communication systems that employ power-efficient nonlinear HPA transmitter.

9.2   IDENTIFICATION AND INVERSE OF COMPLEX-VALUED WIENER SYSTEMS

Throughout this contribution, a CV number $x \in \mathbb{C}$ is represented either by the rectangular form $x = x_R + \mathrm{j}x_I$, where $\mathrm{j} = \sqrt{-1}$, while $x_R = \Re[x]$ and $x_I = \Im[x]$ denote the real and imaginary parts of x, or alternatively by the polar form $x = |x| \cdot \exp(\mathrm{j}\angle^x)$ with $|x|$ denoting the amplitude of x and $\angle^x$ its phase.

9.2.1 The Complex-Valued Wiener System

The generic CV Wiener system considered in this study consists of a cascade of two subsystems, an FIR filter of order L that represents the memory effect on the input signal $x(k) \in \mathbb{C}$, followed by a nonlinear memoryless function $\Psi(\bullet) : \mathbb{C} \to \mathbb{C}$. The system is represented by

$$w(k) = \sum_{i=0}^{L} h_i x(k-i), \text{ with } h_0 = 1 \tag{9.1}$$

$$y(k) = \Psi(w(k)) + \xi(k) \tag{9.2}$$

where $y(k) \in \mathbb{C}$ is the system output, and $\xi(k)$ is a CV white noise sequence independent of $x(k)$ and with $E\big[|\xi_R(k)|^2\big] = E\big[|\xi_I(k)|^2\big] = \sigma_\xi^2$. The z transfer function of the FIR filter is defined by

$$H(z) = \sum_{i=0}^{L} h_i z^{-i}, \text{ with } h_0 = 1 \tag{9.3}$$

with the CV coefficient vector given by $\mathbf{h} = [h_1 \ h_2 \cdots h_L]^\mathrm{T} \in \mathbb{C}^L$. Note that, without loss of generality, we assume that $h_0 = 1$. If this is not the case, h_0 can always be absorbed into the CV static nonlinearity $\Psi(\bullet)$, and the linear filter's coefficients are re-scaled as h_i/h_0 for $0 \le i \le L$.

Without loss of generality, the following assumptions are made regarding the CV Wiener system (9.1) and (9.2).

Assumption 1: $\Psi(\bullet)$ is a one to one mapping, i.e. it is an invertible and continuous function.

Assumption 2: $y_R(k)$, $y_I(k)$, $w_R(k)$, $w_I(k)$ $x_R(k)$ and $x_I(k)$ are upper and lower bounded by some finite real values.

For practical applications, these two assumptions typically hold. Our aim is to identify the above CV Wiener system, i.e. given the input-output data set $D_N = \{x(k), y(k)\}_{k=1}^K$, to identify the underlying nonlinear function $\Psi(\bullet)$ and to estimate the FIR filter parameters $\mathbf{h}$, as well as to provide an accurate inverse of the above Wiener system based on the identified model. Note that the signal $w(k)$ between the two subsystems are unavailable. We will use the CV B-spline neural network approach proposed in Ref. [40] for an efficient identification of this Wiener system and then develop an effective algorithm for an accurate inverse of this Wiener system based on the estimated Wiener model $\widehat{\Psi}(\bullet)$ and $\widehat{\mathbf{h}}$.

9.2.2 Complex-Valued B-Spline Neural Network

The CV B-spline neural network proposed in Ref. [40] is adopted to represent the mapping $\widehat{y} = \widehat{\Psi}(w_R + \mathrm{j}w_I) : \mathbb{C} \to \mathbb{C}$ that is the estimate of the underlying CV nonlinear function $\Psi(\bullet)$. Assume that $U_{\min} < w_R < U_{\max}$ and $V_{\min} < w_I < V_{\max}$, where $U_{\min}$, $U_{\max}$, $V_{\min}$, and $V_{\max}$ are known finite real values.

A set of univariate B-spline basis functions based on w_R is parametrised by the order $(P_o - 1)$ of a piecewise polynomial and a knot vector which is a set of values defined on the real line that break it up into a number of intervals. Suppose that there are N_R basis functions. Then the knot vector is specified by $(N_R + P_o + 1)$ knot values, $\{U_0, U_1, \cdots, U_{N_R+P_o}\}$, with

$$U_0 < U_1 < \cdots < U_{P_o-2} < U_{P_o-1} = U_{\min} < U_{P_o} < \cdots$$
$$< U_{N_R} < U_{N_R+1} = U_{\max} < U_{N_R+2} < \cdots < U_{N_R+P_o} \qquad (9.4)$$

At each end, there are $P_o - 1$ external knots that are outside the input region and one boundary knot. As a result, the number of internal knots is $N_R + 1 - P_o$. Given the set of predetermined knots (9.4), the set of N_R B-spline basis functions can be formed by using the De Boor recursion [27], yielding

$$B_l^{(\Re,0)}(w_R) = \begin{cases} 1, & \text{if } U_{l-1} \le w_R < U_l, \\ 0, & \text{otherwise,} \end{cases} \quad 1 \le l \le N_R + P_o \qquad (9.5)$$

$$B_l^{(\Re,p)}(w_R) = \frac{w_R - U_{l-1}}{U_{p+l-1} - U_{l-1}} B_l^{(\Re,p-1)}(w_R) + \frac{U_{p+l} - w_R}{U_{p+l} - U_l} B_{l+1}^{(\Re,p-1)}(w_R),$$
$$\text{for } l = 1, \cdots, N_R + P_o - p \text{ and } p = 1, \cdots, P_o \qquad (9.6)$$

The derivatives of the B-spline basis functions $B_l^{(\Re,P_o)}(w_R)$ for $1 \le l \le N_R$ can also be computed recursively according to

$$\frac{dB_l^{(\Re,P_o)}(w_R)}{dw_R} = \frac{P_o}{U_{P_o+l-1} - U_{l-1}} B_l^{(\Re,P_o-1)}(w_R)$$
$$- \frac{P_o}{U_{P_o+l} - U_l} B_{l+1}^{(\Re,P_o-1)}(w_R) \qquad (9.7)$$

Similarly, a set of univariate B-spline basis functions based on w_I can be established. Suppose that the order of the piecewise polynomial is again predetermined as $(P_o - 1)$ and there are N_I basis functions. Then the knot vector is defined on the imaginary line in a similar manner, which is specified by the $(N_I + P_o + 1)$ knot values, $\{V_0, V_1, \cdots, V_{N_I+P_o}\}$. Specifically,

$$V_0 < V_1 < \cdots < V_{P_o-2} < V_{P_o-1} = V_{\min} < V_{P_o} < \cdots$$
$$< V_{N_I} < V_{N_I+1} = V_{\max} < V_{N_I+2} < \cdots < V_{N_I+P_o} \qquad (9.8)$$

Again, at each end, there are $P_o - 1$ external knots that are outside the input region and one boundary knot. Consequently, the number of internal knots is $N_I + 1 - P_o$. Similarly, the set of N_I B-spline basis functions are constructed by the De Boor recursion [27] as

$$B_m^{(\Im,0)}(w_I) = \begin{cases} 1, & \text{if } V_{m-1} \le w_I < V_m, \\ 0, & \text{otherwise,} \end{cases} \quad 1 \le m \le N_I + P_o \qquad (9.9)$$

$$B_m^{(\Im,p)}(w_I) = \frac{w_I - V_{m-1}}{V_{p+m-1} - V_{m-1}} B_m^{(\Im,p-1)}(w_I) + \frac{V_{p+m} - w_I}{V_{p+m} - V_m} B_{m+1}^{(\Im,p-1)}(w_I),$$
$$\text{for } m = 1, \cdots, N_I + P_o - p \text{ and } p = 1, \cdots, P_o \qquad (9.10)$$

while the derivatives of the B-spline basis functions $B_m^{(\Im,P_o)}(w_I)$ for $1 \leq m \leq N_I$ are computed recursively according to

$$
\begin{aligned}
\frac{dB_m^{(\Im,P_o)}(w_I)}{dw_I} &= \frac{P_o}{V_{P_o+m-1} - V_{m-1}} B_m^{(\Im,P_o-1)}(w_I) \\
&\quad - \frac{P_o}{V_{P_o+m} - V_m} B_{m+1}^{(\Im,P_o-1)}(w_I)
\end{aligned}
\tag{9.11}
$$

Using the tensor product between the two sets of univariate B-spline basis functions [30], $B_l^{(\Re,P_o)}(w_R)$ for $1 \leq l \leq N_R$ and $B_m^{(\Im,P_o)}(w_I)$ for $1 \leq m \leq N_I$, a set of new B-spline basis functions $B_{l,m}^{(P_o)}(w)$ can be formed and used in the CV B-spline neural network, giving rise to

$$
\begin{aligned}
\widehat{y} = \widehat{\Psi}(w) &= \sum_{l=1}^{N_R} \sum_{m=1}^{N_I} B_{l,m}^{(P_o)}(w)\omega_{l,m} \\
&= \sum_{l=1}^{N_R} \sum_{m=1}^{N_I} B_l^{(\Re,P_o)}(w_R) B_m^{(\Im,P_o)}(w_I)\omega_{l,m}
\end{aligned}
\tag{9.12}
$$

where $\omega_{l,m} = \omega_{R_{l,m}} + j\omega_{I_{l,m}} \in \mathbb{C}$, $1 \leq l \leq N_R$ and $1 \leq m \leq N_I$, are the CV weights. The CV B-spline neural network (9.12) can obviously be decomposed as the following two RV B-spline neural networks

$$
\widehat{y}_R = \sum_{l=1}^{N_R} \sum_{m=1}^{N_I} B_l^{(\Re,P_o)}(w_R) B_m^{(\Im,P_o)}(w_I)\omega_{R_{l,m}}
\tag{9.13}
$$

$$
\widehat{y}_I = \sum_{l=1}^{N_R} \sum_{m=1}^{N_I} B_l^{(\Re,P_o)}(w_R) B_m^{(\Im,P_o)}(w_I)\omega_{I_{l,m}}
\tag{9.14}
$$

Because of the piecewise nature of B-spline functions, for any point evaluation, there are only P_o basis functions with nonzero values for each of the real and imaginary parts, leading to P_o^2 nonzero terms in both (9.13) and (9.14). This is advantageous as P_o can be set to a quite low value. The complexity of the De Boor recursion is in the order of P_o^2, $\mathcal{O}(P_o^2)$. Thus the computational cost of calculating both (9.13) and (9.14) scales up to about three times of the De Boor recursion, including evaluation of both real and imaginary parts as well as the tensor product calculation. Notably, additional cost for derivative evaluation is minimal, as (9.7) and (9.11) are byproducts of the De Boor recursion. Also there are only P_o nonzero first-order derivative terms in each of (9.7) and (9.11). Compared with other CV neural networks based on different spline functions [41, 42, 3], our approach is clearly different in terms of model representation and identification algorithm. The advantages of our CV B-spline neural network are discussed in Ref. [40].

9.2.3   Wiener System Identification

The schematic of CV Wiener system identification is depicted in Fig. 9.1. For the chosen two sets of knots, (9.4) and (9.8), and the polynomial degree P_o, denote the weight vector of the CV B-spline neural network (9.12) as $\boldsymbol{\omega} = \begin{bmatrix} \omega_{1,1} & \omega_{1,2} \cdots \omega_{l,m} \end{bmatrix}$ $\cdots \omega_{N_R,N_I} \end{bmatrix}^{\mathrm{T}} \in \mathbb{C}^N$, where $N = N_R N_I$. Given a set of training input-output data $\{\mathbf{x}(k), y(k)\}_{k=1}^K$, where $\mathbf{x}(k) = [x(k) \ x(k-1) \cdots x(k-L)]^{\mathrm{T}}$, the task is to estimate the parameter vector $\boldsymbol{\theta} = \begin{bmatrix} \theta_1 & \theta_2 \cdots \theta_{2(N+L)} \end{bmatrix}^{\mathrm{T}}$ of the Wiener model, defined as

$$\boldsymbol{\theta} = \begin{bmatrix} \boldsymbol{\omega}_R^{\mathrm{T}} & \boldsymbol{\omega}_I^{\mathrm{T}} & \widehat{\mathbf{h}}_R^{\mathrm{T}} & \widehat{\mathbf{h}}_I^{\mathrm{T}} \end{bmatrix}^{\mathrm{T}} \in \mathbb{R}^{2(N+L)} \tag{9.15}$$

where $\widehat{\mathbf{h}} = \widehat{\mathbf{h}}_R + \mathrm{j}\widehat{\mathbf{h}}_I$ denotes the estimate of $\mathbf{h} = \mathbf{h}_R + \mathrm{j}\mathbf{h}_I$ and $\boldsymbol{\omega} = \boldsymbol{\omega}_R + \mathrm{j}\boldsymbol{\omega}_I$. The CV B-spline neural network used in representing $\Psi(\bullet)$ is given by

$$\widehat{y}(k) = \widehat{\Psi}(\widehat{w}(k)) = \sum_{l=1}^{N_R} \sum_{m=1}^{N_I} B_l^{(\Re,P_o)}(\widehat{w}_R(k)) B_m^{(\Im,P_o)}(\widehat{w}_I(k))\omega_{l,m} \tag{9.16}$$

which is equivalent to the two RV B-spline neural networks

$$\widehat{y}_R(k) = \sum_{l=1}^{N_R} \sum_{m=1}^{N_I} B_l^{(\Re,P_o)}(\widehat{w}_R(k)) B_m^{(\Im,P_o)}(\widehat{w}_I(k))\omega_{R_l,m} \tag{9.17}$$

$$\widehat{y}_I(t) = \sum_{l=1}^{N_R} \sum_{m=1}^{N_I} B_l^{(\Re,P_o)}(\widehat{w}_R(k)) B_m^{(\Im,P_o)}(\widehat{w}_I(k))\omega_{I_l,m} \tag{9.18}$$

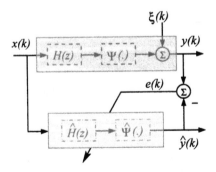

Figure 9.1   Schematic of Wiener system identification. (See color insert.)

where

$$\widehat{w}(k) = [1 \, \widehat{\mathbf{h}}^{\mathrm{T}}]\mathbf{x}(k) = \left(x_R(k) + \sum_{i=1}^{L} \left(\widehat{h}_{R_i} x_R(k-i) - \widehat{h}_{I_i} x_I(k-i) \right) \right)$$

$$+ \mathrm{j}\left(x_I(k) + \sum_{i=1}^{L} \left(\widehat{h}_{R_i} x_I(k-i) + \widehat{h}_{I_i} x_R(k-i) \right) \right) \qquad (9.19)$$

Define the error between the desired output $y(k)$ and the Wiener model output $\widehat{y}(k)$ as $e(k) = y(k) - \widehat{y}(k)$, yielding the sum of squared errors (SSE) cost function

$$J_{\mathrm{SSE}}(\boldsymbol{\theta}) = \sum_{k=1}^{K} |e(k)|^2 = \sum_{k=1}^{K} \left(e_R^2(k) + e_I^2(k) \right) \qquad (9.20)$$

We apply the Gauss–Newton algorithm to minimize the cost function (9.20).

The Gauss–Newton Algorithm   First denote $\boldsymbol{\varepsilon} = [\varepsilon_1 \, \varepsilon_2 \cdots \varepsilon_{2K}]^{\mathrm{T}} \in \mathbb{R}^{2K}$ as

$$\boldsymbol{\varepsilon} = [e_R(1) \, e_R(2) \cdots e_R(K) \, e_I(1) \, e_I(2) \cdots e_I(K)]^{\mathrm{T}} \qquad (9.21)$$

By denoting the iteration step with the superscript $^{(\tau)}$ and with an initial value $\boldsymbol{\theta}^{(0)}$, the iteration formula is given by

$$\boldsymbol{\theta}^{(\tau)} = \boldsymbol{\theta}^{(\tau-1)} - \mu\left(\left(\mathbf{J}^{(\tau)} \right)^{\mathrm{T}} \mathbf{J}^{(\tau)} \right)^{-1} \left(\mathbf{J}^{(\tau)} \right)^{\mathrm{T}} \boldsymbol{\varepsilon}\left(\boldsymbol{\theta}^{(\tau-1)} \right) \qquad (9.22)$$

where $\mu > 0$ is the step size, and $\mathbf{J}^{(\tau)}$ denotes the Jacobian of $\boldsymbol{\varepsilon}\left(\boldsymbol{\theta}^{(\tau-1)} \right)$, which is given by

$$\mathbf{J} = \begin{bmatrix} \frac{\partial \varepsilon_1}{\partial \theta_1} & \frac{\partial \varepsilon_1}{\partial \theta_2} & \cdots & \frac{\partial \varepsilon_1}{\partial \theta_{2(N+L)}} \\ \frac{\partial \varepsilon_2}{\partial \theta_1} & \frac{\partial \varepsilon_2}{\partial \theta_2} & \cdots & \frac{\partial \varepsilon_2}{\partial \theta_{2(N+L)}} \\ \vdots & \vdots & \ddots & \vdots \\ \frac{\partial \varepsilon_{2K}}{\partial \theta_1} & \frac{\partial \varepsilon_{2K}}{\partial \theta_2} & \cdots & \frac{\partial \varepsilon_{2K}}{\partial \theta_{2(N+L)}} \end{bmatrix} \qquad (9.23)$$

The partial derivatives in the Jacobian (9.23) can be calculated as follows. For $1 \leq k \leq K$,

$$
\frac{\partial \varepsilon_k}{\partial \theta_q} =
\begin{cases}
\frac{\partial e_R(k)}{\partial w_{R_{l,m}}} = -B_l^{(\Re,P_o)}(\widehat{w}_R(k)) B_m^{(\Im,P_o)}(\widehat{w}_I(k)), \\
\qquad q = l \cdot m, 1 \leq l \leq N_R, 1 \leq m \leq N_I, \\
\frac{\partial e_R(k)}{\partial w_{I_{l,m}}} = 0, q = N + l \cdot m, 1 \leq l \leq N_R, 1 \leq m \leq N_I, \\
\frac{\partial e_R(k)}{\partial \widehat{h}_{R_i}} = -\sum_{l=1}^{N_R} \sum_{m=1}^{N_I} \left(\frac{dB_l^{(\Re,P_o)}(\widehat{w}_R(k))}{d\widehat{w}_R(k)} B_m^{(\Im,P_o)}(\widehat{w}_I(k)) x_R(k-i) \right. \\
\qquad \left. + B_l^{(\Re,P_o)}(\widehat{w}_R(k)) \frac{dB_m^{(\Im,P_o)}(\widehat{w}_I(k))}{d\widehat{w}_I(k)} x_I(k-i) \right) w_{R_{l,m}}, \\
\qquad q = 2N + i, 1 \leq i \leq L, \\
\frac{\partial e_R(k)}{\partial \widehat{h}_{I_i}} = -\sum_{l=1}^{N_R} \sum_{m=1}^{N_I} \left(-\frac{dB_l^{(\Re,P_o)}(\widehat{w}_R(k))}{d\widehat{w}_R(k)} B_m^{(\Im,P_o)}(\widehat{w}_I(k)) x_I(k-i) \right. \\
\qquad \left. + B_l^{(\Re,P_o)}(\widehat{w}_R(k)) \frac{dB_m^{(\Im,P_o)}(\widehat{w}_I(k))}{d\widehat{w}_I(k)} x_R(k-i) \right) w_{R_{l,m}}, \\
\qquad q = 2N + L + i, 1 \leq i \leq L
\end{cases}
$$

(9.24)

but for $K + 1 \leq k \leq 2K$ and $t = k - K$,

$$
\frac{\partial \varepsilon_k}{\partial \theta_q} =
\begin{cases}
\frac{\partial e_I(t)}{\partial w_{R_{l,m}}} = 0, q = l \cdot m, 1 \leq l \leq N_R, 1 \leq m \leq N_I, \\
\frac{\partial e_I(t)}{\partial w_{I_{l,m}}} = -B_l^{(\Re,P_o)}(\widehat{w}_R(t)) B_m^{(\Im,P_o)}(\widehat{w}_I(t)), \\
\qquad q = N + l \cdot m, 1 \leq l \leq N_R, 1 \leq m \leq N_I, \\
\frac{\partial e_I(t)}{\partial \widehat{h}_{R_i}} = -\sum_{l=1}^{N_R} \sum_{m=1}^{N_I} \left(\frac{dB_l^{(\Re,P_o)}(\widehat{w}_R(t))}{d\widehat{w}_R(t)} B_m^{(\Im,P_o)}(\widehat{w}_I(t)) x_R(t-i) \right. \\
\qquad \left. + B_l^{(\Re,P_o)}(\widehat{w}_R(t)) \frac{dB_m^{(\Im,P_o)}(\widehat{w}_I(t))}{d\widehat{w}_I(t)} x_I(t-i) \right) w_{I_{l,m}}, \\
\qquad q = 2N + i, 1 \leq i \leq L, \\
\frac{\partial e_I(t)}{\partial \widehat{h}_{I_i}} = -\sum_{l=1}^{N_R} \sum_{m=1}^{N_I} \left(-\frac{dB_l^{(\Re,P_o)}(\widehat{w}_R(t))}{d\widehat{w}_R(t)} B_m^{(\Im,P_o)}(\widehat{w}_I(t)) x_I(t-i) \right. \\
\qquad \left. + B_l^{(\Re,P_o)}(\widehat{w}_R(t)) \frac{dB_m^{(\Im,P_o)}(\widehat{w}_I(t))}{d\widehat{w}_I(t)} x_R(t-i) \right) w_{I_{l,m}}, \\
\qquad q = 2N + L + i, 1 \leq i \leq L
\end{cases}
$$

(9.25)

It is seen that the De Boor algorithm, (9.5)–(9.7) and (9.9)–(9.11), is applied in evaluating all entries in the Jacobian. Effectively, this enables stable and efficient evaluations of B-spline functional and derivative values, which could be very difficult for many other nonlinear models, including some spline functions based nonlinear models. The iterative procedure (9.22) is terminated when $\theta^{(\tau)}$ converges or when a predetermined sufficiently large number of iterations has been reached.

Parameter Initialisation for the Gauss–Newton Algorithm   As the cost function (9.20) is highly nonlinear in the parameters, the solution of the Gauss–Newton algorithm depends on the initial condition. It is important to properly initialize $\theta^{(0)}$ so that it is as close as possible to an optimal solution. A simple and effective LS parameter initialization scheme was introduced in Ref. [40], which we adopt in this study.

Initialisation of the Linear Filter Parameters. Denote an estimate of the linear filter parameter vector as $\tilde{\mathbf{h}} = \begin{bmatrix} \tilde{h}_1 & \tilde{h}_2 \cdots \tilde{h}_L \end{bmatrix}^{\mathrm{T}}$ and the inverse function of $\Psi(\bullet)$ as $\varphi(\bullet) = \Psi^{-1}(\bullet) : \mathbb{C} \to \mathbb{C}$. Consider now using the proposed CV B-spline neural network to model $\varphi(\bullet)$. For notational simplicity, assume that the polynomial degree used is still denoted as $P_o - 1$ and the numbers of basis functions used in the modeling of the real and imaginary parts are still denoted as N_R and N_I, respectively. With the two knot vectors for the real and imaginary parts being set based on $y_R(k)$ and $y_I(k)$, respectively, we have an estimate of $\varphi(\bullet)$

$$\tilde{\varphi}(y(k)) = \sum_{l=1}^{N_R} \sum_{m=1}^{N_I} B_{l,m}^{(P_o)}(y(k)) \alpha_{l,m} \tag{9.26}$$

where $\alpha_{l,m} \in \mathbb{C}$, $1 \leq l \leq N_R$ and $1 \leq m \leq N_I$, are CV weights. Let the error between $\tilde{w}(k)$ and $\tilde{\varphi}(y(k))$ be defined as $\epsilon(k) = \tilde{w}(k) - \tilde{\varphi}(y(k))$, where

$$\tilde{w}(k) = x(k) + \sum_{i=1}^{L} \tilde{h}_i x(k - i) \tag{9.27}$$

is used as the target for $\tilde{\varphi}(y(k))$. Thus,

$$\begin{aligned} x(k) &= -\sum_{i=1}^{L} \tilde{h}_i x(k - i) + \sum_{l=1}^{N_R} \sum_{m=1}^{N_I} B_{l,m}^{(P_o)}(y(k)) \alpha_{l,m} + \epsilon(k) \\ &= \left(\mathbf{p}(\underline{\mathbf{x}}(k)) \right)^{\mathrm{T}} \boldsymbol{\vartheta} + \epsilon(k) \end{aligned} \tag{9.28}$$

where

$$\begin{aligned} \underline{\mathbf{x}}(k) &= \begin{bmatrix} x(k - 1) & x(k - 2) \cdots & x(k - L) & y(k) \end{bmatrix}^{\mathrm{T}}, \\ \mathbf{p}(\underline{\mathbf{x}}(k)) &= \begin{bmatrix} -x(k - 1) & -x(k - 2) \cdots -x(k - L) \end{bmatrix} \\ &\quad B_{1,1}^{(P_o)}(y(k)) \, B_{1,2}^{(P_o)}(y(k)) \cdots B_{N_R,N_I}^{(P_o)}(y(k)) \end{bmatrix}^{\mathrm{T}} \\ &= \begin{bmatrix} p_1(\underline{\mathbf{x}}(k)) & p_2(\underline{\mathbf{x}}(k)) \cdots p_{N+L}(\underline{\mathbf{x}}(k)) \end{bmatrix}^{\mathrm{T}} \in \mathbb{C}^{N+L}, \end{aligned}$$

$$\begin{aligned} \boldsymbol{\vartheta} &= \begin{bmatrix} \tilde{h}_1 & \tilde{h}_2 \cdots \tilde{h}_L & \alpha_{1,1} & \alpha_{1,2} \cdots \alpha_{l,m} \cdots \alpha_{N_R,N_I} \end{bmatrix}^{\mathrm{T}} \\ &= \begin{bmatrix} \vartheta_1 & \vartheta_2 \cdots \vartheta_{N+L} \end{bmatrix}^{\mathrm{T}} \in \mathbb{C}^{N+L} \end{aligned}$$

Over the training data set, (9.28) can be written in the matrix form as

$$\overline{\mathbf{x}} = \mathbf{P}\boldsymbol{\vartheta} + \boldsymbol{\epsilon} \tag{9.29}$$

where $\overline{\mathbf{x}} = [x(1) \, x(2) \cdots x(K)]^{\mathrm{T}}$, $\boldsymbol{\epsilon} = [\epsilon(1) \, \epsilon(2) \cdots \epsilon(K)]^{\mathrm{T}}$, and $\mathbf{P}$ is the regression matrix defined as $\mathbf{P} = [\mathbf{p}(\underline{\mathbf{x}}(1)) \, \mathbf{p}(\underline{\mathbf{x}}(2)) \cdots \mathbf{p}(\underline{\mathbf{x}}(K))]^{\mathrm{T}}$. The LS solution for the parameter vector $\boldsymbol{\vartheta}$ is readily given as

$$\boldsymbol{\vartheta}_{\mathrm{LS}} = \left(\mathbf{P}^H \mathbf{P} \right)^{-1} \mathbf{P}^H \overline{\mathbf{x}} \tag{9.30}$$

The sub-vector of the resulting ϑ_{LS}, consisting of its first L CV elements, forms our initial estimate $\widehat{\mathbf{h}}^{(0)} = \widehat{\mathbf{h}}_R^{(0)} + j\widehat{\mathbf{h}}_I^{(0)}$, which are used as the last $2L$ RV elements of $\theta^{(0)}$ in the parameter initialization for the Gauss–Newton iteration procedure.

Initialization of the B-Spline Neural Network Weights. Given the estimate $\widehat{\mathbf{h}}^{(0)}$, generate the auxiliary signal

$$\widehat{w}(k) = x(k) + \sum_{i=1}^{L} \widehat{h}_i^{(0)} x(k-i) \tag{9.31}$$

Using the CV B-spline neural network (9.12) to model the nonlinear static function $\Psi(\bullet)$ based on the training data set $\{\widehat{w}(k), y(k)\}_{k=1}^{K}$ yields

$$y(k) = \sum_{l=1}^{N_R} \sum_{m=1}^{N_I} B_{l,m}^{(P_o)} (\widehat{w}(k)) \omega_{l,m} + \widehat{e}(k) = \left(\mathbf{q}(\widehat{w}(k)) \right)^T \omega + \widehat{e}(k) \tag{9.32}$$

where

$$\mathbf{q}(\widehat{w}(k)) = \left[B_{1,1}^{(P_o)} (\widehat{w}(k))\ B_{1,2}^{(P_o)} (\widehat{w}(k)) \cdots B_{l,m}^{(P_o)} (\widehat{w}(k)) \cdots B_{N_R,N_I}^{(P_o)} (\widehat{w}(k)) \right]^T$$

$$= \left[q_1(\widehat{w}(k))\ q_2(\widehat{w}(k)) \cdots, q_N(\widehat{w}(k)) \right]^T \in \mathbb{R}^N$$

Over the training data set, (9.32) can be written in the matrix form

$$\mathbf{y} = \mathbf{Q}\omega + \widehat{\mathbf{e}} \tag{9.33}$$

with $\mathbf{y} = [y(1) \cdots y(K)]^T, \widehat{\mathbf{e}} = [\widehat{e}(1) \cdots \widehat{e}(K)]^T$ and $\mathbf{Q} = [\mathbf{q}(\widehat{w}(1)) \cdots \mathbf{q}(\widehat{w}(K))]^T$. The LS solution for $\omega \in \mathbb{C}^N$

$$\omega_{LS} = \left(\mathbf{Q}^T \mathbf{Q} \right)^{-1} \mathbf{Q}^T \mathbf{y} \tag{9.34}$$

is used as the initial estimate of $\omega^{(0)} = \omega_R^{(0)} + j\omega_I^{(0)}$ that forms the first $2N$ RV elements of $\theta^{(0)}$ for the parameter initialization of the Gauss–Newton algorithm.

The LS estimates $\widehat{\mathbf{h}}^{(0)}$ and $\omega^{(0)}$ are generally not consistent. This is because the B-spline regressors in (9.26) and (9.32) are subject to the output noise which will in general propagate to the parameter estimates, yielding a bias. However, this estimate represents an excellent initialization for the Gauss–Newton algorithm. The final parameter estimate via minimizing (9.20) is optimal in the sense that it is the maximum likelihood estimate in the case that $\xi(t)$ is Gaussian.

9.2.4 Wiener System Inverse

For the CV Wiener system (9.1) and (9.2), there are two types of inverse as depicted in Fig. 9.2. The "pre-inverse" can be found for example in the digital predistorter design for compensating the Wiener HPA [34, 35, 36, 37, 38, 39], while the "post-inverse" is typically found in the deconvolution or equalization applications [2, 3].

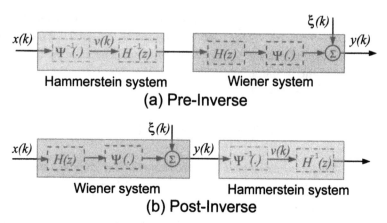

Figure 9.2   Schematic of inverse for a Wiener system. (See color insert.)

Note that in either case, the exact inverse of the Wiener system is a Hammerstein system consisting of a nonlinear static function followed by a linear filter. The difference between these two cases is that in the pre-inverse case, the input to the Hammerstein model is a clean, i.e. noise-free, signal, while in the post-inverse case, the input signal to the Hammerstein model is corrupted by the noise. Without significant loss of generality, we consider the pre-inverse case in this study.

Inverse of Wiener System's Static Nonlinear Function   Given the CV Wiener system's static nonlinearity $\Psi(\bullet)$, we wish to compute its inverse defined by $v(k) = \Psi^{-1}(x(k))$. This task is identical to find the CV root of $x(k) = \Psi(v(k))$, given $x(k)$. In Subsection 9.2.3, the estimate $\widehat{\Psi}(\bullet)$ for $\Psi(\bullet)$ has been obtained based on the CV B-spline neural network with the aid of the De Boor algorithm. We now show that $\widehat{\Psi}^{-1}(\bullet)$ can be effectively obtained with the aid of the inverse of De Boor algorithm. Given $\widehat{\Psi}(\bullet)$ of (9.17) and (9.18), we have

$$\widehat{x}_R(k) = \sum_{l=1}^{N_R} \sum_{m=1}^{N_I} B_l^{(\Re,P_o)}(v_R(k)) B_m^{(\Im,P_o)}(v_I(k)) \omega_{R_{l,m}} \qquad (9.35)$$

$$\widehat{x}_I(t) = \sum_{l=1}^{N_R} \sum_{m=1}^{N_I} B_l^{(\Re,P_o)}(v_R(k)) B_m^{(\Im,P_o)}(v_I(k)) \omega_{I_{l,m}} \qquad (9.36)$$

Define $\zeta(k) = x(k) - \widehat{x}(k)$ and the squared error (SE)

$$S(k) = \zeta_R^2(k) + \zeta_I^2(k) \qquad (9.37)$$

If $S(k) = 0$, then $v(k)$ is the CV root of $x(k) = \widehat{\Psi}(v(k))$. Thus, the task is equivalent to the one that minimizes the SE (9.37). We propose to use the following Gauss–Newton algorithm to solve this optimization problem with the aid of the inverse of De Boor algorithm.

By denoting again the iteration step with the superscript $^{(\tau)}$ and giving a random initialization of $v^{(0)}(k)$ that satisfies $U_{\min} < v_R^{(0)}(k) < U_{\max}$ and $V_{\min} < v_I^{(0)}(k) < V_{\max}$, the iterative procedure is given by

$$
\begin{bmatrix} v_R^{(\tau)}(k) \\ v_I^{(\tau)}(k) \end{bmatrix} = \begin{bmatrix} v_R^{(\tau-1)}(k) \\ v_I^{(\tau-1)}(k) \end{bmatrix} - \eta\left((\mathbf{J}_v^{(\tau)})^{\mathrm{T}}\mathbf{J}_v^{(\tau)}\right)^{-1}(\mathbf{J}_v^{(\tau)})^{\mathrm{T}}\begin{bmatrix} \zeta_R^{(\tau-1)}(k) \\ \zeta_I^{(\tau-1)}(k) \end{bmatrix}
$$
(9.38)

where $\eta > 0$ is the step size, $\zeta^{(\tau)}(k) = x(k) - \widehat{x}^{(\tau)}(k)$ with $\widehat{x}^{(\tau)}(k) = \widehat{\Psi}(v^{(\tau)}(k))$, and $\mathbf{J}_v^{(\tau)}$ is the 2×2 Jacobian matrix given by

$$
\mathbf{J}_v^{(\tau)} = \begin{bmatrix} \frac{\partial \zeta_R(k)}{\partial v_R(k)} & \frac{\partial \zeta_R(k)}{\partial v_I(k)} \\ \frac{\partial \zeta_I(k)}{\partial v_R(k)} & \frac{\partial \zeta_I(k)}{\partial v_I(k)} \end{bmatrix}_{|v(k)=v^{(\tau)}(k)}
$$
(9.39)

The entries in (9.39) are given by

$$
\frac{\partial \zeta_R(k)}{\partial v_R(k)} = -\sum_{l=1}^{N_R}\sum_{m=1}^{N_I} \frac{dB_l^{(\Re,P_o)}(v_R(k))}{dv_R(k)} B_m^{(\Im,P_o)}(v_I(k))\omega_{R_{l,m}},
$$

$$
\frac{\partial \zeta_R(k)}{\partial v_I(k)} = -\sum_{l=1}^{M_R}\sum_{m=1}^{N_I} B_l^{(\Re,P_o)}(v_R(k))\frac{dB_m^{(\Im,P_o)}(v_I(k))}{dv_I(k)}\omega_{R_{l,m}},
$$

$$
\frac{\partial \zeta_I(k)}{\partial v_R(k)} = -\sum_{l=1}^{N_R}\sum_{m=1}^{N_I} \frac{dB_l^{(\Re,P_o)}(v_R(k))}{dv_R(k)} B_m^{(\Im,P_o)}(v_I(k))\omega_{I_{l,m}},
$$

$$
\frac{\partial \zeta_I(k)}{\partial v_I(k)} = -\sum_{l=1}^{N_R}\sum_{m=1}^{N_I} B_l^{(\Re,P_o)}(v_R(k))\frac{dB_m^{(\Im,P_o)}(v_I(t))}{dv_I(k)}\omega_{I_{l,m}}
$$
(9.40)

for which the De Boor algorithm, (9.5)–(9.7) and (9.9)–(9.11), can be used for their calculation efficiently. The algorithm is terminated when $S(k) < \rho$, where ρ is a preset required precision, e.g. $\rho = 10^{-8}$, or when τ reaches a predetermined maximum value.

Inverse of Wiener System's Linear Filter   The identification algorithm presented in Subsection 9.2.3 also provides the estimate of the Wiener system's linear filter $\widehat{H}(z) = 1 + \sum_{i=1}^{L} \widehat{h}_i z^{-i}$. Let the transfer function of the Hammerstein model's linear filter be

$$
G(z) = z^{-\iota} \cdot \sum_{i=0}^{L_g} g_i z^{-i}
$$
(9.41)

where the delay $\iota = 0$ if $H(z)$ is minimum phase. The solution of the Hammerstein model's linear filter $\mathbf{g} = [g_0\ g_1 \cdots g_{L_g}]^{\mathrm{T}}$ can readily be obtained by solving the set of linear equations specified by

$$
G(z) \cdot \widehat{H}(z) = z^{-\iota}
$$
(9.42)

To guarantee an accurate inverse, the length of $\mathbf{g}$ should be chosen to be three to four times of the length of $\mathbf{h}$. Note that $g_0 = 1$ as $h_0 = 1$.

9.3 APPLICATION TO DIGITAL PREDISTORTER DESIGN

HPA is an indispensable component in any wireless communication system. The operation of HPAs in modern wireless systems may introduce serious memory effects and nonlinear distortions [32, 33, 43, 44], causing intersymbol interference and adjacent channel interference that degrade the system's achievable bit error rate (BER) performance. The problem becomes particularly acute, as the recent green-radio initiative [45] places the emphasis on the energy-efficiency aspect of communication. To achieve high-energy efficiency, HPAs should operate at their output saturation regions, but this operational mode could not accommodate high-bandwidth-efficiency single-carrier high-order quadrature amplitude modulation (QAM) signals [46] as well as multi-carrier orthogonal frequency division multiplexing (OFDM) signals [47], which are essential modern transmission technologies. It is therefore critical to compensate the distortions caused by the HPA with a digital predistorter in the design of a wireless system [34, 35, 36, 37, 38, 39].

9.3.1 High-Power Amplifier Model

A widely used model for HPAs is the Wiener model [32]. Without loss of generality, we consider single-carrier QAM systems [46], but our approach is equally applicable to multi-carrier OFDM systems [47]. The CV input signal to the HPA, $x(k)$, where k denotes the discrete time or symbol index, takes the values from the CV M-QAM symbol set

$$\mathbb{S} = \{d(2l - \sqrt{M} - 1) + jd(2q - \sqrt{M} - 1), 1 \leq l, q \leq \sqrt{M}\} \qquad (9.43)$$

where $2d$ is the minimum distance between symbol points. The 16-QAM symbol constellation is illustrated in Fig. 9.3. The memory effect of the Wiener HPA can be modeled by the FIR filter (9.1), while the nonlinear saturating distortion of the

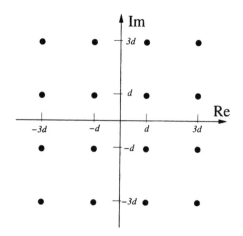

Figure 9.3   16-QAM symbol constellation.

Wiener HPA can be represented by the static nonlinearity (9.2). Note that in practical HPAs, the noise $\xi(k)$ is often negligible, that is, σ_ξ^2 is zero or extremely small. Two typical CV nonlinearities $\Psi(\bullet)$ of HPAs are the traveling-wave tube (TWT) nonlinearity [43] and the nonlinearity of solid-state power amplifiers [44]. Nonlinear characteristics of these two types of HPAs are similar. The static nonlinearity of the HPA considered in this study is the TWT nonlinearity, but the approach is equally applicable to the other type of nonlinearity.

Express the (unavailable) input signal $w(k)$ to the static nonlinearity part $\Psi(\bullet)$ of the HPA by

$$w(k) = r(k) \cdot \exp(j\psi(k)) \qquad (9.44)$$

with the amplitude $r(k) = |w(k)|$ and phase $\psi(k) = \angle w(k)$. The input signal $w(k)$ is affected by the nonlinear amplitude and phase functions of the HPA, and the output signal $y(k)$ is distorted mainly depending on the input signal amplitude $r(k)$, yielding

$$y(k) = |y(k)| \cdot \exp(j\angle y(k)) = A(r(k)) \cdot \exp(j(\psi(k) + \Phi(r(k)))) \qquad (9.45)$$

The output amplitude $A(r(k))$ and the phase $\Phi(r(k)) = \angle y(k) - \psi(k)$ of the HPA are specified respectively by [43, 32, 39]

$$A(r) = \begin{cases} \frac{\alpha_a r}{1 + \beta_a r^2}, & 0 \le r \le r_{\text{sat}}, \\ A_{\max}, & r > r_{\text{sat}} \end{cases} \qquad (9.46)$$

$$\Phi(r) = \frac{\alpha_\phi r^2}{1 + \beta_\phi r^2} \qquad (9.47)$$

where the saturating input amplitude is defined as

$$r_{\text{sat}} = \frac{1}{\sqrt{\beta_a}} \qquad (9.48)$$

while the saturation output amplitude is given by

$$A_{\max} = \frac{\alpha_a}{2\sqrt{\beta_a}} \qquad (9.49)$$

The underlying physics require that $A_{\max} > r_{\text{sat}}$ and the input amplitude r meets the condition $r < R_{\max}$, where $R_{\max}$ is some large positive number. The TWT nonlinearity is specified by the positive RV parameter vector $\mathbf{t} = [\alpha_a \ \beta_a \ \alpha_\phi \ \beta_\phi]^{\text{T}}$. The operating status of the HPA is specified by the input back-off (IBO), which is defined as

$$\text{IBO} = 10 \cdot \log_{10} \frac{P_{\text{sat}}}{P_{\text{avg}}} \qquad (9.50)$$

where $P_{\text{sat}} = r_{\text{sat}}^2$ is the saturation input power and P_{avg} is the average power of the signal at the input of the TWT nonlinearity. Note that here P_{avg} is defined as the average power of $w(k)$, which is equal to the average power of $x(k)$ scaled by the linear filter power gain $1 + \|\mathbf{h}\|^2$. A small IBO value indicates that the HPA operates in the highly nonlinear saturation region.

9.3.2   A Novel Digital Predistorter Design

Based on the technique developed in Section 9.2 for identification and inverse of the CV Wiener system, a novel digital predistorter can readily be designed to compensate the distortions caused by the HPA. Because both the predistorter and the HPA are operating at the transmitter, the input M-QAM signal $x(k)$ to the HPA and the HPA's output signal $y(k)$ are readily available to identify the Wiener HPA model $\widehat{H}(z)$ and $\widehat{\Psi}(\bullet)$ using the Gauss–Newton method based on the De Boor algorithm of Subsection 9.2.3. Since the distributions of $x_R(k)$ and $x_I(k)$ are symmetric, the distributions of $w_R(k)$ and $w_I(k)$ are also symmetric. Furthermore, from the underlying physics of the HPA, R_{max} is known or can easily be found. Therefore, the two knot sequences (9.4) and (9.8) can be chosen to be identical with $U_{max} = V_{max} = R_{max}$, $U_{min} = V_{min} = -R_{max}$ and $N_R = N_I = \sqrt{N}$. In practice, $P_o = 4$ is sufficient, and an appropriate value of $\sqrt{N}$ can be chosen by trail and error. Specifically, the number of internal knots should be sufficient to provide good modeling capability but should not be too large in order to avoid overfitting.

Based on the estimated $\widehat{\Psi}(\bullet) = \widehat{\Psi}_R(\bullet) + j\widehat{\Psi}_I(\bullet)$, an accurate inverse to $\Psi(\bullet) = \Psi_R(\bullet) + j\Psi_I(\bullet)$ can readily be obtained. Note that over the input range, $\Psi_R(\bullet)$ and $\Psi_I(\bullet)$ are monotonic. Since $\widehat{\Psi}(\bullet)$ is an accurate estimate of $\Psi(\bullet)$, $\widehat{\Psi}_R(\bullet)$ and $\widehat{\Psi}_I(\bullet)$ can also be assumed to be monotonic over the input range. Therefore, the Gauss–Newton method of Subsection 9.2.4 based on the inverse of De Boor algorithm converges to the unique solution $\widehat{\Psi}^{-1}(\bullet)$. For the M-QAM signal (9.43), there are M different symbol points $x(k)$. Thus, $v(k) = \widehat{\Psi}^{-1}(x(k))$ has M distinct values, and these values can be precalculated off-line and stored for on-line transmission. Therefore, our proposed digital predistorter solution has extremely low on-line computational complexity, which is critically important for high-throughput wireless systems.

9.3.3   A Simulation Example

We considered the single-carrier 16-QAM system with the static nonlinearity of the Wiener HPA described by (9.46) and (9.47). The parameters of the Wiener HPA were given as

$$\begin{aligned} \mathbf{h}^T &= [0.75 + j0.2\; 0.15 + j0.1\; 0.08 + j0.01], \\ \mathbf{t}^T &= [2.1587\; 1.15\; 4.0\; 2.1] \end{aligned} \tag{9.51}$$

The serious nonlinear and memory distortions caused by this memory HPA are illustrated in Figs. 9.4 and 9.5. Note that, for IBO= 0 dB, the HPA is operating well into the saturation region.

Results of Wiener HPA Identification   The 16-QAM training sets each containing $K = 3000$ data samples were generated given the HPA's parameters (9.51) and with the HPA operating at the IBO values of 4 dB and 0 dB, respectively, where the power of the CV output measurement noise $\xi(k)$ was $2\sigma_\xi^2$. Note that since the identification is carried out at the transmitter, both the HPA's input $\mathbf{x}(k)$ and the corresponding

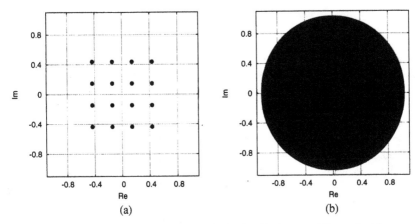

Figure 9.4   The case of IBO = 4 dB: (a) the HPA's input $x(k)$, marked by •, and (b) the HPA's output $y(k)$, marked by ×.

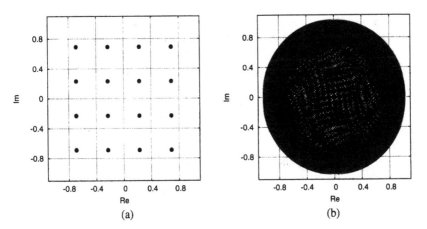

Figure 9.5   The case of IBO = 0 dB: (a) the HPA's input $x(k)$, marked by •, and (b) the HPA's output $y(k)$, marked by ×.

HPA's output measurement $y(k)$ are available. Furthermore, the measurement $y(k)$ can usually be considered as noise free. However, to demonstrate the effectiveness of the proposed CV B-spline identification approach, we considered both the noise-free and noisy measurement cases with $2\sigma_\xi^2 = 0.0$ and $2\sigma_\xi^2 = 0.01$, respectively.

The piecewise cubic polynomial ($P_o = 4$) was chosen as the B-spline basis function, and the number of B-spline basis functions was set to $\sqrt{N} = 8$. For this HPA, we set $R_{\max} = 1.2$, and used the empirically determined knot sequence

$$\{-12.0, -6.0, -2.0, -\mathbf{1.2}, -0.6, -0.3, 0.0, 0.3, 0.6, \mathbf{1.2}, 2.0, 6.0, 12.0\}$$

The Gauss–Newton identification algorithm with the LS parameter initialization, as described in Subsection 9.2.3, was carried out. The results obtained are summarized in Table 9.1 and illustrated in Figs. 9.6 to 9.9, which confirm that an accurate CV B-spline neural network model can be obtained for the HPA even in the cases that the measurements $y(k)$ are corrupted by noise.

In order to achieve an accurate identification of a nonlinear system, the nonlinear system should be sufficiently excited over all the amplitudes concerned by the input signal, which is known as the "persistent excitation" condition. Note that, under the identification condition of IBO= 4 dB, there were relatively few data points which yielded the signal amplitude $r(k) = |w(k)|$ with the values near or over the saturation value r_{sat}. Consequently, the amplitude response and phase response of the estimated B-spline neural network $\widehat{\Psi}(\bullet)$ exhibits noticeable deviation from the HPA's true amplitude response $A(r)$ and true phase response $\Phi(r)$ in the region $r > R_{\text{max}}$, as can be seen from Figs. 9.7 and 9.9. This of course does not matter, as this region is well beyond the operating region of the HPA. Interestingly, under the operating condition of IBO $= 0$ dB, the deviation between the estimated response and the true response at the region of $r > R_{\text{max}}$ is no longer noticeable, as can be noted from Figs. 9.6 and 9.8, because of the better excitation of the input signal. From Figs. 9.7 and 9.9, it can be seen that the noise $\xi(k)$ mainly affects the estimated phase response at the region of the signal amplitude $r(k)$ near zero. Note that this relatively poor accuracy of the estimated phase response under the noisy measurement condition at $r(k)$ near zero does not matter at all. This is because the estimated $\widehat{\Psi}(\bullet)$ is used to design $v(k) = \widehat{\Psi}^{-1}(x(k))$ for the 16-QAM signal $x(k)$, whose amplitude $|x(k)|$ is much larger and is well over this near zero region.

Results of Digital Predistorter Solution   We employed the estimated CV B-spline Wiener HPA model obtained under the condition of noise-free measurement ($2\sigma_\xi^2 = 0.0$) to design the predistorter. Note that we only needed to calculate the 16 points of $v(k) = \widehat{\Psi}^{-1}(x(k))$ for the 16-QAM constellation using the Gauss–Newton algorithm based on the De Boor inverse, as described in Subsection 9.2.4. The length

Table 9.1   Identification results for the linear filter part, **h**, of the HPA

true parameter vector: $\mathbf{h}^{\text{T}} = \begin{bmatrix} 0.7500 + \text{j}0.2000 \ 0.1500 + \text{j}0.1000 \ 0.0800 + \text{j}0.0010 \end{bmatrix}$
estimate under IBO $= 0$ dB and $2\sigma_\xi^2 = 0.0$: $\widehat{\mathbf{h}}^{\text{T}} = \begin{bmatrix} 0.7502 + \text{j}0.1996 \ 0.1499 + \text{j}0.0999 \ 0.0800 + \text{j}0.0008 \end{bmatrix}$
estimate under IBO $= 0$ dB and $2\sigma_\xi^2 = 0.01$: $\widehat{\mathbf{h}}^{\text{T}} = \begin{bmatrix} 0.7519 + \text{j}0.1963 \ 0.1510 + \text{j}0.1000 \ 0.0814 + \text{j}0.0014 \end{bmatrix}$
estimate under IBO $= 4$ dB and $2\sigma_\xi^2 = 0.0$: $\widehat{\mathbf{h}}^{\text{T}} = \begin{bmatrix} 0.7502 + \text{j}0.2001 \ 0.1501 + \text{j}0.1001 \ 0.0800 + \text{j}0.0011 \end{bmatrix}$
estimate under IBO $= 4$ dB and $2\sigma_\xi^2 = 0.01$: $\widehat{\mathbf{h}}^{\text{T}} = \begin{bmatrix} 0.7533 + \text{j}0.1978 \ 0.1518 + \text{j}0.1002 \ 0.0810 + \text{j}0.0019 \end{bmatrix}$

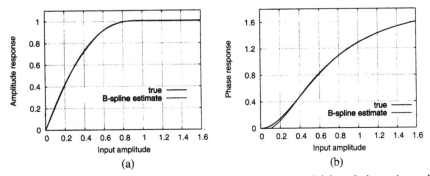

Figure 9.6 Comparison of the HPA's static nonlinearity $\Psi(\bullet)$ and the estimated static nonlinearity $\widehat{\Psi}(\bullet)$ under IBO = 0 dB and $2\sigma_\xi^2 = 0.0$: (a) the amplitude response, and (b) the phase response.

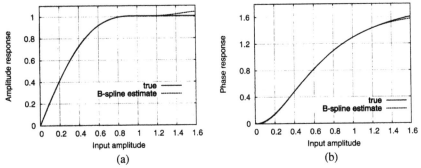

Figure 9.7 Comparison of the HPA's static nonlinearity $\Psi(\bullet)$ and the estimated static nonlinearity $\widehat{\Psi}(\bullet)$ under IBO = 4 dB and $2\sigma_\xi^2 = 0.0$: (a) the amplitude response, and (b) the phase response.

of the predistorter's inverse filter was set to $L_g = 12$. The outputs of the combined predistorter and Wiener HPA are depicted in Fig. 9.10 for the HPA's operating conditions of IBO = 4 dB and 0 dB, respectively. Compared with the outputs of the HPA as plotted in Fig. 9.4 (b) and Fig. 9.5 (b), it can be seen that the designed predistorter successfully removes the serious distortions caused by the HPA. The achievable performance of the designed predistorter was further assessed using the MSE metric defined by

$$\text{MSE} = 10\log_{10}\left(\frac{1}{K_{\text{test}}}\sum_{k=1}^{K_{\text{test}}}|x(k) - y(k)|^2\right) \tag{9.52}$$

and the system's BER, where K_{test} was the number of test data, $x(k)$ was the 16-QAM input and $y(k)$ was the output of the combined predistorter and HPA system. The channel signal-to-noise ratio (SNR) in the simulation was given by SNR $= 10\log_{10}\left(\text{E}_b/\text{N}_o\right)$, where E_b was defined as the energy per bit and N_o the power of the channel's additive white Gaussian noise (AWGN).

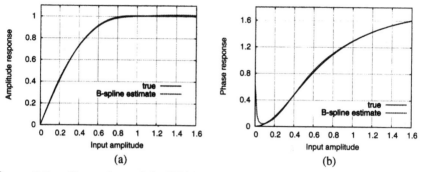

Figure 9.8 Comparison of the HPA's static nonlinearity $\Psi(\bullet)$ and the estimated static nonlinearity $\hat{\Psi}(\bullet)$ under IBO = 0 dB and $2\sigma_\xi^2 = 0.01$: (a) the amplitude response, and (b) the phase response.

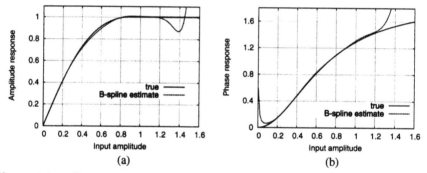

Figure 9.9 Comparison of the HPA's static nonlinearity $\Psi(\bullet)$ and the estimated static nonlinearity $\hat{\Psi}(\bullet)$ under IBO = 4 dB and $2\sigma_\xi^2 = 0.01$: (a) the amplitude response, and (b) the phase response.

With $K_{\text{test}} = 10^5$, 16-QAM data were passed through the combined predistorter and HPA system to compute the MSE (9.52), and the resulting MSE as the function of IBO is plotted in Fig. 9.11. The output signal after the HPA was then transmitted over the AWGN channel, and the BER was then determined at the receiver. The results so obtained are plotted in Fig. 9.12, in comparison with the benchmark BER curve of the ideal AWGN channel. It can be seen from Fig. 9.12 that the BER performance of the combined predistorter and HPA system is practically indistinguishable from those of the ideal AWGN channel even under the operating condition of IBO = 0 dB. The achievable BER performance of the combined predistorter and HPA system are further illustrated in Fig. 9.13 for the three values of the channel SNR.

9.4   CONCLUSIONS

Identification and inverse of complex-valued Wiener systems have been proposed based on the complex-valued B-spline neural network approach. Our contribution is twofold. Firstly, the complex-valued nonlinear static function in the Wiener system is modelled based on the tensor product from two univariate B-spline neural networks that are constructed using the real and imaginary parts of the system input. The Gauss-Newton algorithm, aided by an least squares parameter initialization scheme, has been applied to estimate the model parameters that include the complex-valued linear dynamic model coefficients and B-spline neural network weights. The identification algorithm naturally incorporates the efficient De Boor algorithm with both the B-spline curve and first-order derivative recursions. Secondly, an accurate inverse technique has been developed for the complex-valued Wiener model. In particular, the inverse of the complex-valued nonlinear static function in the Wiener system is calculated effectively using the Gauss-Newton algorithm based on the estimated B-spline neural network model with the aid of the inverse of De Boor algorithm that again utilises naturally both the B-spline curve and first-order derivative recursions. An application to digital predistorter design for high-power amplifiers with memory has been used to demonstrate the effectiveness of our approach for modeling and inverse of complex-valued Wiener systems.

REFERENCES

1. S. Chen, S. McLaughlin, and B. Mulgrew. Complex-valued radial basis function network, Part I: Network architecture and learning algorithms. *Signal Processing*, 35(1): 19–31, 1994.

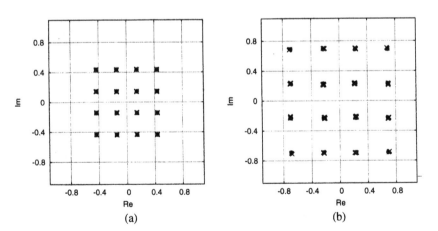

Figure 9.10   The output of the combined predistorter and HPA $y(k)$, marked by ×, for the 16-QAM input signal $x(k)$, marked by •: (a) the IBO of 4 dB, and (b) the IBO of 0.0 dB.

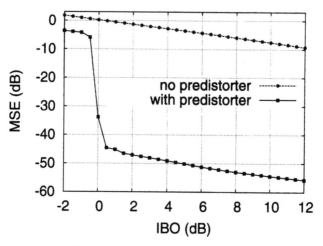

Figure 9.11   The mean square error versus IBO performance.

2. S. Chen, S. McLaughlin, and B. Mulgrew. Complex-valued radial basis function network, Part II: Application to digital communications channel equalisation. *Signal Processing*, 36(2): 175–188, 1994.

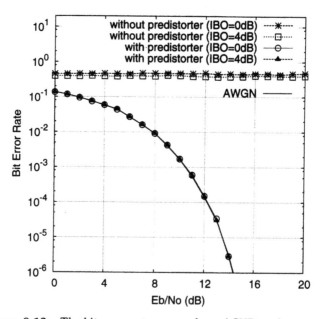

Figure 9.12   The bit error rate versus channel SNR performance.

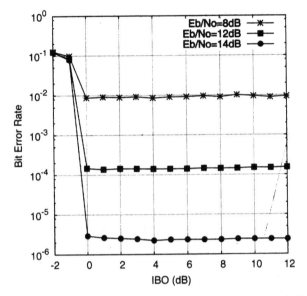

Figure 9.13   The bit error rate versus IBO performance of the combined predistorter and HPA for three values of the channel SNR.

3. A. Uncini, L. Vecci, P. Campolucci, and F. Piazza. Complex valued neural networks with adaptive spline activation function for digital radio links nonlinear equalization. *IEEE Transactions on Signal Processing*, 47(2): 505–514, 1999.

4. T. Kim and T. Adali. Approximation by fully complex multilayer perceptrons. *Neural Computation*, 15(7): 1641–1666, 2003.

5. C.-C. Yang and N. K. Bose. Landmine detection and classification with complex-valued hybrid neural network using scattering parameters dataset. *IEEE Transactions on Neural Networks*, 16(3): 743–753, 2005.

6. M. B. Li, G. B. Guang, P. Saratchandran, and N. Sundararajan. Fully complex extreme learning machine. *Neurocomputing*, 68: 306–314, 2005.

7. A. Hirose. *Complex Valued Neural Networks*. Springer-Verlag, Berlin, 2006.

8. S. Chen, X. Hong, C. J. Harris, and L. Hanzo. Fully complex-valued radial basis function networks: Orthogonal least squares regression and classification. *Neurocomputing*, 71(16–18): 3421–3433, 2008.

9. T. Nitta, editor. *Complex-Valued Neural Networks: Utilizing High-Dimensional Parameters*. Information Science Reference, New York, 2009.

10. A. S. Gangal, P. K. Kalra, and D. S. Chauhan. Inversion of complex valued neural networks using complex back-propagation algorithm. *International Journal of Mathematics and Computers in Simulation*, 3(1): 1–8, 2009.

11. M. Kobayashi. Exceptional reducibility of complex-valued neural networks. *IEEE Transactions on Neural Networks*, 21(7): 1060–1072, 2010.

12. S. A. Billings. Identification of nonlinear systems – A survey. *IEE Proceedings D*, 127(6): 272–285, 1980.

13. E. W. Bai. An optimal two-stage identification algorithm for Hammerstein–Wiener non-linear systems. *Automatica*, 34(3): 333–338, 1998.

14. Y. Zhu. Estimation of an N-L-N Hammerstein–Wiener model. *Automatica*, 38(9): 1607–1614, 2002.

15. J. Schoukens, J. G. Nemeth, P. Crama, Y. Rolain, and R. Pintelon. Fast approximate identification of nonlinear systems. *Automatica*, 39(7): 1267–1274, 2003.

16. K. Hsu, T. Vincent, and K. Poolla. A kernel based approach to structured nonlinear system identification part I: algorithms. in *Proceedings of the 14th IFAC Symposium on System Identification* (Newcastle, Australia), March 29–31, 2006, 6 pages.

17. K. Hsu, T. Vincent, and K. Poolla. A kernel based approach to structured nonlinear system identification part II: convergence and consistency. in *Proceedings of the 14th IFAC Symposium on System Identification* (Newcastle, Australia), March 29–31, 2006, 6 pages.

18. I. W. Hunter and M. J. Korenberg. The identification of nonlinear biological systems: Wiener and Hammerstein cascade models. *Biological Cybernetics*, 55(2–3): 135–144, 1986.

19. A. Kalafatis, N. Arifin, L. Wang, and W. R. Cluett. A new approach to the identification of pH processes based on the Wiener model. *Chemical Engineering Science*, 50(23): 3693–3701, 1995.

20. A. D. Kalafatis, L. Wang, and W. R. Cluett. Identification of Wiener-type nonlinear systems in a noisy environment. *International Journal of Control*, 66(7): 923–941, 1997.

21. Y. Zhu. Distillation column identification for control using Wiener model. in *Proceedings of the 1999 American Control Conference* (San Diego, USA), June 2–4, 1999, pp. 3462–3466.

22. J. C. Gomez, A. Jutan, and E. Baeyens. Wiener model identification and predictive control of a pH neutralisation process. *IEE Proceedings on Control Theory and Applications*, 151(3): 329–338, 2004.

23. A. Hagenblad, L. Ljung, and A. Wills. Maximum likelihood identification of Wiener models. *Automatica*, 44(11): 2697–2705, 2008.

24. W. Greblicki. Nonparametric identification of Wiener systems. *IEEE Transactions on Information Theory*, 38(5): 1487–1493, 1992.

25. I. Skrjanc, S. Blazic, and O. E. Agamennoni. Interval fuzzy modeling applied to Wiener models with uncertainties. *IEEE Transactions on Systems, Man and Cybernetics, Part B*, 35(5): 1092–1095, 2005.

26. G. Farin. *Curves and Surfaces for Computer-Aided Geometric Design: A Practical Guide*. Fourth Edition. Academic Press, Boston, 1996.

27. C. De Boor. *A Practical Guide to Splines*. Spring Verlag, New York, 1978.

28. T. Kavli. ASMOD – an algorithm for adaptive spline modelling of observation data. *International Journal of Control*, 58(4): 947–967, 1993.

29. M. Brown and C. J. Harris. *Neurofuzzy Adaptive Modelling and Control*. Prentice Hall, Englewood Cliffs, NJ, 1994.

30. C. J. Harris, X. Hong, and Q. Gan. *Adaptive Modelling, Estimation and Fusion from Data: A Neurofuzzy Approach*. Springer-Verlag, Berlin, 2002.

31. Y. Yang, L. Guo, and H. Wang. Adaptive statistic tracking control based on two-step neural networks with time delays. *IEEE Transactions on Neural Networks*, 20(3): 420–429, 2009.

32. C. J. Clark, G. Chrisikos, M. S. Muha, A. A. Moulthrop, and C. P. Silva. Time-domain envelope measurement technique with application to wideband power amplifier modeling. *IEEE Transactions on Microwave Theory and Techniques*, 46(12): 2531–2540, 1998.

33. J. H. K. Vuolevi, T. Rahkonen, and J. P. A. Manninen. Measurement technique for characterizing memory effects in RF power amplifiers. *IEEE Transactions on Microwave Theory and Techniques*, 49(8): 1383–1389, 2001.

34. C.-H. Lin, H.-H. Chen, Y.-Y. Wang, and J.-T. Chen. Dynamically optimum lookup-table spacing for power amplifier predistortion linearization. *IEEE Transactions on Microwave Theory and Techniques*, 54(5): 2118–2127, 2006.

35. B. Ai, Z.-Y. Yang, C.-P. Pan, S.-G. Tang, and T. T. Zhang. Analysis on LUT based predistortion method for HPA with memory. *IEEE Transactions on Broadcasting*, 53(1): 127–131, 2007.

36. L. Ding, G. T. Zhou, D. R. Morgan, Z. Ma, J. S. Kenney, J. Kim, and C. R. Giardina. A robust digital baseband predistorter constructed using memory polynomials. *IEEE Transactions on Communications*, 52(1): 159–165, 2004.

37. D. Zhou and V. E. DeBrunner. Novel adaptive nonlinear predistorters based on the direct learning algorithm. *IEEE Transactions on Signal Processing*. 55(1): 120–133, 2007.

38. V. P. G. Jiménez, Y. Jabrane, A. G. Armada, and B. Ait Es Said. High power amplifier pre-distorter based on neural-fuzzy systems for OFDM signals. *IEEE Transactions on Broadcasting*, 57(1): 149–158, 2011.

39. S. Chen. An efficient predistorter design for compensating nonlinear memory high power amplifier. *IEEE Transactions on Broadcasting*, 57(4): 856–865, 2011.

40. X. Hong and S. Chen. Modeling of complex-valued Wiener systems using B-spline neural network. *IEEE Transactions on Neural Networks*, 22(5): 818–825, 2011.

41. B. Igelnik. Kolmogorov's spline complex network and adaptive dynamic modeling of data. in T. Nitta, editor. *Complex-Valued Neural Networks: Utilizing High-Dimensional Parameters*, Information Science Reference, New York, 2009, pp. 56–78.

42. M. Scarpiniti, D. Vigliano, R. Parisi, and A. Unicinis. Flexible blind signal separation in the complex domain. in T. Nitta, editor *Complex-Valued Neural Networks: Utilizing High-Dimensional Parameters*, Information Science Reference, New York, 2009, pp. 284–323.

43. A. A. M. Saleh. Frequency-independent and frequency-dependent nonlinear models of TWT amplifiers. *IEEE Transactions on Communications*, COM-29(11): 1715–1720, 1981.

44. M. Honkanen and S.-G. Häggman. New aspects on nonlinear power amplifier modeling in radio communication system simulations. in *Proceedings on PIMRC'97* (Helsinki, Finland), September 1–4, 1997, pp. 844–848.

45. P. M. Grant, S. McLaughlin, H. Aghvami, and S. Fletcher. Green radio – towards sustainable wireless networks. *Mobile VCE Core 5 Programme* Presentation, April 2009. Available on-line from http://www.ee.princeton.edu/seminars/iss/Spring2009/sl

46. L. Hanzo, S. X. Ng, T. Keller, and W. Webb. *Quadrature Amplitude Modulation: From Basics to Adaptive Trellis-Coded, Turbo-Equalised and Space-Time Coded OFDM, CDMA and MC-CDMA Systems*. John Wiley, Chichester, UK, 2004.

47. L. Hanzo, M. Münster, B. J. Choi, and T. Keller. *OFDM and MC-CDMA for Broadband Multi-User Communications, WLANs and Broadcasting*. John Wiley, Chichester, UK, 2003.

CHAPTER 10

QUATERNIONIC FUZZY NEURAL NETWORK FOR VIEW-INVARIANT COLOR FACE IMAGE RECOGNITION

WAI KIT WONG,[1] GIN CHONG LEE,[1] CHU KIONG LOO,[2] WAY SOONG LIM,[1] AND RAYMOND LOCK[1]

[1] Multimedia University, Melaka, Malaysia
[2] University of Malaya, Kuala Lumpur, Malaysia

People always to recognize, identify, and distinguish individuals based on face. Conventional face recognition algorithms employ simple geometric models. However, recently developed face recognition processes have emerged into the advancement of sophisticated mathematical representations and pattern matching processes. This book presents an effective color image processing system of view-invariant person face image recognition for the Max Planck Institute Kybernetik (MPIK) dataset. The proposed system can recognize face images of a view-invariant person by correlating the input face images with the reference face image and classifying them according to the correct persons name/ID indeed. This has been carried out by constructing a complex quaternion correlator and a max-product fuzzy neural network classifier. Two classification parameters, namely discrete quaternion correlator output (p-value) and the peak-to-side-lobe ratio (PSR), were used in classifying the input face images to categorize it to the authentic class or not. Besides, a new parameter called G-value is also introduced in the proposed view-invariant color face image recognition system for better classification purpose. Experimental results show that the proposed view-invariant color face image recognition system outperforms the conventional non-negative matrix factorization (NMF), block diagonal non-negative matrix factor-

Complex-Valued Neural Networks: Advances and Applications. Edited by Akira Hirose
Copyright © 2013 The Institute of Electrical and Electronics Engineers, Inc.

ization (BD-NMF), and hyper-complex Gabor filter in terms of consumption of enrolment time, recognition time and accuracy in classifying MPIK color face images which are view-invariant, noise-influenced, and scale-invariant.

10.1   INTRODUCTION

Face recognition has been applied in many areas such as face search in databases, authentication in security system, smart user interfaces, robotics and so on. Conventional face recognition methods normally focus on grayscale face image recognition. However in recently, there are more and more researchers switch to focus on color information of the face images to improve the performance of recognition algorithm due to the reasons that color face images offer more information for face recognition task in contrast to grayscale face images.

A simple color face recognition system was first proposed by Torres et al. [1] based on the PCA (principal component analysis) method. The method is based on the representation of the facial images using eigenfaces. The information of three different channels (R, G, B) of color face images are first represented in the form of eigenvectors respectively; and the recognition is implemented separately on each color channel. However, it is found out that the information of different color channels that utilized separately would destroy the structural integrality of the color information and make it hard to learn the facial features (variation in expression, poses and illuminations). Rajapakse et al. [2] presented a parallel work based on NMF (non-negative matrix factorization) for color face recognition. In their work, color information on face images of different channels were treated separately too. Some observed advantages of NMF method on face recognition are more robust to occlusion, variation of expressions and poses. However, since the NMF method also treats information of different color channels separately, just like the PCA method, it would also destroy the structural integrality of color information and the correlation among the color information.

In order to preserve the integrality of color information on different channels in the color face recognition system, Wang et al. [3] proposed a supersedable NMF method, which is the block diagonal non-negative matrix factorization (BDNMF). Inspired by the NMF method, BDNMF also separated color information into different color channels, but it uses block diagonal matrix to simultaneously encode color information of different channels, hence preserving the integrality of color information. However, BDNMF method has the demerit of complex enrollment/training stage. In BDNMF, unsupervised multiplicative learning rules are used iteratively to update the parameters such as basis image matrix (W) and encoding image (H). Therefore, longer enrollment time is required for this method. Another demerit of BDNMF is that an additional coined block diagonal constraint is imposed on the factorization part to construct the BDNMF algorithm. This makes the computation more complex compared to the conventional NMF method.

Another recently developed color face recognition method is the use of hypercomplex Gabor filters [4]. Conventional Gabor filters are used in many face recognition applications [5–7] and they are proven to obtain good recognition performance due to its inherent merits of insensitivity to illumination and pose variation. In Ref.4, the author further extended conventional Gabor filter into hypercomplex (quaternion) domain to perform color based feature extraction. Experimental results in Ref.4 showed that the conventional Gabor filter feature extraction achieved significant improvement in face matching accuracy over the monochromatic case. However, hypercomplex Gabor filter required a large number of different kernels, and hence the length of the feature vectors in quaternion domain would increase dramatically. Also, hypercomplex Gabor filter is twice the size of filter structure compared to those used in the conventional Gabor filters.

Most of the proposed algorithms for color face recognition treat the three color channels (R, G, B) separately and apply grayscale face recognition methods [8, 9] to each of the channels and then combine the results at last. But with the quaternion correlation techniques [10], it processes all color channels jointly by using its quaternion numbers. Quaternion numbers are the generalization of complex numbers. It is a number which consists of one real part and three orthogonal imaginary parts. RGB color face image can be represented using quaternion representation by inserting the value of three color channels into the three imaginary parts of the quaternion number respectively. Therefore, in this book chapter, the concept of quaternion is proposed for view-invariant color face image recognition system.

An advanced correlation filter named as unconstrained optimal tradeoff synthetic discriminant (UOTSDF) [11, 12], is also applied in the proposed view-invariant color face image recognition system. The goal of the filter is to produce sharp peak that is similar to 2-D delta-type correlation outputs when the input face image belongs to the class of the reference face image that was used to train the input face image; and, this provides automatic shift-invariance. A strong and sharp peak can be observed in the output correlation plane when the input face image comes from the authentic class (input face image matches with a particular training/reference face image stored in database) and no discernible peak if the input face image comes from the imposter class (input face image does not matches with the particular reference face image).

Three classification parameters are in concern in classifying whether an input face image belongs to the authentic class or not. They are the real-to-complex ratio of the discrete quaternion correlator output (ρ-value) [10], peak-to-sidelobe ratio (PSR) [13] and the max product fuzzy neural network classifier value (G-value). ρ-value has been introduced in Ref.10, which is used in measuring the correlation output between the colors, shape, size, and brightness of input image and a particular reference image. PSR is another parameter introduced in Ref.13 for a better recognition due to the reason that it is more accurate if we consider the peak value with the region around the peak value, rather than a single peak point. The higher the value of PSR, the more likely the input face image belongs to the referenced image class. In this chapter, both the ρ-value and the PSR are combined, normalized and applied with Gaussian distribution function in the max-product fuzzy neural network classifier. This technique is producing a new parameter, so-called the G-value. This new parameter as well as the new algorithm is applied in view-invariant color face image recognition system for better classification purposes. The same technique had been applied in the machine condition monitoring [14] and it yields high success rate in classifying machine conditions. It is good to be implemented for color face image recognition.

In this chapter, a quaternion-based fuzzy neural network classifier is proposed for MPIK data sets view-invariant color face image recognition. A ten thousand repeated images generated/collected from the 7 different position color face images of 200 people in MPIK data set were used for evaluated the system performance. Among the 10,000 repeated color face images, 5000 are normal MPIK color face images; 2500 are normal MPIK color face images embedded with noise features such as "salt and pepper," "poisson," and "speckle noise" as provided in Matlab image processing toolbox; and 2500 are normal MPIK color face images with scale invariance (shrink or dilation). The performance of the proposed quaternion-based fuzzy neural network classifier is compared to NMF, BDNMF, and hypercomplex Gabor filter. Experimental results showed that the quaternion-based fuzzy neural network classifier outperforms conventional NMF, BDNMF, and hypercomplex Gabor filter in terms of enrollment time consumption, recognition time consumption and accuracy in classifying view-invariant, noise-influenced, and scale-invariant MPIK color face images.

This chapter is organized as follows: Section 10.2 briefly discusses face recognition system and some conventional face recognition methods, such as PCA, NMF, and BDNMF methods. Section 10.3 comments on the proposed view-invariant color face image recognition model and the quaternion-based color face image correlator. Section 10.4 describes the enrollment stage and recognition stage for the algorithm of the proposed quaternion-based color face image correlator. Then in Section 10.5, the structure of fuzzy max-product neural network classifier will be described. Section 10.6 contains the experimental results. Finally, in Section 10.7, the work is summarized and envisages some future work.

10.2   FACE RECOGNITION SYSTEM

Humans often had the inherent ability to distinguish and recognize between individual faces, however, computers starting from the mid-1960s have shown the same ability. In the mid-1960s, researchers began using the computer to work on face recognition. Since then, computerized facial recognition has started. During 1964, Bledsoe and Chan worked on using the computer to recognize human faces [15–17]. They were proud of these works, however, due to the reason that an unnamed intelligence agency was funded their research, they did not allow much dissemination, and only little of the work was published. According to their work, given a big database of images and a photograph, the problem was to pick from the database on a small set of records such that one of the image records matched the photograph. The success rate is measured in terms of the ratio of the answer list to the number of records in the database. Bledsoe labeled the facial recognition system as man–machine system [16] due to the reason that the coordinates of a set of features from the photographs will be extracted out based on human images, which will later be applied by the computer for recognition. The following difficulties were discovered in Ref.16:

1. Face recognition is hard with the great variability in head rotation and tilt, angle and lighting intensity, aging, facial expression, etc.

2. The correlation method on unprocessed optical data is inevitably failed on cases with great variability. The correlation between two images of the same person with two different head rotations is very low.

In 1970s, Goldstein et al. [18] applied 21 specific subjective markers such as lip thickness and hair color to run the automated face recognition. The problem of this face recognition method was that the measurements and locations were manually computed. However in 1987, Sirovich and Kirby [19] applied a standard linear algebra technique, so called the "principal components analysis" for grayscale face recognition.

10.2.1 Principal Component Analysis (PCA) Method

Principal Components Analysis (PCA) is a statistical method used in face recognition, image compression, and high-dimensional pattern searching. In face recognition, PCA, by the application of eigenfaces (eigenvectors of the set of faces) is the technique first developed by Sirovich and Kirby for grayscale face recognition in 1987. It was later improved by Turk and Pentland [20] to extend to multiple-view face recognition, as well as by Torres et al. [1] in the color face recognition system.

In PCA face recognition system [1], every face image is represented as a vector and expressed in an orthogonal basis, computed from the training images set. Suppose there are N training vectors $\bar{x}_1, \bar{x}_2, \ldots, \bar{x}_N$, the covariance matrix C can be estimated by

$$C \approx \frac{1}{N} \sum_{k}^{N} (\bar{x}_k - \bar{\mu})(\bar{x}_k - \bar{\mu})^T \tag{10.1}$$

where $\bar{\mu}$ is the estimation of the training vectors expectation. The $N-1$ eigenfaces e_i can be computed and sorted by descending module of their eigenvalues $\lambda_1 \geq \lambda_2 \geq \cdots \geq \lambda_{N-1}$. Once the corresponding eigenfaces are computed, they are used to represent the training and test faces to be identified. This is done by a projection on the eigenfaces applying a scalar product. Any training image can be obtained by a linear combination of the eigenfaces:

$$\bar{x} = \bar{\mu} + \sum_{i=1}^{N-1} \hat{x}_i \bar{e}_i \tag{10.2}$$

where $\hat{x}_i = \bar{x}_i . \bar{e}_i$. The first eigenfaces contain the most information, in the root mean square sense, so that a test vector $\bar{y}$ can be expressed in the eigenspace, to express it in term of the principal components of the training vectors [1]:

$$\bar{y} = \bar{\mu} + \sum_{i=1}^{N-1} \hat{y}_i \bar{e}_i \tag{10.3}$$

The training and test vectors can be rewritten as

$$\bar{\hat{x}} = \begin{pmatrix} \hat{x}_1 \\ \cdot \\ \cdot \\ \cdot \\ \hat{x}_{N-1} \end{pmatrix} \text{ and } \bar{\hat{y}} = \begin{pmatrix} \hat{y}_1 \\ \cdot \\ \cdot \\ \cdot \\ \hat{y}_{N-1} \end{pmatrix} \tag{10.4}$$

Then the recognition is performed using the maximum likelihood principle by a distance computation. The selected training image is the one which have the minimal distance under the eigenbasis:

$$k_o = arg \min_{1 \le k \le K} d(\bar{\hat{x}}_k, \bar{\hat{y}}) \tag{10.5}$$

where $d(\bar{\hat{x}}, \bar{\hat{y}}) = \sqrt{\sum_{i=1}^{N-1} \frac{(\hat{y}_i - \hat{x}_i)}{\lambda_i}}$ is the Mahalanobis distance. In summary, PCA is holistic algorithm which learns facial features of the whole image. It uses a linear combination of a set of orthogonal bases to describe a whole face image. The essence of the algorithm makes it hard to learn local facial features for recognition [21]. Hence, face recognition approach based on it is more prone to be affected by the variation of poses, expressions and illuminations.

10.2.2   Non-negative Matrix Factorization (NMF) Method

Rajapakse et al. [2] present a color face recognition method based on non-negative matrix factorization (NMF). In their work, color information from different channels (R, G, B) is treated separately. Face images of different color channels are factorized using NMF algorithm respectively and base images on each channel are computed. The projection coefficients of color face samples extracted from the base images are used as the facial features for recognition. Given a data matrix $F = \{F_{ij}\}_{n \times m}$, non-negative matrix factorization refers to the decomposition of the matrix F into two matrices W and H of size $n \times r$ and $r \times m$, respectively, such that

$$F = WH \tag{10.6}$$

where the elements in W and H are all positive values. From this decomposition, a reduced representation is achieved by choosing the rank r, such that $r < n$ and $r < m$. The reconstruction of an object is performed only by adding its representative parts collectively. Each column in the matrix H is called an encoding and each column in the matrix W is called a basis image. An image (column) in F can be reconstructed by linearly combining the coefficients in an encoding with the basis images. The encodings influence the activation of pixels in the original matrix via basis images.

According to Ref.22, each element in the matrix F can be written as $F_{ij} = \sum_{\rho=1}^{r} W_{i\rho} H_{\rho j}$, where r represents the number of basis images and the number of coefficients in an encoding. The following unsupervised multiplicative learning rules are used iteratively to update W and H:

$$H_{\rho j} \leftarrow H_{\rho j} \sum_{i=1}^{n} \left(\frac{W_{i\rho} F_{ij}}{\sum_{k=1}^{r} W_{ik} H_{kj}} \right) \tag{10.7}$$

$$W_{i\rho} \leftarrow W_{i\rho} \sum_{j=1}^{m} \left(\frac{F_{ij} H_{\rho j}}{\sum_{k=1}^{r} W_{ik} H_{kj}} \right) \tag{10.8}$$

$$W_{i\rho} \leftarrow \frac{W_{i\rho}}{\sum_{k=1}^{n} W_{k\rho}} \tag{10.9}$$

The initial values of W and H are fixed randomly. At each iteration, a new value for W or H is evaluated. Each update consists of a multiplication and sums of positive factors, With these iterative updates, the approximation of (10.6) improves with a guaranteed convergence to a locally optimal matrix factorization [23].

10.2.2.1 Color Image Representation and Training for Face Recognition In color images, a set of 3 data matrices F^l is constructed where $l \in \{ R,G,B \}$ such that each color channel, l, of training face images occupies the columns of the $F^l = [f^l_1 f^l_2 ... f^l_m]$, $l \in \{ R,G,B \}$ matrices. Let the set of faces be $\Gamma = \{ f_1, f_2, ..., f_m \}$, then the data matrices, $F^l = [f^l_1 f^l_2 ... f^l_m]$. Learning is done using (10.7) – (10.9) to decompose each matrix F^l into two matrices, H_l and W_l. Let the basis images be $W^l = [w^l_1 w^l_2 ... w^l_r]$ and encodings be $H^l = [h^l_1 h^l_2 ... h^l_m]$. Each face f^l_i in F can be approximately reconstructed by linearly combining the basis images, and the corresponding encoding coefficients $c = (h^l_{1i} h^l_{2i} ... h^l_{ri})$. Hence, a face can be modeled in terms of a linear superposition of basis functions together with color encodings as follows:

$$f^l_i = W^l h^l_i \tag{10.10}$$

For each face f_i in the training set and test set, the corresponding encoding coefficients are calculated for each color channel. The basis images in W^l are generated from the set of training faces, Γ^{train}. The corresponding color encodings, h^l_i of each training face f_i is given by

$$h^l_i = (W^l)^t f^l_i \tag{10.11}$$

where W^t is computed pseudo-inverse matrix of the basis matrix W. Once trained, the face image set, Γ^{train}, is represented by a set of encodings $\{h^l{}_1\ h^l{}_2 \ldots h^l{}_m\}$ with a reduced dimension of rank r.

10.2.2.2 Color Face Image Recognition
Given a face image f, a representative color encodings for it can be found by

$$h^l = (W^l)^t f^l \tag{10.12}$$

Cosine angle distance measure is used to calculate the similarity between encodings of a trained image $h_i = \Gamma^{train}$ and a test image $h = \Gamma^{test}$.

The cosine angle between the two data vectors is taken as the similarity measure:

$$s_i = \sum_{l \in R,G,B} s^l_i = \frac{h^l h^l{}_i}{|h^l||h^l{}_i|} \tag{10.13}$$

The similarity measure s_i determines the matching score between the encodings h and h_i corresponding to 2 faces f and f_i. The optimum matching encoding of a trained image can be given as h_{i*} where

$$i^* = arg \max_i s_i \tag{10.14}$$

In summary, NMF algorithm imposes non-negative constraint on base image matrix and coefficient matrix. In the algorithm, there are only additive operations and no subtractive operations. It is more accordant to the basic idea of linear combination. It can learn facial features of facial part and then construct the part-based representation. The pros of NMF algorithm in face recognition is more robust to occultation, variation of expression and poses. But as on color face image, Rajapakse et. al. applied NMF algorithm to different channels separately which would destroy the integrality of color information and the correlation among them as the work of Torres et. al. does on PCA method.

10.2.3 Block Diagonal Non-negative Matrix Factorization (BDNMF) Method

Inspired by the NMF algorithm, a novel approach on block diagonal non-negative matrix factorization (BDNMF) is proposed by Wang and Bai [3] for color face representation and recognition. In order to preserve the integrality of color information of different channels, BDNMF method exploits block diagonal matrix to encode the color information for different channels (R, G, B) simultaneously. BDNMF imposes an additional coined block diagonal constraint on base image matrix and coefficient matrix based on the basic constraint of NMF, and it is applied to compute factorization coefficients and color base images. To preserve the integrality of color information no each channels (R, G, B), the mode of block diagonal matrix is proposed in [3] to encode color information of different channel simultaneously.

Let F denote a color face image with size $n = n_1 \times n_2$. $(F^{(R)}, F^{(G)}, F^{(B)})$ are data matrices corresponding to three color channels (R, G, B), respectively $(F^{(R)}, F^{(G)}, F^{(B)}$ $\Re^{n_1 \times n_2})$. These component data corresponding to the three color channels are arranged in the place of principal diagonals of a matrix and used to represent a color face:

$$F = \begin{bmatrix} F^{(R)} & 0 & 0 \\ 0 & F^{(G)} & 0 \\ 0 & 0 & F^{(B)} \end{bmatrix} \tag{10.15}$$

In order to exploit the BDNMF algorithm to compute the coefficient matrix and the base image matrix, color faces in training set are first combined together to form the block diagonal matrix of training set [3]:

$$V = \begin{bmatrix} X^{(R)} & 0 & 0 \\ 0 & X^{(G)} & 0 \\ 0 & 0 & X^{(B)} \end{bmatrix} \tag{10.16}$$

where $X^{(l)} = [X_1{}^{(l)}, X_2{}^{(l)}, ..., X_m{}^{(l)}]$, $l \in \{R,G,B\}$, for m color faces, and each column of the sub-matrix $X^{(l)}$ represents the component data corresponding to channel l of one color face, i.e., $X^{(l)}$ is the vector mode of component data matrix $F_i{}^{(l)}$.

Similar to the conventional NMF algorithm, BDNMF algorithm's goal is to factorize block diagonal matrix V into the multiplication of two non-negative matrices W (basis images) and H (encodings/coefficients):

$$V_{i\mu} \approx (WH)_{i\mu} = \sum_{k=1}^{3r} W_{ik} H_{k\mu} \tag{10.17}$$

where $3r$ is the rank of BDNMF and r is the rank of sub-matrix in the place of principal diagonal. The most essential difference between BDNMF and conventional NMF algorithm is that the constraint imposed on the basis image matrix W and encoding/coefficient matrix H are different. As seen in (10.16), most elements in V are zeros except for three sub-matrices in the place of the principal diagonal, and the elements of each sub-matrix belong to the same color channel. Herein, as to the same rank r, BDNMF imposes an additional block diagonal constraint on the basis image matrix W and encoding/coefficient matrix H, i.e., W and H must be in block diagonal matrices as well:

$$W = \begin{bmatrix} W^{(R)} & 0 & 0 \\ 0 & W^{(G)} & 0 \\ 0 & 0 & W^{(B)} \end{bmatrix} \tag{10.18}$$

$$H = \begin{bmatrix} H^{(R)} & 0 & 0 \\ 0 & H^{(G)} & 0 \\ 0 & 0 & H^{(B)} \end{bmatrix} \tag{10.19}$$

where $W^{(l)} \in \Re^{n \times r}$, $H^{(l)} \in \Re^{n \times r} (l \in \{R, G, B\})$. Then BDNMF algorithm is transformed into the following optimal problem:

$$\arg_{min} D(V \| WH), \ s.t. \ W \geq 0, H \geq 0; \quad (10.20)$$
$$W \text{ and } H \text{ meet conditions } (10.18) \text{ and } (10.19)$$

In summary, it is deserved to be mentioned that V, W, and H have a lot of elements equaling zero respectively. It would be time-consuming to compute each element during the process of optimizing subjective function (10.20). Therefore, longer enrollment time is required for this method. Another demerit of BDNMF is that an additional coined block diagonal constraint is imposed on the factorization part to construct the BDNMF algorithm. This makes the computation more complex compared to the conventional NMF method. Therefore, in this chapter, a concept applying the quaternion approach is proposed for view-invariant color face image recognition system. The proposed quaternionic-based face recognition system processes all color channels jointly by using its quaternion numbers.

10.3 QUATERNION-BASED VIEW-INVARIANT COLOR FACE IMAGE RECOGNITION

In this subchapter, quaternion-based view-invariant color face image recognition will be briefly discussed. Section 10.3.1 will introduce what is quaternion. Section 10.3.2 will discuss the quaternion Fourier transform and Section 10.3.3 will indicate the newly developed quaternion-based view-invariant color face image correlator.

10.3.1 Quaternion

In mathematics, complex number is viewed as points in a plane. It consists of a real part and an imaginary part. However, a quaternion is number system that extends the complex number into space. A quaternion consists of a real part and three imaginary parts. From the quaternion, it gave birth to quaternion algebra. Quaternion algebra was first introduced by Sir William Rowan Hamilton, an Irish mathematician, in 1843 [24]. Sir Hamilton discovered that points in space can actually be described by their coordinates that are with triples of numbers (i, j, k). He was later carving the formulas for adding multiplying and dividing those triples of numbers (quaternion).

The quaternion and quaternion algebra were first applied to mechanics literature on its three-dimensional space studies. In the modern world today, the quaternion also is useful in theoretical mathematics and applied mathematics for three-dimensional rotations calculations such as in 3D computer vision and computer graphics. Some elementary properties of quaternion numbers and the operations of quaternion arithmetic are shown below:

Extending the complex number: A triples example $p + q.i + r.j = (p, q, r)$ where i and j are distinct and independent.

Breaking commutatively: Two triples x and x^*.

$$x = p + q.i + r.j = (p, q, r), x^* = p - q.i - r.j = (p, -q, -r) \qquad (10.21)$$
$$xx^* = p^2 + q^2 + r^2 - 2ijqr$$

The result has an extra product term $(-2ijqr)$.

Sir Hamilton resolves this problem by regarded them as two terms: $(-ijqr)$ and $(-jiqr)$. If somebody breaks the commutative law of multiplication and claims that $ij = -ji$, then $(-2ijqr)$ term vanishes, but it turns out that there still maintain a consistent number:

$$ij.ij = i(ji)i = -i(ij)j = -(i^2)(j^2) = -(-1)(-1) = -1 \qquad (10.22)$$

which means $ij = \sqrt{-1}$, which is still a root of -1. If this root is name as k, then the extension from triples to quadruples is straightforward:

$$p + q.i + r.j + s.k = (p, q, r, s) \qquad (10.23)$$

which means that the following relationships hold:

$$ij = k, \; jk = i, \; ki = j, \; ji = -k, \; kj = -i, \; ik = -j \qquad (10.24)$$
$$i^2 = j^2 = k^2 = ijk = -1$$

Sir Hamilton named these extended numbers as quaternions.

Addition and subtraction for quaternions:

$$Let \; x = (p, q, r, s) = p + 9.i + r.j + s.k$$
$$and \; y = (a, b, c, d) = a + b.i + c.j + d.k, \; then$$
$$x + y = (p + a, \; q + b, \; r + c, \; s + d)$$
$$= (p + a) + (q + b).i + (r + c).j + (s + d).k$$
$$x - y = (p - a, q - b, r - c, s - d)$$
$$= (p - a) + (q - b).i + (r - c).j + (s - d).k \qquad (10.25)$$

Multiplication of a quaternion with a real number:

$$Let \; x = (p, q, r, s), \; and \; y \; is \; a \; real \; number, \; then$$
$$yx = xy = (yp, yq, yr, ys) = yp + (yq).i + (yr).j + (ys).k \qquad (10.26)$$

Alternate representation of a quaternion:

$$Let \; x = (p, q, r, s)$$

where the real part p can be separate from the purely imaginary part $\nu = (p, q, r)$

$$x = (p, \nu)$$

If there is another quaternion, $y = (a, \mathbf{u})$ where $\mathbf{u}$ is another purely imaginary part, then

$$x + y = (p, \nu) + (a, \mathbf{u}) = (p + a, \nu + \mathbf{u}) \tag{10.27}$$

Conjugation and absolute value of a quaternion:

$$Let\ x = (p, q, r, s) = p + q.i + r.j + s.k$$
$$and\ its\ conjugate\ x^* = (p, -q, -r, -s) = p - iq - jr - ks$$
$$or\ x^* = (p, -\nu)$$
$$The\ absolute\ value\ |x| = \sqrt{(p^2 + q^2 + r^2 + s^2)} = \sqrt{xx^*} \tag{10.28}$$

Multiplication of a quaternion:

$$Let\ x = (p, q, r, s)\ and\ y = (a, b, c, d),$$
$$xy = (p + q.i + r.j + s.k)(a + b.i + c.j + d.k)$$
$$= p(a + b.i + c.j + d.k) + q.i(a + b.i + c.j + d.k) +$$
$$r.j(a + b.i + c.j + d.k) + s.k(a + b.i + c.j + d.k)$$
$$= pa + pb.i + pc.j + pd.k + qa.i - qb + qc.k - qd.j +$$
$$ra.j - rb.k - rc + r.i + sa.k + sb.j - sc.i - sd$$
$$= (pa - qb - rx - sd, pb + qa + rd - sc, pc - qd + ra + sb,$$
$$pd + qc - rb + sa)$$

Another representation way: $x = (p, \nu),\ y = (a, \mathbf{u})$

$$xy = (pa - \nu.\mathbf{u}, p\mathbf{u} + a\nu + \nu X \mathbf{u}) \tag{10.29}$$

where X is the vector cross product. From this representation, it shows that quaternion multiplication is not commutative (change the order of operands will change the end result).

Squaring the quaternion: Let $x = (p, q, r, s) = (p, \nu)$

$$x^2 = (p^2 - \nu.\nu, 2p\nu) \tag{10.30}$$

since the cross product of any vector with itself is zero.

Inverse and division of a quaternion:

$$xx^* = x^*x = |x|^2 \text{ and thus}$$
$$\frac{xx^*}{|x|^2} = \frac{x^*x}{|x|^2} = 1$$
$$\frac{x}{y} = xy^{-1} \text{ or } \frac{y}{x} = x^{-1}y \qquad (10.31)$$

Real and complex subspaces for quaternions:

$$e.g. \ (p, 0, 0, 0) = p,$$
$$(p, q, 0, 0) = p + q.i,$$
$$(p, 0, r, o) = p + r, j,$$
$$(p, 0, 0, s) = p + s.k \qquad (10.32)$$

For more understanding and studies on quaternion and its properties, see Ref.25.

10.3.2 Quaternion Fourier Transform

There are many types of Quaternion Fourier Transform introduced, the earliest definition of QFT is the two-side form as below:

$$H_{(q)}(\omega, \nu) = \int_{-\infty}^{\infty} \int_{-\infty}^{\infty} e^{-i\omega x}.h(x, y).e^{-j\nu y} \, dxdy \qquad (10.33)$$

It can be generalized as

$$H_{(q)}(\omega, \nu) = \int_{-\infty}^{\infty} \int_{-\infty}^{\infty} e^{-\mu_1 \omega x}.h(x, y).e^{-\mu_2 \nu y} \, dxdy \qquad (10.34)$$

where μ_1 and μ_2 are two pure quaternion units (the quaternion equation with real part equal to zero) that are orthogonal to each other:

$$\mu_1 = \mu_{1,i} + \mu_{1,j}.j + \mu_{1,k}.k$$
$$\mu_2 = \mu_{2,i} + \mu_{2,j}.j + \mu_{2,k}.k$$

Recently, the left-side form of QFT was introduced:

$$H_{(q)}(\omega, \nu) = \int_{-\infty}^{\infty} \int_{-\infty}^{\infty} e^{-\mu_1(\omega x + \nu y)}.h(x, y) \, dxdy \qquad (10.35)$$

The right-side QFT can also define as the transpose transform of the left-side form of QFT. Therefore, it can be concluded that there are at least three types of QFT:

1. Type 1 QFT (two-side):

$$H_{(q1)}(\omega, \nu) = \int\limits_{-\infty}^{\infty} \int\limits_{-\infty}^{\infty} e^{-\mu_1 \omega x} h(x, y) e^{-\mu_2 \nu y} \; dx dy$$

2. Type 2 QFT (left-side):

$$H_{(q2)}(\omega, \nu) = \int\limits_{-\infty}^{\infty} \int\limits_{-\infty}^{\infty} e^{-\mu_1(\omega x + \nu y)} h(x, y) \; dx dy$$

3. Type 3 QFT (right-side):

$$H_{(q3)}(\omega, \nu) = \int\limits_{-\infty}^{\infty} \int\limits_{-\infty}^{\infty} h(x, y) e^{-\mu_1(\omega x + \nu y)} \; dx dy \qquad (10.36)$$

The inverse quaternion Fourier transform (IQFT) are as below:

1. Type 1 IQFT (two-side):

$$h(x, y) = (4\pi^2)^{-1} \int\limits_{-\infty}^{\infty} \int\limits_{-\infty}^{\infty} e^{\mu_1 \omega x} H_{(q1)}(\omega, \nu) e^{\mu_2 \nu y} \; d\omega d\nu$$

2. Type 2 IQFT (left-side):

$$h(x, y) = (4\pi^2)^{-1} \int\limits_{-\infty}^{\infty} \int\limits_{-\infty}^{\infty} e^{\mu_1(\omega x + \nu y)} H_{(q2)}(\omega, \nu) \; d\omega d\nu$$

3. Type 3 IQFT (right-side):

$$h(x, y) = (4\pi^2)^{-1} \int\limits_{-\infty}^{\infty} \int\limits_{-\infty}^{\infty} H_{(q3)} e^{\mu_1(\omega x + \nu y)} \; d\omega d\nu \qquad (10.37)$$

For continuous QFT, there are also at least three types of discrete quaternion Fourier transform (DQFT):

1. Type 1 DQFT (two-side):

$$H_{(q1)}(p, s) = \sum_{m=0}^{M-1} \sum_{n=0}^{N-1} e^{-\mu_1 2\pi(pm/M)} h(m, n) e^{-\mu_2 2\pi(sn/M)}$$

2. Type 2 DQFT (left-side):

$$H_{(q2)}(p, s) = \sum_{m=0}^{M-1} \sum_{n=0}^{N-1} e^{-\mu_1 2\pi((pm/M)+(sn/M))} h(m, n)$$

3. Type 3 DQFT (right-side):

$$H_{(q3)}(p, s) = \sum_{m=0}^{M-1} \sum_{n=0}^{N-1} h(m, n) e^{-\mu_1 2\pi((pm/M)+(sn/M))} h(m, n) \quad (10.38)$$

QFT and DQFT are useful for color image processing, especially for the color-sensitive smoothing, but research on the algorithms of QFT and DQFT are not sufficient enough and thus limit the utilities of QFT and DQFT. Therefore, efficient algorithms of all types of QFT will be developed. With the algorithms, the QFT can be implemented by using the structure of the original FFT directly [26]. As the efficient algorithms of DQFT are very similar to the continuous QFT, therefore we will only discuss the efficient algorithms of the continuous QFT.

10.3.2.1 Implementation of Type 1 QFT   To simplify the discussion, we begin with a special case that $\mu_1 = i$ and $\mu_2 = j$. If:

$$H_c(\omega, \nu) = \int_{-\infty}^{\infty} \int_{-\infty}^{\infty} e^{-i\omega x} . h(x, y) . e^{-i\nu y} \, dx dy \quad (10.39)$$

then

$$\frac{[H_c(\omega, \nu) + H_c(\omega, -\nu)]}{2} = \int_{-\infty}^{\infty} \int_{-\infty}^{\infty} e^{-i\omega x} h(x, y) . \cos(\nu y) \, dx dy$$

$$\frac{[H_c(\omega, \nu) + H_c(\omega, -\nu)]}{2} = \left[\int_{-\infty}^{\infty} \int_{-\infty}^{\infty} e^{-i\omega x} h(x, y) \sin(\nu y) \, dx dy \right] . i \quad (10.40)$$

and therefore,

$$\frac{[H_c(\omega, \nu) + H_c(\omega, -\nu)]}{2} + \frac{[H_c(\omega, \nu) + H_c(\omega, -\nu)]}{2} . (k)$$

$$= \int_{-\infty}^{\infty} \int_{-\infty}^{\infty} e^{-i\omega x} h(x, y) e^{-ij\nu y} \, dx dy \quad (10.41)$$

thus,

$$H_{(q1)}(\omega, \nu) = \frac{[H_c(\omega, \nu)(1 - k) + H_c(\omega, -\nu)(1 + k)]}{2} \qquad (10.42)$$

Hence, to compute the QFT, it can first compute complex 2-D FT of input function as stated in (10.39) and then use (10.42) to compute the QFT. Note that in (10.39), the input $h(x, y)$ is a quaternion function and not a complex function; therefore one complex 2-D FT is impossible to implement it. Hence, $h(x, y)$ first decompose as

$$h(x, y) = h_a(x, y) + h_b(x, y).j \qquad (10.43)$$

where $h_a(x, y) = h_r(x, y) + h_i(x, y).i$, $h_b(x, y) = h_j(x, y) + h_k(x, y).i$. Then, (10.39) can be rewritten as

$$
\begin{aligned}
H_c(\omega, \nu) &= \int_{-\infty}^{\infty}\int_{-\infty}^{\infty} e^{-i\omega x} h_a(x, y) e^{-i\nu y}\, dx dy + \int_{-\infty}^{\infty}\int_{-\infty}^{\infty} e^{-i\omega x} h_b(x, y).j e^{-i\nu y}\, dx dy \\
&= \int_{-\infty}^{\infty}\int_{-\infty}^{\infty} e^{-i\omega x} h_a(x, y) e^{-i\nu y}\, dx dy + \int_{-\infty}^{\infty}\int_{-\infty}^{\infty} e^{-i\omega x} h_b(x, y).e^{-i\nu y}.j\, dx dy \\
&= \int_{-\infty}^{\infty}\int_{-\infty}^{\infty} e^{-i\omega x} e^{-i\nu y} h_a(x, y)\, dx dy + \left[\int_{-\infty}^{\infty}\int_{-\infty}^{\infty} e^{-i\omega x} e^{-i\nu y} h_b(x, -y)\, dx dy\right] j
\end{aligned}
$$

$$(10.4\qquad$$

In summary, there are 3 steps to follow to compute the type 1 QFT:

1. Decompose the input function as Eq.(10.43).

2. Calculate $H(\omega, \nu)$ from Eq.(10.44).

3. Calculate the transform result of QFT from $H(\omega, \nu)$.

If the $x, y, \omega,$ and v axes are sampled as

$$
\begin{aligned}
x &= m\Delta_x,\ y = n\Delta_y,\ \omega = p\Delta_\omega \\
\nu &= q\Delta_\nu,\ m,\ p \in [-M_0, M_0],\ n,\ q \in [-N_0, N_0] \\
\Delta_x.\,\Delta_\omega &= \frac{2\pi}{M},\ \Delta_y.\Delta_\nu = \frac{2\pi}{N},\ M = 2M_0 + 1,\ N = 2N_0 + 1
\end{aligned}
$$

$$(10.45)$$

then (10.44) can be implemented as below:

$$H_{(q1)}(p\Delta_\omega, q\Delta_\nu) = \sum_{m=-M_0}^{M_0} \sum_{n=-N_0}^{N_0} e^{-i((2\pi pm)/M + (2\pi qm)/N)} h_a(m\Delta_x, n\Delta_y)$$

$$+ (\sum_{m=-M_0}^{M_0} \sum_{n=-N_0}^{N_0} e^{-i((2\pi pm)/M + (2\pi qm)/N)} h_a(m\Delta_x, n\delta_y))j$$

$$(10.46)$$

QFT can be implemented by two $M \times N$ point 2-D DFTs. Each 2-D DFT requires $MN \times \log_2 MN$ real number multiplications. Hence, to implement QFT, it is totally require $2MN \times \log_2 MN$ real number multiplications. For the discussion above, it is the special case where $\mu_1 = i$ and $\mu_2 = j$. Hence, for general case, suppose that

$$\mu_1 = \mu_{1,1}.i + \mu_{1,2}.j + \mu_{1,3}.k,$$
$$\mu_2 = \mu_{2,1}.i + \mu_{2,2}.j + \mu_{2,3}.k,$$
$$\mu_3 = \mu_{3,1}.i + \mu_{3,2}.j + \mu_{3,3}.k$$

$$(10.47)$$

Then, $h(x, y)$ rewritten as below:

$$h(x, y) = h_r(x, y) + h_1(x, y)\mu_1 + h_2(x, y)\mu_2 + h_3(x, y)\mu_3 \qquad (10.48)$$

and

$$\begin{bmatrix} h_1(x,y) \\ h_2(x,y) \\ h_3(x,y) \end{bmatrix} = \begin{bmatrix} \mu_{1,1} & \mu_{2,1} & \mu_{3,1} \\ \mu_{1,2} & \mu_{2,2} & \mu_{3,2} \\ \mu_{1,3} & \mu_{2,3} & \mu_{3,3} \end{bmatrix} \begin{bmatrix} h_i(x,y) \\ h_j(x,y) \\ h_k(x,y) \end{bmatrix} \qquad (10.49)$$

Then, the type 1 QFT can be implemented as follows [26]:

1. Decompose input function as

$$h(x, y) = h_a(x, y) + h_b(x, y)\mu_2 \qquad (10.50)$$

where $h_a(x, y) = h_r(x, y)h_1(x, y).\mu_1, h_b(x, y) = h_2(x, y) + h_3(x, y).\mu_1$

2. Calculate $H(\omega, \nu)$, where

$$H_c(\omega, \nu) = \int_{-\infty}^{\infty}\int_{-\infty}^{\infty} e^{-\mu_1(wx+vy)}.h_a(x, y) \ dxdy$$

$$+ \left(\int_{-\infty}^{\infty}\int_{-\infty}^{\infty} e^{-\mu_1(wx+vy)}.h_d(x, -y) \ dxdy \right)\mu_2 \quad (10.51)$$

3. Calculate transform result of QFT by

$$H_{q1}(\omega, \nu) = H_c(\omega, \nu)\frac{1 - \mu_3}{2} + H_c(\omega, -\nu)\frac{1 + \mu_3}{2} \qquad (10.52)$$

10.3.2.2 *Implementation of Type 2, 3 QFT* The following process shows the implementation of type 2 and type 3 QFT:

1. Find a unit pure quaternion μ_2 orthogonal to μ_2, as below:

$$\mu_1 = \mu_{1,i}.i + \mu_{1,j}.j + \mu_{1,k}.k,$$
$$\mu_2 = \mu_{2,i}.i + \mu_{2,j}.j + \mu_{2,k}.k,$$
$$\mu_{1,i}.\mu_{2,i} + \mu_{1,j}.\mu_{2,j} + \mu_{1,k}.\mu_{2,k} = 0 \qquad (10.53)$$

μ_3 defined as product of μ_1 and μ_2.

2. Decompose input function $h(x, y)$ into $h_a(x, y)$ and $h_b(x, y)$.

3. Calculate transform result. Type 2 QFT:

$$
\begin{aligned}
H_{(q2)}(\omega, \nu) \;=\; & \int_{-\infty}^{\infty}\int_{-\infty}^{\infty} e^{-\mu_1(\omega x + \nu y)} h_a(x, y)\ dx dy \\
& + \left(\int_{-\infty}^{\infty}\int_{-\infty}^{\infty} e^{-\mu_1(\omega x + \nu y)} h_b(x, y)\ dx dy \right).\mu_2 \quad (10.54)
\end{aligned}
$$

Type 3 QFT:

$$
\begin{aligned}
H_{(q3)}(\omega, \nu) \;=\; & \int_{-\infty}^{\infty}\int_{-\infty}^{\infty} e^{-\mu_1(\omega x + \nu y)} h_a(x, y)\ dx dy \\
& + \left(\int_{-\infty}^{\infty}\int_{-\infty}^{\infty} e^{-\mu_1(\omega x + \nu y)} h_b(x, y)\ dx dy \right)\mu_2 \quad (10.55)
\end{aligned}
$$

The amount of real multiplications required for the QFT of types 2 and 3 are same as type1 QFT. The similar way as in type 1 can be used to implement IQFT of types 2 and 3 except that:

1. The roles of $h(x, y)$ and $H_{q2,3}(\omega, \nu)$ are exchanged

2. The signs of μ_1 in Eqs.(10.54) and (10.55) are opposite.

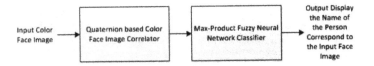

Figure 10.1   View-invariant color face image recognition system.

10.3.3   Quaternion-Based View-Invariant Color Face Image Recognition System Model

The proposed view-invariant face recognition system model considered in this chapter is shown in Fig. 10.1.

The view-invariant input color face image is first supplied to the quaternion-based color face image correlator. The quaternion-based color face image correlator is used to obtain correlation plane for each correlated input face image with reference face images stored in a database to calculate out some classification characteristics such as the real to complex ratio of the discrete quaternion correlator (DQCR) output, p-value, and the peak-to-sidelobe ratio, PSR. These classification characteristic will later be input to the max-product fuzzy neural network to perform classification. Below is the detailed discussion on the quaternion-based color face image correlation.

The referenced face image after performing discrete quaternion Fourier transforms (DQFT) [10]:

$$I(m,n) = I_R(m,n).i + I_G(m,n).j + I_B(m,n).k \qquad (10.56)$$

where m and n are the pixel coordinates of the reference face image. R, G, B parts of reference face image are represented by $I_R(m,n)$, $I_G(m,n)$, and $I_B(m,n)$, respectively, and $i-, j-, k-$ are the imaginary parts of a quaternion complex number [27] and the real part of it is set to zero. Similarly, $h_i(m,n)$ is used for representing input face image. Then, we can produce output $b(m,n)$ to conclude whether the input face image matches the reference face image or not. If $h_i(m,n)$ is the space shift of the reference face image:

$$h_i(m,n) = I(m-m_0,n-n_0) \qquad (10.57)$$

Then after some calculation,

$$\max(b_r(m,n)) = b_r(-m_0,n_0) \qquad (10.58)$$

where $b_r(m,n)$ means the real part of $b(m,n)$ and

$$b_r(-m_0,n_0) = \sum_{m=0}^{M-1}\sum_{n=0}^{N-1} |I(m,n)|^2 \qquad (10.59)$$

where M, N is the image x-axis, y-axis dimension. At the location $(-m_0, n_0)$, the multiplier of $i-$, $j-$, $k-$ imaginary part of $b(-m_0, n_0)$ are equal to zero:

$$b_i(-m_0, n_0) = b_j(-m_0, n_0) = b_k(-m_0, n_0) = 0 \tag{10.60}$$

Thus, the process as below can be followed for face image correlation [10]:

1. Calculate energy of reference face image $I(m, n)$:

$$E_I = \sum_{m=0}^{M-1} \sum_{n=0}^{N-1} |I(m, n)|^2 \tag{10.61}$$

Then the reference face image and the input face image are normalized as:

$$I_s(m, n) = I(m, n)/\sqrt{E_1} \tag{10.62}$$

$$H_s(m, n) = h_i(m, n)/\sqrt{E_1} \tag{10.63}$$

2. Calculate the output of discrete quaternion correlation (DQCR):

$$g_s(m, n) = \sum_{\tau=0}^{M-1} \sum_{\eta=0}^{N-1} I_s(\tau, \eta) . \overline{H_s(\tau - m, \eta - n)} \tag{10.64}$$

where the bar means the quaternion conjugation operation and perform the space reverse operation:

$$g(m, n) = g_s(-m, -n) \tag{10.65}$$

3. Perform an inverse discrete quaternion Fourier transform (IDQFT) on (65) to obtain the correlation plane $P(m, n)$.

4. Search all the local peaks on the correlation plane and record the location of the local peaks as (m_s, n_s).

5. Then at all the location of local peaks (m_s, n_s) found in step 4, calculate the real to complex value of the DQCR output:

$$p = \frac{|P_r(m_s, n_s)|}{|P_r(m_s, n_s)| + |P_i(m_s, n_s)| + |P_j(m_s, n_s)| + |P_k(m_s, n_s)|} \tag{10.66}$$

where $P_r(m_s, n_s)$ is the real part of $P(m_s, n_s)$. $P_i(m_s, n_s)$, $P_j(m_s, n_s)$ and $P_k(m_s, n_s)$ are the $i-$, $j-$, $k-$ parts of $P(m_s, n_s)$, respectively. If $p \geq d_1$ and $c_1 < |P(m_s, n_s)| < c_2$, then it can conclude that at location (m_s, n_s), there is a face image that has the same shape, size, color, and brightness as the reference face image. $d_1 < 1$, $c_1 < 1 < c_2$ and c_1, c_2, and d_1 are all with values near to 1. The value of p decays faster with the color difference among the match face image to the reference face image.

Another classification characteristic that can be applied in quaternion-based color face image correlation is the peak-to-sidelobe ratio (PSR). A strong peak can be observed in the correlation output if the input face image comes from imposter class. A method of measuring the peak sharpness is the PSR, which is defined as below [13,28]:

$$PSR = \frac{peak - mean(sidelobe)}{\sigma(sidelobe)} \qquad (10.67)$$

where $peak$ is the value of the peak on the correlation output plane. $sidelobe$ is a fixed-sized surrounding area off the peak. $mean$ is the average value of the sidelobe region. σ is the standard deviation of the sidelobe region. Large PSR values indicate the better match of the input face image and the corresponding reference face image.

The quaternion-based color face image correlator involved 2 stages: (1) enrollment stage and (2) recognition stage. During the enrollment stage, one or multiple face images of each person in database are acquired. These multiple reference face images have the variability in the angle of turning faces (e.g., 90 deg to left, 60 deg to left, 30 deg to left, 0 deg facing in front, 30 deg to right, 60 deg to right, 90 deg to right, etc.). The DQFT of the reference face images are used to train the fuzzy neural network and determine correlation filter coefficients for each possible persons set. During the recognition stage, sample face images will be input and the DQFT of such images are correlated with the DQFT form of the reference face images stored in the database together with their corresponding filter coefficients, and the inverse DQFT of this product results in the correlation output for that filter. Enrollment stage and recognition stage are discussed in detail in the following section.

10.4 ENROLLMENT STAGE AND RECOGNITION STAGE FOR QUATERNION-BASED COLOR FACE IMAGE CORRELATOR

This section describes the enrollment stage and recognition stage for the algorithm of the proposed quaternion based color face image correlator.

10.4.1 Enrollment Stage

The schematic of the enrollment stage is shown in Fig. 10.2. During the enrollment stage, the reference face images for each person set in database are partitioned according to S different angle face image. These partitioned reference face images are then encoded into a two-dimensional quaternion array (QA) as follows:

$$I_{s(t_1)} = I_{sr(t_1)} + I_{sR(t_1)}.i + I_{sG(t_1)}.j + I_{sB(t_1)}.k \qquad (10.68)$$

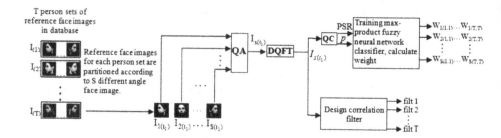

Figure 10.2   Schematic of the enrollment stage. (See color insert.)

where $t_1 = 1, 2, ..., T$ represents the number of person subscribe to the database, $I_{sr(t_1)}$ represents the real part of a quaternion array of an s-th face image for person set t_1, $s = 1, 2, ..., S$ represents the number of face images in different angle for a particular person. $I_{sR(t_1)}$, $I_{sG(t_1)}$, and $I_{sB(t_1)}$ each represents the $i-, j-, k-$ imaginary part of an s-th face image for person t_1, respectively.

The quaternion array in (10.68) then performs a discrete quaternion Fourier transform (DQFT) to transform the quaternion image to the quaternion frequency domain. A two-side form of DQFT has been proposed by Ell [29, 30] as follows:

$$I_{s(t_1)}(m, n) = \sum_{\tau=0}^{M-1} \sum_{\eta=0}^{N-1} e^{-\mu_1 2\pi(m\tau/M)} . I_{s(t_1)}(\tau, \eta) . e^{-\mu_2 2\pi(n\eta/N)} \quad (10.69)$$

where e is an exponential term, and μ_1 and μ_2 are two units pf pure quaternion (the quaternion unit with real part equal to zero) that are orthogonal to each other [26]:

$$\mu_1 = \mu_{1,i}.i + \mu_{1,j}.j + \mu_{1,k}.k,$$
$$\mu_2 = \mu_{2,i}.i + \mu_{2,j}.j + \mu_{2,k}.k,$$
$$\mu_{1,i}^2 + \mu_{1,j}^2 + \mu_{1,k}^2 = \mu_{2,i}^2 \mu_{2,j}^2 + \mu_{2,k}^2 = 1$$
$$(\text{i.e.} \mu_1^2 = \mu_2^2 = -1),$$
$$\mu_{1,i}.\mu_{2,i} + \mu_{1,j}.\mu_{2,j} + \mu_{1,k}.\mu_{2,k} = 0 \quad (10.70)$$

The output of DQFT, $I_{s(t_1)}$ is used to train the max-product fuzzy neural network classifier and design the correlation filter.

10.4.1.1   *Quaternion Correlator (QC)*   To train the max-product fuzzy neural network classifier, the output of the DQFT is first passed to a quaternion correlator (QC)

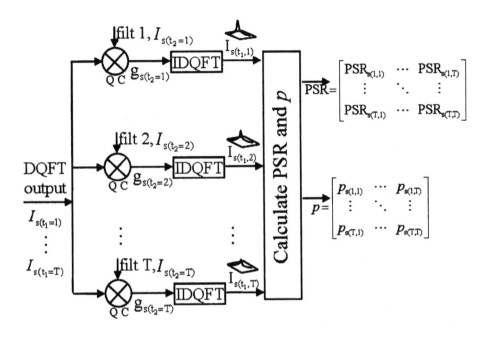

Figure 10.3   Quaternion correlator (QC)

as shown in Fig. 10.3. The function of the QC is summarized as below: For DQFT output of s-th face image, perform discrete quaternion correlation (DQCR) [31, 32] on reference face image $I_{s(t_1)}$ with reference face image $I_{s(t_2)}$ and multiply with corresponding filter coefficients ($filt_{(t2)}$):

$$g_{s(t_1,t_2)}(m,n) = \sum_{\tau=0}^{M-1} \sum_{\eta=0}^{N-1} I_{s(t_1)} . \overline{I_{s(t_2)}(\tau-m,\eta-n)} . filt_{t_2} \qquad (10.71)$$

where $t_1, t_2 = 1, 2, ..., T$ are the number of person subscribe to the database. After that, (10.71) is performing inverse DQFT to obtain the correlation plane function:

$$P_{s(t_1 t_2)}(m,n) = \frac{1}{4\pi^2} \sum_{\tau=0}^{M-1} \sum_{\eta=0}^{N-1} e^{-\mu_1 2\pi(m\tau/M)} . g_{s(t_1,t_2)}(m,n) . e^{-\mu_2 2\pi(n\eta/N)}$$

$$(10.72)$$

The correlation plane is a collection of correlation values, each one obtained by performing a pixel-by-pixel comparison (inner product) of two images ($I_{s(t_1)}$ and

$I_{s(t_2)}$). A sharp peak in the correlation plane indicates the similarity of $I_{s(t_1)}$ and $I_{s(t_2)}$, while the absence of lower value of such a peak indicate their dissimilarity $I_{s(t_1)}$ and $I_{s(t_2)}$.

Calculate $p_{s(t_1,t_2)}$ and $PSR_{s(t_1,t_2)}$ from the correlation plane as in (10.72) using (10.66) and (10.67), respectively. $p_{s(t_1,t_2)}$ means that p-values of reference face image $I_{(t_1)}$ correlate with reference face image $I_{(t_2)}$ in s-th angle, while $PSR_{s(t_1,t_2)}$ means that PSR values of reference face image $I_{(t_1)}$ correlate on reference face image $I_{(t_2)}$ in s-th angle. These values are then fed into max-product fuzzy neural network classifier to perform training and calculate weight, which will be discussed in Section 10.5.

10.4.1.2 Correlation Filter

Conventional filtering methods [33] are emphasizing on applying matched filters. Matched filters are optimal for detecting a known reference image in additive white Gaussian noise environment. If the input image changes slightly from the known reference image (scale, rotation, and pose invariant), the detection of the matched filters degrades rapidly. However, the emergence of correlation filter designs [34] have changed to handle such types of distortions. The minimum average correlation energy (MACE) filters [35] are one of such design and show good results in the field of automatic target recognition and applications in biometric verification [13, 36]. MACE filters are different from matched filters in that more than one reference image are used to synthesize a single filter template, therefore making its classification performance invariant to shift of the input image [34].

There are two types of MACE filters in general, namely: (1) Conventional MACE filter [35] and (2) Unconstrained MACE (UMACE) filter [37], both with the goal to produce sharp peaks that resemble two-dimensional delta-type correlation outputs when the input image belongs to the authentic class and low peaks in imposter class. Conventional MACE filter [35] minimizes the average correlation energy of the reference images while constraining the correlation output at the origin to a specific value (usually 1), for each of the reference images. Lagrange multiplier is used for optimization, yielding

$$filt_{MACE} = D^{-1}X(X'D^{-1}X)^{-1}c \qquad (10.73)$$

This equation is the closed form solution to be the linear constrained quadratic minimization. D is a diagonal matrix with the average power spectrum of the reference images placed as elements along diagonal of the matrix. X contains a Fourier transform of the reference images lexicographically reordered and placed along each column. As an example, if there are T sets of reference face images, each with size $256 \times 1792 (= 458752)$, then X will be a $458792\,T$ matrix. X is the matrix transpose of X. c is a column vector of length T with all entries equal to 1.

The second type of MACE filter is the unconstrained MACE (UMACE) filter [37]. Just like a conventional MACE filter, UMACE filter also minimizes the average correlation energy of the reference images and maximizes the correlation output at the origin. The difference between a conventional MACE filter and a UMACE filter is the optimization scheme. A conventional MACE filter uses a Lagrange multiplier but a UMACE filter uses a Raleigh quotient that leads to the following equation:

$$filt_{UMACE} = D^{-1}m \qquad (10.74)$$

where D is the diagonal matrix which is the same as that in conventional MACE filter. m is a column vector containing the mean values of the Fourier transform of the reference images.

Besides MACE filters, there is a type of correlation filter, namely the unconstrained optimal tradeoff synthetic discriminant filter (UOTSDF) shown by Refreiger [38] and Kumar et al. [11] has yielding good verification performance. The UOTSDF is by

$$filt_{UOTSDF} = (\alpha D + \sqrt{1 - \alpha^2 C})^{-1}m \qquad (10.75)$$

where D is a diagonal matrix with average power spectrum of the training image placed along the diagonal elements, m is a column vector containing the mean values of the Fourier transform of the reference images and C is the power spectral density of the noise. For most of the applications, a white noise power spectral density is for assumption, therefore C reduces to the identity matrix. The α term is typically set to be close to 1 to achieve good performance even in the presence of noise, but it also helps improve generalization to distortions outside the reference images.

By comparing the three correlation filters listed above, conventional MACE filter is complicated to implement whereby it requires many inversion of $T \times T$ matrices. UMACE filter is simpler to implement from a computational viewpoint as it involves inverting diagonal matrix only, and the performance was close to the conventional MACE but poorer than UOTSDF. Therefore, this chapter extends UOTSDF into a quaternion version to use in the quaternion-based face image correlator for the recognition of a view invariant person face since it is less complicated in computational viewpoint than is a conventional MACE filter and achieves good performance.

10.4.2 Recognition Stage

The schematic of recognition stage for classification of color face image by quaternion correlation is shown in Figure 10.4. During the recognition stage, an input view invariant face image is first encoded into a two-dimensional quaternion array (QA) as follows:

$$h_{(i)} = h_{r(i)} + h_{R(i)}.i + h_{G(i)}.j + h_{B(i)}.k \qquad (10.76)$$

where i represents the input face image, $h_{r(i)}$ represents the real part of a quaternion array for input face image i. $h_{R(i)}$, $h_{G(i)}$, and $h_{B(i)}$ each represents the $i-, j-, k-$ imaginary part for input face image i, respectively.

The quaternion array in (10.76) is then performing DQFT to transforms the quaternion image to the quaternion frequency domain. A two-side form of DQFT is used:

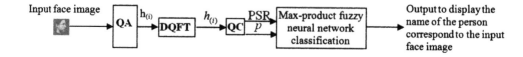

Figure 10.4   Schematic of recognition stage. (See color insert.)

$$h_{(i)}(m,n) = \sum_{\tau=0}^{M-1} \sum_{\eta=0}^{N-1} e^{-\mu_1 2\pi(m\tau/M)} . h_{(i)}(\tau,\eta) . e^{-\mu_2 2\pi(n\eta/N)} \qquad (10.77)$$

where e is exponential term, and μ_1 and μ_2 are two pure quaternion units as shown in (10.70), respectively. The output of the DQFT, $h_{(i)}$, is cross-correlated with every quaternion correlation filter in the database using the quaternion correlator (QC) just as the one shown in Fig. 10.3, but the DQFT output is now. The QC performs quaternion correlation with $h_{(i)}$ with reference face images $I_{s(t_2)}$ from the database, and it is multiplied with corresponding filter coefficients $filt_{(t1)}$:

$$g_{s(i,t_2)}(m,n) = \sum_{\tau=0}^{M-1} \sum_{\eta=0}^{N-1} h_{(i)} . \overline{I_{s(t_2)}(\tau-m,\eta-n)} . \dot{filt}_{t_2} \qquad (10.78)$$

After that, (10.78) is performing inverse DQFT to obtain the correlation plane function:

$$P_{s(i,t_2)}(m,n) = \frac{1}{4\pi^2} \sum_{\tau=0}^{M-1} \sum_{\eta=0}^{N-1} e^{-\mu_1 2\pi(m\tau/M)} . g_{s(i,t_2)}(m,n) . e^{-\mu_2 2\pi(n\eta/N)}$$

$$(10.79)$$

Calculate $p_{s(i,t_2)}$ and $PSR_{s(i,t_2)}$ from the correlation plane as in (10.79) using (10.66) and (10.67), respectively. $p_{s(i,t_2)}$ means that p-values of input face image $h_{(i)}$ correlate with an s-th reference face image in $I_{(t_2)}$, while $PSR_{s(i,t_2)}$ means that PSR values of input image $h_{(i)}$ correlate with an s-th reference face image in $I_{(t_2)}$. These values are then fed into a max-product fuzzy neural network classifier to perform classification for view invariant face images, which will be discussed in the next section.

10.5   MAX-PRODUCT FUZZY NEURAL NETWORK CLASSIFIER

Fuzzy logic is a type of multivalued logic that derived from fuzzy set theory to deal with approximate reasoning. Fuzzy logic provides a high-level framework for approximate reasoning that can appropriately handle both the uncertainty and imprecision in linguistic semantics, model expert heuristics, and provide requisite high-level organizing principles [39]. Neural network in the engineering field refers to a mathematical/computational model based on biological neural network. Neural network provides self-organizing substrates for low-level representation of information with adaptation capabilities. Fuzzy logic and neural network are complementary technologies. Therefore, it is plausible and justified to combine both these approaches in the design of classification systems. Such integrated system is referring to a fuzzy neural network classifier [39]. This section will discuss the fuzzy neural network system and the Max-Product fuzzy neural network classification.

10.5.1 Fuzzy Neural Network System

Fuzzy neural network system refers to the combinations of fuzzy logic and artificial neural network system. Fuzzy neural network system was first proposed by Jyh-Shing Roger Jang [40]. Conventional fuzzy systems have limitation of low capabilities for learning and adaptation. An improvement done in Ref.40 combines conventional fuzzy technology with neural network technology to form an innovative technological field, so called fuzzy neural networks (FNNs). Fuzzy mathematics gives an inference mechanism for approximate reasoning under cognitive uncertainty, while neural networks have the abilities of pattern recognition, optimization, and decision making [41]. A combination of these two technological innovations gives birth to a new technology in which the explicit knowledge representation of fuzzy logic is improved by the learning power of simulated neural networks [41].

A normal fuzzy logic system can take linguistic information (linguistic rules) from human experts, in which it incorporates the human-like reasoning style of fuzzy systems through the application of fuzzy sets and linguistic model consisting of a set of fuzzy IF-THEN rules. However, fuzzy logic system has the limitation of no learning capability. On the other hand, an artificial neural network system is with learning capability but cannot take linguistic information directly. Jyh-Shing Roger Jang in his work [40] had formalized a hybrid model for both fuzzy logic and artificial neural network, so called the fuzzy neural network which not only can take in linguistic information (rules) from human experts, but also has learning capability to adapt itself using numerical data (input/output pairs) to achieve better performance. The main strength of the developed fuzzy neural network systems is that they are universal approximators together with the ability to seek for interpretable IF-THEN rules.

The framework for a fuzzy neural network system is introduced below. This type of network system normally referred to by practitioners as adaptive Neuro-Fuzzy Inference System (ANFIS) [42–44]. The ANFIS architecture will be described below. For simplicity, an example of two inputs (x and y) and one output (f) fuzzy inference system is under consideration. For a simple radial basis function model [45–47], a normal rule set with two fuzzy IF-THEN rules under max-min composition [48–50] can be expressed as

$$RULE\ 1: IF\ x\ is\ A_1\ and\ y\ is\ B_1,\ THEN\ f_1 = \min(p_1 x, q_1 y)$$
$$RULE\ 2: IF\ x\ is\ A_2\ and\ y\ is\ B_2,\ THEN\ f_2 = \min(p_2 x, q_2 y) \quad (10.80)$$

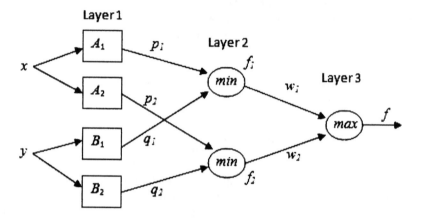

Figure 10.5   Fuzzy radial basis function model with max–min composition.

where p_i and q_i are modifiable parameters, $i = 1, 2$. Figure 10.5 illustrates the ANFIS architecture for the fuzzy radial basis function model with max–min composition.

Layer 1: Each node i in this layer is an adaptive node with node output:

$$O_{1,i} = \mu_{A_i}(x) \quad \text{for i} = 1, 2$$
$$O_{1,i} = \mu_{B_{i-2}}(y) \quad \text{for i} = 3, 4 \tag{10.81}$$

where x (or y) is the input to layer 1 node and A_i (or B_{i-2}) is the fuzzy set related with this node. The outputs of layer 1 are the membership functions for A_i and B_i correspondingly, can be any parametrized membership functions. For example, A_i can be characterized by the Gaussian function:

$$\mu_{A_i}(x) = \exp\left[\frac{-(x - c)^2}{\sigma^2}\right] \tag{10.82}$$

where $\{c, \sigma\}$ are the parameters set. Parameters in this layer are named as premise parameters.

Layer 2: Each node in this layer is a fixed node labeled min, which compares the incoming signals and output the minimum one.

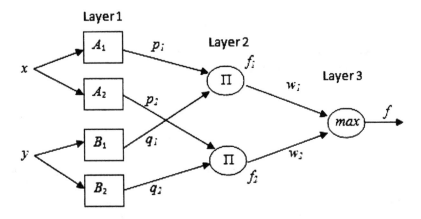

Figure 10.6   Fuzzy radial basis function model with max-product composition.

$$O_{2,i} = f_i = \min(\mu_{A_i}(x), \mu_{B_i}(y)) \quad \text{for i} = 1, 2 \qquad (10.83)$$

Layer 3: The single node in this layer is a fixed node labeled max which computes the overall output as the maximum one chosen:

$$O_{3,i} = f = \max(w_1 f_1, w_2 f_2) \qquad (10.84)$$

Next, another study case for a normal rule set with two IF-THEN rules under max-product composition [51, 52] in an example of two inputs (x and y) and one output (f) fuzzy inference system can be expressed as

$$Rule\ 1: \ IF\ x\ is\ A_1\ and\ y\ is\ B_1,\ THEN\ f_1 = p_1 x \times q_1 y$$
$$Rule\ 2: \ IF\ x\ is\ A_2\ and\ y\ is\ B_2,\ THEN\ f_2 = p_2 x \times q_2 y$$

$$(10.85)$$

where p_i and q_i are modifiable parameters, $i = 1, 2$. Figure 10.6 illustrates the ANFIS architecture for the fuzzy radial basis function model with max-product composition.

Layer 1: Each node i in this layer is an adaptive node with node output:

$$O_{1,i} = \mu_{A_i}(x) \quad \text{for i} = 1, 2$$
$$O_{1,i} = \mu_{B_{i-2}}(y) \quad \text{for i} = 3, 4 \qquad (10.86)$$

Layer 2: Each node in this layer is a fixed node labeled "Π," which multiplies the incoming signals and outputs the product.

$$O_{2,i} = f_i = \mu_{A_i}(x) \times \mu_{B_i}(y) \quad \text{for i} = 1, 2 \tag{10.87}$$

Layer 3: The single node in this later is a fixed node labeled "max," which computes the overall output as the maximum one chosen:

$$O_{3,i} = f = \max(w_1 f_1, w_2 f_2) \tag{10.88}$$

There are various fuzzy neural network classifiers proposed in the literature [53–56], and there has been much interest in many fuzzy neural networks applying max-min composition as functional basis [48–50]. However, Leotamonphong and Fang [52] mention that the max-min composition is suitable only when a system allows no compensatability among the elements of a solution vector. He proposed to use max–product composition in fuzzy neural network rather than max–min composition. Another work by Bourke and Fisher [51] also comments that the max-product composition gives better results than the traditional max–min operator. Therefore, efficient learning algorithms have been studied by others [57, 58] using the max-product composition afterwards.

10.5.2 Max-Product Fuzzy Neural Network Classification

In this chapter, a fuzzy neural network classifier using max-product composition will be proposed for a view-invariant color face image classification system. The max-product composition is the same as a single perceptron except that summation is replaced by maximization, and in the max–min threshold unit, min is replaced by product.

10.5.2.1 Define T Classes, for T Persons' Sets of View-Invariant Face Images
The reference face images for all T persons in database will be assigned with a *Unique Number* started from 1 till $T \times S$. *Class* number is assigned starting from 1 till T. The same person's face images in a different angle of view will be arranged in sequence according to the unique number assigned and classified in the same *Class* number.

10.5.2.2 Training Max-Product Fuzzy Neural Network Classifier The training of the max-product of fuzzy neural network is done with 4 steps:

1. $PSR_{s(t_1,s_2)}$ and $p_{s(t_1,s_2)}$ output from the quaternion correlator of the enrollment stage are fuzzified through the activation functions (Gaussian membership function):

$$G_{PSR_{s(t_1,t_2)}} = \exp\left[\frac{-(PSR_{s(t_1,t_2)} - 1)^2}{\sigma^2}\right] \tag{10.89}$$

$$G_{p_{s(t_1,s_2)}} = \exp\left[\frac{-(p_{s(t_1,s_2)} - 1)^2}{\sigma^2}\right] \tag{10.90}$$

where σ is the smoothing factor, that is the deviation of the Gaussian functions.

2. Calculate the G-value, which is the product value for the s-th reference face image of the fuzzy neural network classifier at each correlated images:

$$G_{s(t_1,t_2)} = G_{PSR_{s(t_1,t_2)}} \times G_{p_{s(t_1,s_2)}} \qquad (10.91)$$

3. Gather and store the product values in an array:

$$F = \begin{bmatrix} G_{s(1,1)} & G_{s(1,2)} & \cdots & G_{s(1,T)} \\ G_{s(2,1)} & G_{s(2,2)} & \cdots & G_{s(2,T)} \\ \vdots & \vdots & \vdots & \vdots \\ G_{s(T,1)} & G_{s(T,2)} & \cdots & G_{s(T,T)} \end{bmatrix} \qquad (10.92)$$

The output will be set so that it will output 1 if it is authentic class and 0 if it is imposter class, and it is in an array $Y_{identity}$, whereby it is an identity matrix of dimension $T \times T$. To calculate the weight w for the s-th angle face image, the equation is

$$w_s = X_{straining}^{-1} Y_{identity} \qquad (10.93)$$

10.5.2.3 Max-Product Fuzzy Neural Network Classification
The max-product fuzzy neural network classification is with 7 steps:

1. $PSR_{s(i,s_2)}$ and $p_{s(i,s_2)}$ output from the quaternion correlator of the recognition stage are fuzzified through the activation functions (Gaussian membership function):

$$G_{PSR_{s(i,t_2)}} = \exp\left[\frac{-(PSR_{s(i,t_2)} - 1)^2}{\sigma^2}\right] \qquad (10.94)$$

$$G_{p_{s(i,s_2)}} = \exp\left[\frac{-(p_{s(i,s_2)} - 1)^2}{\sigma^2}\right] \qquad (10.95)$$

2. Calculate the product value of the fuzzy neural network classifier at an input face image on the training face images in th database:

$$G_{s(i,t_2)} = G_{PSR_{s(i,t_2)}} \times G_{p_{s(i,s_2)}} \qquad (10.96)$$

3. Gather and store the product values in an array:

$$X_{s\ classification} = [G_{s(i,1)} \ G_{s(i,1)} \ \ldots \ G_{s(i,T)}] \qquad (10.97)$$

4. Obtain the classification outcomes by multiplying (97) with the weight trained at (93):

$$Y_{classification} = X_{s\ classification} \times w_s \qquad (10.98)$$

5. Classify the input face image with the person it belongs to by using max composition:

$$Output = \max\{Y_{classification}\} \qquad (10.99)$$

6. Determine whether the face image is in the database or not:
   IF normalized output $\leq Thresh_{output}$
   THEN conclude that the face is not in the database.
   ELSE determine which element in $Y_{classification}$ matrix matches with output:
   ψ = the position number of element in $Y_{classification}$ matrix which has the equal value with output.

   $Thres_{output}$ is the threshold value of an output to indicate that a face is not in the database. ψ corresponds to the assigned number of reference image in the database.

7. Based on T sets of fuzzy IF-THEN rules, perform defuzzification:

$$R^{(l)} : IF\ \psi\ is\ match\ with\ the\ Unique\ Number\ stored\ in\ Class\ l,$$
$$THEN\ display\ name\ of\ person\ correspond\ to\ Class\ l$$
$$(10.100)$$

where $l = 1, 2, ..., T$.

10.6   EXPERIMENTAL RESULTS

In this section, the application of a quaternion-based face image correlator together with a max-product fuzzy neural network classifier for a view-invariant face recognition system will be briefly illustrated. Here, some experiments are used to prove the algorithms introduced in Sections 10.4 and 10.5.

10.6.1   Database of Reference Face Images for 200 Persons

A database with view-invariant color face images provided by the Max-Planck Institute for Biological Cybernetics in Tuebingen Germany [59] is used to test the proposed view-invariant color face image recognition system. The database contains color face images of 7 views of 200 laser-scanned (Cyberware TM) heads without hair. These model 200 persons' sets of color face images, each with view-invariant/angle of different: facing 90 deg to left, facing 60 deg to left, facing 30 deg

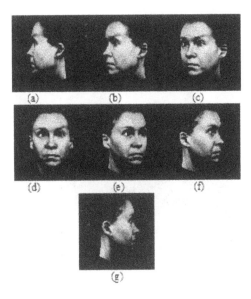

Figure 10.7   An example of a person set with view-invariant face images (a) facing 90° to left, (b) facing 60° to left, (c) facing 30° to left, (d) facing 0° in-front, (e) facing 30° to right, (f) facing 60° to right, and (g) facing 90° to right. (See color insert.)

to left, facing 0 deg in-front, facing 30 deg to right, facing 60 deg to right, and facing 90 deg to right. Hence, $S = 7$ since there are 7 view-invariant images for 1 person set. An example of a person set with view-invariant face images are shown in Fig. 10.7. The dimension of each image is 256 horizontal pixels × 256 vertical pixels.

10.6.2   Quaternion-Based Face Image Correlation Using Unconstrained Optimal Tradeoff Synthetic Discriminant Filter (UOTSDF)

In the evaluation experiment, $T = 180$ MPIK persons' faces are used to train the system during the enrollment stage. $T \times S = 1260$ reference face images are used in the database to synthesize a single UOTSDF using (75). D and m are calculated from the reference images, and C is an identity matrix of dimension 1260×1260 and α set to 1. These values are substituted into (75) to calculate out the filter coefficients. Then in the enrollment stage, for each filter line as in Fig. 10.3, perform cross-correlations of all the DQFT form of reference face images in database $I_{s(t_1)}$ with the DQFT form of reference face image in database as well $I_{s(t_2)}$, and multiply the output value with corresponding filter coefficients respectively, where

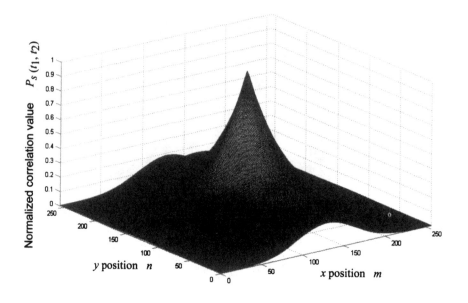

Figure 10.8 Sample correlation plane for input face image matching with the exact reference face image of the same person class in the database (authentic case). (See color insert.)

$t_1, t_2 = 1, 2, ..., 180$; $s = 1, 2, ..., 7$. In the recognition stage, for each filter line, perform cross-correlation of the DQFT form of input face image $(h_{(i)})$ with the DQFT form of reference face images in database $(I_{s(t_2)})$ and multiply the output value with the corresponding filter coefficient respectively. For an authentic case (good match in between two face images), the correlation plane should have sharp peaks and it should not exhibit such strong peaks for the imposter case (bad match in between two face images). These two cases will be investigated below:

Authentic case: Figure 10.8 shows the samples correlation plane for input face image matching with the exact reference face image of the same person in the database. Since the face images are in good match, the observed correlation plane is having a smooth and sharp peak.

Imposter case: Fig. 10.9 show the sample correlation plane for input face image matching with one of the reference face image of different person in the database. Since the face images are not in good match, the observed correlation plane is having a lower and round peak as compared to those in good match.

Table 10.1 shows the PSR and p-value for both authentic and imposter case as in Fig. 10.8 and Fig. 10.9. Note that the sharp correlation peak resulted in large normalized PSR and p-value in the authentic case, whereas small PSR and p-value are exhibited in the imposter case.

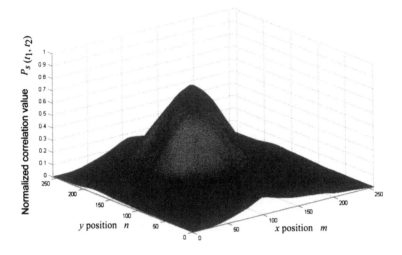

Figure 10.9 Sample correlation plane for input face image matching with one of the reference face image of different person in the database. (See color insert.)

Table 10.1 Normalized PSR and p-value for both authentic and imposter case

Case	Normalized PSR	Normalized p-value
Authentic case	1.0000	0.7905
Imposter case	0.7894	0.5083

To indicate that a face is not in the database, a threshold, $Thres_{output}$, is implemented on the normalized output value at Step 6 in Section 10.5.2.3. The 20 persons' faces samples excluded from the training database are input to the trained system to run for accuracy test on different normalized output value ranges from 0.05 to 1.0. The plot is shown in Fig. 10.10. From the plot, the optimum $Thres_{output}$ is at 0.6.

10.6.3 Efficiency of the View-invariant Color Face Image Recognition System

The view-invariant color face image recognition system was evaluated with respect to random picking 10,000 repeated input face images from database (with mixing up the trained $T = 180$ people's faces plus 20 more people's faces excluded from the training database sets) and input to the view-invariant color face image recogni-

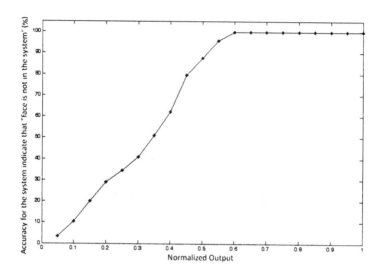

Figure 10.10 Plot of accuracy versus normalized output.

tion system to run test. The graph of accuracy versus number of person sets in the database is plotted in Fig. 10.11.

From the plot, it can be observed that as the number of persons in the database increases, the performance drop is actually not much if the G-value is applyied in the proposed view-invariant color face image recognition system. Among the 10,000 input face images, 9,973 were tracked perfectly (output human names/ID agreed by the input images) in a database of 10 persons, i.e. an accuracy of 99.73%, while 9,821 were tracked perfectly in a database of 200 persons, i.e. an accuracy of 98.21%. The performance drops if the proposed face recognition system is only applying PSR value (no G-value and p-value) whereas the accuracy is 99.62% in a database of 10 persons but is 97.73% in a database of 200 persons. The performance drop almost 0.24-fold more compared to the system that applies G-value. The performance drops in the face recognition system, applying only p-value (no G-value and PSR-value), is rather significant. The accuracy is 99.50% in a database of 10 persons but is 97.04% in a database of 200 persons. It is almost 0.62 fold more the performance drop compared to the system that applies G-value. From the experiment results, it can be concluded that with the implementation of the G-value and the fuzzy neural network classifier, it helps boost up the accuracy of view-invariant color face image recognition.

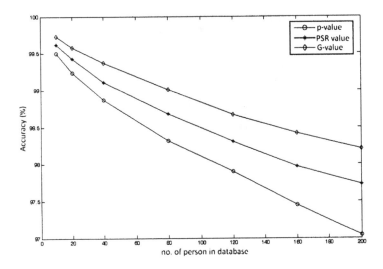

Figure 10.11   Plot of accuracy versus number of person sets in database.

10.6.4   Comparative Study with the Parallel Method

For comparative study, the proposed quaternion based fuzzy neural network classifier is compared with conventional NMF, BDNMF, and hypercomplex Gabor filter. For conventional NMF, the reference face images as in Section 10.6.1 database has been extracted and used. There are seven training sets, each set exclusively containing the color face images for every person in different positions (facing 90 deg to left, facing 60 deg to left, facing 30 deg to left, facing 0 deg in-front, facing 30 deg to right, facing 60 deg to right, and facing 90 deg to right). For each training set, three different basis matrices and encodings were extracted for each color channel in the RGB scheme, F^l, where $l \in \{R, G, B\}$ is constructed such that each color channel, l, of training color face images occupies the columns of F^l matrices. The rank r of factorization is generally chosen so that [60]

$$r < \frac{nm}{n+m} \tag{10.101}$$

In this case, $n = 7$ and $m = 180$, $r < 6.74$. Hence, r is set to 6. The experiment was carried out to test the enrollment stage time consumption and the classification stage time consumption. The recorded time consumption is normalized and recorded in Table 10.2. For the recognition accuracy, a total of 10000 randomly selected and repeated MPIK color face images with mixing up the trained $T = 180$ persons faces plus 20 more persons faces excluded from the training database sets are tested. These also distributed to 5000 are normal MPIK color face images, 2500 are normal

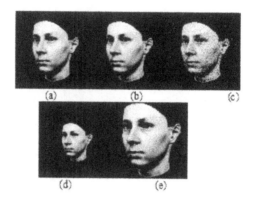

Figure 10.12   An example of a person set (a) original image (b) embedded with mild salt and pepper noise, (c) embedded with heavy salt and pepper noise, (d) shrink (e) dilation. (See color insert.)

MPIK color face images embedded with noise features such as "salt and pepper," "poisson," and "speckle noise" in Matlab image processing toolbox, and 2500 are normal MPIK color face images with scale invariance (shrink or dilation), some examples are shown in Fig. 10.12. The recognition accuracy (percentage of total correct recognized images 10,000 tested images) is recorded in Table 10.2.

For the BDNMF method, to evaluate the performance on different color spaces, the color faces are separated into RGB spaces and face recognition experiment using BDNMF algorithm is conducted. The rank of factorization r is set to 6 as well. In the experiment, all the seven color face images of each person in different position are used to constitute the training/enrollment set. For the testing/classification set, a total of 10,000 face images used in testing the conventional NMF method are used. The results of the identification test including the enrollment stage time consumption (normalized), classification stage time consumption (normalized), and matching accuracy are shown in Table 10.2.

To evaluate the effectiveness of the hypercomplex Gabor filter proposed by Jones and Abbott [4] for feature extraction used in this comparative study, the hypercomplex Gabor filter is operated on all the MPIK RGB data set color face images as in Section 10.6.1. Each color face image was analyzed at a total of 24 landmark location, determined by the statistical analysis of the MPIK face image population. Since Mahalanobis distance applied in Ref.4 yields higher accuracies compared to the normal Euclidean distance approach, matching in this comparative study was performed using Mahalanobis distance classification. The jets extracted at the chosen

Table 10.2   Normalized enrollment stage time consumption, normalized classification stage time consumption, and matching accuracy for different color face classification method

Color face classification method	Enrollment stage normalized time consumption (for training all data sets in database)	Classification stage normalized time consumption (for matching 10,000 tested image)	Accuracy (output human names/ID match with the correspondence input images)
Conventional NMF	2.76	1.39	80.18%
BDNMF	3.51	1.55	83.37%
Hypercomplex Gabor filter (Mahalanobis distance classification)	1.36	1.20	86.13%
Quaternion-based fuzzy neural network classifier	1.00	1.00	92.06%

face landmark locations was used for face matching, and the Mahalanobis distance was computed using the global covariance matrix for all the color face landmarks. During classification, jets derived from color face images in a database were matched against models consisting of jets extracted from a set of 10,000 color face images used in testing both conventional NMF and BDNMF above, for accuracy measurement. The results of the identification test including the normalized enrollment stage time consumption, normalized classification stage time consumption, and matching accuracy are shown in Table 10.2.

From the experimental results in Table 10.2, it is observed that a quaternion-based fuzzy neural network classifier has the fastest enrollment time and classification time. This was followed by a hypercomplex Gabor filter using Mahalanobis distance classification, conventional NMF, and the slowest BDNMF. Conventional NMF and BDNMF are slow due to the reason that they required an iterative training stage for enrollment, which is time-consuming in comparison with the proposed quaternion-based fuzzy neural network classifier and hypercomplex Gabor filter. Comparing between conventional NMF and BDNMF, the BDNMF algorithm imposes an additional constraint, which is the block diagonal constraint, on the base image matrix and coefficient matrix slowing down the enrollment processes. However, with the block diagonal constraint, BDNMF can preserve the integrity of color information better in different channels for color face representation, hence achieving higher accuracy in color face recognition. In comparison to the fuzzy neural network, the Gabor filter required a large number of different kernels, and hence the length of the feature vectors in quaternion domains would increase dramatically. Therefore, the Gabor filter required more time in enrollment and classification compared to the fuzzy neural network. In terms of recognition accuracy, the proposed quaternion-based fuzzy neural network outperformed the hypercomplex Gabor filter, conventional NMF, and BDNMF in recognizing view-invariant, noise influenced and scale-invariant MPIK color face images.

10.7 CONCLUSION AND FUTURE RESEARCH DIRECTIONS

This chapter presents a system capable of recognizing view-invariant color face images from MPIK dataset, using quaternion-based color face image correlator and max-product fuzzy neural network classifier. One of the advantages of using quaternion correlator rather than a conventional correlation method is that quaternion correlation method deals with color images without converting them into gray-scale images. Hence important color information can be preserved. Also the proposed max-product fuzzy neural network provides high-level framework for approximate reasoning, since it is best suitable to apply in face image classification. Our experimental results show that the proposed face recognition systems perform well with a very high accuracy of 98% from a data set of 200 persons each with 7 view-invariant images. In comparative study with parallel work, experimental results also show that the proposed face recognition system outperforms conventional NMF, BD-NMF, and hypercomplex Gabor filter in terms of consumption of enrollment time, recognition time, and accuracy in classifying view-invariant, noise influenced, and scale-invariant color face images from MPIK. Since an artificial data set (MPIK) was used in the experiments, which might be impractical, this work creates a number of avenues for further work. Direct extensions of this work may fall into three main sorts in future. Firstly, more rigorous work is necessary on investigating the system performance in realistic environment, and the system should be extended to consider variations that include translation, facial expression, and illumination. Real face images such as FERET dataset might be employed in the training as well as empirical tests. Secondly, facial image preprocessing mechanisms, mainly eye detection, and geometric and illumination normalization, might be employed to ease the image acquisition. A large scale of facial images acquisition and storage of facial data might raise security concerns in terms of identity theft. Third extension might fall in the employment of cancelable face data as a step to reinforce the system security.

REFERENCES

1. L. Torres, J. Y. Reutter, and L. Lorento. The importance of the color information in face recognition. *In Proceedings of the International Conference on Systems, Man and Cybernetics*, 3: 627–631, 1999.

2. M. Rajapakse, J. Tan, and J. Rajapakse. Color channel encoding with NMF for face recognition. *In International Conference on Image Processing (ICIP 2004)*, 2007–2010, 2004.

3. C. Wang, and X. Bai. Color face recognition based on revised NMF algorithm. *In 2nd International Conference on Future Information Technology and Management Engineering*, 2009, pp. 455–458.

4. C. Jones III, and A. L. Abbott. Color face recognition by hypercomplex Gabor analysis, *In Proceedings of the 7th International Conference on Automatic Face and Gesture Recognition (FGR '06)*, 2006, pp. 1–6.

5. L. Skott, J. Fellous, N. Kruger, and C. V. D. Malsburg. Face recognition by elastic bunch graph matching. *In Intelligent Biometric Techniques in Fingerprint and Face Recognition*, CRC Press, Boca Raton, FL, 1999, pp. 355–396.

6. B. Due, S. Fischer, and J. Bigun. Face authentication with Gabor information on deformable graphs. *IEEE Transaction on Image Processing*, 8(4): 504–516 1999.

7. C. Liu, and H. Wechsler. A Gabor feature classifier for face recognition. *In Proceedings of Eighth IEEE International Conference on Computer Vision*, 2: 270–275, 2001.

8. S. Lawrence, C. L. Giles, A. C. Tsoi, and A. Back. Face recognition: A convolutional neural network approach. *IEEE Transactions On Neural Networks*, 8(1): 98–113, 1997.

9. I. Paily, A. Sachenko, V. Koval, and Y. Kurylyak. Approach to Face Recognition Using Neural Networks. *IEEE Workshop on Intelligent Data Acquisition and Advanced Computing Systems: Technology and Applications, Sofia, Bulgaria*, 2005, pp. 112–115.

10. S. C. Pei, J. J. Ding, and J. Chang. Color pattern recognition by quaternion correlation", *In Proceedings of International Conference on Image Processing*, 1: 894–897, 2001.

11. B.V.K. Kumar, D.W. Carlson, and A. Mahalanobis. Optimal trade-off synthetic discriminant function filters for arbitrary devices. *Optics Letters*, 19(19): 1556–1558, 1994.

12. S. Kumar. *Neural Networks: A Classroom Approach*. International Editions, McGraw Hill, New York, 2004.

13. D.V.K. Vijaya Kumar, M. Savvides, K. Venkataramani and C. Xie. Spatial frequency domain image processing for biometric recognition. *In Proceedings of International Conference on Image Processing*, 1: 2002, pp. I53–I56

14. W. K. Wong, C. K. Loo, W. S. Lim, and P. N. Tan. Quaternion based thermal condition monitoring system. *In Fourth International Workshop on Natural Computing (IWNC 2009), Himeiji, Japan*, 2009, pp.317–327.

15. W. W. Bledsoe. The model method in facial recognition. Technical Report PRI 15, Panoramic Research Inc., Palo Alto, California, 1964.

16. W. W. Bledsoe, and H. Chan. A man-machine facial recognition system. Technical Report PRI 19A, Panoramic Research Inc., Palo Alto, California, 1965.

17. W. W. Bledsoe. Semiautomatic facial recognition. Technical Report SRI Project 6693, Stanford Research Institute, Menlo Park, California, 1968.

18. A. J. Goldstein, L. D. Harmon, and A. B. Lesk. Identification of human faces. *In Proceedings of the IEEE*, 59(5): 748–760, 1971.

19. L. Sirovich, and M. Kirby. A low-dimensional procedure for the characterization of human faces. *Journal of the Optical Society of America A*, 4(3): 519–524, 1987.

20. M. A. Turk, and A. P. Pentland. Face recognition using eigenfaces. *In Proceedings of the IEEE*, 586–591, 1991.

21. S. Z. Li, X. W. Hou, H. J. Zhang, and Q. S. Cheng. Learning spatially localized, parts-based representation. *CVPR, Hawaii*, 2001.

22. D. D. Lee, and H. S. Seung. Learning the parts of objects by non-negative matrix factorization. *Nature*, 401: 788-791, 1999.

23. D. D. Lee and H. S. Seung. Algorithms for non-negative matrix factorization. *In Proceedings of NIPS*, 2000, pp. 556-562.

24. M. Hazelwinkel, N. M. Gubareni, N. Gubareni, and V. V. Kirichenko. *Algebras, Rings and Modules*. Springer, Berlin, 2004.

25. J. B. Kuipers. *Quaternions and Rotation Sequences*, Princeton University Press, Princeton, NJ, 1998.

26. S. C. Pei, J. J. Ding, and J. Chang. Efficient implementation of quaternion Fourier transform, convolution, and correlation by 2-D complex FFT. *IEEE Transactions on Signal Processing*, 49(11): 2783–2797, 2001.

27. W. R. Hamilton. *Elements of Quaternions*, London, U.K., Longmans, Green, 1866.

28. C. Xie, M. Savvides, and B. V. Kumar. Quaternion correlation filters for face recognition in wavelet domain. *International Conference on Accoustic, Speech and Signal Processing (ICASSP 2005)*, 2005, pp.II85–II88,.

29. T. A. Ell. Hypercomplex spectral transforms. PhD dissertation, University of Minnesota, Minneapolis, 1992.

30. T. A. Ell. Quaternion-Fourier transforms for analysis of two-dimensional linear time-invariant partial differential systems. *In Proceedings of 32nd Conference on Decision Control*, 1993, pp. 1830–1841,

31. S. J. Sangwine, and T. A. Ell. Hypercomplex auto- and cross-correlation of colour images. *In Proceedings of International Conference on Image Processing, (ICIP 1999)*, 1999, pp. 319–323.

32. T. A. Ell, and S. J. Sangwine. Colour sensitive edge detection using hypercomplex filters. *EUSIPCO 2000*, 2000, pp. 151–154.

33. A. Vanderlugt. Signal detection by complex spatial filtering. *IEEE Transactions on Information Theory*, 10: 139–145, 1964.

34. M. Saviddes, K. Venkataramani, and B. V. Kumar. Incremental updating of advanced correlation filters for biometric authentication systems. *In Proceedings of International Conference on Multimedia and Expo (ICME 2003)*, 3: 229–232, 2003.

35. A. Mahalanobis, B. V. K. Vijaya Kumar, and D. Casasent. Minimum average correlation energy filters. *Applied Optics*, 26: 3633–3640, 1987.

36. M. Savvides, B. V. K. Vijaya Kumar, and P. Khosla. Face verification using correlations filters. *In Proceedings of 3rd IEEE Automatic Identification Advanced Technologies, Tarrytown, NY*, 2002, pp. 56–61.

37. A. Mahalanobis, B. V. K. Vijaya Kumar, S. R. F. Sims, and J. F. Epperson. Unconstrained correlation filters. *Applied Optics*, 33: 3751–3759, 1994.

38. P. Refreiger. Filter design for optical pattern recognition: multi-criteria optimization approach. *Optics Letters*, 15: 854–856, 1990.

39. S. Kumar, *Neural Networks: A Classroom Approach*, International Editions, McGraw Hill, New York, 2004.

40. J. S. R. Jang. Fuzzy modeling using generalized neural networks and Kalman filter algorithm. *In Proceedings of 9th National Conference on Artificial Intelligence (AAAI-91)*, 1991, pp. 762–767.

41. S. S. Bhatti. What is neuro fuzzy-logic? The Tribune, Chandigarh, India, 2002.

42. J. S. R. Jang. ANFIS: Adaptive-network-based fuzzy inference systems. *IEEE Transactions on Systems, Man, and Cybernetics*, 23:, 665–685, 1993.

43. P. K. Ciji, V. I. George, B. Jayadev, and S. A. Radhakrishna. ANFIS model for the time series prediction of interior daylight illuminance. *AIML Journal*, 6(3): 35–40, 2006.

44. T. Pejman, and H. Ardeshir. Application of adaptive neuro-fuzzy inference system for grade estimation: case study, Sarcheshmeh Porphyry Copper Deposit, Kerman, Iran. *Australian Journal of Basic and Applied Sciences*, 4(3): 408–420, 2010.

45. M. Sushmita, and B. Jayantha. FRBF: A fuzzy radial basis function network. *Neural Computing and Applications*, 10: 244–252, 2001.

46. Y. Sun, Y. Xu, and L. Ma. The implementation of fuzzy RBF neural network on indoor location. *In Pacific-Asia Conference on Knowledge Engineering And Software Engineering*, 2009, pp. 90–93.

47. F. Du, and W. Du. New Smith predictor and FRBF neural network control for networked control systems. *In Eighth IEEE/ACIS International Conference on Computer and Information Science*, 2009, pp. 210–214,.

48. H. K. Kwan, and Y. Cai. A fuzzy neural network and its application to pattern recognition. *IEEE Transactions on Fuzzy Systems*, 2(3): 185–193, 1997.

49. G. Z. Li, and S. C. Fang. Solving interval-valued fuzzy relation equations. *IEEE Transactions on Fuzzy Systems*, 6(2): 321-324, 1998.

50. R. Ostermark. A fuzzy neural network algorithm for multigroup classification. *Elsevier Science, Fuzzy Sets and Systems*, 105· 113–122, 1999,

51. M. M. Bourke, and D. G. Fisher. A predictive fuzzy relational controller. *In the Proceedings of the Fifth International Conference on Fuzzy Systems*, 1996, pp. 1464–1470.

52. J. Leotamonphong, and S. Fang. An efficient solution procedure for fuzzy relation equations with max product composition. *IEEE Transactions on Fuzzy Systems*, 7(4):441–445, 1999.

53. J. J. Buckley, and Y. Hayashi. Fuzzy neural networks: A survey. *Fuzzy Sets and Systems*, 66: 1–13, 1994.

54. C. T. Lin, and C. S. G. Lee. *Neural Fuzzy Systems: A Neuro-Fuzzy Synergism to Intelligent Systems*. Prentice Hall, Upper Saddle River, NJ, 1996.

55. D. Nauck, F. Klawonn, and R. Kurse. *Foundations of Neuro-Fuzzy Systems*, Wiley, Chichester, UK, 1997.

56. S. K. Pal, and S. Mitra. *Neuro-Fuzzy Pattern Recognition: Methods in Soft Computing*. Wiley, Chichester, UK, 1999.

57. M. M. Bourke, and D. G. Fisher. Solution algorithms for fuzzy relational equations with max-product composition. *Fuzzy Sets Systems*, 94: 61–69, 1998.

58. P. Xiao, and Y. Yu. Efficient learning algorithm for fuzzy max-product associative memory networks. *SPIE*, 3077: 388–395, 1997.

59. N. Troje, and H. H. Bulthoff. Face recognition under varying poses: the role of texture and shape. *Vision Research*, 36: 1761–1771, 1996. Redirected from http://faces.kyb.tuebingen.m

60. D. D. Lee, and H. S. Seung. Learning the parts of objects by non-negative matric factorization. *Nature*, 401: 788–791, 1999.

INDEX

Complex-Valued Neural Networks: Advances and Applications. Edited by Akira Hirose
Copyright © 2013 The Institute of Electrical and Electronics Engineers, Inc.

IEEE Press Series on
COMPUTATIONAL INTELLIGENCE

Series Editor, **David B. Fogel**

The IEEE Press Series on Computational Intelligence includes books on neural, fuzzy, and evolutionary computation, and related technologies, of interest to the engineering and scientific communities. Computational intelligence focuses on emulating aspects of biological systems to construct software and/or hardware that learns and adapts. Such systems include neural networks, our use of language to convey complex ideas, and the evolutionary process of variation and selection. The series highlights the most-recent and groundbreaking research and development in these areas, as well as the important hybridization of concepts and applications across these areas. The audiences for books in the series include undergraduate and graduate students, practitioners, and researchers in computational intelligence.